The Future of Career

The fragmented nature of modern working life is leading to fundamental changes in our understanding of the term 'career'. Few people now expect to have a lifetime of continuous employment, regardless of their qualifications or the sector they work in. This book presents a kaleidoscopic view of the concept of career, reviewing its past and considering its future. International specialists in psychology, sociology, counselling, education, and human resource management offer a multi-layered examination of career theories and practice, identifying the major changes taking place in the world of work that are challenging and extending the meaning of the word 'career'. The overall aim is to redefine it in ways that are relevant to the newly emerging network society of the twenty-first century. The chapters are wide-ranging, exploring topics such as the changing contexts of career, individual career experiences, women's careers, multicultural issues, and implications for practice and policy-making.

AUDREY COLLIN is Professor of Career Studies at De Montfort University, Leicester. She is editor, with Richard Young, of *Interpreting career: Hermeneutical studies of lives in context* (1992).

RICHARD YOUNG is Professor of Counselling Psychology at the University of British Columbia. He has also edited, with William Borgen, *Methodological approaches to the study of career* (1990).

The Future of Career

Edited by

Audrey Collin and Richard A. Young

CAMBRIDGE
UNIVERSITY PRESS

PUBLISHED BY THE PRESS SYNDICATE OF THE UNIVERSITY OF
CAMBRIDGE
The Pitt Building, Trumpington Street, Cambridge, United Kingdom

CAMBRIDGE UNIVERSITY PRESS
The Edinburgh Building, Cambridge CB2 2RU, UK   www.cup.cam.ac.uk
40 West 20th Street, New York, NY 10011-4211, USA   www.cup.org
10 Stamford Road, Oakleigh, Melbourne 3166, Australia
Ruiz de Alarcón 13, 28014 Madrid, Spain

First published 2000

Printed in the United Kingdom at the University Press, Cambridge

Typeset in Plantin 10/12pt [VN]

A catalogue record for this book is available from the British Library

Library of Congress Cataloguing in Publication data

The future of career/edited by Audrey Collin and Richard A. Young.
    p.   cm.
Includes index.
ISBN 0 521 64021 0 (hardback) – ISBN 0 521 64965-X (paperback)
1. Career development – Forecasting. I. Collin, Audrey, 1935– . II. Young,
Richard A. (Richard Anthony), 1942–
HF5381 .F87 2000
331.7 – dc21   99-057076

ISBN 0 521 64021 0 hardback
ISBN 0 521 64965 X paperback

Contents

Notes on contributors

MICHAEL B. ARTHUR Michael Arthur is Professor of Management at Suffolk University in Boston. He is an editor of *The boundaryless career* (with Denise Rousseau, Oxford University Press, 1996), *The handbook of career theory* (with Douglas T. Hall and Barbara Lawrence, Cambridge University Press, 1989), and a co-author of *The new careers* (with Kerr Inkson and Judith Pringle, Sage, 1999). Michael has been a Visiting Professor at the University of Warwick, the University of Auckland, and London Business School. He holds a Ph.D. in Management from Cranfield University, UK.

PAT HORNBY ATKINSON Pat Hornby Atkinson is a Senior Lecturer in organisation studies at Bolton Institute, UK. She has an M.Sc. in Occupational Psychology. Pat has published articles on human and organisational issues in system design, and more recently she has become concerned with the changing nature of careers and the impact of relationships on the career progression of women and men. She lives with her partner Norman and her son Conor.

AUDREY COLLIN Audrey Collin, Ph.D., is Professor of Career Studies at De Montfort University, Leicester. Her interests are in interpretative approaches to career research, mentoring, the role of organisations in the construction of career, and the development of appropriate research approaches for career practitioners. Some of her published work has been in collaboration with Richard Young, with whom she also co-edited *Interpreting career: hermeneutical studies of lives in context* (Praeger, 1992). She has specialised in teaching organisation studies to Business School post-graduate, post-experience students. A member of the Institute of Personnel and Development, she began her career in personnel management, and studied mid-career change for her doctorate.

YVAN COMEAU Yvan Comeau teaches in the Faculté des sciences de l'éducation at Université Laval. He holds a master's degree in social work and has worked in the field of community organisation in Quebec and Africa for several years. He also holds a doctorate in sociology and conducts research on social movements, associations, and collective enterprises. He coordinates an inter-university research team on social economics and is a member of the Centre interdisciplinaire de recherche et d'information sur les entreprises collectives (CIRIEC-Canada). He is also editor of the journal *Economie et Solidarités*.

MIKE DOYLE Mike Doyle is Senior Lecturer in the Department of Human Resource Management at De Montfort University, Leicester. After some twenty years in line management roles, in both public and private sector organisations, he now teaches on post-graduate, post-experience management programmes in the areas of management development, organisational development, and change management. His current research interests revolve around researching the 'lived experience' of organisational change with a focus on the selection, development, and support of change agents.

PAUL J. HARTUNG Paul J. Hartung, Ph.D., is Assistant Professor of Behavioral Sciences at Northeastern Ohio Universities College of Medicine and Adjunct Assistant Professor of Guidance and Counseling at the University of Akron. His scholarship focuses on developmental career theory, assessment, and counselling, career decision making, multicultural issues, and physician career development. Dr Hartung serves on the editorial boards of the *Career Development Quarterly* and the *Journal of Career Assessment*.

HEATHER HÖPFL Heather Höpfl is Professor of Organisational Psychology and Head of the School of Operations Analysis and Human Resource Management at Newcastle Business School, University of Northumbria. She is a member of the Board of the Standing Conference on Organisational Symbolism (chair 1995–1998). She is a Visiting Professor of the Academy of Entrepreneurship in Warsaw and an Adjunct Professor of the University of South Australia. Her current research interests are in the vernacular aspects of organisation. She is married to Harro Höpfl, a political theorist at Lancaster University, and has two children, George and Max.

BILL LAW Bill was for twelve years a schoolteacher. He was appointed Senior Fellow in the National Institute for Careers Education and Counselling (NICEC) in 1975. His work, undertaken worldwide, includes programme-, organisation- and staff-development work in career education. His doctoral research examined role conflicts for career educators. He has published a number of influential theoretical perspectives on career development in early years and young adulthood. He has developed professional material for career educators – notably the Department for Education and Employment's open-learning pack *Careers Work*. Since 1992 he has become an independent education consultant. He edits NICEC's *Careers Education and Guidance Bulletin*.

FREDERICK T. L. LEONG Frederick Leong is an Associate Professor of Psychology at The Ohio State University. He has authored or co-authored over seventy publications in various counselling and psychology journals, and thirty book chapters. Dr Leong is also associate editor of the *Encyclopedia of psychology* which will be published by the American Psychological Association and Oxford University Press. He is the editor of a book series from Sage Publications on Racial and Ethnic Minority Psychology. Dr Leong is a Fellow of the American Psychological Association. He is the 1998 recipient of the Asian American Psychological Association Distinguished Contributions Award. His major research interests are in vocational psychology, cross-cultural psychology (particularly culture and mental health), and organisational behaviour.

SUELLEN M. LITTLETON Suellen M. Littleton is the NatWest Research Fellow at the London Business School and part-time lecturer at London School of Economics and Birkbeck College, University of London. Her research interests include employment relationship issues that focus on aspects of the psychological contract and the changing nature of careers.

MARIE-FRANCE MARANDA Marie-France Maranda holds a Ph.D. in Sociology and teaches in the Département d'orientation of the Faculté des sciences de l'éducation at Université Laval, Quebec City, Canada. Her research examines the interplay of the psychodynamics of work and mental health, particularly alcohol and drug consumption. She is affiliated with the Education Faculty's Centre de recherche sur le développement de carrière (CERDEC) and is a member of research teams in the field of work and mental health.

DAMIAN O'DOHERTY Damian O'Doherty is a Lecturer in organisational analysis in the School of Management at University of Manchester Institute of Science and Technology. Damian graduated from the University of Warwick in 1991 with an MA in Industrial Relations and is currently writing up his doctoral thesis. His thesis explores the nature of order and disorder in the organisation of employment relations and addresses issues of conflict, fragility, and breakdown in the management of the labour process. Damian is also preparing a paper on the relevance of Maurice Blanchot for organisation theory and hopes to restore an interest in transgression and covert forms of resistance and revolt in the fields of organisation and management studies.

WENDY PATTON Wendy Patton is Associate Professor in the School of Learning and Development at the Queensland University of Technology in Australia. She coordinates the Master of Education in Career Guidance programme. Dr Patton has an extensive background researching in the psychology of youth unemployment, and in the need for career guidance for the unemployed. With Dr Mary McMahon, she has developed an integrative framework for career theories (*Career development and systems theory: A new relationship*, Brooks/Cole, 1999). She is also editor of the *Australian Journal of Career Development*.

MARY SUE RICHARDSON Mary Sue Richardson is a Professor in the Department of Applied Psychology in the School of Education, New York University. Currently she serves as the Director of Counseling Programs, including both a Ph.D. programme in counselling psychology and an MA programme in counsellor education. Her professional interests encompass work and relationships in people's lives, psychoanalytic theory and psychotherapy, feminist perspectives on theory, research, and practice, group process in the classroom, and qualitative inquiry.

DANIELLE RIVERIN-SIMARD Danielle Riverin-Simard received her doctorate in Educational Sciences and has been a Professor at Université Laval since 1978. Previously, she was a counsellor and a professor–researcher at the Université du Québec. From 1989 to 1992, she was the founding scientific director of the Centre for Research in Career Development at the Université Laval. Since 1991, she has been an associate researcher in the Laboratoire des sciences de l'éducation at the Université Rabelais, France. From 1995 to 1998, she was a member of the Social Sciences and Humanities Research Council of Canada. Her scholarly contributions on adult vocational development include more than 100 books, book chapters, and articles.

IAN ROBERTS Ian Roberts has a B.Sc. in Management Science and an MA in Industrial Relations, both from Warwick University. After leaving the music industry in 1991 he joined De Montfort University, Leicester, as a Lecturer in organisational behaviour and human resource management. He has published in the areas of management development, career theory, and reward management. Ian currently has a research grant to study the professional and personal development of university students on work placements, and is involved in on-going research into performance management in commercial organisations. He is a member of the Institute of Personnel and Development and a management consultant.

DENISE M. ROUSSEAU Denise Rousseau is H. J. Heinz II Professor of Organizational Behavior at Carnegie Mellon University, jointly in the Heinz School of Public Policy and Management and in the Graduate School of Industrial Administration. Her research focuses on the changing psychological contract at work, and the impact of employment relations on firm effectiveness.

MARK L. SAVICKAS Mark Savickas, Ph.D., is Professor and Chair in the Behavioral Sciences Department at the Northeastern Ohio Universities College of Medicine and Adjunct Professor of Counselor Education in the College of Education at Kent State University. He has served as editor for the *Career Development Quarterly* (1991–1998) and is currently editor for the *Journal of Vocational Behavior*.

JULIE STOREY Julie Storey is a Principal Lecturer in the Department of Human Resource Management at De Montfort University, Leicester, teaching employee resourcing and personnel management on a range of post-graduate and professional courses. Before embarking on an academic career she worked in both retail and personnel management so has enjoyed a variety of career experiences. Her interest in the subject of career was sparked by attendance at the symposium 'The Future of Career: Death or Transfiguration' and this was followed up with a Master's dissertation on women's careers in personnel management. In addition, she has researched and published in other human-resource-related areas such as recruitment and selection and personnel practices in non-union firms.

LADISLAV VALACH Ladislav Valach, D.Phil., is a psychologist at Buerger Hospital, Solothurn, and University Hospital, Bern, Switzerland. He serves on the editorial board of the *Journal of Health Psychology* and is a board member of the European Health Psychology Society. His professional interests include goal-directed systems, counselling, psychotherapy, health psychology. His publications have been on topics that relate to goal-directed action, career, coping with illnesses, health promotion, culture, and neuropsychology. He has authored or co-authored chapters in *Methodological approaches to the study of career* (Praeger, 1990), *Representation, health, illness and handicap* (Harwood Academic, 1995), *Handbook of career counseling theory and practice* (Davies-Black, 1996), *Career choice and development* (Jossey-Bass, 1996); and other books.

A. G. WATTS Tony Watts is Director of the National Institute for Careers Education and Counselling, a network organisation initiated and sponsored by the Careers Research and Advisory Centre (of which he was a co-founder) in Cambridge. He is also Visiting Professor of Career Development at the University of Derby.

RICHARD A. YOUNG Richard Young is Professor in the Department of Educational and Counselling Psychology and Special Education at the University of British Columbia. A Fellow of the Canadian Psychological Association, Professor Young's interest and expertise are in the fields of career theory and career development, among others. With a number of colleagues, he has extended the application of action theory to topics in career development, health promotion, and particularly parent–adolescent communication. These applications have included the refinement of a qualitative research method based on action theory as well as its use in cultural studies. With W. A. Borgen, he edited *Methodological approaches to the study of career* (Praeger, 1990), and with A. Collin, *Interpreting career: Hermeneutical studies of lives in context* (Praeger, 1992).

Acknowledgements

The origin of this book lies in a symposium convened by Audrey Collin on 'The Future of Career: Death or Transfiguration?' that took place at De Montfort University, Leicester, in July 1993. Several of the contributors to this book participated in it: Bill Law, Ian Roberts, Mark Savickas, Julie Storey, Tony Watts, and Richard Young. The two other participants were Sue Bloy of De Montfort University, and Martin Shuttleworth of the National Examination Board in Occupational Safety and Health. Together we began to identify the 'fracture lines of career', which Julie Storey took as the starting-point for her chapter.

We would like to thank Mark Savickas. Through the symposium on 'The Birth and Death of Career' at the 1996 annual convention of the American Psychological Association in Toronto, which he initiated and chaired, and which raised awareness of the need to consider the future of career, he has contributed to a favourable climate for this book.

We want to express our appreciation for the support we have received from De Montfort University, which funded the Leicester symposium, enabled Audrey Collin to attend the Toronto, and other, conferences, and appointed Richard Young a Visiting Professor from 1995 to 1998.

We are greatly indebted to Margaret Spence of De Montfort University for her unfailing help and magnificent computer skills. We wish to thank our editors at Cambridge University Press. Others we wish to acknowledge are Beth Haverkamp, whom we consulted on a specialist matter, and Hayley Turkel, who assisted in constructing the index, both of the University of British Columbia.

Above all, we need to thank our contributors for their effort, and often forbearance, in meeting our demands for chapters that would make the book a coherent whole, and for their commitment to this project.

1   Introduction: framing the future of career

Richard A. Young and Audrey Collin

Career has been a key notion in twentieth-century Western societies. Although 'career' is often used as a short-hand term for work histories and patterns, it has also served more significant purposes. Many in our complex and highly differentiated society use it to attribute coherence, continuity, and social meaning to their lives. By tying people to labour markets and employment in ways that are both personally meaningful and beneficial to work organisations and society, career is also part of the rhetoric that supports the ideologies of society and thereby contributes to its stability. Thus, the future of career has implications not only for individuals, including their personal identity and meaning, but also for groups and institutions, and for society itself.

Like so many words in the English language, 'career' is flexible and elastic, enabling it to adapt well to a variety of functions and contexts. This makes it a term of multi-layered richness and ambiguity, which is a 'major source of its power' (Watts, 1981, p. 214). As we shall discuss here and, indeed, encounter in the various chapters of this book, 'career' is used in various ways: as a concept, and as a construct in lay, professional, and academic discourses. It is the future of this overarching notion of career that is the subject of this book.

Whatever the specific context in, or function for which, career is used, to date it has involved a representation or construction of actions and events, and in some instances, the self, across time. Janus-like, career relates the past and present to the future, including our planning for and anticipation of the future, and also addresses how the future motivates action and the construction of meaning in the present. It makes a construction of the future possible. However, profound and widespread change is both anticipated and being realised; from today's perspective, the future looks very different from the past and present. Hence, the purpose of this book is to consider the future of career, for career, in part, constructs our futures.

The present interest in the future of career

Many in the lay, professional, and academic literature are also attempting to come to terms with formidable changes in many aspects of our world and their impact on work and career. Castells (1996, 1997, 1998) and others (e.g. Rifkin, 1995) point us to future changes, and also provide us with an understanding and interpretation of the present that will serve to construct the future. Castells has been particularly comprehensive in his analysis of a new world that is coming into being. He attributes it to the confluence of three independent processes: 'the information technology revolution; the economic crises of both capitalism and statism, and their subsequent restructuring; and the blooming of cultural and social move- ments, such as libertarianism, human rights, feminism, and environment- alism' (1998, p. 336). These processes have had profound effects on our society. According to Castells, they have brought into being 'a new social structure, the network society; a new economy, the informational global economy; and a new culture, the culture of real virtuality' (1998, p. 336). The changes he documents have converged in 'a historical redefinition of the relationship of production, power, and experience on which society is based' (1998, p. 340). We infer that this redefinition will be critically important to career. In particular, the capability of one's career to provide continuity is being challenged. Has career outlived its usefulness? It is a construct that grew up largely in industrial society and as that society has changed and continues to change in so many fundamental ways, perhaps it no longer offers a range of useful meanings with which to understand and interpret our own and others' experience and behaviour.

The initial impetus for this book was a symposium held at De Montfort University in 1993 (NICEC Bulletin, 1994), but we are not alone in asking about the future of career. Other recent publications that have also addressed it include, notably *The career is dead: Long live the career: A relational approach to careers*, by Hall and Associates (1996); Rifkin's (1995) *The end of work*; *Managing careers in 2000 and beyond* (Jackson, Arnold, Nicholson, & Watts, 1996); *The boundaryless career: A new employment principle for a new organizational era* (Arthur & Rousseau, 1996); and *The corrosion of character: The personal consequences of work in the new capitalism* (Sennett, 1998). In comparison to these, this book addresses what is happening to the overarching notion of career from a range of multi-disciplinary perspectives.

The range of meanings of career

Arthur, Hall, and Lawrence (1989) identified ten viewpoints on career each tied to a particular discipline. Thus in order to address the future of this adaptive and flexible notion, we begin by clarifying some of its common and long-established meanings in the academic and professional literature and in lay usage.

In the abstract, as a concept, career can refer to the individual's movement through time and space. It can also focus on the intersection of individual biography and social structures. One way that the term 'career', or more specifically 'careers', is used in several chapters of this book is to refer to the patterns and sequences of occupations and positions occupied by people across their working lives. While this is a common meaning attributed to career in the academic and professional literature, it is even more so in lay understanding. Moreover, 'careers' and 'occupations' are often used synonymously.

Career is also used as a construct in academic, professional and lay discourse. By drawing on common understanding of individual and shared motivations and institutional and organisational practices, 'career' provides a prevailing discourse that allows both lay persons and professionals to create meaning.

The construct of career is also used in organisational and social rhetoric (e.g. Gutteridge, Leibowitz, & Shore, 1993). At times, its rhetorical use may disguise its ideological underpinnings. Career can be used to motivate and persuade employees. It has been used to refer to the work experiences of some groups of people and not others, and thus is considered to be an elitist term. Those excluded include those in occupations without the likelihood of promotions, in occupations that have excluded women and persons from some ethno-cultural groups, and those who do not participate in the paid labour force. Many occupations have undoubtedly offered elitist careers, having limited entry and selective progress along recognisable paths, in which the ascent of organisational ladders has also been restricted to a few. However, since the mid twentieth century, this in general has not been the message society has disseminated. Career has been a powerful symbol of a meritocratic and increasingly complex and differentiated industrial society, in which individual status no longer depends on ascription but could be achieved through education, effort, and social mobility achieved, epitomised in career. Although those without traditional careers or traditional career aspirations have been recognised in some branches of the literature, for example, Hearn's (1977) 'careerless', 'uncareerist', and 'non-careerist', the message to them that careers are normal and desirable has been a strong one. Watts (1981) following Wilensky (1968), indeed, suggests that the 'term [career] is sufficiently wedded to the work ethic to hold considerable potential for social control' (p. 214). Arthur and Lawrence (1984) suggest that 'the term "career" should be applicable to anyone who works, and to any succession of work roles that a person may hold' (p. 2). Further, in order to improve their citizens' life-chances and work prospects, many governments provide career guidance and placement services directly or through the educational system. This encourages the view that, so powerful has been the rhetoric of career, even those who had been denied either access to certain occupations or progression within them may still aspire to having a career of some kind.

The rhetorical use of the construct of career has been particularly strong in bureaucratic organisations (Gowler & Legge, 1989). Their hierarchical structure has provided 'a potential career ladder and thus a reward mechanism for individuals' (Watson, 1980, p. 210). Thus, although the majority who started on the bottom rungs may have had no chance whatsoever of reaching the higher levels, this may not have been known by them until much later in their organisational life, perhaps on reaching a 'career plateau' (Ference, Stoner, & Warren, 1977). Many have been encouraged in this aspiration, and many organisations have used these career potentials as inducement to generate motivation, effort, and commitment. More recently, many large organisations have used their equal opportunities policies and practices to remove some of the barriers to their career ladders. However, not all forms of career are rooted in organisations. For example, Kanter (1989) identified the bureaucratic, professional, and entrepreneurial forms of career, some of which lie outside the organisations. Other careers, as we shall point out, are not related to occupations at all.

Career can embrace a longer period of the life span than membership in employing organisations. According to Hall (1976), career is 'the individually perceived sequence of attitudes and behaviors associated with work-related experiences and activities over the span of the person's life' (p. 4). It weaves together the individual's occupational, professional, and organisational experiences with other strands of their life, as in Super's (1980) 'life-career rainbow'. Career is 'nothing narrower than certain significant relationships between the individual and work, and the individual, work and wider life over an extended period of time' (Hearn, 1977, p. 275). Smelser (1980, p. 10) equates 'personal career' with 'life history'. Career is 'coming to be used . . . in a broadened sense to any social strand of any person's course through life' (Goffman, 1959, p. 123). This is the kind of career of which Roth (1963) wrote in his classic study of the 'career' of the TB patient. It is movement through 'a series of situations which bestow identity on us' (Watson, 1980, p. 47). For people who 'do not have careers in the sense that professional and business people have them' (Becker & Strauss, 1968, p. 320), a career may be based on 'positional passage', not in employment, but in 'domestic, age, and other escalators'. Barley (1989) observed that sociologists in the

Chicago School, including Hughes, Becker, and Roth, used career as the basis for a wide range of studies other than those of occupational careers, including, for example, the careers of marijuana users.

Career also refers to more than objective pathways or movements. It can involve self-identity, and reflect individuals' sense of who they are, who they wish to be, and their hopes, dreams, fears, and frustrations. This is reflected in a foundational description of career given by Goffman (1959) when discussing the 'moral career of the mental patient': 'One value of the concept of career is its two-sidedness. One side is linked to internal matters held dearly and closely, such as image of self and felt identity; the other side concerns official positions, jural relations, and style of life, and is part of a publicly accessible institutional complex' (p. 123). This distinction between the 'objective' and the 'subjective' career is well established in the literature (e.g., Campbell & Moses, 1986; Stebbins, 1970). The subjective and objective careers are blended in the living of one's life, as Cochran (1991) noted, 'A career is a person's life, and in that usage, there is one career for every person' (p. 7).

Overall, career can be seen as an overarching construct that gives meaning to the individual's life. Young and Valach (1996) described it as a superordinate construct that allows people to construct connections among actions, to account for effort, plans, goals, and consequences, to frame internal cognitions and emotions, and to use feedback and feed-forward processes.

Issues and questions about the future of career

Because career is associated with work, among the factors that precipitated concern about the future of career are the changes in the world of work – career has been and is enmeshed in notions of work, employment, occupations, and jobs. It is difficult to overestimate the centrality of work in human life and society: Applebaum (1992) describes it as a condition of life. Notwithstanding that the rhetoric of career was useful for some members of society, many have viewed their jobs as a means of making money for subsistence, consumption, and leisure, rather than providing intrinsic satisfaction and fulfillment. Major studies in the early 1970s reported many people's overall dissatisfaction with their occupational roles (e.g. O'Toole et al., 1973; Terkel, 1972). However, it was not their dissatisfaction that has led to what Rifkin (1995) has suggested is the end of work and the beginning of a jobless society. His specific hypothesis is that the effects of information technology will be massive unemployment. Clearly information technology is one of the most salient factors in the change in work – a shift that several observers have noted is from industrialism to informationalism. What is critical from Castells's (1996) perspective is that the revolution in information technology has made possible the globalisation of the economy, and hence he calls this new era 'informationalism' rather than 'post-industrialism.' The premise of informationalism, as Castells speculates, is that the source of productivity and growth lies in the generation of knowledge and extends 'to all realms of economic activity through information processing' (p. 203) – production will be organised by maximising 'knowledge-based productivity'. In turn, knowledge-based productivity is itself maximised through human resources, and hence has implications for career.

Ericson and Haggerty (1997) provide an excellent example of how informationalism has effected changes in policing, including the activity of policing, the careers of police, and police organisations. They argue that the police now spend relatively little time dealing directly with crime. Notwithstanding the media image of the police as crime fighters, Ericson and Haggerty consider them as knowledge workers in a complex system of embedded communication formats and technologies. The purpose of this system is to provide institutions and individuals with information and knowledge about risk in areas relevant to the police's jurisdiction. They also contend that the effect of this shift on the occupational culture and the self is to undermine individual autonomy and discretion.

Informationalism raises several questions related to the future of career. The first is whether an information society will result in proportionately more information-rich occupations (managers, professionals, technicians) or whether, as in the case of the police cited above, the nature of particular occupations change. At the same time in an information society, there may be real growth in unskilled and semiskilled jobs so that an increasingly polarised social structure could result were the middle of the occupational structure to give way to the poles. If so, career, by being attributed to people at only one pole of this social structure, could assume the 'elite' connotation described earlier. Irrespective of whether the hypothesis of increased polarisation of the occupational structure is eventually supported by the data, we seem to be facing a world in which occupation and employment will not serve to grade and group people to the extent, or in the same way, that was possible under industrialism.

Informationalism also suggests a scenario in which future societies may have to address both massive unemployment and sharp divisions between the employed and unemployed/occasional workers. Moreover, it implies a redefinition of work and employment, involving a full restructuring of social and cultural values, as Castells suggests (1996). It is clear that career is one construct that connects social and cultural values and the specifics of work and employment and thus is critical to both scenarios. As seriously as we should heed these predictions, we also need to be cognisant of Organisation for Economic Co-operation and Development (1994, reported in Castells, 1996) employment projections for the United States, Japan, and the European Community as a net increase of over 38 million jobs to the year 2005. Moreover, Castells (1996) maintains 'that there is no systematic structural relationship between the diffusion of information technologies and the evolution of employment trends in the economy as a whole' (p. 263).

A further characteristic of change in the information society is that there will be greater opportunity for self-employment and flexible occupations and work (in terms of location, time of day, season, or longer time periods).

At another level, the information society has substantial implications for identity and the self. Castells (1997) refers to identity as 'the source of meaning and experience' (p. 6). Giddens (1991) suggested that, as a result of tradition losing its hold and the ensuing interplay between the local and the global, there is a greater need for reflexivity – that characteristic of the self that allows one 'to know . . . both what one is doing and why one is doing it' (p. 35). He pointed to reflexively organised life planning as a central feature of structuring self-identity and spoke of the need to 'negotiate lifestyle choices among a diversity of options' (p. 32). Castells, in turn, suggested that the systemic disjunction between the local and the global is such for most individuals as to make reflexive life planning impossible. As career has been traditionally closely implicated in the issue of personal identity, the implications for career of both positions are substantial. At the same time, because of the close connection between personal identity and career, one cannot question the viability of the latter, as many of the contributors of this book do, without also challenging the construct of personal identity.

The issue of identity in the information society cannot be restricted to the identity that emerges from our engagement in occupation and work. Irrespective of our own particular occupations and work, our life career and identities are substantially influenced by informationalism. For example, as Ericson and Haggerty (1997) argue, information is the basis for categorising our life careers as employed or unemployed, patients or healthy, victims or survivors. Information also has the capacity to create population-based identities, as, for example, the police frequently use age-based, ethnic, and racial classifications.

At first glance, it appears that the future of career and the personal identity associated with it are driven by factors such as informationalism, globalisation, and technology. However, at the heart of the issue of identity are philosophical questions. Among many other 'deaths' that have been announced recently, the alleged death of philosophy, which Heidegger proclaimed in 1966, assumes a particular salience for identity and the self, and, thus, for the issues addressed in this book. Heidegger's point, as recounted by Cahoone (1988), was that philosophy had been subsumed by modern science, that the work of philosophy had been relegated to an analysis of language and literary criticism. Taylor (1989) suggested that the 'disengaged, instrumental mode of life' (p. 499) that empties life of meaning is compounded by philosophy's inability to agree on what constitutes 'the good' in moral life. Cahoone comments that the 'death' of philosophy is evident in the 'subordination of communal–symbolic processes and socio-cultural activities to economic processes' (p. 227). The result, he observes, is that the technical–productive–administrative sector becomes regarded as the only source of benefit and value to society. The discussion of career in several chapters of this book reflects the tacit tension between career as an artefact of the technical–productive–administrative sector and as representative of broader social and moral processes. This tension, which is encapsulated in career, is at the heart of the modern dilemma of identity.

These issues culminate in the question of the extent to which our understanding and experience of career in the future will be continuous and discontinuous with our understanding and experience of it in the past and present. In his discussion of work in the new capitalism, Sennett (1998) identified several factors that contribute to the discontinuity endemic in the present context. These include the following experiences of importance from the career perspective: the experience of disjointed time, 'threatening the ability of people to form their characters into sustained narratives' (p. 31); the different and often conflicting directions of institutional change; the lack of sustained human relations and durable purposes; and the absence of a shared narrative of difficulty and a shared fate. Ultimately, there is a lack of guidance in how to conduct the ordinary life. Not being able to locate oneself in time and space, as discussed by Collin in chapter 6, also erodes the usefulness of the career construct.

The experience of discontinuity challenges the fundamental principles and standards on which career theory, research, and practice have stood. Discontinuity is also a common theme in the postmodern world of language, science, and practice, not the least of which is the decline of the idea of progress; an idea that itself is enmeshed with the expectations of industrialism, science, and technology. Legge (1995) epitomises the issues of continuity by asking the question, in reference to human resource management, whether it is a modernist project or a postmodern discourse. The same question could also be asked of career. Thus, we need to ask not only whether career provides people with continuity of their experiences across a lifetime. We also need to ask, if the dire descriptions of the present are accurate, whether, and if so on what grounds, the notion of career can be revitalised to address the very problems that seem to be contributing to its demise. It must also be questioned whether the career experiences themselves which, in the ideal, have been assumed to be continuous, are now and can be expected to be increasingly discontinuous.

We need to know what the implications of the broader changes that are taking place in society are for career. We need to consider how to interpret what is happening, and the extent to which it calls into question our earlier conceptualisation of career. Will career lose – or change – its former significance to individuals, organisations, and society as a whole? Are we witnessing the virtual 'death' of career, or should we rather understand what is happening as 'transfiguration', a change of form or appearance? The contributors individually and jointly address these and the following questions:

> How is our understanding of the future of career informed by existing disciplines, theories, and constructions?
>
> In what way are the contexts of career changing?
>
> How are individuals experiencing career in these changing contexts and what interpretations can be made of these new experiences?
>
> What are the new challenges for policy, education, career counselling, and human resource development in light of these anticipated changes in career?
>
> What are the implications for research and theory? What new constructions of career are emerging?

In light of the above, what future does career have? What are the themes, issues, and implications that are likely to characterise it in the twenty-first century?

Overview

Several chapters of this book, notably the chapters by Maranda and Comeau (chapter 3), Savickas (chapter 4), Collin (chapter 11), Richardson (chapter 13), and Young and Valach (chapter 12), provide an overview of the relatively recent history of career. These chapters include references to the rise of career in concert with the industrial revolution, the influence of individualism, the period of the bureaucratic career, and the development of career guidance as a social movement. However, developments in the most recent past, including the loss of respect for authority, the growth of the women's movement, the increased application and use of information technology, the emergence of capitalism as virtually the only world economic system, and globalisation of business and industry, are having profound effects on career. Against this backdrop, several chapters document how this history has engendered and influenced our understanding and use of career as a construct in research and practice. Other chapters address the present situation and the effects of the enormous changes that are occurring in society. Although the history of career is pertinent to the discussion herein, this book examines career from many different perspectives in order to understand how the varieties and patterns of practice and different discourses are articulated.

This articulation is critical to an appreciation of the future of career precisely because career has the range of meaning and usage we have identified. In this book, career discourse, conceptualisations, and practices are discussed. The book offers a range of perspectives from various disciplines and applied areas such as psychology, sociology, education, and career guidance. There are also discussions of organisational and multi-cultural contexts, women's careers, and the perspectives of counselling practice, management, education, and social policy. As well, chapters come from European, Australian, and North American contributors. This book includes both modernist and postmodernist viewpoints although exclusive categorisation of most chapters as one or the other is not possible. Thus, this book, rather than undertaking a homogenising or unifying stance, addresses the future of career in its diversity. It proposes a number of tentative and interrelated arguments for the nature and use of the career construct in the future. Notwithstanding this broad range of perspectives and specific references to globalisation, this book provides a largely Western view, which, of course, is prevalent in the construct itself.

Part 1   Changing contexts

Part 1 addresses the changing contexts of career by examining broad changes in both the economic and social environments and the academic and practitioner contexts. The initial chapter by Julie Storey (chapter 2) identifies current and emerging economic, social, and demographic changes that are creating 'fracture lines' in labour markets, organisations, and employment, disturbing this field. In doing so, she sets the stage for a more detailed examination of the historical and changing perspectives in two disciplines that have largely been involved in the study of career: sociology (Marie-France Maranda and Yvan Comeau), and vocational psychology (Wendy Patton and Mark Savickas in separate chapters).

Psychology and sociology have contributed significantly to what we know about career. Although each with its own goals, methods, and audiences, and notwithstanding fragmentation within and between them, these disciplines, together with others, have co-constructed and continue to re-construct career and the professional practice associated with it. They provide both contexts in which and means through which the future of career will be known. Maranda and Comeau (chapter 3) argue that sociology has been uniquely able to contextualise career broadly by showing how successive sociological theories, that can be used to explain career, responded specifically to the social and economic contexts in which they arose. They conclude in favour of a current theory, the psychodynamics of work, that, in their view, best responds to both the complexity of the current situation and the need for social responsibility in it. Savickas (chapter 4) examines how vocational psychology as a discipline and practice emerged in concert with the development of work organisations and the organisational career in twentieth-century America. He also demonstrates how vocational psychology has developed a range of both substantial constructs and alternative theories to respond effectively to the changing career realities.

Deeply embedded in these changing contexts are the values that influence both career and the lives of human beings. Weber's (1950) analyses of the Protestant work ethic and the spirit of capitalism delineate the relationship that has existed, from the time of the Reformation, between economic and personal values and the notion of a 'calling' to one's work or profession. Patton (chapter 5) argues for the life–work intersection as a renewed place for the examination of values. She introduces broad social values into the discussion of the future of career and also considers the study of values in career research and practice. Audrey Collin (chapter 6) identifies the changing construction of time and space as an even broader context in which we need to understand career. Her premise is that career has been one of the resources that people in the twentieth century have used to locate themselves in time and space, and, in particular, to construct, in concert, both their future and their identity. However, social and cultural change is resulting in what Collin describes as shifts to a present rather than a future orientation, and from a temporal to a spatial focus. These shifts challenge an accepted under-standing of career as a personal temporal trajectory.

Part 2 New perspectives

Part 2 offers new constructions of, and perspectives on, career. These chapters are based on theoretical as well as empirical analyses and represent a variety of disciplines and the experience of people from different groups. Interpretation and experience are interactive and inter-dependent in a variety of ways. We see, for example, in chapter 7 by Suellen Littleton, Michael Arthur, and Denise Rousseau, how the career experiences of people in two diverse industries, the computer industry and the film industry, allow career to be reinterpreted. They describe and illustrate a recent notion in the organisational literature: the boundaryless career. This form of career is in contrast to an earlier form, now fading in some sectors, that fit for relatively stable and unchanging occupations. Using Weick's (1979, 1995) social psychological theory, Littleton, Arthur, and Rousseau show how the enactment of career reflects an intersection of self-organising and social phenomena.

Similarly, Danielle Riverin-Simard's (chapter 8) extensive data on the career experiences of older adults leads her to argue that, in contrast to the linear and stable career patterns identified in earlier theories and research, career in the future will incorporate 'non-linear, unstable, and even chaotic elements'. Her interpretation leads her to apply chaos theory to career behaviour.

Heather Höpfl and Pat Hornby Atkinson (chapter 9) take a critical perspective, drawing on the literature on gender and work to examine the issue of power in the workplace and its implications for women's career. They rely on evidence on the way women experience work and career in the context of their lives and examine underlying assumptions about women and work in organisational theories and practice. Höpfl and Hornby Atkinson point to a future in which the meaning conferred by career is apt to disintegrate unless the ambivalence that is at the root of women's engagement with work is addressed.

In chapters 10 and 11, the authors rely on literary and other disciplines and discourses that have drawn extensively on postmodernist and post-humanist philosophy and critical theory both to challenge current, and to propose new, perspectives for career. Damian O'Doherty and Ian Roberts (chapter 10) take up a speculative approach to address the ontological insecurity implicit in career, as individuals struggle to make sense of their world and themselves. They argue that the career literature is based on Western reason and rationality that is coming under increased scrutiny. In its place, they propose a postmodern approach in which one's understanding of life is not only tentative and local (circumscribed by time and place), but characterised by experiment, contingency, and flux.

A literary theme is taken up by Audrey Collin (chapter 11) who uses a discussion of the traditional epic, the novel and the modern epic to examine the construct and rhetoric of career. The classical epic, for

Collin, is analogous to the traditional understanding of career that includes notions of destiny, duty, and linear teleology. In contrast, the modern epic is composed of fragments, teleology is 'replaced by the perpetual digression of exploration'. This, she suggests, expresses more of the contradiction, complexity, and diversity of postmodern life. Collin concludes by asking whether career will contribute to the new rhetorics of the future.

Part 3 New directions for theory, practice, and policy

Part 3 is written from the perspectives of experts grappling with the changing fields of career theory, practice, and policy. It proposes several ways forward for the problems addressed in this book. Several authors in this section anticipate the demise of career as a useful construct unless it is broadened to include other aspects of life. They further develop the understanding of career expressed by Super (1980) in his life-career rainbow by showing its social and political implications.

In chapter 12, Richard A. Young and Ladislav Valach re-conceptualise career theory and research in a way that is grounded conceptually and empirically and, at the same time, remains close to human experience and responsive to the issues identified in this book. In their integrated approach that has substantial implications for research, counselling, and other domains of practice, they link career to the constructs of action and project as representing both the social-embedded and goal-directed behaviours of short, intermediate, and long duration.

Career has been and is a construct about human action. Thus, it has specific implications in the domain of practice. Counselling is one of those actions. It has been viewed for the last half of the twentieth century as an effective means of helping people who are experiencing difficulties in their careers or who want assistance with plans, goals, and decisions for the future. The challenge to the process and practice of counselling, which has long been a major element in the repertoire of North American career practitioners, is brought into relief by Mary Sue Richardson in chapter 13 and Fred Leong and Paul Hartung in chapter 14. Richardson envisages a different future for career counselling by shifting the focus from career to the 'place of work in people's lives'. This shift in perspective addresses the career ideology of work and thereby speaks to the concerns of those who have judged career to be elitist, sexist, and racist. She challenges counsellors to consider counselling practice as 'significant social practice' that not only provides services but also asks fundamental questions about people and work. Leong and Hartung begin by identifying a new 'multi-cultural mindset' in American society that is the basis for their proposal of a specific approach to career counselling that addresses the cultural diversity of the United States, and, by extension, other countries. Their approach, grounded in developments in a wide range of multi-cultural career research and interventions, is integrative and can be used for career counselling practice and assessment as well as research with culturally distinct clients.

Another area of practice significantly affected by current change is the 'management of careers' that occurs in organisations. Mike Doyle in chapter 15 bases his analysis on the changing nature of both the organisation and the psychological contract. He recognises that a number of career development practices have been imported by organisations in recent years and questions whether organisations can and should 'manage careers'. The nature of the changing employment relationship is captured, for Doyle, in notions of the psychological contract that demands new skills and competencies of managers and new opportunities for negotiation among employees.

In chapter 16, Bill Law interweaves policy and practice in arguing for and delineating the critical place that education has in the future of career, and more particularly in the future of work. This place is based on the notion of the transfer of learning as the key concept in relating education to working life – linking purpose to process not only in vocational education, but in general and liberal education as well. Law contends that by linking purpose to process in education, it may be possible to locate 'learning for work' in a 'thoughtful democracy' and, at the same time, to ensure its transferability and cultural relevance – dimensions he considers critical for the future.

In chapter 17, Tony Watts identifies the challenges that changes in career pose to government and proposes a direction for social policy in light of them. He characterises the major change for career as greater labour market flexibility, which, he argues, makes it possible for more individuals to achieve their potential than has been the case in the past. However, this will happen only if there is a new concept of career embedded in a social policy supporting career flexibility across the life span. He promotes a strong and renewed place for career guidance and counselling services.

Finally in chapter 18, we, as editors, take up the varied issues raised by our contributors that we depict as multi-perspectival and multi-layered. In pulling together the various threads of this book, we identify substantial and recurrent themes raised about career. We also attempt to put these perspectives in a larger context by examining them in light of broader and longer-term issues and their implications for various stakeholders in career. From these we begin to reframe career in a way that addresses the world at the beginning of the twenty-first century. This revised interpretation of career acknowledges its duality as both rhetoric and praxis. It provides the basis for a way forward, or ways forward, that involve constructing career in its social context, recognising the roles of experience and language in the construction of meaning, and elucidating cultural variability. These ways forward represent fundamental shifts from the individualism, mono-culturalism, and objectivism that have been implicit in much career theory, practice, and rhetoric since the inception of the modern Western use of this construct. They allow the opportunity to ground the understanding of career in human experience, and through it to achieve emancipatory praxis.

REFERENCES

Applebaum, H. (1992). *The concept of work: Ancient, medieval, and modern.* Albany, NY: State University of New York Press.
Arthur, M. B., Hall, D. T., & Lawrence, B. S. (1989). Generating new directions in career theory: The case for a transdisciplinary approach. In M. B. Arthur, D. T. Hall, & B. S. Lawrence (Eds.), *Handbook of career theory* (pp. 7–25). Cambridge: Cambridge University Press.
Arthur, M. B. & Lawrence, B. S. (1984). Perspectives on environment and career: An introduction. *Journal of Occupational Behaviour, 5*, 1–8.
Arthur, M. B. & Rousseau, D. M. (Eds.) (1996). *The boundaryless career: A new employment principle for a new organizational era.* New York: Oxford University Press.
Barley, S. R. (1989). Careers, identities, and institutions: The legacy of the Chicago School of Sociology. In M. B. Arthur, D. T. Hall, & B. S. Lawrence (Eds.), *Handbook of career theory* (pp. 41 65). Cambridge: Cambridge University Press.
Becker, H. S. & Strauss, A. L. (1968). Careers, personality, and adult socialization. In B. L. Neugarten (Ed.), *Middle age and aging* (pp. 311–320). Chicago: University of Chicago Press.
Cahoone, L. E. (1988). *The dilemma of modernity: Philosophy, culture, and anti-culture.* Albany, NY: State University of New York Press.
Campbell, R. J. & Moses, J. L. (1986). Careers from an organizational perspective. In D. T. Hall (Ed.), *Career development in organizations* (pp. 274–309). San Francisco: Jossey-Bass.
Castells, M. (1996). *The information age: Economy, society and culture. Vol. I: The rise of the network society.* Malden, MA: Blackwell.
    (1997). *The information age: Economy, society and culture. Vol. II: The power of identity.* Malden, MA: Blackwell.
    (1998). *The information age: Economy, society and culture. Vol. III: End of millennium.* Malden, MA: Blackwell.
Cochran, L. (1991). *Life-shaping decisions.* New York: Peter Lang.
Ericson, R. V. & Haggerty, K. D. (1997). *Policing the risk society.* Toronto: University of Toronto Press.

Ference, T. P., Stoner, J. A. F., & Warren, E. K. (1977). Managing the career plateau. *Academy of Management Review, 2,* 602–612.

Giddens, A. (1991). *Modernity and self-identity: Self and society in the late modern age.* Cambridge: Polity Press.

Goffman, E. (1959). The moral career of the mental patient. *Psychiatry, 22,* 123–142.

Gowler, D. & Legge, K. (1989). Rhetoric in bureaucratic careers: Managing the meaning of management success. In M. B. Arthur, D. T. Hall, & B. S. Lawrence (Eds.), *Handbook of career theory* (pp. 437–453). Cambridge: Cambridge University Press.

Gutteridge, T. G., Leibowitz, Z. B., & Shore, J. E. (1993). *Organizational career development: Benchmarks for building a world-class workforce.* San Francisco: Jossey-Bass.

Hall, D. T. (1976). *Careers in organizations.* Pacific Palisades, CA: Goodyear.

Hall, D. T., & Associates. (1996). *The career is dead: Long live the career: A relational approach to careers.* San Francisco: Jossey-Bass.

Hearn, J. (1977). Toward a concept of non-career. *Sociological Review, 25,* 273–288.

Heidegger, M. D. (1966/1977). The end of philosophy and the task of thinking. In D. Krell (Ed.), *Basic writings* (pp. 369–392). New York: Harper.

Jackson, C., Arnold, J., Nicholson, N., & Watts, A. G. (1996). *Managing careers in 2000 and beyond.* Brighton: The Institute for Employment Studies.

Kanter, R. M. (1989). Careers and the wealth of nations: A macro-perspective on the structure and implications of career forms. In M. B. Arthur, D. T. Hall, & B. S. Lawrence (Eds.), *Handbook of career theory* (pp. 506–521). Cambridge: Cambridge University Press.

Legge, K. (1995). *Human resource management: Rhetorics and realities.* London: Macmillan.

NICEC Bulletin (1994) Summer *42.* Cambridge: National Institute for Careers Education and Counselling.

O'Toole, J., Hansot, E., Herman, W., Herrick, N., Liebow, E., Lusignan, B., Richman, H., Sheppard, H., Stephansky, B., & Wright, J. (1973). *Work in America: Report of a special task force to the Secretary of Health, Education and Welfare.* Cambridge, MA: MIT Press.

Rifkin, J. (1995). *The end of work: The decline of the global labor force and the dawn of the post-market era.* New York: G. P. Putnam's Sons.

Roth, J. A. (1963). *Timetables: Structuring the passage of time in hospital treatment and other careers.* Indianapolis: Bobbs-Merrill.

Sennett, R. (1998). *The corrosion of character: The personal consequences of work in the new capitalism.* New York: W. W. Norton.

Smelser, N. J. (1980). Issues in the study of work and love in adulthood. In N. J. Smelser & E. H. Erikson (Eds.), *Themes of work and love in adulthood* (pp. 1–26). London: Grant McIntyre.

Stebbins, R. A. (1970) Career: The subjective approach. *Sociological Quarterly, 11,* 32–49.

Super, D. E. (1980). A life-span, life-space approach to career development. *Journal of Vocational Behavior, 13,* 282–298.

Taylor, C. (1989). *Sources of the self: The making of the modern identity*. Cambridge, MA: Harvard University Press.

Terkel, S. (1972). *Working: People talk about what they do all day and how they feel about what they do*. New York: Pantheon.

Watson, T. J. (1980). *Sociology, work and industry*. London: Routledge and Kegan Paul.

Watts, A. G. (1981). Career patterns. In A. G. Watts, D. E. Super, & J. M. Kidd (Eds.), *Career development in Britain: Some contributions to theory and practice* (pp. 213–245). Cambridge: CRAC/Hobsons.

Weber, M. (1950). *The Protestant work ethic and the spirit of capitalism* (T. Parsons, trans.). New York: Scribner's.

Weick, K. E. (1979). *The social psychology of organizing* (2nd edn). Reading, MA: Addison-Wesley.

(1995). *Sensemaking in organizations*. Thousand Oaks, CA: Sage.

Wilensky, H. L. (1968). Orderly careers and social participation: The impact of work history on social integration in the middle mass. In B. L. Neugarten (Ed.), *Middle age and aging* (pp. 321–340). Chicago: University of Chicago Press.

Young, R. A. & Valach, L. (1996). Interpretation and action in career counseling. In M. L. Savickas and W. B. Walsh (Eds.), *Handbook of career theory and practice* (pp. 361–375). Palo Alto, CA: Davies-Black.

Part 1

Changing contexts

2   'Fracture lines' in the career environment

Julie A. Storey

The recent plethora of books concerned with 'new' interpretations of career (e.g. Arnold, 1997; Hall & Associates, 1996; Herriot & Pemberton, 1995) is indicative of a growing awareness that the concept is undergoing a fundamental, and some would say irreversible, transformation. Nor is this view restricted to academics: the demise of traditional careers forms the cornerstone of the UK Government's Lifelong Learning initiative. Expectations about jobs for life and opportunities for progression with a single employer are seen as no longer tenable in contemporary society and the vocabulary used to describe careers has changed dramatically: career, ladders, employer, job, progression, rising income, and security are 'out' whilst portfolio, bridges, customer, adding value, project team roles, personal growth, and maintaining employability are 'in' (Association of Graduate Recruiters (AGR), 1994).

The 'environment' of careers has largely been neglected by mainstream career theorists (Collin, 1997) but in recent years the transformation of careers has frequently been attributed to external factors: 'we are in an era of unprecedented changes, at both global and local levels, which have the capacity to transform the nature and structure of careers' (Jackson, Arnold, Nicholson, & Watts, 1996, p. 9). These views are echoed elsewhere (e.g. AGR, 1994; Institute of Personnel and Development (IPD), 1998) and are indicative of a growing recognition that careers cannot be considered in isolation. But what exactly are these factors and to what extent are they responsible for the radical shift in careers? Are we in danger of exaggerating the extent and inevitability of this transformation? In addressing these questions, this chapter explores the contextual factors frequently attributed to the transformation of careers and attempts to gauge the overall impact on the concept of career.

Fracture lines

A number of key contextual factors are frequently attributed to the transformation of careers in the UK and elsewhere, including: globalisation; advances in technology; changes in labour markets and organisational structures; changing employment patterns and increased job insecurity; changes in societal values (see, for example, Arnold, 1997; IPD, 1998; Jackson *et al.*, 1996). Developments in these and other areas since the early 1980s have led some commentators to predict the death of careers and, in some instances, of the job itself (e.g. Bridges, 1995). Whilst it is impossible to ignore these changes it is somewhat harder to determine past and future effects on careers. One way to attempt this is to borrow the idea of 'fracture lines' and explore the degree to which these factors have resulted in radically altering the concept of career. 'Fracture lines' are defined as 'those points of change and transformation that have the potential to alter the nature of whole industries, services and their constituent organisations' (Morgan, 1988, p. xii) but can also be described as 'discontinuities, breakpoints and sheers' (p. 26).

The concept was devised by Morgan to encourage senior executives to explore the implications of key environmental trends for the future of their organisations. However, the identification of 'fracture lines' as a means of examining those external factors with the greatest potential to effect change seems particularly appropriate in a study of career, a concept which appears to have undergone such radical alteration over recent years. This approach enables one not only to identify specific external factors but also to consider their cumulative impact on career. In this way one is able to appreciate something of the complexity inherent within the environment of careers. This chapter therefore considers a number of key contextual factors and discusses their potential to alter the nature of careers and the extent to which this has happened in practice in the UK. The chapter's focus is predominantly on the UK but it is hoped that the discussion will also have relevance for a wider readership.

Globalisation

Globalisation, in terms of major developments in the internationalisation of markets and competition, has the potential to impact heavily on careers because of its effects on the structure of organisations and the nature and form of work. Increased competition and the availability of wider product and labour markets have triggered the emergence of new 'inter-firm' forms via mergers, joint ventures, and strategic alliances and changes in 'intra-firm forms' evidenced by delayering and downsizing (Sparrow, 1998). These changes have the potential to alter dramatically the nature and experience of work, simultaneously widening and restricting opportunities for employment. On the one hand, organisations have considerable freedom of choice about where their goods are produced which can lead to the relocation of production to areas where labour is relatively cheap, resulting in reduced job opportunities in 'expensive' countries. On the other hand, the growth of multi-national corporations can provide more opportunities for appropriately skilled individuals to enhance their personal growth with the experience of international assignments.

The extent to which globalisation is fulfilling this potential is perhaps harder to assess. There is little doubt that many organisations are becoming more international; 17 of *The Times* Top 100 Companies now employ the majority of their workforce outside the UK (Keep & Mayhew, cited in AGR, 1994) and a number of organisations undertake activities in various parts of the world (for example, British Airways' financial processing is undertaken in India). At the same time it is rare to find examples of truly global organisations along the lines described by Ohmae (1990) in which nations are unimportant to organisations either as a home base or as a source of identity. Multi-national enterprises (MNEs) still tend to retain a strong national identity and less than half of the top 50 MNEs have more than 50% of sales outside their home country (Hornby, Gammie, & Wall, 1997). In addition, it should be remembered that globalisation does not necessarily affect all parts of the economy equally; for example, much of the UK service sector, including the law and delivery of care for the elderly, is perceived as being outside the remit of a global market (Hutton, 1995).

The sustainability of global pressure is also open to debate. Globalisation is a relatively new phenomenon and, despite its immediate impact, some commentators would suggest that it is nothing more than a brief episode in the evolution of the world economy (Gray, 1998). Recent financial crises in the Far East and the resulting economic and social problems have raised awareness of the possible long-term consequences of global free markets; particularly the potentially harmful effects on social cohesion world-wide (Elliott, 1998; Gray, 1998). Warnings about the disastrous consequences of doing nothing to restrict market forces are now frequently accompanied by calls for greater regulation, thus challenging assumptions about the long-term sustainability of world-wide free markets.

In many ways the impact of globalisation on careers is indirect in that global market forces have been seen as the cause of much of the workforce restructuring undertaken by organisations in their efforts to become more competitive and responsive to an increasingly turbulent environment. The potential impact of organisational restructuring on careers will be discussed later in the chapter but at this point it is worth noting that the effect of globalisation is not necessarily towards greater homogeneity of organisational form. Schein (1996) outlines three possible future scenarios with the potential to impact on careers: firstly, domination by a small number of very large global organisations with centralised key functions which would have the capacity to offer lifetime employment and develop broad career policies; secondly, the pre-dominance of smaller, more varied, and constantly changing organisations which would mainly offer temporary employment and portfolio careers; and thirdly, a combination of scenarios one and two. As it is possible to see elements of both scenarios one and two at the present time, it seems reasonable to suppose that the third scenario will continue to feature, suggesting a continuation of organisational diversity offering a variety of careers for individuals rather than the dominance of one extreme or the other.

Deregulation of labour markets

Within the UK the rationalisation associated with global competition in the private sector has been facilitated by deregulation of the labour market in various ways: the extension of the qualifying period for (fairly basic) employment rights; the abolition of the Wages Councils; and the imposition of restrictions on trade union activities. The main effect of this deregulation has been the shifting of balance from employment protection towards employment flexibility (Noon & Blyton, 1997). Such deregulation has the potential to reduce job security and notions of the permanency of employment and, in terms of impact on careers, can be seen as a contributor to the demise of lifetime employment and an intensification of the need to maintain employability. However, there are two major qualifiers to this: firstly, the UK labour market has always been relatively free of regulation and so little has changed for many people; and secondly, bodies like the Wages Councils mainly served individuals in low-paid positions who, even if in permanent long-term employment, often had little access to traditional careers.

Privatisation

The effects of deregulation have also been experienced in the public sector in the UK through privatisation of public utilities and national institutions such as British Telecom, British Rail, and British Airways. In addition, those parts of the public sector which have not been fully privatised (such as local authorities, hospitals, and schools) 'have been encouraged to act like private companies by purchasing goods and services from different operating units, and obliged to contract out their operations wherever financially advantageous, through the process of compulsory competitive tendering' (Noon & Blyton, 1997, p. 18). As in private companies the effect on careers has largely been through the reduction of job security and the need to adapt to more flexible forms of working. The shedding of labour associated with the introduction of commercial pressures has also considerably reduced employment opportunities; at the beginning of the 1990s the privatised utilities and telecommunications alone lost over 100,000 people in five years (Ruddle, Stewart, & Dopson, 1998). Although the effects of privatisation on employment are similar to the effects of deregulation of the labour market, the impact on traditional careers appears more significant because of common perceptions about the stability of employment and promotions based on length of service previously offered in the public sector.

Technological advances

Advances in communication and information technology, allowing the almost instantaneous transmission of information world-wide, have facilitated the internationalisation of organisations. Technological advances in other areas have led to radical changes in organisational structures (such as flatter, leaner structures and the devolution of decision-making to business units) and working methods; for example, the automation of formerly labour-intensive processes is displacing people and their skills, particularly in manufacturing (Jackson et al., 1996) and financial services. Technological advances have also had an impact on the make-up of certain sectors of the economy; for example, reduced entry costs have enabled small businesses to compete against large corporations in sectors such as publishing and investment analysis with the net effect of increasing the diversity of organisations and intensifying the complexity and changeability of patterns of employment (Jackson et al., 1996).

Changing employment patterns

Within the UK there is evidence of increased utilisation of more flexible forms of work, particularly temporary and part-time work and self-employment. In 1996, part-time work accounted for 29% of employment (an increase from 21% in 1981) and was evident particularly in the retailing, hotel and catering, and financial service sectors. Temporary working, whilst less pervasive, has increased significantly and accounted for 7% of employment in 1996 (Sly & Stillwell, 1997). Self-employment grew faster in the UK than in any other European Union country during the 1980s and is predicted to account for 16% of all employment by 2006 (Meager & Evans, 1997). As permanent, full-time employment has commonly been seen as a characteristic of traditional careers it is easy to associate the rise of flexible forms of work with their demise. However, on further analysis the picture becomes more complex.

There is a higher incidence of flexible working but few organisations have embraced flexible forms of work to any great degree; only 4% of workplaces have more than 5% of their workforce on temporary contracts (Casey, Metcalf, & Millward, 1997). In any case, temporary working does not necessarily prevent access to conventional careers as a fifth of employers use temporary jobs to trial for permanent positions (Atkinson & Rick, 1996). Paradoxically, temporary work does not necessarily equate with short-term employment; 12% of people in temporary positions have been with their employer for more than five years (Emmott & Hutchinson, 1998). In addition, although there is a greater incidence of part-time and temporary working, there is less evidence of these flexible forms of working having significant impact on the bastion of traditional careers, i.e. management positions. It is possible to find some examples of temporary posts at senior management level (e.g. Houlder, 1997) but they are relatively atypical; the majority of managers still have open contracts and 'by implication, the prospect of a job for life' (Guest & Mackenzie Davey, 1996).

Changing organisational forms and structures

The prevailing trend for many organisations over recent years has been towards 'downsizing' and 'delayering', i.e. reducing both the size of the workforce and the number of hierarchical tiers within the organisational structure. In general, this restructuring has been driven by demands for greater flexibility in the face of intensified competition. Miles and Snow (1996) perceive changes of organisational form and structure in North America as moving away from large bureaucratic structures towards more fluid structures such as 'networked' and 'cellular' organisations. Network structures describe a number of interrelated independent firms in a specific value chain, each contributing their own area of expertise. Such structures may include large organisations outsourcing certain functions to smaller companies as well as smaller firms linking together to strengthen their competitive position, thus enabling 'small firms in newer industries to act big and the older firms in hyper-competitive industries to act small' (Miles & Snow, 1996, p. 103). The cellular structure consists of a number of individual 'cells', e.g. self-managing teams, autonomous business units that could exist independently but 'by interacting with other cells can produce a more potent and competent organism' (p. 109). A similar transformation has been predicted in the UK. Guest and Mackenzie Davey (1996) describe three potential stages of organisational change: from 'Traditional' structures which embrace concepts of bureaucracy, hierarchy, job security, and careers; through a 'Transitional' phase, involving downsizing, restructuring, heightened job insecurity and uncertainty on the part of individuals; towards 'Transformed' (new) organisations which are flat, flexible learning organisations with an emphasis on project-based work.

Miles and Snow (1996) associate different types of careers with each phase of organisational change: traditional hierarchical career progression is the dominant form in bureaucratic organisations; whereas in networked organisations the emphasis is on horizontal progression between interrelated firms; and in cellular structures the emphasis is on individual self-development. Similarly, Guest and Mackenzie Davey (1996) identify a number of implications from organisational change including increased emphasis on development and marketability and a greater demand for interpersonal and networking skills. Thus, in theory, changes to organisational forms and structures have the potential to transform careers but the extent to which this is actually happening is harder to determine.

There is little doubt that many organisations have experienced change during the 1990s: almost half of companies in a UK survey had undergone some sort of restructuring in the previous year and a similar number the year before; some organisations had to cope with almost constant restructuring for the last ten years (Incomes Data Services, 1995). However, whilst the changes have undoubtedly occurred, the effect of these changes on careers is open to widely differing interpretation. For example, on the one hand some commentators suggest a dramatic transformation (e.g. Bridges, 1995; Handy, 1994) whereas other research suggests the impact is minimal. Guest and Mackenzie Davey (1996) found that many organisations in their study had moved from the 'Traditional' to the 'Transitional' phase but had then reverted to the 'Traditional' form, leaving the researchers to conclude that 'for the core of key managers, the traditional career is therefore still intact and hierarchy remains in place, albeit somewhat reduced' (p. 23). This view is echoed elsewhere, for example an Incomes Data Study (IDS, 1995) concludes that the upheavals associated with restructuring appear to have had little actual impact on executive career patterns to date although the study concedes that this may change in the future.

These contradictory opinions may result from researching different types and sizes of organisation. The Guest and Mackenzie Davey study (1996) involved a number of leading private and public sector companies and one may infer from this that the participants were likely to be fairly large organisations; whereas Handy (1994) bases his predictions on the assumption that work will increasingly centre around small organisations. Newer and smaller firms are likely to experience change more quickly than larger, longer-established organisations; for example, since the late 1980s management profiles have altered more radically in small firms than in larger organisations (IDS, 1995). Small firms account for a significant part of the UK's economy: of the 992,000 enterprises with employees operating in Britain at the end of 1993, four out of five employed fewer than 100 people (Noon & Blyton, 1997) but large organisations still account for about half of all employment. This diversity suggests that it is too simplistic to attempt universal descriptions and predictions about organisational forms and consequent effects on career patterns because it is possible to find examples of both transformation and continuity.

Demographic and labour market changes

The demographic profile of the UK population has undergone significant change in terms of age, gender, and ethnic composition. The UK population is ageing and this is impacting on the labour force: by 2006 it is estimated that the number of over-35s in the labour force will rise by 2.3 million whilst there will be 1.1 million fewer under-35s (Ellison *et al.*, 1997). Women's participation in the labour force has been increasing steadily since the 1960s and this trend is set to continue, so that by 2006 women will account for almost half the total labour force. Members of non-white ethnic minority groups are younger on average than the white population and so they also have the potential to make up an increasing proportion of the workforce of the future. There is, however, considerable variation in the economic participation of different minority groups with Black-African and Pakistani men and women suffering significantly higher rates of unemployment than white men and women (Sly, Price, & Risdon, 1997). Despite the increased diversity of the workforce there is still evidence of labour market segregation and white males still hold the majority of management and professional positions.

As well as increased diversity in terms of age, gender, and ethnic origin, there is also evidence of changes in household structures. Such changes include significant increases in the numbers of single person households, dual-career couples, and single-parents. Many women are delaying having children or choosing not to have them at all. In addition, the ageing population has led to a rise in the number of people with elderly dependants. These factors can all affect an individual's attitudes to and expectations of work and careers and, by doing so, have as much potential to impact on peoples' choices and opportunities as the organisation-led factors (such as flexible employment) discussed earlier.

In addition, labour markets have been increasingly localised by developments during the 1990s. Professional and graduate recruitment was traditionally carried out nationally but experience of boom and bust in the housing market, particularly volatile in the 1980s, has left many professionals reluctant or unable to move and the expansion of higher education and restrictions on student finance have made many graduates less inclined to move from their home locality: 'It may seem paradoxical that in a period where all the talk is of the global market, global technology and global change, employers should need to focus more closely on local conditions but that is the reality of the labour market' (IDS, 1996, p. 8). Once again, these trends seem to point to an increasing diversity of career patterns, sometimes from choice, sometimes from necessity. For example, those with no family ties or those who bought property at the 'right time' may have the freedom to pursue careers which involve working in various locations, whereas others may be forced to take a number of relatively insecure jobs because they are unable to move from a specific locality. Some people may choose to remain with one company because of the employment prospects offered whilst others may be forced to stay because of the lack of other viable options.

Changing balance of work and non work life

The emerging dominance of market forces in the 1980s typified by the 'greed is good' ethic of Gordon Gecko, in *Wall Street*, has been somewhat tempered by an increased emphasis on quality of life in the 1990s. There appears to be a trend towards viewing work as just one component of life rather than the 'be-all and end-all'. The demands of permanent employment and steady progression up a career ladder can be perceived as overly restrictive and some organisations attempt to counter this by offering career-break schemes and sabbaticals which allow individuals to develop by undertaking some non-work activity, such as travel. At the same time, the assumptions frequently underpinning traditional careers are those of full-time employment, often involving long hours, undertaken by one individual from a family unit (usually male) who is able to separate work from domestic duties which are dealt with by someone else. In the light of greater numbers of dual-career couples and the decline of the nuclear family these fundamental assumptions become increasingly untenable.

It is often assumed that attitudes towards work and careers change from generation to generation. Children of Generation X, born between 1965 and 1981, can have very different attitudes to their predecessors, the Baby Boomers (1943–1964). Work undertaken by the University of Southern California, reported in the UK press (Summers, 1998), highlighted a number of traits which have implications for the way Generation X-ers view their careers. Firstly, they want to balance work and private life, build more traditional families and be more available for their children; secondly, they want independence and mobility and perceive loyalty as something due only to self and team-mates, not organisations; and thirdly, they prefer workplaces that feel like a community. These desires are consistent with portfolio working rather than traditional careers but are not necessarily applicable to everyone. There may be room for ambiguity within these stereotypes: for example, many of the Baby Boomers who are in employment will not necessarily wholeheartedly embrace the values of Generation X, but some might in order to rebalance their lives. By the same token, not all Generation X will want to live in the more contingent world of short-term contracts and portfolio work and some may seek a more stable career pattern.

Changing psychological contracts

Many of the discussions around the transformation of work in the UK have centred around the concept of the psychological contract (see, for example, Guest, Conway, Briner, & Dickman, 1996; Herriot & Pemberton, 1995), referring to the implicit mutual expectations of employer and employee. Much of the change from traditional to new forms of career has been typified by a transition from a long-term 'relational' psychological contract, i.e. the promise of job security in exchange for loyalty to the organisation, towards a more short-term 'transactional' contract 'based on more explicit negotiation between individual and organisation concerning what each side expects to give and receive in return' (IPD, 1998). This shift appears to be reflected by the findings of a study undertaken by the business research organisation, the Conference Board, and reported in the UK press (Summers, 1997). Only 6% of the 92 organisations in the study still retained 'a contractual or tacit understanding with employees that promised a secure job in exchange for loyal and dedicated service' whereas 67% had once had this type of agreement but no longer did so. This seems to indicate a dominant trend but the shift cannot be assumed to be universal; the remaining 27% of respondents said that this type of agreement had never existed in their companies.

Problems also arise because of the ambiguity in interpretations of the psychological contract as 'relational' or 'transactional' (Arnold, 1997); for example, training can be seen as part of a 'relational' contract because it suggests commitment to employee development but the same activity can also be seen as 'transactional' if it helps someone to work more effectively. The unwritten, and often unspoken, nature of the psychological contract also means that individuals are often only aware of it once it has been breached (Sparrow, 1998). Because the contract is based on individual expectations, perceptions, and interpretations it can be infinitely variable which makes broad generalisations problematic.

Increased job insecurity

Perceptions of heightened job insecurity form a significant component of the changing psychological contract. Organisational downsizing and delayering of the 1980s and early 1990s increased fears over job security particularly in certain sectors, such as financial services, which had previously had a reputation for safe and secure employment. As with changes in organisational form discussed earlier, evidence regarding changes in job security is mixed and potentially contradictory. On the one hand, many people either have personally experienced redundancy or know someone who has, as between 1990 and 1995 over 4 million redundancies occurred in Britain (Noon & Blyton, 1997). The causes of redundancy can also appear more threatening than in the past. Instead of being used only as an extreme measure when an organisation was in economic difficulty, redundancies have more recently been used as an immediate cost-cutting measure even when the organisation is relatively healthy, with the likely effect of making 'job insecurity a more prominent concern to workers in contemporary workplaces than it was to the majority of their counterparts a generation ago' (Noon & Blyton, 1997, p. 32).

On the other hand, feelings of greater job insecurity are not necessarily reflected in any dramatic reductions in job tenure in the UK. In 1968, 37.7% of men had been with the same employer for ten years or more and the equivalent figure for 1993 was still 36% (IDS, 1995). In fact, improved maternity provision has given women greater job stability over recent years. General statistics may obscure the complete picture by not taking account of increasing balkanisation in the job market; whilst a significant proportion of those in employment are still able to build up long service with a single employer, for others, work has become a much more 'precarious affair with insecurity, redundancy, temporary contracts and unemployment contributing to a fragmented, rather than a unified working life' (Noon & Blyton, 1997).

Job insecurity impacts on careers by removing the foundations of long-term career planning and shifting the emphasis away from employment to employability and to the need for individuals to take control of their own development. However, in considering its overall effect one needs to strip away some of the mythology of the past and assess how different things really are. Much of the hype has concerned the end of lifetime employment but this has never been the reality for the majority of people: in the 1960s half of male manual workers and two-thirds of women workers had been with the same employer for five years or less (IDS, 1995). Job insecurity might now be a new experience for some groups of workers but it has always been a fact of life for many others.

Changes in education

A significant long-term change has been the rise in the level of educational attainment: two thirds of the UK population now hold at least some qualifications compared to about a third in the late 1970s (Jackson *et al.*, 1996). There has also been considerable expansion in higher education. These changes have been accompanied by increased complexity in labour markets as the traditional distinctions between graduate and non-graduate jobs and between jobs that demanded some form of educational qualification and those that did not have become blurred. Even within the lifetime of many people currently in employment, the boundaries were quite marked: the segregation of children by examination results at the age of eleven often had considerable influence on future career opportunities. Those who failed the 'Eleven Plus' examination and attended secondary modern schools were largely expected to go into manual or trade positions, whereas those who attended grammar schools were considered suitable for university and/or the minor professions; with top positions open to those with a public school or university education. In the current climate, graduates are increasingly likely to be unemployed or under-employed in 'non-graduate' jobs: a recent survey within the financial services industry found that 45% of graduates recruited in a twelve-month period were employed in 'unmodified, clerical jobs for which a degree was not required' (AGR, 1994, p. 13).

Educational attainments in the UK still lag some way behind other major international competitors and a persistent preoccupation of recent governments has been the status of Britain as a 'low-skill, low quality' economy. Initiatives to raise the overall standard via the introduction of work-based, vocational qualifications have been introduced. These initiatives have the potential to encourage individuals to take responsibility for their own development and improve employability through the demonstration of transferable skills (Jackson *et al.*, 1996) but they have yet to have any marked impact.

Transformation of careers?

So, to what extent have these contextual factors transformed careers? For the purposes of analysis each factor has been discussed separately but it is important to recognise the direct and indirect relationship among the factors. Both individually and cumulatively these factors can be consider-ed as 'fracture lines' because each has the potential to alter careers significantly in some way. Taken together the overall effect is to increase the pace and intensity of change but the impact on the concept of career is harder to determine. Currently, the prevailing view is that careers have undergone a radical shift: for example, 'in the new world of work, careers are very different' (AGR, 1994); and 'it seems very clear that in the twenty first century the pattern of career paths will continue to be transformed' (IPD, 1998). The main emphasis of this shift is away from a narrow interpretation of career as steady, upward progression with a single employer towards a broader definition which embraces 'any sequence of employment-related positions' (Arnold, 1997, p. xiii).

The broadening of the concept of career to embrace the greater diversity of career patterns is seen as increasingly necessary (e.g. Jackson *et al.*, 1996) but this type of definition is not new, it has just been largely ignored in the past: twenty years ago Hearn (1977) defined career as 'nothing narrower than significant relationships between the individual and work, and the individual, work and wider life over an extended period of time' (p. 275). Furthermore, there is nothing new about diversity in career patterns. Much of the attention surrounding the transformation of careers has concentrated on the decline of traditional, bureaucratic careers but this type of career has always been the preserve of a relatively select group, mainly managerial and professional employees. Concentra-tion on these groups of workers for the study of career has meant considerable neglect for other groups including women and members of ethnic minorities who, until fairly recently, had little access to such positions (and some would say have only limited access now). It has also meant neglect for substantial numbers of men: the experiences of the self-employed, those in non-managerial positions (including unskilled, part-time, and temporary employment), have always been outside any narrow definition of career. There may be increased incidence of atypical forms of work in the UK but they are not new working practices for many people. At the other end of the spectrum, portfolio working, increasingly seen as the way forward (e.g. Handy, 1994), is not necessarily a new experience but rather one that has been experienced by many 'high-fliers' in the past.

A greater awareness of diversity is also reflected in a raised awareness of 'subjective' career (Collin, 1986), i.e., an individual's perceptions of their own career and life experiences and a reduced emphasis on 'objective' career, i.e., the observed progress of an individual through an organisation or occupation. It is difficult to generalise on the impact of external circumstances whichever interpretation is adopted. For example, using the objective interpretation, factors such as organisational delayering might have a negative impact on the career of a manager who faces redundancy but may have a positive impact on the subordinate who is subsequently given greater responsibility and enhanced development opportunities. Using a more subjective interpretation, the same event can be perceived in diverse ways; the loss of a job might be viewed positively and negatively by those affected: some may fear the uncertainty of redundancy and potential loss of income, whereas others might welcome the opportunity to change direction and expand into new fields. Individual perceptions of events may also alter over time. Much of the talk of transformation of careers is based on a comparison of current and past events but careers can be perceived very differently when considered with the benefit of hindsight. Job changes which can appear *ad hoc* and random at the time can be rationalised into a career path when viewed overall.

If the overall impact of contextual change has been to increase awareness that a multitude of work and life experiences can be classed as careers then all well and good, but this hardly constitutes a radical shift. The current emphasis is in danger of emphasising only the discontinuity and failing to acknowledge the continuity; increased diversity means that traditional careers, even if experienced by smaller numbers than in the past, still have a role to play and reports of the 'death' of career have been somewhat exaggerated. The overall impact of external factors is less a transformation from one type of career to another but rather continuous evolution within a complex concept which contains many layers of meaning. To this extent, this exploration of some of the commonly perceived 'fracture lines' has enabled us to consider the longevity of multiple meanings of career rather than limit our vision to a more immediate focus on contemporary changes.

REFERENCES

Arnold, J. (1997). *Managing careers into the 21st century*. London: Paul Chapman.
Association of Graduate Recruiters (1994). *Skills for graduates in the twenty first century*. Cambridge: Author.

Atkinson, J. & Rick, J. (1996). *Temporary work and the labour market.* IES Report no. 311. Brighton: Institute for Employment Studies.

Bridges, W. (1995). *Jobshift: How to prosper in a workplace without jobs.* London: Nicholas Brealey.

Casey, B., Metcalf, H., & Millward, N. (1997). *Employers' use of flexible labour.* Policy Studies Institute Report no. 837. London: Policy Studies Institute.

Collin, A. (1986). Career development: The significance of the subjective career. *Personnel Review, 15* (2), 22–28.

(1997). Career in context. *British Journal of Guidance and Counselling, 25,* 435–446.

Elliott, L. (1998). Flat earth gurus convert. *The Guardian,* 2 February.

Ellison, R., Tinsley, K., & Houston, N. (1997). British labour force projections: 1997–2006. *Labour Market Trends,* 105, 51–67.

Emmott, M. & Hutchinson, S. (1998). Employment flexibility: Threat or promise? In P. Sparrow & M. Marchington (Eds.), *Human resource management: The new agenda* (pp. 229–244). London: Financial Times Management.

Gray, J. (1998). Global cooling. *The Guardian,* 17 March.

Guest, D., Conway, N., Briner, R., & Dickman, M. (1996). *The state of the psychological contract in employment,* Issues in People Management no. 16. London: IPD.

Guest, D. & Mackenzie Davey, K. (1996). 'Don't write off the traditional career'. *People Management, 2* (4), 23–26.

Hall, D. T., & Associates (1996). *The career is dead – long live the career: A relational approach to careers.* San Francisco: Jossey-Bass.

Handy, C. (1994). *The empty raincoat.* London: Hutchinson.

Hearn, J. (1977). Toward a concept of non-career. *Sociological Review, 25,* 273–288.

Herriot, P. & Pemberton, C. (1995). *New deals: The revolution in managerial careers.* Chichester: John Wiley & Sons.

Hornby, W., Gammie, B., & Wall, S. (1997). *Business economics.* London: Longman.

Houlder, V. (1997). When even the boss is a temp. *Financial Times,* 11 August.

Hutton, W. (1995). *The state we're in.* London: Vintage.

Incomes Data Services (1995). *IDS Focus 74: The Jobs Mythology,* March.

(1996). *IDS Focus 80,* December.

Institute of Personnel and Development (1998). *The IPD guide on career management in organisations.* London: Author.

Jackson, C., Arnold, J., Nicholson, N., & Watts, A.G. (1996). *Managing careers in 2000 and beyond.* Report no. 304. Brighton: IES/CRAC.

Meager, N. & Evans, C. (1997). United Kingdom. *Employment Observatory Trends, 29,* Winter, 58–63.

Miles, R. & Snow, C. (1996). Twenty first century careers. In M. Arthur & D. Rousseau (Eds.), *The boundaryless career: A new employment principle for a new organizational era* (pp. 97–115). New York: Oxford University Press.

Morgan, G. (1988). *Riding the waves of change.* San Francisco: Jossey-Bass.

Noon, M. & Blyton, P. (1997). *The realities of work.* Basingstoke: Macmillan.

Ohmae, K. (1990). *The borderless world.* London: Collins.

Ruddle, K., Stewart, R., & Dopson, S. (1998). From downsizing to revitalisation, *Financial Times*, 27 February, 12.

Schein, E. (1996, November). Career anchors revisited: Implications for career development in the 21st century. *Academy of Management Executive*, special issue: Careers in the 21st century, *10* (4), 80–89.

Sly, F., Price, A., & Risdon, A. (1997). Trends in labour market participation of ethnic groups 1984–1996. *Labour Market Trends*, *105*, 295–303.

Sly, F., & Stillwell, D. (1997). Temporary workers in Great Britain. *Labour Market Trends*, *105*, 347–354.

Sparrow, P. (1998). New organisational forms, processes, jobs and psychological contracts: Resolving the HRM issues. In P. Sparrow & M. Marchington (Eds.), *Human resource management: The new agenda* (pp. 117–144). London: Financial Times Management.

Summers, D. (1997). Career-fit worker seeks insecure post. *Financial Times*, 25 April.

(1998). Generation X comes of age. *Financial Times*, 16 February.

3 Some contributions of sociology to the understanding of career

Marie-France Maranda and Yvan Comeau

This chapter examines career from a sociological perspective, with emphasis on the changes that have affected employment and work organisation during recent decades. First, we argue that the context of the 1950s and 1960s, which was characterised by economic prosperity, made two quite different sociological theories plausible. While status attainment theory asserts that motivation allows people to seize the opportunities offered by the labour market, reproduction theory maintains that far from being chosen, a career is assigned on the basis of an individual's social and economic origin. The first theory implies that individuals have to adapt through adequate socialisation and the second suggests that societal structures be transformed. Secondly, the employment crisis of the 1980s and 1990s is described and new theories such as human capital theory, segmentation theory, and regulation theory, which attempt to provide an explanation of career interruptions, are presented. Thirdly, courses of action for interventions in career based on these recent theories are formulated.

In sociology, career is usually examined in terms of social mobility, which describes the movement of individuals or family units within the system of occupational categories or the social class system (Boudon & Bourricaud, 1994). The concept of mobility has been used as an indicator of the relative rigidity of both structures and the social order, and has been linked with career prospects. According to Emile Durkheim (1858–1917), who represents an early theoretical perspective emphasising social structure, people had little scope for action when it came to occupational choice. He maintained that social facts represent 'ways of acting or thinking with the peculiar characteristic of exercising a coercive influence on individual consciousness' (Durkheim, 1964, p. liii). A second perspective proposed that social order was maintained through control, exploitation, and domination (Karl Marx, 1818–1883), thus provoking freedom movements and transformation of the system (Marx & Engels, 1982). Yet a third perspective emphasised the meanings that people give to their actions and the relative choices that they can make.

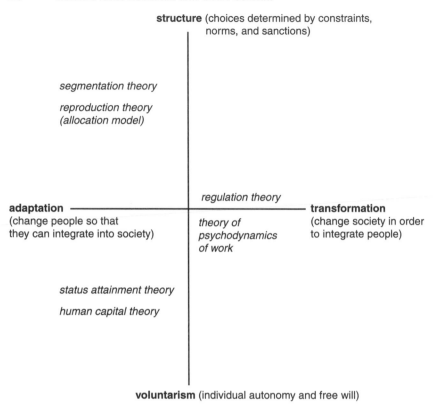

structure (choices determined by constraints, norms, and sanctions)

segmentation theory

*reproduction theory
(allocation model)*

regulation theory

adaptation ———————————————— **transformation**
(change people so that   *theory of*   (change society in order
they can integrate into society) *psychodynamics*   to integrate people)
                                 of work

status attainment theory

human capital theory

voluntarism (individual autonomy and free will)

Figure 3.1. Classification of selected career theories based on different viewpoints

The sociologist Max Weber (1864–1920) analysed different forms of rationality and the meaning of social action (Weber, 1968). The theorists who drew inspiration from Weber, such as members of the Chicago School in the 1920s and 1930s, gave considerable importance to meanings and the social construction of reality (Berger & Luckmann, 1980). Finally, a fourth perspective brought out social equilibrium and people's adaptation to the social system according to principles corresponding to individual and public interest. Talcott Parsons (1902–1979) showed how the division of labour and different occupational forms ensure that society operates through the interdependence of functions (Parsons, 1951).

The objective of this chapter is to examine a number of theoretical approaches in the field of career along two axes illustrated in figure 3.1. The first focuses on employment and work from a structural as opposed to an individual perspective (the structure–voluntarism axis). The second contrasts the idea of adapting to the environment with action seeking to transform it (the adaptation–transformation axis). Although at first glance, the various sociological viewpoints regarding career may appear to be antagonistic, their complementarity becomes more evident when they are viewed from the perspective of understanding the complex relations between individuals and context. To sum up this complexity briefly, it can be said that the individual's autonomy and free will come up against the constraints imposed by social structure, and the forces of transformation and change act as a counterbalance to the tendency towards a conformist type of adaptation to established powers. A social interpretation of the problems affecting employment and work is relevant to the argument of this chapter and thus encourages the development of dynamic interventions in the field of guidance and counselling that take into account the complex nature of reality. This interpretation opts neither for the evolutionism that presumes that societies change through an ongoing process of improvement and perfection (Touraine, 1977), nor for the structural deterministic approaches that leave individuals and social groups no room for action.

Full employment and predictability in the 1950s and 1960s

Ever since industrialisation first emerged in the eighteenth century, the capitalist economy has undergone cyclical crises and recurrent periods of unemployment. The Fordist wage relation model was set up soon after the Second World War leading to a period of unprecedented economic prosperity from 1945 to 1973–4. During this post-war period, opportunities for advancement in a trade or profession began to increase. Thus, the Fordist model can be characterised as follows: first, the dominant form of work organisation devised by the scientific management approach and epitomised by assembly line work (Taylorism); second, growth of mass consumption in line with growth of productivity, which was made possible by assembly-line work; third, relatively full employment; and fourth, methods of regulating tensions and conflicts through collective bargaining and the welfare state.

At the same time, occupational choices opened up considerably compared to earlier periods. The marked development of the state in Western countries and the employment created in state and public bodies provided young people with career opportunities and the chance to make choices with the help of career guidance and counselling professionals. Since this was a period characterised by relatively full employment, individuals could also cut short their academic studies and still find a job requiring fewer skills and qualifications, as in the case of assembly-line work.

During this period, three dominant sociological viewpoints seeking to explain occupational mobility co-existed: status attainment theory and allocation model theory dominated the English-language literature; and social reproduction theory the French-language literature. These three viewpoints are restated by various authors. For example, Hotchkiss and Borow (1990) identify a theory (status attainment theory) and an approach (structural approach); and Kerckhoff (1976) distinguishes between two processes, socialisation and allocation.

Status attainment theory

This theory was developed during a period characterised by almost uninterrupted economic prosperity in North America from the Second World War onwards. The theory was very popular among sociologists in the United States and provided the inspiration for several empirical studies during the 1970s (Abbott, 1993). The favourable economic context reinforced this position insofar as greater opportunities for mobility made it possible to link occupational aspirations with social status, at least on a conceptual level. According to this theory,[1] the father's education and occupation influence the children's educational attainment, the first job they hold and, to a large extent, their subsequent jobs. The theory is based on the following postulates: the socialisation process establishes a link between social origin and status attainment; motivations are particularised by the individual's scope for action; individual preferences and characteristics can be matched with society's labour force requirements through the labour market; and everyone has more or less the same opportunities.

Critiques of the theory then prompted its refinement in terms of its explanation of how variables related to social origin influence future mobility (Colclough & Horan, 1983). Family social status and intellectual characteristics determine sociological and psychological processes, such as young people's educational and occupational aspirations on the one hand, and the type of encouragement provided by parents, teachers, and peers on the other. Ultimately, these processes influence educational attainment and career. This theory, therefore, adopts a voluntarist viewpoint since it is motivation that defines the career plan to be achieved. It is less a question of transforming the labour market than one of matching people's preferences to job opportunities.

[1] The theory as presented here is based on its original formulation by Blau and Duncan in their book *The American occupational structure*, first published in 1967.

Reproduction or allocation model theory

At the same time that theoretical development and the empirical studies of status attainment theory were taking place, a more structural viewpoint was being articulated. In the 1960s, sociologists examined how one's career in school was determined, and characterised social class origin by living conditions, an ethos, and a distinctive cultural and social capital (Bourdieu & Passeron, 1983).

A few years later, Kerckhoff (1976) showed that societal forces select, classify, and assign people a place based on imposed criteria. Instead of attributing status attainment to motivations and learned abilities, Kerckhoff associated occupation with structural limits and selectivity. These constraints involved race, institutional phenomena, and a region's economy, which determined the availability of jobs.

The allocation model theory was developed in reaction to status attainment theory because the latter attributes an intentionality to people that disregards institutional mechanisms related to social stratification and sectors of economic activity. Among these, sex and race are two obvious elements of social stratification that have an influence on career. According to this perspective, career choice results from the process of systemic discrimination based on complex external and internal rules of the game through which the reproduction of social classes is perpetuated. The institutional mechanisms of entering an occupation start with social origin, continue as individuals go through the educational system, and are still operating as they get their first and then subsequent jobs. According to structural explanations, these mechanisms are either levers or restraints to educational and occupational development (Kerckhoff, 1995) and play a determining role in social mobility since they act as mechanisms of opportunity for some and of selection and exclusion for others.

In the mid-1970s, both status attainment theory and the structural viewpoint were criticised. In a new economic context in which the opportunities of a greater number of people were limited, an explanation based on motivation, which did not take structural change in society into consideration, proved to be inadequate (Abbott, 1993). Structuralism was criticised for denying the role of individual consciousness and rationality (Javeau, 1997). Radical structuralism as well did not succeed in incorporating free will as an element of social transformation (Castoriadis, 1975). In short, it was as if a paradigmatic shift displaced these theories and underpinned the development of a model that could launch a new generation of empirical studies (Colclough & Horan, 1983). The structural viewpoint was pitted against voluntarism, and vice versa, but neither was intrinsically formulated to take the complexity that characterises our era into consideration. Nor did either approach adequately reflect the dynamic character of the interrelationship between the individual and society.

The employment crisis of the 1980s and 1990s

The last two decades have been characterised by economic upheavals, which have altered the structure and nature of jobs. On the one hand, economic globalisation and the restructuring of firms (mergers, horizontal and vertical integrations, and, more recently, re-engineering) have resulted in the loss of millions of jobs, rising unemployment, and precarious employment for many in Western industrialised societies.[2] On the other hand, the development of automated technology, which replaces human labour, and the growth of services, which tend to diversify and intensify work schedules, have been the main economic factors fuelling the strong demand for flexibility. The latter is defined as 'a greater ability on the part of firms to adapt to an unstable and continually changing environment' (Burrows, Gilbert, & Pollert, 1992). The accompanying demand for numerical flexibility (the number of jobs and the employment relationship) and functional flexibility (changes in work organisation) gave rise to a structural and cultural crisis that can be seen in labour market segmentation and the reorganisation of work and firms.

There was increasing acknowledgement of the structural nature of the employment crisis. Jobs linked to heavy technologies disappeared and the skills and qualifications of the workers affected became obsolete (De Coster, 1992). New jobs emerged but they did not compensate for the job losses incurred, and, more particularly, the unemployed, without the skills and qualifications required by the new technologies, were left out. Workers who lost their jobs tended to be older, with work experience limited to Taylorised tasks. In the absence of policies for further on-the-job training, they had little chance of one day holding the required skills and qualifications. Moreover, unemployment tended to be a 'long-term' situation, a new reality which was a break with previous periods in which it was largely either a temporary or a cyclical experience. For some, such a long, unproductive period leads to a withdrawal, resulting in social exclusion and disaffiliation (Castel, 1995). Workers affected by this form of unemployment also have to live with precarious employment, with no guarantee of keeping a job, and, thus, no guarantee of a steady income.

The employment crisis was accompanied by a labour crisis character-

---

[2] The Organisation for Economic Cooperation and Development estimated that in 1996 there were 33 million unemployed people in the industrialised world, or 8% for the countries as a whole, compared to 24 million in 1990 (France Press, 1996).

ised by the transformation of work organisation. Firms counted on a rapid shift from mass production to one that was flexible and specialised (Storper & Salais, 1997). As a result, priority was given to technological changes with a highly automated content and to reorganising work groups on the basis of a sustained increase in productivity. The creation of semi-autonomous teams, standardisation and normalisation of quality criteria by the International Standards Organisation, multi-skilling, and programmes of excellence are but a few examples of the organisational innovations instituted in the search for more flexibility – in this case, functional flexibility.

Viewed positively, these changes provide an opportunity for people to redefine work, inspired by an ethic centred on the individual but using team work. The nature of tasks was being transformed and thus instead of carrying out the type of repetitive, monotonous tasks required by assembly-line work of the Fordist era, the technical system resulted in growing abstraction and complexity, for example, in data interpretation, description of circuits and processes at work, adjustment, diagnosis, anticipation of dysfunction, and problem resolution. Multi-skilling became both horizontal and vertical. Mobilising workers around the objectives of quality and productivity gave them more responsibilities, autonomy, and control. The worker was no longer excluded or marginalised from the production process but became a manufacturing worker (or technologist) with a management function (Coriat, 1991). In brief, such changes gave rise to a new type of workplace relationship that should have resulted in increased democratisation of work. Furthermore, experiments in the third sector, that is, the social economy, may provide the basis for methods to democratise firms (Anheier & Seibel, 1990). The social economy includes firms that generally have the status of cooperatives or non-profit organisations and operate democratically by encouraging participation by workers and even by the public, giving priority to the latter in surplus redistribution.

Viewed negatively, people who are concerned about job security can be manipulated by playing on their fear of losing their livelihood. Thus, 'survivors' are ashamed to complain and somehow adapt to the context of precarious employment. Work can become a place where paradox and suffering are rife because workers are seduced by the new elements of work reorganisation (for example, autonomy, team concept and total quality) but are also often disappointed with the way managers change individual and group aspirations into production goals. The ideology of excellence tends to merge and confuse the firm's requirements with the desires of employees, since firms are more interested in increasing productivity than in their workers' quality of work life. The managerial ideology of 'always wanting more' has multiple effects on health, the signs of which are fatigue, exhaustion, disillusionment, and, in short, demoralised troops. In those contexts where material factors compensate for poor working conditions and where there is a strong culture of consumption, people defend themselves in individual ways, some of which are ultimately harmful to them (alcoholism and drug abuse, isolation). In this context of adaptation to economic globalisation, individual career aspirations as well as social mobility become more fragile in the face of market forces.

Human capital theory

During the 1980s, the economic approach of human capital theory (Becker, 1993) has in a way succeeded status attainment theory (Abbott, 1993). Both these theories share several common features. The model of classical (and neo-classical) economic theory regards *homo oeconomicus* as an economic agent, or a social actor, who is guided by a defined rationality. From this perspective, economic and social progress is based on market and industrial development. The position of an individual is that of a rational being who wishes to maximise his or her investments for future gains. One of the premises of this model is that the most qualified individuals, in terms of education and experience, will hold the best-paid jobs with the most favourable working conditions (Krahn & Lowe, 1993). According to this theory, the individual invests in his or her intellectual capital, education, training, and productivity (through efforts to be flexible and mobile) and invests in health through the quality of food and leisure. Each person makes a decision to accept a level of costs for his or her education based on preferences and capacities while assessing the benefits that education might bring to the labour market. This theory is situated in the voluntarism–adaptation sector of figure 3.1 because it favours individual decision and suggests that people adopt strategies so that they can get the best out of any situation.

This conservative explanation supports the notion of career in terms of adapting to the labour market since it considers that stratification and social inequalities are necessary components of the social order. However, in the context of the end of this century, which is marked by liberalisation and deregulation, the foundations of human capital theory, which is based on the market economy model, have turned out to be socially unsatisfactory (Krahn & Lowe, 1993). Not unlike status attainment theory, which was examined above, this perspective of market adaptation disregards the market's imperfections and dysfunctions, organisational instability, and cultural and individual differences such as race, gender, and ethnic group

(Fitzgerald & Betz, 1994). Moreover, given the wide disparity between available jobs and skills and qualifications, individuals are unlikely to have much confidence in this theory's virtues when the cost is too high for its returns.

Segmentation theory

Piore and Sabel (1984), the principal proponents of segmentation theory, traced the contours of the segmented society, which is divided into two types of labour market: the primary market, which consists of good jobs, and the secondary market, which is characterised by precarious and unstable employment. The transition from mass to flexible production gave rise to this dual-market model. In economic terms, dual theories show that there are at least two segments, or realities, in the labour market: the core and the periphery. The core is made up of large firms, which are either monopolistic or oligopolistic, use leading-edge technology, and offer favourable working conditions and career opportunities to a stable core of skilled workers responsible for regular production. The periphery includes small firms which offer lower wages and less occupational mobility for non-permanent employees. This segmentation is also present in firms, giving rise to a model of concentric circles which embeds the existence of a permanent core of qualified workers carrying out regular production and the establishment of peripheral classes of temporary surplus workers who are meant to provide, on command, the supplementary amount of work necessary to meet the imperatives of a flexible production that is delivered just in time and adapted to clients' requirements (Pollert, 1991). The dual society, or society 'at two or three speeds', as Gorz (1988) called it, is thus a reality in many industrialised countries.

Just like theories of reproduction and allocation, segmentation theory incorporates the idea of structural determinants which restrict career opportunities. Middle-aged white males are most often found in the primary market, the sector of unionised large firms, whereas women, youths, Blacks, and ethnic minorities are more heavily concentrated in small- and medium-sized businesses in the secondary market where jobs are precarious and there are fewer career advancement opportunities.

However, two important elements are missing from this theory: on the one hand, the unemployed, who end up on social security and disaffiliated (Castel, 1995); and, on the other hand, holders of capital, that is, bankers, rich shareholders, annuitants, etc. (De Bandt, Dejours, & Dubar, 1995). Segmentation theory, which derives from Marxism (Edwards, Gordon, & Reich, 1973), is useful in pointing out the existence of segmented markets, but it does not explain the causes of segmentation, nor does it question its bases. It is at the top of figure 1 because it neither refers to sociological and political systems nor hints at the notion of social transformations.

Regulation theory

Regulation theory combines the basic notions of Marxist economics and the sociology of social movements to explain the historical alternations between periods of relative stability and change, and the mechanisms through which rules regulating the divergent interests and conflicts in society are instituted.

In order to face competition, firms carry out two types of change: those related to work organisation and those related to the institutional aspect of firms (Bélanger, Grant, & Lévesque, 1994). Organisational changes address the actual work and production activities, whereas institutional changes deal with the firm's political system, that is, the distribution of power and rules of the game (laws, collective agreement, and government regulations). Firms act according to at least two logics: a Taylorist logic and an alternative logic. The Taylorist logic of labour management provides for organisational innovations to increase productivity that sometimes reduce workers' power. Demands at work are increased while work autonomy is not, thus giving rise to destructive situations (Karasek & Theorell, 1990). The alternative logic emphasises institutional changes by granting more power to workers, for example, through collective ownership of firms and workers' participation in strategic decision making (Comeau & Lévesque, 1993). When managements adopt the alternative logic, they are making a major political compromise, because they believe in doing so that they are giving themselves an advantage over their competitors by strongly motivating and integrating the work force into the firm.

To explain labour force mobility, regulation theory takes into account both economic and social determinants, and the possibility of enlightened collective action to guide economic development and career opportunities. In figure 3.1, regulation theory is situated near the 'transformation' pole, because industrialised countries are following two strategies in managing the economy. The first involves increasing competitiveness and flexibility by reinforcing the neo-liberal project and giving priority to de-regulation, globalisation, free trade, and disengagement of the state. The second strives to develop more power for citizens through the democratisation of society and a balanced adjustment between economic and social activities. This second choice, supported by the Group of Lisbon (1995), heralds the emergence of a new international civil society whose social contract stresses the imposition of minimum standards, co-operation, thinking globally (in terms of ethics and respect for human rights), and acting locally. This new world-society would provide the scope for a more active citizenship. In other words, the economy should reclaim its place in society but it should not dominate to the exclusion of all other factors.

Technical production capacities are reaching such a level, moreover, that the central role of paid work is being called into question. Some foresee 'the end of work' (Rifkin, 1995) while others insist that human labour should be returned to the centre of economic activities (De Bandt, Dejours, & Dubar, 1995), hence the necessity to redefine the notion of work so as to include all of society's production activities. For example, would it be possible for domestic or mutual help activities to be henceforth recognised and valorised to the same extent as paid work? And why not recognise and develop training time as well, since it is beneficial for firms? Could production capacities provide a decent standard of living for everybody? How might the economy operate then and what role would the state play in sharing and redistributing wealth? These are the many questions raised by sociology and which have a significant impact on the notion of career.

Courses of action in the career field

As was seen above, in the career field, sociology offers various theories, each with its own way of interpreting career-related phenomena. This multi-paradigmatic situation may be seen as a richness that can help inspire courses of action with the ability to capture the complex reality of the career field. Making the transition from general theories to intervention is, however, not self-evident and is examined here.

First, the scope of changes affecting employment and work requires that psychometric tests be used wisely. Positivism, a current of thought that seeks the truth through the formulation of universal theories and the focus on quantitative and statistical methods to make predictions, has enjoyed a privileged position in twentieth-century scientific thought. In career counselling, it encourages the use of matching: people are classified objectively into categories (of interests, abilities and values, systematically correlated to the traits needed to take up a particular craft or profession); and individuals are matched to occupations and the technical division of labour (Granovetter, 1981). The idea that in looking to their future, people adapt and match themselves to the environment, is apparently realised in the science of counselling, but it becomes a problem as soon as individuals are asked to adapt to the 'unadaptable'. Roberts (1981) maintains that the assumption of career choice, self-achievement, *and* equal opportunity have paradoxically led to a fatalistic acceptance of market forces. Harmon (1996) conjures up a disturbing portrait of the disparity between this idealist career aim and the real world of hegemonic economic rationality and resultant social exclusion. These considerations provide the disciplines of psychology and sociology with the opportunity to pool their ideas so as to develop a perspective that once again considers tools as means rather than ends in themselves.

Second, the institutional dimension of career should be given greater consideration in intervention. Guidance counsellors must develop analytical abilities that allow them to understand, anticipate, and act in the environment (sociological and economic analyses, consideration of multicultural diversity, identification of problematic institutional practices, establishment of facilitative action, etc.). The existence of institutional barriers and the practices of educational institutions and employers that give rise to unemployment and racial and sexual discrimination are all elements that reinforce and contribute to the reproduction of a structure of privileges for some (the elite, a minority) and a hard reality for others (Thomas, 1996). Unless the rules of the game are changed, today's society will continue to be stratified into a structure of unequal opportunities, and institutions will continue to operate according to a division of labour that confers these inequalities.

Third, experiments in career counselling that favour dynamic types of intervention should be developed. More concretely, practitioners should gather information about the links between the social organisation, the power relationships it produces, and personality development. This will help them see submissive behaviours as unhealthy and understand the mistrust of people who are disadvantaged. Practitioners will be better able to play the role of advocate of or with the client. Finally, they can strive to empower clients by helping them to act before acting for them. The increase in power in turn encourages the establishment of a dialogic relationship. In this sense, the act of intervening is not neutral. Indeed, it can be said that the claim of neutrality strives to camouflage the practitioners' true options (Freire, 1973).

For an interactionist and contextualist approach to develop, sociology must be better able to take human subjectivity into consideration. The psychodynamics of work constitutes a theory and a clinical approach to the work place (Dejours 1993) that draw on comprehensive sociology, psychoanalysis, and Habermas's action theory (1984) in order to understand better the subjective and intersubjective relations between people who work together, as well as how identity is constructed in the work place. The examination of pleasure and suffering in the working environment provides an innovative way of understanding work organisation and the defence mechanisms people set up to protect themselves at work. In figure 3.1, this theory is placed in the sector defined by individual antonomy and social transformation because the psychodynamics of work provide a means to break the cycle of individual adjustment to bad working conditions. When the corrective measures that need to be made in a work organisation are examined, the action has to take place at the collective level, to go beyond the limits of the individual client–counsellor relationship.

Finally, practitioners' knowledge of personal, group, organisational, and institutional issues leads to consideration of the group as the preferred system of intervention. The group represents a source of support, a means to self-improvement, self-development, and a way to share certain concerns, ideas, and goals; it constitutes a source of identity and social recognition. The solidarity resulting from this affiliation with a group increases the intensity of convictions and multiplies the strength of collective power. Holding clinics in the work place as a method of group intervention allows practitioners and group members to go beyond the limits of individual client–counsellor relationships with regard to ident-ifying and applying solutions to work organisations.

Many professionals in the field of workplace mental health face an impasse when it comes to changing the pathogenic elements of work organisation that cause stress, depression, burn-out, alcoholism and drug addiction, and family problems. Very often, supportive action is limited to such interventions as individual therapy, medication, suggestions for relaxation exercises and stress management courses, without considering how the work environment itself can be improved. More often than not the advice to leave the work environment has been the principal method of regulation. The time has come for researchers and career practitioners to ask themselves whether it is still relevant to encourage individuals to adapt to an unhealthy environment (work overload, precarious work, disrupted work schedules). In the context of profound employment changes, it is worth considering new courses of intervention that take into account both the individual and social costs resulting from the pathogenic effects of work organisations and institutions. Surely, it is worthwhile to contribute to changes that promote both individual and collective well being.

Conclusion

Although its theories have inspired many empirical studies, sociology as a discipline has not been drawn upon enough in developing paradigms and approaches in the career field. Because it identifies contradictions and paradoxes, sociology challenges routines by situating practices in the broader context of important contemporary changes. However, any paradigm renewal in the career field cannot afford to overlook sociology, with its projects for democratisation, promotion of integration and skill building, and transformations of dehumanising conditions.

As profound changes are currently affecting social mobility and career development, career counselling professionals must recognise the fact that people's employment situations are the result of both constraints due to the economic context and more or less strategic individual and collective behaviour. It is therefore suggested that the type of action favoured by the theory of the psychodynamics of work be placed at the centre of figure 3.1. It is at the centre, not for reasons of political expediency, but to give this action the best conditions under which practitioners and researchers can face complexity and at the same time can fulfil their social responsibility.

REFERENCES

Abbott, A. (1993). The sociology of work and occupations. *Annual Review of Sociology, 19,* 187–209.

Anheier, H. K. & Seibel, W. (Eds.) (1990). *The third sector. Comparative studies of nonprofit organizations.* Berlin/New York: Walter de Gruyter.

Becker, G. S. (1993). *Human capital* (3rd edn). Chicago: University of Chicago Press.

Bélanger, P. R., Grant, M., & Lévesque, B. (1994). *La modernisation sociale des entreprises.* Montreal: Presses de l'Université de Montréal.

Berger, P. L. & Luckmann, T. (1980). *The social construction of reality: A treatise in the sociology of knowledge.* New York: Irvington Publishers.

Blau, P. M. & Duncan, O. (1967). *The American occupational structure.* New York: John Wiley & Sons.

Boudon, R. & Bourricaud, F. (1994). *Dictionnaire critique de la sociologie.* Paris: Presses universitaires de France.

Bourdieu, P. & Passeron, J. C. (1983). *La reproduction: éléments pour une théorie du système d'enseignement.* Paris: Editions de Minuit. (Original work published 1970.) (Trans. (1977) *Reproduction in education, society and culture.* London/Beverly Hills: Sage Publications.)

Burrows R., Gilbert, N., & Pollert, A. (1992). Introduction: Fordism, Post-Fordism and economic flexibility. In N. Gilbert, R. Burrows, & A. Pollert (Eds.), *Fordism and flexibility* (pp. 1–9). New York: St Martin's Press.

Castel, R. (1995). *Les métamorphoses de la question sociale.* Paris: Librairie Arthème Fayard.

Castoriadis, C. (1975). *L'institution imaginaire de la société.* Paris: Seuil.

Colclough, G. & Horan, P. M. (1983). The status attainment paradigm: An application of a Kuhnian perspective. *Sociological Quarterly, 24,* 25–42.

Comeau, Y. & Lévesque, B. (1993). Workers' financial participation in the property of enterprises in Quebec. *Industrial and Economic Democracy, 14* (2), 233–250.

Coriat, B. (1991). *Penser à l'envers, travail et organisation du travail dans l'entreprise japonaise.* Paris: Bourgeois.

De Bandt, J., Dejours, C., & Dubar, C. (1995). *La France malade du travail.* Paris: Bayard Editions.

De Coster, M. (1992). La division technique du travail. In D. G. Tremblay (Ed.), *Travail et société, une introduction à la sociologie du travail* (pp. 117–150). Quebec City: Editions Agence d'Arc et Télé-Université.

Dejours, C. (1993). Contributions of the psychodynamic analysis of work situations to the study of organizational crises. *Industrial and Environmental Crisis Quarterly, 7,* 2.

Durkheim, E. (1964). *The rules of sociological method* (first Free Press paperback edn.) Trans. S. A. Solovay & J. H. Mueller, ed. George E. G. Catlin. New York: The Free Press.

Edwards, M., Gordon, D., & Reich, M. (1973). A theory of labor market segmentation. *American Economic Review, 63* (2), 359–365.

Fitzgerald, L. F. & Betz, N. E. (1994). Career development in cultural context: The role of gender, race, class, and sexual orientation. In M. L. Savickas & R.W. Lent (Eds.), *Convergence in career development theories: implications for science and practice* (pp. 103–117). Palo Alto, CA: CPP Books.

France Press (1996, 25 March). *Organisation for Economic Cooperation and Development. Le Soleil,* p. A13.

Freire, P. (1973). *Pédagogie des opprimés.* Paris: Maspéro.

Gorz, A. (1988). *Métamorphoses du travail: quête du sens. Critique de la raison économique.* Paris: Galilée.

Granovetter, M. (1981). Toward a sociological theory and income differences. In I. Berg (ed.), *Sociological perspectives on labor markets* (pp. 12–43). London: Academic Press.

Group of Lisbon (1995). *Limits to competition.* Cambridge, MA: MIT Press.

Habermas, J. (1984). *The theory of communicative action.* Boston: Beacon Press.

Harmon, L. W. (1996). A moving target: The widening gap between theory and practice. In. M. L. Savickas & W. B. Walsh (Eds.), *Handbook of career counseling theory and practice* (pp. 37–54). Palo Alto, CA: Davies-Black Publishing.

Hotchkiss, L. & Borow, H. (1990). Sociological perspectives on work and career development. In D. Brown & L. Brooks (Eds.), *Career choice and development. Applying contemporary theories to practice* (pp. 262–307). San Francisco/ Oxford: Jossey-Bass Publishers.

Javeau, C. (1997). *Leçons de sociologie.* Paris: Armand Colin.

Karasek, R. & Theorell, T. (1990). *Healthy work: Stress, productivity, and the reconstruction of working life.* New York: Basic Books.

Kerckhoff, A. C. (1976). The status attainment process: Socialization or allocation? *Social Forces, 55* (2), 368–381.

(1995). Institutional arrangements and stratification processes in industrial societies. *Annual Review of Sociology, 15,* 323–347.

Krahn, H. J. & Lowe, G. S. (1993). *Work, industry, and Canadian society* (2nd edn). Scarborough, Ontario: Nelson Canada.

Marx, K. & Engels, F. (1982). *L'idéologie allemande.* Paris: Essentiel, Editions sociales.

Parsons, T. (1951). *The social system.* Glencoe, IL: Free Press.

Piore, M. J. & Sabel, C. F. (1984). *The second industrial divide.* New York: Basic Books.

Pollert, A. (1991). *Farewell to flexibility.* Oxford/Cambridge, MA: Blackwell.

Rifkin, J. (1995). *The end of work: The decline of the global labor force and the dawn of the post-market era.* New York: G. P. Putnam's Sons.

Roberts, K. (1981). The sociology of work entry and occupational choice. In A. G. Watts, D. E. Super, & J. M. Kidd (Eds.), *Career development in Britain: Some contributions to theory and practice.* Cambridge: CRAC/Hobsons Press.

Storper, M. & Salais, R. (1997). *Worlds of production: The action frameworks of the economy.* Cambridge, MA: Harvard University Press.

Thomas, S. C. (1996). A sociological perspective on contextualism. *Journal of Counseling and Development, 74,* 525–536.

Touraine, A. (1977). *The self-production of society.* Chicago: University of Chicago Press.

Weber, M. (1968). *Economy and society* (3 vols.). New York: Bedminster Press.

4 Renovating the psychology of careers for the twenty-first century

Mark L. Savickas

Scrutinising the psychology of careers during the twentieth century requires a close examination of the cultural context in which organisational careers emerged, then flourished, and now languish. Following this analysis, the present chapter discusses how vocational psychology, a discipline born early in the twentieth century, has responded to cultural transformations that, as they reshape work and its social organisation, demand renovations in the psychology of careers.

The context for career

The editors of this volume define career broadly, 'as the engagement of the individual with society through involvement in the organisation of work'. They do so to allow chapter authors to specify manifold meanings for career. Yet, in so doing, they highlight the very essence of career, the social context of work. Different social contexts condition different social arrangements of work. The dominant arrangements that have characterised a particular historical era and specific society have been usefully designated by different concepts, including vocation, craft, and career. From this perspective, my understanding of career has a particular meaning, embedded in twentieth-century culture and society in North America. This historical era gave rise to the essential structure that required most workers to construct careers within bureaucratic boundaries, thus defining the concept of career with a very specific meaning. Now, changes in that cultural context may be devitalising the concept and experience of career, or at least redefining its core meaning.

To trace the rise and fall of career in North America, I examine social conventions, shared assumptions, and implicit values surrounding survival and procreation, that is work and family as central concerns of people. By focusing on the evolution of work and family across three cultural eras in American history, we can examine how worklives were shaped by agrarian, urban, and global economies. In so doing, I will propose that urban society provided the medium in which organisations fashioned the concept of career and substantiated its meaning. Before considering this proposal in more detail, let us review the predecessor of career – that is, vocation.

Agrarian economy and vocations

Throughout most of American history, individuals lived in an agricultural economy. For example, during the 1800s, more than half of the population in the United States lived and worked on farms. The agrarian culture moulded work and family roles to fit its needs. The dominant social institution was the family – a large, multigenerational labour unit and production team who worked together in the fields or cottages. The family healed the sick, educated the young, nursed the elderly, and laboured to support itself. If there was schooling outside the family, that education occurred in a one-room school house operated by the smartest or most sophisticated person in town. Work, school, and family were interwoven, with the family itself being the major social institution.

When the time came to earn a livelihood, young people typically just inherited their parents' occupation. For example, people born on farms became farmers and children of crafts workers joined the guild. Occasionally, a family member heard a *calling* from the church, the court, or the village and left the family to become a minister, lawyer, or merchant. Thus, the work ethic of the time came to be referred to as a calling or vocation. The secular version of vocation was often called a craft, and individuals followed their calling or pursued their craft.

Urban economy and careers

With the advent of American industrial society at the end of the nineteenth century, cultural changes occurred in the institutions of work, school, and family. Jobs were relocated from farms to urban areas. As people moved from farms to the hubs of modern industry they, together with a throng of immigrants, formed large metropolitan cities. Rather than working for themselves or a small business, more and more people moved to cities, many of them securing employment in large, bureaucratic organisations. These organisations gave birth to the concept of career as individual worklives followed a predictable course up an organisation's ladder. Career path replaced vocation as the dominant metaphor. As the fundamental social identity of individuals in urban economies became linked to work performed rather than family of origin, one's occupation changed from a calling to what one was called (e.g., Miller, Smith, Cook, Farmer, etc.).

Because the fundamental form of modern twentieth-century organisations was hierarchical, career connotes a vertical perspective, one that
defined career success as individual advancement up the corporate ladder.
Entry-level positions in most occupations were linked systematically to a
sequence of future positions, each with more responsibility and greater
rewards. For example, at mid-century a high-school graduate in Montana
could begin employment as a labourer in a copper mine, with good wages
and the prospect of a 2 or 3% salary increase each year along with the
opportunity to move up the ladder from labourer, to heavy equipment
operator, to blaster, and eventually (say at about the age of thirty-five)
contract miner. Wages for contract miners matched or exceeded the
wages earned by college graduates in white-collar positions. Workers
learned the skills necessary to climb the blue-collar career ladder on the
job by watching or assisting more senior workers perform the skills. Night
school and advanced education were unnecessary.

As working changed at the beginning of the industrial era, so did
schooling. Schools became institutions that educated people for the
industrial society. School structure imitated the model of the factory, with
graded class rooms and specialised teachers replacing one-room school-
houses and generalist teachers. One system fit all students as a teacher,
who was expert in a subject matter or type of student, stood in front of
thirty students sitting in rows and quietly working on individual tasks.
These schools systematically socialised students for assembly lines and
organisational life. Psychologists did not need to research problems in
school-to-work transitions, these transitions were small changes for which
students were well prepared.

In addition to restructuring schools, the movement to urban jobs also
restructured American families – after all, when you went to Detroit to
make automobiles you did not take twenty people with you. The industrial
economy's need for mobile workers changed multigenerational families
on farms into nuclear families in cities. Like assembly line jobs, the
functions of the family became specialised. Urban schools educated
children, metropolitan hospitals cured the sick, county nursing homes
cared for the elderly, and companies provided work. The nuclear family,
relieved of its critical work functions, focused almost exclusively on
reproduction, now emphasising procreation, sex, romance, and compan-
ionship. City people married for romantic love, rather than to merge
farms. Furthermore, urban families had fewer children; even today, family
size continues to shrink.

Modern society no longer expected people to select a livelihood by
following family traditions or praying for spiritual inspiration. Those who
continued to make their choice in this traditional manner were labeled as

immature and enmeshed. Instead of following the family tradition, students were encouraged by their teachers to choose an occupation autonomously from the hundreds of specialised and compartmentalised jobs engendered by industrialisation and its assembly lines. A new occupation even emerged to help them choose – vocational guidance counsellor (Bloomfield, 1915). Guidance counsellors applied – and continue to do so – the viewpoint of positivist science and its technical procedures to help individuals choose occupations rationally.

Frank Parsons (1909) devised the paradigm for modern vocational guidance in urging counsellors to objectify a client's abilities and interests and then use 'true reasoning' to match these traits to occupations with corresponding requirements and rewards. Parsons's matching paradigm for guiding occupational choice remains the most widely used approach to career counselling. Today individuals describe themselves in responding to interests inventories and ability tests, and then a computer compares these responses to occupational profiles in its data banks. The computer produces a profile that portrays objectively the degree of fit between an individual and dozens of different occupations. After discussing these empirical findings and objective facts with a counsellor, clients select a few occupations for in-depth exploration, leading to a final choice. Parsons's 'true reasoning' paradigm provides career counsellors with a rational and objective model along with scientifically reliable and valid methods for helping individuals choose occupations in a society where occupations have become overly specialised. This matching person-to-position paradigm has served twentieth-century organisations and individuals well, but it relies on stable occupations and predictable career paths.

Global economy and worklives

The end of the twentieth century finds US industrial society becoming an information society. As part of this change, large industrial organisations such as IBM, US Steel, and General Motors are shrinking and reshaping themselves. Daily newspapers are replete with stories of 're-engineering organisations', 'downsizing', 'learning organisations', 'dejobbing', and 'contingent workers'. Fewer and fewer companies promise life-time employment following a career path. Increasingly, individuals working at overspecialised jobs that involve a single task are being replaced by employees who work in teams with each member performing many tasks. As the information age sweeps away the old hierarchies, its computer technology flattens organisations, breaks middle management rungs off the career ladder, and hires 'contingent workers' for term-specific contracts. Job security is history. Without the hierarchical, bureaucratic organisations that gave form to careers, career paths themselves seem to be disappearing. In 1996, the incumbent US Labor Secretary, Robert Reich, observed that 'Twenty years ago, you could fairly easily plot a career. It might have had a few twists and turn, but you would progress though a hierarchy of positions that were more or less predetermined. Career paths are now gone. They're not even trails. . . The lack of a career path means that people . . . are more on their own' (Brazaitis, 1996).

In the emerging employment compact, employees are urged to view themselves as 'self-employed', with employers being their customers. Because employees can anticipate losing several jobs (or working for several customers) during their worklives, they must focus on developing and maintaining skills that enhance their current performance and can get the next job. This means that, to maintain their employability, contemporary workers must manage their own careers, with résumés becoming a list of transferable skills and adaptive strengths. For their part, employers should provide constructive feedback about employee performance and offer developmental opportunities. Given this transformation in society and its occupations, life-time employment must become life-time employability.

As the economy changes and careers fracture, so does America's nuclear family. Vice-President Gore at his Family Reunion Conference in Nashville (26 June 1996), stated the obvious when he said, 'We have a workplace crunched by change. It is creating profound anxiety. Work and family are in fierce competition. Lifetime job security is a thing of the past. The family is the shock absorber for this tremendous social change.' For the last twenty years, the fit between work and family has been grinding like gears that do not mesh. The emergence of family-friendly companies, that will give workplace flexibility and leave time to address family responsibilities, is an external band-aid for a nation experiencing internal haemorrhaging. Some families find that the schools are not educating their children, hospitals are not admitting their spouses, and nursing homes will not accept their impoverished parents. With work harder to find and paying less, there are increasing numbers of dual-earner, single-parent, and alternative families. Thus, US society is engaged in a redefinition of the family unit to include a variety of structures.

Most surviving and thriving organisations have realised that the only realistic adaptation is to live with change; they have accepted permanent internal reorganisation as a way of life. They realise that, in a complex and fast changing marketplace, the bureaucratic form is maladaptive because the top of the hierarchy does not know what the bottom is doing. Organisations are breaking the middle management rungs off the career ladder, thereby destroying the ladder itself. Instead of looking up, employees are being taught to look over to colleagues and to move diagonally across departments. Even academia is starting to downsize and place its professors in transdisciplinary teams rather than specialised departments. Tenure as a form of life-time employment is being replaced with five-year contracts.

Unfortunately for many communities, individual workers do not seem to be adapting as quickly as organisations. Laid-off workers need new skills, the most important being new cultural skills with which to adapt to the information era and the global economy. Because the family form is connected to how people work, families too must adapt. Society must become more open to multiple forms of family with diverse structures. Schools also need to diversify, no longer can they consist of uniform classrooms that produce standardised graduates for a stable labour market. Just as there will be multiple forms of families, there must be multiple forms of schooling. Whatever the outcome may be, cultural transformation is in full progress.

Vocational psychology's response to cultural changes in career

Vocational psychologists have made noteworthy contributions in helping to shape the societal meaning of career and fostering career development among individuals. Now, some of these contributions require renovation or replacement to keep pace with the changing structure of work and new global economy (Savickas, 1993, 1994, 1995). The decline of organisational careers directly affects career counselling as a specialised occupation. As vocational psychologists move into the information age their viewpoint must change. Like that of other occupations, vocational psychology's perspective has been conditioned by tradition and training. These social practices have produced a psychology of careers and counselling methods highly related to the modern industrial era. Vocational psychologists' self-defining commitment has been to objectively measuring individual differences, studying occupations, and scientifically matching people to positions. These commitments have led them to privilege the core values of rational decision making, independence, planning, individual achievement, advancement up the hierarchy, and personal success and satisfaction.

As the culture that embeds vocational psychologists' scientific ideals and objective practices changes, it is hard for them to stand outside their training and traditions. However, psychologists must because modern career education and counselling, based on linear projections of career, no longer seem as useful to postmodern workers who encounter twists and turns, with both good and bad surprises. Accordingly, vocational psychologists must participate in a re-vision and re-interpretation that responds to these cultural changes and the new difficulties that students and workers encounter. Vocational psychology's self-interpretation is at a turning point as its practitioners re-examine their ideals, reflect on their models, and choose new values to emphasise.

The core constructs that have been the foundation of modern vocational psychology are already being re-examined and, in many instances, transformed. At first blush, the cultural revolution seems to have separated vocational psychologists into two camps – those who defend the numerous accomplishments of objectivism in producing trait-and-factor models and methods for career counselling versus those who devise constructivist methods for career intervention that are more sensitive to the needs of diverse clients and individuals who are at the margins of objectivist career theory and practice. However, this dichotomy is simplistic. I have never heard a vocational psychologist call for constructivist models and methods to replace objectivist theory and techniques. There is no attack on the trait-and-factor camp. On the contrary, leading constructivist career theorists (e.g. Cochran, 1997) continue to applaud and build upon the accomplishments of trait-and-factor models as they produce supplemental models and materials. Hopefully, this means that vocational psychologists can quickly renovate career psychology for a second century of distinguished service to its clients and country. Let us examine, in a little more detail, how constructivist and objectivist vocational psychologists are responding to the changes in the meaning of career.

Constructivist responses to changes in career

The change in the structure of work and its social organisation means that the modern paradigm of matching people to positions needs to be expanded to address individuals as managers of their own worklives, drawing meaning from the role of work in their lives, not from an organisational culture. Career must become more personal and self-directed to flourish in the postmodern information age. We have already begun to use the phrase 'career management' to replace 'career planning'. The emphasis on personal meaning and becoming an agent in one's own life draws inspiration and support from constructivist metatheory. The lens of constructivism allows counsellors to view career, not as a life-time employment on an organisational ladder, but as a carrier of personal meaning that defines and structures significant events in a life (Carlsen, 1988, p. 186). Rather than looking just at how people fit into the occupational structure, constructivists envision how work fits into people's lives (Richardson, 1993).

Constructivism provides a viewpoint from which to conceptualise careers in post-industrial societies. Constructivism represents a meta-theory and epistemologic stance that emphasises self-conceiving, self-organising, and proactive features of human knowing (Neimeyer, 1995). From this perspective, career may become a framework for personal meaning and self-management, rather than a path through an organisation. Constructive methods enable people to fashion careers that carry meaning for their lives and impose personal direction on their vocational behaviour (Miller-Tiedeman & Tiedeman, 1985). According to Young and Valach (1996, p. 364) career will become a process that 'people intentionally engage in to acquire social meaning within the framework of their lives'. From this perspective, career counselling should aim to increase self-reflection about meaning and prompt exploration of and experimentation with other ways of seeing and doing. In the words of Peavy (1993) constructivist career counselling is a 'process which enables individuals to review, revise, and reorient how they are living their lives'.

Constructivist metatheory has already produced three compelling models for expanding and improving career theory and practice (Savickas, 1997a). The personal construct, biographical-hermeneutic, and narrative models for career counselling comfortably and comprehensively meet the needs of clients who must make career decisions and plan their lives during a time of rapid change in society and its occupations. Constructivism's concentration on self-conceiving, self-organising processes enables counsellors to focus on the subjective meaning with which their clients imbue work and career. For example, Cochran (1997) has published a narrative approach to career counselling that emphasises meaning-making, personal development, and identity by focusing on purpose, passion, and life history. This new concentration on subjective careers is revitalising the interest of counsellors in their clients' work roles by making career counselling more complex, personal, and therapeutic. Just as objectivist theory with its trait-and-factor methods fit the modern industrial society of the twentieth century, so may constructivist theory with its interpretive methods fit the postmodern information society of the twenty-first century.

Objectivist responses to changes in career

While constructivist researchers attend to expanding contemporary career counselling by emphasising the subjective perspective on worklife, traditional objectivist researchers are expanding the meaning and contemporary applicability of core concepts in career psychology. Let us examine a few concepts and how they are being renovated or replaced.

Career salience and work importance

Work as the central life role has long been a pillar of career counselling. Occupational roles tie individuals to reality and confer social identity. The career ethic emphasises individualism and competitive self-advancement. Today, some psychologists call for a new work ethic, one that requires a shift from assuming that occupation is the most salient social role for every individual to recognising how individuals position their occupation in a constellation of important life roles. This transformation moves from assuming that occupation is the central life role to examining the role of work in each individual's life. This examination includes an emphasis on charting a life course, with attention to multiple roles and work–family interactions not just occupational roles. This focus on life rather than work benefits from the insights provided by multicultural specialists who emphasise the diverse ways in which different segments of the population structure the roles and functions involved in love and work. To further this transformation, prominent career theorists have developed new psychometric instruments to measure these variables; including the Salience Inventory (Nevill & Super, 1986a), which measures commitment to and participation in five life roles, and the Career Attitudes and Strategies Inventory (Holland & Gottfredson, 1994; Gottfredson, 1996), which measures traditional variables such as job satisfaction and work involvement yet also measures skill development, interpersonal abuse, and family commitment. This new perspective on multiple roles, rather than a concentration on just the work role, has prompted some career theorists to reconsider their fundamental postulates. For example, following such a reconsideration, Super (1990) embedded his psychology of careers into a broader life-space model in which importance of the work role is contextualised relative to other life roles. Other theorists such as Brown (1988) and Hansen (1997) have urged counsellors to transform career counselling into life planning.

Career development theories

Career development theories are also being modified in response to the changing economy. For example, Super's twin constructs of career patterns (1954) and career maturity (1955) seem to be in the process of being renovated into a new construct called career adaptability (Super & Knasel, 1981; Savickas, 1997b). This new construct is informed by contemporary advances in developmental psychology, and serves as an example of vocational psychologists trying to link their theories and research back to mainstream psychology (Savickas, in press). The trend to reconnect with mainstream psychology is manifest in projects such as linking the structure of vocational interests to the Big Five personality factors (Costa & McCrae, 1992), applying Bandura's (1997) social cognitive theory to the career domain, and comparing vocational development tasks to the construct of psychosocial identity (Holland, Gottfredson, & Power, 1980).

Career counselling

A few vocational psychologists have begun to focus attention on career counselling theory, as distinct from career development theory (Swanson, 1995). The major career development theories of the twentieth century comprehend how individuals develop an occupational choice and adjust to work; they do not instruct counsellors in effective techniques for working with clients. Models and methods for counselling with clients about managing their worklives address the relationship and communication dimensions of the process. Three new theories of career counselling have recently emerged. Krumboltz (1996) has constructed a learning theory of career counselling 'to facilitate the learning of skills, interests, beliefs, values, work habits, and personal qualities that enable each client to create a satisfying life within a constantly changing work environment' (p. 61). Chartrand (1996) has devised a sociocognitive–interactional theory of career counselling that focuses on counsellors' reactions to a client's career-specific cognitions and interpersonal functioning. Fouad and Bingham (1995) have developed a 'culturally appropriate career counseling model' that incorporates cultural variables into a method for career intervention characterised by seven specific steps. All three of these new theories emphasise counselling process and outcomes rather than decision making and developmental tasks.

Rational and autonomous decision making

Long a cornerstone of career psychology, autonomous and rational decision making is now being challenged as the sole method for choosing. Parsons's method of 'true reasoning' fits a more stable and predictable economy. Careers today do not follow a fixed course. In this new era, flexibility and adaptability may be more important than autonomy and rationality. For example, rather than independence being the goal, maybe the goal should be interdependence or the judicious expression of dependence and independence contingent upon the situation. Regarding rational decision making, Phillips (1997) has recently emphasised the need to investigate the role of intuition and 'other-than-rational' methods in career decision making as well as the circumstances under which they may be beneficially employed.

Occupational interests

Another cornerstone of modern career counselling has been the administration and interpretation of vocational interest inventories. Since their inception early in the twentieth century, interest inventories and vocational guidance itself have focused on 'constant' rather than 'variable' occupations (Ayres, 1915). Today, as occupations become less stable, it is more difficult to know which occupational titles to include in an interest inventory. Furthermore, occupational titles themselves become problematic as items in interest inventories because the occupations involve a set of activities under continual transformation.

The empirical scales in interest inventories such as the Kuder Occupational Interest Scale (Kuder & Zytowski, 1991) and the Strong Interest Inventory (Harmon, Hansen, Borgen, & Hammer, 1994) directly measure occupational interests. These scales are composed of heterogeneous items and the resulting scale scores indicate similarity or degree of fit between an individual's interest pattern and the interest patterns empirically identified for selected occupational groups such as engineers and psychologists. For example, a score on the Lawyer Scale of the Strong Interest Inventory indicates how well a client's pattern of choices resembles the choice pattern that characterises lawyers. Thus scores from empirical scales do not represent a client's interests, rather they indicate the similarity of that client's interests to those of selected occupational groups. Recognising this distinction, Campbell, Borgen, Eastes, Johansson, and Peterson (1968, p. 1) asked rhetorically, 'What does it mean to have interests similar to lawyers?' They developed basic interest scales for the Strong Interest Inventory to address this question. These basic interest scales consist of clusters of related interests which clearly specify the pattern of work activities that an individual likes. Day and Rounds (1997) argued persuasively that because homogenous basic interest scales actually measure interests as dispositional traits, these scales may be more meaningful to clients and thus should play a central role in career counselling for a global economy. Basic interests group together work activities that can generalise across different occupational situations. For example, *writing* maximises meaningfulness in comparison to the general factor of *artistic* interests and the occupational title *reporter*.

Kuder (1977) recommended an even more fundamental innovation to interest inventory scoring when he suggested matching an individual's interest pattern to the interest patterns collected from a large number of diverse individuals, rather than to group patterns for several occupations. Interpretation of such scores would indicate to clients which individuals they closely resemble and then inform clients about vocational biographies of their 'person-matches' (Hornaday & Gibson, 1995). This process aims to provide clients with suitable role models and a wide variety of occupational possibilities to consider.

Skills confidence

A few psychologists who have devoted decades of sustained research to studying vocational interests are now re-emphasising the need to assess functional skills, in addition to interests. Currently, vocational psychologists are focusing much attention on self-estimates of abilities and skills confidence. In 1981, Hackett and Betz, applying self-efficacy theory (Bandura, 1977, 1997) to the career domain, proposed that self-efficacy, or skill self-confidence, mediates the processes of career choice and adjustment. Subsequent research has shown that combining interest inventory results with self-estimates of abilities or assessments of skills confidence increases the predictive validity of interest inventory results (Prediger & Brandt, 1991). Accordingly, Betz, Borgen, and Harmon (1996) have constructed the Skills Confidence Inventory, and Osipow, Rooney, and Temple developed the Task-Specific Occupational Self-Efficacy Scale (Osipow & Temple, 1996). Using a similar rationale, Prediger (1989) constructed a method for estimating career-related skills, a method that coordinates with American College Testing's world-of-work map. The revitalised focus on inter-domain assessments that include interests and skills bodes well for the future of career assessment in a global economy.

Work values

In the middle of the twentieth century, Super linguistically explicated the construct of work values (Zytowski, 1994) and later operationally defined the construct with the Work Values Inventory (Super, 1970). Late in his own career, when he noted the changing culture and the importance of life-role salience, Super replaced the Work Values Inventory with the Values Scale (Nevill & Super, 1986b) which does not privilege the occupational role. This innovation recognises that individuals can gratify important values in roles other than work. Accordingly, career counsellors can now assess life values and then discuss with clients which values will be fulfilled in which roles. For example, achievement can be gained at work, altruism satisfied in the community, nurturance fulfilled in the family, and creativity expressed in hobbies. This increasing attention to values in career assessment and counselling fits well with postmodern concentration on meaning-making and the quest for significance as well as the emphasis on work as a contribution to a social community.

Career education

Career education in the schools, since the 1970s, has focused on preparing individuals for a linear career in stable organisations. Now, necessarily, attention is shifting away from developing autonomy, rational decision making, and linear plans to developing employability skills, life-long learning strategies, and flexibility. Vocational psychologists are just now starting to attend to the very real and complex problems that youths encounter as they try to move from school to work (Blustein, Phillips, Jobin-Davis, Finkelberg, & Roarke, 1997; Worthington & Juntunen, 1997). The school-to-work transition has become particularly problematic because the instructional methods and materials in the schools have become increasingly dissociated from the requirements of post-industrial organisations. Thus, since the late 1980s, more and more students have encountered turmoil as they leave school and try to secure meaningful employment.

Conclusion

Vocational psychologists realise that society is in the middle of a cultural revolution that is radically changing their own worklives as well as those of their clients. Whether they consciously attend to it or not, most vocational psychologists are adapting their thinking and doing to reflect the new realities. It might be beneficial for vocational psychologists to become more explicitly and systematically self-reflective as they renovate career psychology for the twenty-first century.

REFERENCES

Ayres, L. P. (1915). *Constant and variable occupations and their bearing on problems of vocational education*. Russell Sage Foundation Publications.

Bandura, A. (1977). Self-efficacy: Toward a unifying theory of behavioral change. *Psychological Review, 84*, 191–215.

(1997). *Self-efficacy: The exercise of control*. New York: W. H. Freeman.

Betz, N. E., Borgen, F. H., & Harmon, L. W. (1996). *Skills Confidence Inventory: Applications and technical guide*. Palo Alto, CA: Consulting Psychologists Press.

Bloomfield, M. (1915). *Readings in vocational guidance.* Boston: Ginn and Company.

Blustein, D. L., Phillips, S. D., Jobin-Davis, K., Finkelberg, S. L., & Roarke, A. E. (1997). A theory-building investigation of the school-to-work transition. *Counseling Psychologist, 25,* 364–402.

Brazaitis, T. (1996). Career paths are gone. *Cleveland Plain Dealer,* 10 March, C-3.

Brown, D. (1988). *Life-role development and counseling.* Paper presented at the meeting of the National Career Development Association, Orlando, FL.

Carlsen, M. B. (1988). *Meaning-making: Therapeutic processes in adult development.* New York: Norton.

Campbell, D. P., Borgen, F. H., Eastes, S. H., Johansson, C. B., & Peterson, R. A. (1968). A set of basic interest scales for the Strong Vocational Interest Blank for Men. *Journal of Applied Psychology Monographs, 52* (6, whole no. 2), 1–54.

Chartrand, J. M. (1996). Linking theory with practice: A sociocognitive interactional model for career counseling. In M. L. Savickas & W. B. Walsh (Eds.), *Handbook of career counseling theory and practice* (pp. 121–134). Palo Alto, CA: Davies-Black.

Cochran, L. (1997). *Career counseling: A narrative approach.* Thousand Oaks, CA: Sage.

Costa, P. T., Jr. & McCrae, R. R. (1992). Four ways five factors are basic. *Personality and Individual Differences, 13,* 653–665.

Day, S. X. & Rounds, J. (1997). 'A little more than kin, and less than kind': Basic interests in vocational research and career counseling. *Career Development Quarterly, 45,* 207–220.

Fouad, N. A. & Bingham, R. P. (1995). Career counseling with racial and ethnic minorities. In W. B. Walsh & S. H. Osipow (Eds.), *Handbook of vocational psychology* (2nd edn, pp. 331–365). Mahwah, NJ: Lawrence Erlbaum Associates.

Gottfredson, G. D. (1996). The assessment of career status with the Career Attitudes and Strategies Inventory. *Journal of Career Assessment, 4,* 363–381.

Hackett, G. & Betz, N. E. (1981). A self-efficacy approach to the career development of women. *Journal of Vocational Behavior, 18,* 326–339.

Hansen, L. S. (1997). *Integrative life planning: Critical tasks for career development and changing life patterns.* San Francisco: Jossey-Bass.

Harmon, L. W., Hansen, J. C., Borgen, F. H., & Hammer, A. C. (1994). *SII applications and technical guide.* Palo Alto, CA: Consulting Psychologists Press.

Holland, J. L. & Gottfredson, G. D. (1994). *Career Attitudes and Strategies Inventory: An inventory for understanding adult careers.* Odessa, FL: Psychological Assessment Resources.

Holland, J. L., Gottfredson, G. D., & Power, P. G. (1980). Some diagnostic scales for research in decision making and personality. *Journal of Personality and Social Psychology, 39,* 1191–1200.

Hornaday, J. & Gibson, L. A. (1995). *The Kuder book of people who like their work.* Amherst, MA: Motivation Press.

Krumboltz, John D. (1996). A learning theory of career counseling. In M. L. Savickas & W. B. Walsh (Eds.), *Handbook of career counseling theory and practice* (pp. 55–80). Palo Alto, CA: Davies-Black.

Kuder, F. (1977). Career matching. *Personnel Psychology, 30,* 1–4.

Kuder, F. & Zytowski, D. G. (1991). *Kuder Occupational Interest Survey: General manual.* Monterey, CA: CTB/McGraw-Hill.

Miller-Tiedeman, A. & Tiedeman, D. (1985). Educating to advance the human career during the 1980s and beyond. *Vocational Guidance Quarterly, 34,* 15–30.

Neimeyer, R. A. (1995). An appraisal of constructivist psychotherapies. In M. J. Mahoney (Ed.), *Cognitive and constructive psychotherapies: Theory, research, and practice* (pp. 163–194). New York: Springer Publishing.

Nevill, D. D. & Super, D. E. (1986a). *The Salience Inventory: Theory, application, and research manual.* Palo Alto, CA: Consulting Psychologists Press.

(1986b). *The Values Scale: Theory, application and research manual.* Palo Alto, CA: Consulting Psychologists Press.

Osipow, S. H. & Temple, R. D. (1996). Development and use of the Task-Specific Occupational Self-Efficacy Scale. *Journal of Career Assessment, 4,* 445–456.

Parsons, F. (1909). *Choosing a vocation.* New York: Agathon Press.

Peavy, R. V. (1993). *Envisioning the future: Sociodynamic counselling.* Paper presented at the meeting of the International Association for Educational and Vocational Guidance, Budapest, Hungary, October.

Phillips, S. D. (1997). Toward an expanded definition of adaptive decision making. *Career Development Quarterly, 45,* 275–287.

Prediger, D. J. (1989). *Estimating your career-related abilities.* Iowa City, IA: American College Testing.

Prediger, D. J. & Brandt, W. E. (1991). Project CHOICE: Validity of interest and ability measures for student choice of vocational program. *Career Development Quarterly, 40,* 132–144.

Richardson, M. S. (1993). Work in people's lives: A location for counseling psychologists. *Journal of Counseling Psychology, 40,* 425–433.

Savickas, M. L. (1993). Career counseling in the postmodern era. *Journal of Cognitive Psychotherapy: An International Quarterly, 7,* 205–215.

(1994). Vocational psychology in the postmodern era: Comment on Richardson (1993). *Journal of Counseling Psychology, 41,* 105–107.

(1995). Current theoretical issues in vocational psychology: Convergence, divergence, and schism. In W. B. Walsh & S. H. Osipow (Eds.), *Handbook of vocational psychology: Theory, research, and practice* (2nd edn, pp. 1–34). Mahwah, NJ: Lawrence Erlbaum Associates.

(1997a). Constructivist career counseling: Models and methods. In R. Neimeyer & G. Neimeyer (Eds.), *Advances in personal construct psychology* (vol. IV, pp. 149–182). Greenwich, CT: JAI Press.

(1997b). Adaptability: An integrative construct for life-span, life-space theory. *Career Development Quarterly, 45,* 247–259.

(in press). Toward a comprehensive theory of careers: Dispositions, concerns, and narratives. In F. T. L. Leong & A. Barak (Eds.), *Contemporary models in vocational psychology: A volume in honor of Samuel H. Osipow*. Mahwah, NJ: Lawrence Erlbaum Associates.

Super, D. E. (1954). Career patterns as a basis for vocational counseling. *Journal of Counseling Psychology*, *1*, 12–19.

(1955). The dimensions and measurement of vocational maturity. *Teachers College Record*, *57*, 151–163.

(1970). *The Work Values Inventory manual*. New York: Houghton Mifflin.

(1990). A life-span, life-space approach to career development. In D. Brown, L. Brooks, & Associates, *Career choice and development: Applying contemporary theories to practice* (2nd edn, pp. 197–261). San Francisco, CA: Jossey-Bass.

Super, D. E. & Knasel, E. G. (1981). Career development in adulthood: Some theoretical problems and a possible solution. *British Journal of Guidance and Counselling*, *9*, 194–201.

Swanson, J. L. (1995). Process and outcome research in career counseling. In W. B. Walsh & S. H. Osipow (Eds.), *Handbook of vocational psychology* (2nd edn, pp. 217–259).

Worthington, R. L. & Juntunen, C. L. (1997). The vocational development of non-college-bound youth: Counseling psychology and the school-to-work transition movement. *Counseling Psychologist*, *25*, 323–363.

Young, R. A. & Valach, L. (1996). Interpretation and action in career counseling. In M. L. Savickas & W. B. Walsh (Eds.), *Handbook of career counseling theory and practice* (pp. 361–375). Palo Alto, CA: Davies-Black.

Zytowski, D. G. (1994). A Super contribution to vocational theory: Work values. *Career Development Quarterly*, *43*, 25–31.

5   Changing career: the role of values

Wendy Patton

The changing work place – a combination of economic, demographic, technological, and social changes – continues to have far-reaching effects on work, family, and other life roles of individuals. Changing definitions of career reflect the complex combination of work and non-work roles which are increasingly a feature of life (Collin & Watts, 1996; Super, 1990; Watts, 1997). These definitions incorporate the themes of multiple roles and individual responsibility for career. Super (1980, p. 282) referred to the 'combination and sequence of roles played by a person during the course of a lifetime'. More recent definitions emphasise that individuals must review their perception of their career as an individual rather than organisational phenomenon – 'individuals should regard themselves as being self-employed' (Collin & Watts, 1996, p. 391). Changes in the future of career – in the way individuals engage in society through work – and in its relationship with other life roles prompt a re-examination of values and personal meanings in role involvement.

Most writers would agree that the meaning we ascribe to values is constructed within the contexts in which we live (e.g. Gergen, 1985; Nord, Brief, Atieh, & Doherty, 1990). Our values and the meanings we attach to life roles change in concert with changes in culture and society, but the extent to which this happens is unclear (Kopper, 1993). In a post-traditional context, Giddens (1991) suggests that the radical alteration in the way we engage with society individually and collectively, so that individual and society reflexively interact, encourages a construction of a narrative of self-identity so that the self becomes a reflexive project. He notes that 'the altered self has to be explored and constructed as part of a reflexive process of connecting personal and social change' (p. 33). In this context of change, reflexive self-identity plays an important role in connecting past and present and providing unity and coherence. This interconnection between the personal and the social is reflected in the broader understanding of career that incorporates multiple life roles. This emphasises that the traditional focus on work values also needs to be broader, and we need to explore life values in our study of the future of career (Brief & Nord, 1990; Brown, 1996).

Criticisms of the domain of values and work values focus on the complex nature of definitions (Nord *et al.*, 1990), the unresolved nature of many theoretical assumptions (Zytowski, 1994), and the need for refinement in measurement of the construct (Brown, 1996; Feather, 1992; Krumboltz, 1994). In this chapter I will set the changing discussion of values in the career literature within the context of world-of-work changes. Conceptualising values, including work values, will be discussed, followed by a review of empirical findings illustrating the construct of work values as it is presently understood. The career theory literature will be briefly reviewed, outlining the changing place of values and work values in our understanding of career, and focusing on the need to reconceptualise our understanding of the meaning of values within future career contexts. Finally, the relationship between our understanding of values and our strategies for measuring them will be reviewed, pointing to new directions in incorporating values into career research and counselling. Overall the chapter takes the view that the way values are now conceptualised in career does not take into account the narrative of career, that is the individual's own construction of meaning in the changing nature of personal and social interaction with local and global systems (Giddens, 1991).

Conceptualising values

A substantial literature supports the importance of values in career and other life-role decisions (Dawis & Lofquist, 1984; Judge & Bretz, 1992); however, a number of researchers and theorists have emphasised how little work has focused on values in contrast to other related constructs, such as interests (Brown, 1996; Brown & Crace, 1996; Feather, 1992). Feather asserted that the sparcity of attention to values, and in particular to the relations between values and actions, is due to problems in conceptualising and measuring values, and in constructing a theoretical bridge between values and actions.

A number of conceptualisations of values have been proposed. The seminal discussions of Rokeach (1973, 1979) emphasised the centrality of values to the self-concept. He contended that values are relatively stable across the lifespan, transcending different situations, but they are not, however, immune to change. Because our values represent what is important to us, they are influential in most life decisions, including career decisions. They are also influential in the relative importance we place on work in relation to other roles in life. Values are constructs that cannot be observed but they are recognised through the goals an individual strives to attain in life, such as physical and mental health, security (including financial security), social status, and self-fulfilment.

A second conceptualisation addresses needs, values, and interests. This relationship is beset with conceptual confusion in the literature, and the terms are often used interchangeably. Super (1995) developed a model which distinguished these three concepts and provided greater clarity to their individual meaning and to the relationship between them. He defined needs as 'wants, manifestations of physiological conditions such as hunger, and they are related to survival . . . values are the result of further refinement through interaction with the environment . . . The need for help thus becomes love, and the need to help becomes altruism. Interests are the activities within which people expect to attain their values and thus satisfy their needs' (p. 5). In a further elaboration, Brown and Crace (1996) defined values as

cognized representations of needs that, when developed, provide standards for behavior, orient people to desired end states, . . . and form the basis for goal setting. Values are the major factor in motivation because they form the basis for attributing worth to situations and objects . . . Moreover, values serve as the basis for self-regulating cognitions and provide the basis for judging the utility of external reinforcers. (pp. 11–12)

The limitation of these definitions, however, is that they do not acknowledge the active role individuals have in giving meaning to experiences and constructing their own values.

Values need to be conceptualised as socially constructed notions; they are a function of context as they are rarely settled upon introspectively. Individuals construct reality through interactions with a changing society, culture, and economy. Narratives of self-identity, including an understanding of personal values, reflexively interact with these changing institutions as an individual works to construct and reconstruct personal self-identities (Giddens, 1991). In the career literature, Young and Valach (1996) emphasised the role of individual action in the development of values, and suggested that their construction is through the individual actively constructing meaning through interaction with the context.

Values and work values

A number of writers have emphasised that work values are a subset of broader value perspectives (Brown, 1996; Judge & Bretz, 1992). Work values can be defined as 'the end states people desire and feel they ought to be able to realise through working' (Nord et al., 1990, p. 21). Work values are constructed by individuals as they make meaning of the experience of work in their lives. Discussions about the future of career (e.g. Collin & Watts, 1996) suggest that as the place of work in individuals' lives changes, so too will the relationship between work values and broader 'lifestyle' values. The importance of work to individuals' well being and social stability is a key element of the organisational behaviour literature. There are four relevant perspectives on work values in this literature. Within the first perspective, the traditional perspective, work values are related to worker behaviour and satisfaction. The second perspective emphasises the relationship between work values and different times and cultures. The relationship between work values and social institutions such as family, community, and religion is discussed within the third perspective. Finally, the individual's active role in constructing work values is embodied in the fourth perspective. Each of these perspectives will be discussed.

Within the traditional perspective, certain work values are seen as some kind of goal to which individuals should aspire, as reflective of a 'good' and 'bad' worker. Given the only slight correlations reported, Nord *et al.* (1990) question the emphasis given to the relationship between job satisfaction and performance in the organisational behaviour literature. They note that such research has the potential to be used to exercise control over worker behaviour, with assumptions that work values are related to worker performance. Recent work has been critical of the generally accepted view that work values are predictors of job satisfaction and performance. O'Brien (1992) concluded that there is no evidence of a causal relationship between work values and performance and only a weak relationship between work values and job satisfaction. Hunt (1991) emphasised that many other factors (for example, environmental contingencies) need to be included in the analysis. Nord and his colleagues concluded that the focus on this relationship is an attempt 'to find a way to think of work so that it appears to be a less coercive activity than it is for many people. In other words, work values have received so much attention because they have reduced the need to confront the potential disquieting realities of work in our society' (p. 56).

The second perspective holds that work values develop in concert with other constructs and individuals, across different situations, times, and cultures. Thus it would be reasonable to expect a considerable number and richness of work values. This perspective, where individuals construct their own meanings of work values, also suggests that there is less potential for an ideological manipulation and bias in work values than with the traditional perspective. In acknowledging the contextual basis of values, there is less scope for values being related to narrow confining views about work, and less potential for certain values to be viewed as prerequisites for worker performance.

Taking this broader social and cultural perspective emphasises that individuals' values vary according to the social context in which they live. Regardless of changes in employment opportunities in our post-industrial age, studies continue to show that people place a high importance on work (Meaning of Work International Research Team (MOW), 1987), although it may not assume the role of the central life interest (O'Brien, 1992). Studies show that people would continue to work irrespective of financial necessity (MOW, 1987). A recent major cross-cultural study exploring values and role salience showed that self-realisation values (personal development, ability utilisation, and achievement) are among the highest-ranked in all countries (Super & Sverko, 1995). This was the case for both adolescents and adults.

Other research challenges the previously assumed universality of work values, showing support for a variation in values, such as hierarchy and democracy, across times and cultures. Studies have illustrated significant cultural differences among adolescents and adults (Kopper, 1993; Schulenberg, Bachman, Johnston, & O'Malley, 1995; Super & Sverko, 1995); however Elizur, Borg, Hunt, and Beck (1991) commented that cultural differences were 'minor variations within a much broader pattern . . . of similarity' (p. 36), a view echoed by Super and Sverko. The Schulenberg et al. report, based on extensive longitudinal data gathered from American adolescents and young people, showed small but consistent declines in young people's expectations of work over time. This study showed both gender and cohort effects, reporting a slight decrease in the centrality of work in life, especially among males, and an increase in self-oriented work values and associated decrease in other-oriented work values until the late 1980s, and a reversal of this trend during the early 1990s. These data indicate the complex social and economic context in which values are embedded.

In focusing on role salience, a measure of the value or importance of work (as opposed to work values) in relation to other life roles, the Super & Sverko (1995) study revealed substantial age differences, the pattern of which was substantially similar across several countries. Adolescents (secondary and higher education students) in all countries ranked leisure as their most important role, followed by work, home and family, and study, which were closely ranked, and community service ranking last. In contrast, adults, including unemployed adults, ranked work and home-making as their most important life roles. Age differences were also apparent within the adult group, with younger workers attaching relatively greater importance to leisure than older workers.

Research with Generation X (young people born in the 1960s and 1970s) attributes these differences in work values and the importance of work to the context of the world of work. Lankard (1995) asserts that Generation X views the concept of career differently from its predecessors; for example, job changing is an indication of this generation's perception that job security comes from adaptability and transferability of skills. A focus on generational differences in work values betrays the traditional controlling approach to the nature of work. Young people not exhibiting the same values as older generations, for example in terms of organisational loyalty, may cause concern about the structural role of work in society.

Super and Sverko (1995) emphasise that life roles may also change according to the individual's life stage, although the data may indicate an overall change in work values and the importance of work. They note that observations made in the 1970s showed similar findings to their 1995 data, and that the young people of those earlier studies were likely to be the adults of their 1995 studies. However, it must be remembered that although Rokeach (1973) emphasised the relative stability of values, work values are sensitive to change in work and related social conditions over time (Kopper, 1993; Nord et al., 1990). This argument is supported by data which indicated a 'strong reciprocal relationship between economic conditions and individual work values' (Pine & Innis, 1987, p. 285).

The third perspective on work values focuses on the relationship between work values and other social institutions, such as the family, community, and religion. A number of writers have commented on the limitation of studying work values within the confines of the workplace (e.g. Nord et al., 1990). For example, family and work remain separate in the lives of many workers and in much of the organisational literature. Fletcher and Bailyn (1996) comment on the 'paradoxical vision of boundaryless organisations filled with workers who have the skills to capture the synergy in crossing functional and occupational boundaries, but who nonetheless feel the need to maintain the strict separation of work and family' (p. 257). Moreover, Lankard (1995) suggests that Generation X focuses more on a balance between work and family. It would seem that in the changing context of work, the relationship between work and other social institutions will also change.

In the three perspectives discussed thus far, work values represent an apparent contradiction for many social scientists. While these perspectives acknowledge that much work is not a positive experience for many people, nevertheless, in their conceptualisations of work values, there is embedded the idealisation of work. A different perspective is that work values are actually attempts by workers to give work their own meaning, both within the workplace and in its relationships to other aspects of their lives (Jackall, 1978). That is, individuals construct work values in relationship with their work experience rather than seek work that realises and idealises their work values. Such a perspective is reflected in the changing work values of Generation X discussed above. For example, Richardson (1993) argued for a new understanding of career in which we relocate the importance of work in people's lives rather than focus on constructions based on traditional and idealised notions of career. Therefore it is important to conceptualise work values as personal and social constructions rather than as ideals to be achieved in a world-of-work environment which denies many traditional work values (such as prestige and security). This conceptualisation is in accord with the constructivist position that life and career values cannot be separated.

There is increasing criticism that work values have been treated as a psychological phenomenon only, without adequate regard for historical, sociological, philosophical, and economic processes which are intrinsic to an understanding of the world of work and its place in individuals' lives. Early work did not focus on the relationships between the work place and other contexts, and, until recently, the changes in the work place and the related changes in social contexts. The third and fourth perspectives discussed demand that the study of values be broader than the study of work values alone (Brief & Nord, 1990; Brown, 1996). If we accept that the new career will demand a stronger relationship between work and other life roles, and that the construct of values needs to be more broadly considered, then it needs a firmer place in career development theories. It is to this development in career theory that I now turn.

Values and career theory

There has long been a recognition in career theory of the importance of values in career development. As Patton and McMahon (1999) report, major theorists accorded values a place in their work, although values did not assume a central place in theory until the recent work of Brown (1995, 1996; Brown & Crace, 1996). This section gives a brief overview of the attention to values in the career theory literature, and will focus specifically on Brown's emerging theory which adopts a trait-and-factor approach.

Historically, the trait-and-factor theorists included values along with needs, interests, and aptitudes as important factors to consider when exploring career development. Thus theorists such as Ginzberg, Ginsburg, Axelrad, and Herma (1951) asserted that values were causally 'related to the different satisfactions individuals will seek and derive from work' (p. 216). Holland (1992) affirmed both that interests grow out of values, and that individuals seek out work environments which are compatible with their attitudes and values and allow them to use their skills and abilities. Similarly, the work adjustment theory of Dawis & Lofquist (1984) asserted that individuals strive for congruence, or correspondence, between occupational characteristics and their own needs and values. Super's (1990) developmental approach also asserts that individuals aim to satisfy their values in making career decisions and included them as personality attributes alongside needs, interests, and the self-concept.

Other more recent theoretical formulations, for example the social cognitive career theory (SCCT; Lent & Brown, 1996; Lent, Brown, & Hackett, 1994, 1996; Lent & Hackett, 1994) continue the early conceptualisation of values. Lent *et al.* (1994) suggest that, while values are important to the development of interests, they are mediated by self-efficacy and outcome expectations. SCCT conceptualises work values within outcome expectations, that is they are related to preferences for particular work conditions and perceived reward, and the extent to which the individual believes they are part of certain jobs.

Brown's values-based career theory (Brown, 1996; Brown & Crace, 1996) adopts a holistic approach, that is while it emphasises the importance of particular traits, values, it also acknowledges the concept of development and the context in which individuals live. Brown and Crace assert that individuals judge their own performance and that of others against a core set of beliefs or values, which are important not only in the selection of life roles but also in the satisfaction derived from life roles. They claim that 'values form the basis for attributing worth to situations and objects' (p. 212). Thus they draw attention to the function of values in decision making and career counselling, and set values into the broader context of life roles and life space.

Brown proffers several concepts. Fundamental to this model is the understanding that each person develops a relatively small number of values 'as a result of the interaction between inherited characteristics and experience' (Brown, 1996, p. 340). Cultural background, gender, and socioeconomic status influence opportunities and social interaction and thus there is variation of values both within and between subgroups of society.

Brown includes life roles other than those of worker, and the interaction of these roles, as an integral part of his theory. His work, which has strong ties to the trait-and-factor approach, reflects an advancement in career theory. Thus while he emphasises the broader context of social influence, and focuses on life roles in career development, he retains an emphasis on a core set of values which need to be prioritised, and perceives values as traits which can be measured. While Brown acknowledges the social and cultural influences on values, and hence the variation in them, his adherence to a trait-and-factor approach does not adequately provide for the recognition of the social construction of values in which individual and society reflexively interact (Giddens, 1991), which seems likely to underpin any future understanding of career. In addition, Brown views values in a unidirectional causal relationship, related to the selection of life roles. This view does not account for how individuals construct work values to make sense of their work experience. As the literature on the work values of Generation X discussed earlier illustrates, young people are constructing work and broader life values in relation to their experience of the world of work.

Measuring values and using them in practice

Assessment of values has traditionally been through the use of quantitative inventories which can be categorised into two groups. The first category includes work value inventories which aim to measure work satisfaction and success. These inventories are used to guide career exploration in determining which jobs might best meet individuals' needs. Examples include the Work Values Inventory (WVI; Super, 1970), the Minnesota Importance Questionnaire (MIQ; Weiss, Dawis, & Lofquist, 1971), and the Work Aspect Preference Scale (WAPS; Pryor, 1983). The second category of measures includes values inventories which aim to measure values associated with all aspects of life. Such instruments assist in assessing the relative importance of values which are met by the worker role and others. These include the Values Scale (Super & Nevill, 1985), and the more recent Life Values Inventory (LVI; Crace & Brown, 1995). In terms of the fourth perspective, that individuals construct values to make meaning of career experiences, these inventories have a limited usefulness. They presuppose a predetermined set of values in contrast to individuals' ongoing construction of their own meaning of work.

Each of the above measures uses varying assessment strategies, including self-report, pair-comparisons, ratings, and repertory grids. Reviews of the varying approaches suggest that each strategy yields slightly different information (Zytowski, 1994). While these measures have been predominantly used in research which has focused on group (e.g. age and gender) and cultural differences, evidence is also supportive of their usefulness in counselling (Niles & Goodnough, 1996). For example, values and salience scores may identify potential problem areas (e.g. role conflict between home and work) and uncover possible issues in career development (e.g. limited life-role salience). However the fourth constructionist perspective on work calls for more idiographic approaches. Of the four assessment strategies above, the repertory grid (Kelly, 1955) is the most appropriate as it encourages each individual to select those dimensions which are relevant to a uniquely derived value system.

Understanding values in the career of the future will demand more individually based career practices and assessment strategies. Changes in the world of work identified throughout this book are dictating that adults, who may have had limited career guidance and who entered the work force with the expectation of a job for life, need more help than ever with career issues (Kerka, 1995). In terms of age and life experience, the adult group is even more heterogeneous than a group of high-school or college adolescents. Even for adolescents, limited exposure to realities of the work role means that the realistic attention to completion of measures of objective lists of values (and other variables) is going to be a less than meaningful activity. In addition, there are problems in generalisation across age, gender, and ethnicity with many traditional measures (Marsella & Leong, 1995). Our understanding of the contextual basis for constructing our life meanings demands strategies that go beyond decontextualised objective instruments. Counsellors need to work with individuals to explore life themes and focus on 'lives in progress rather than [act] as actuaries who count interests and abilities' (Savickas, 1992, p. 338).

Increasingly, counsellors and researchers include qualitative methods of assessment in their practice. These include autobiographies, early recollections, guided imagery, narratives, and life-stories. Such methods allow individuals to be engaged as themselves and to focus on their own lives and perhaps identify values which are not tapped by traditional methods. Recognising the power of stories to convey meaning and to set values in a meaningful context, Krumboltz, Blando, Hyesook, & Reikowski (1994) reported differences in work values between females and males and several ethnic groups in their study which made use of narrative. The methodology was seen as a useful research strategy, in addition to having considerable potential for group and individual counselling in offering varying narratives and in exploring emerging values further.

Conclusion

The values construct is receiving renewed prominence in the career literature, in theory, research, and practice. This is partially related to the increasing attention to the work–life intersection (Mirvis & Hall, 1996), and the focus on the integration between life and career: the lifecareer (Miller-Tiedeman, 1988). These notions emphasise the changes in the world of work, from organisationally driven careers to careers constructed by individuals. As individuals construct a place for work in their lives, a place that may alter with work changes, so too will their construction of values vary. What is clear in our understanding of the future of career is that individual values about work will experience shifts, that is they will be constructed differently as experiences change. These shifts will be both subtle and large. Thus, we need to focus on not only work values, but work values in concert with other life values. As individuals construct their own careers, so too will they need to construct their own meaning about the values they attach to work roles and other life roles.

These changes also place demands on theorists, practitioners, and researchers involved in career development work. Theorists acknowledge the importance of theory which can be constructed by individuals to explain relevant experiences within their lives (Miller-Tiedeman, 1988; Patton & McMahon, 1999). They emphasise the need for holistic models which focus on creating a synergy between interrelated life roles. Practitioners will need to work with individuals using narratives and stories to assist them to make meaning of the experiences of work in their whole lives. Narrative can be used in individual career counselling as well as in career education programmes (Cochran, 1998). Researchers will need to work with different methodologies, for example stories and narratives, in order to understand how experiences with work are being understood by individuals.

REFERENCES

Brief, A. P. & Nord, W. R. (1990). Work and meaning: Definitions and interpretations. In A. Brief & W. Nord (Eds.), *Meanings of occupational work: A collection of essays* (pp. 1–20). Lexington, MA: D. C. Heath.

Brown, D. (1995). A values-based approach to facilitating career transitions. *Career Development Quarterly, 44*, 4–11.

(1996). Brown's values-based, holistic model of career and life role choices and satisfaction. In D. Brown, L. Brooks, & Associates, *Career choice and development* (3rd edn, pp. 337–372). San Francisco: Jossey-Bass.

Brown, D. & Crace, R. K. (1996). Values and decision making: A conceptual model. *Career Development Quarterly, 44*, 11–23.

Cochran, L. (1998). A narrative approach to career education. *Australian Journal of Career Development, 7* (2), 12–16.

Collin, A. & Watts, A. G. (1996). The death and transfiguration of career – and of career guidance? *British Journal of Guidance and Counselling, 24*, 385–398.

Crace, R. K. & Brown, D. (1995). *Life Values Inventory*. Minneapolis, MN: National Computer Systems.

Dawis, R. V. & Lofquist, L. H. (1984). *A psychological theory of work adjustment*. Minneapolis, MN: University of Minnesota Press.

Elizur, D., Borg, I., Hunt, R., & Beck, I. M. (1991). The structure of work values: A cross cultural comparison. *Journal of Organizational Behavior, 12*, 21–38.

Feather, N. T. (1992). Values, valences, expectations, and actions. *Journal of Social Issues, 48*, 109–124.

Fletcher, J. K. & Bailyn, L. (1996). Challenging the last boundary. In M. B. Arthur & D. M. Rousseau (Eds.), *The boundaryless career: A new employment principle for a new organizational era* (pp. 256–267). Oxford: Oxford University Press.

Gergen, K. (1985). The social constructionist movement in modern psychology. *American Psychologist, 40*, 266–275.

Giddens, A. (1991). *Modernity and self-identity: Self and society in the late modern age*. Cambridge: Polity Press.

Ginzberg, E., Ginsburg, S. W., Axelrad, S., & Herma, J. L. (1951). *Occupational choice: An approach to a general theory*. New York: Columbia University Press.

Holland, J. L. (1992). *Making vocational choices: A theory of careers* (2nd edn). Englewood Cliffs, NJ: Prentice-Hall.

Hunt, R. G. (1991). Work values and work performance: Critical commentary from a comparative perspective. In G. M. Green & F. Baker (Eds.), *Work, health, and productivity* (pp. 198–214). Oxford: Oxford University Press.

Jackall, R. (1978). *Workers in a labyrinth*. New York: Universe Books.

Judge, T. A. & Bretz, R. D., Jr (1992). Effects of work values on job choice decisions. *Journal of Applied Psychology, 77*, 261–271.

Kelly, G. S. (1955). *The psychology of personal constructs*. New York: Norton.

Kerka, S. (1995). *Adult career counseling in a new age*. ERIC Digest no. 167. Columbus, OH: ERIC Clearinghouse on Adult, Career, and Vocational Education.

Kopper, E. (1993). Swiss and Germans: Similarities and differences in work-related values, attitudes, and behaviour. *International Journal of Intercultural Relations, 17*, 167–184.

Krumboltz, J. D. (1994). Improving career development from a social learning perspective. In M. L. Savickas & R. W. Lent (Eds.), *Convergence in career development theories: Implications for science and practice* (pp. 9–32). Palo Alto, CA: CPP Books.

Krumboltz, J. D., Blando, J. A., Hyesook, K., & Reikowski, D. J. (1994). Embedding work values in stories. *Journal of Counseling and Development, 73*, 57–62.

Lankard, B. A. (1995). *Career development in Generation X: Myths and realities*. Columbus, OH: ERIC Clearinghouse on Adult, Career, and Vocational Education.

Lent, R. W. & Brown, S. D. (1996). Social cognitive approach to career development: An overview. *Career Development Quarterly, 44*, 310–321.

Lent, R. W., Brown, S. D., & Hackett, G. (1994). Toward a unifying theory of career and academic interest, choice and performance. *Journal of Vocational Behavior, 45,* 79–122.

(1996). Career development from a social cognitive perspective. In D. Brown, L. Brooks, & Associates, *Career choice and development* (3rd edn, pp. 373–421). San Francisco: Jossey-Bass.

Lent, R. W. & Hackett, G. (1994). Sociocognitive mechanisms of personal agency in career development: Pantheoretical aspects. In M. L. Savickas & R. W. Lent (Eds.), *Convergence in career development theories: Implications for science and practice* (pp. 259–271). Palo Alto, CA: CPP Books.

Marsella, A. J. & Leong, F. T. L. (1995). Cross-cultural issues in personality and career assessment. *Journal of Career Assessment, 3* (2), 202–218.

Miller-Tiedeman, A. (1988). *Lifecareer: The quantum leap into a process theory of career.* Vista, CA: Lifecareer Foundation.

Mirvis, P. H. & Hall, D. T. (1996). New organizational forms and the new career. In D. T. Hall & Associates, *The career is dead: Long live the career: A relational approach to careers* (pp. 72–101). San Francisco: Jossey-Bass.

MOW International Research Team (1987). *The meaning of working.* London: Academic Press.

Niles, S. G. & Goodnough, G. E. (1996). Life-role salience and values: A review of recent research. *Career Development Quarterly, 45,* 65–86.

Nord, W. R., Brief, A. P., Atieh, J. M., & Doherty, E. M. (1990). Studying meanings of work: The case of work values. In A. Brief & W. Nord (Eds.), *Meanings of occupational work: A collection of essays* (pp. 21–64). Lexington, MA: D. C. Heath.

O'Brien, G. E. (1992). Changing meanings of work. In J. F. Hartley & G. M. Stephenson (Eds.), *Employment relations: The psychology of influence and control at work* (pp. 44–66). Oxford: Blackwell.

Patton, W. & McMahon, M. (1999). *Career development and systems theory: A new relationship.* Pacific Grove, CA: Brooks/Cole.

Pine, G. P. & Innis, G. (1987). Cultural and individual work values. *Career Development Quarterly, 35,* 279–287.

Pryor, R. G. L. (1983). *Work Aspect Preference Scale manual.* Sydney: Australian Council for Educational Research.

Richardson, M. S. (1993). Work in people's lives: A location for counseling psychologists. *Journal of Counseling Psychology, 40,* 425–433.

Rokeach, M. (1973). *The nature of human values.* New York: Free Press.

(1979). *Understanding human values.* New York: Free Press.

Savickas, M. L. (1992). New directions in career assessment. In D. H. Montross & C. J. Shinkman (Eds.), *Career development* (pp. 336–355). Springfield, IL: Charles C. Thomas.

Schulenberg, J., Bachman, J. G., Johnston, L. D., & O'Malley, P. M. (1995). American adolescents' views on family and work: Historical trends from 1976–1992. In P. Noack, M. Hofer, & J. Youniss (Eds.), *Psychological responses to social change: Human development in changing environments* (pp. 37–64). New York: Walter de Gruyter.

Super, D. E. (1970). *The Work Values Inventory.* Boston, MA: Houghton Mifflin.

(1980). A life-span, life-space approach to career development. *Journal of Vocational Behavior, 13*, 282–298.

(1990). A life-span, life-space approach to career development. In D. Brown, L. Brooks, & Associates, *Career choice and development: Applying contemporary theories to practice* (2nd edn, pp. 197–262). San Francisco: Jossey-Bass.

(1995). Values: Their nature, assessment, and practical use. In D. E. Super & B. Sverko (Eds.), *Life roles, values, and careers: International findings of the Work Importance Study* (pp. 54–61). San Francisco: Jossey-Bass.

Super, D. E. & Nevill, D. D. (1985). *Values Scale*. Palo Alto, CA: Consulting Psychologists Press.

Super, D. E. & Sverko, B. (Eds.) (1995). *Life roles, values, and careers: International findings of the Work Importance Study*. San Francisco: Jossey-Bass.

Watts, A. G. (1997). Careerquake. *Australian Journal of Career Development, 6* (2), 36–40.

Weiss, D. J., Dawis, R. V., & Lofquist, L. H. (1971). *The Minnesota Importance Questionnaire*. Minneapolis, MN: University of Minnesota Press.

Young, R. A. & Valach, L. (1996). Interpretation and action in career counseling. In M. L. Savickas & W. B. Walsh (Eds.), *Handbook of career counseling theory and practice* (pp. 361–375). Palo Alto, CA: Davies-Black.

Zytowski, D. G. (1994). A Super contribution to vocational theory: Work values. *Career Development Quarterly, 43*, 25–31.

6   Dancing to the music of time

Audrey Collin

The return of the comet Hale-Bopp in 1997 connected us to a far distant past and future. By making the sweep of time and space visible in the heavens to the naked eye, it offered some measure and meaning of the vastness of time, and spoke of our lineage as human beings on our planet in space. In contrast, in the run-up to the new millennium, our apocalyptic vision was of the havoc to be wrought should computers fail to recognise the start of the year 2000, and no longer be able to translate the future into the present. Today's experiences of time are 'increasingly instantaneous and glacial or evolutionary' (Lash & Urry, 1994, p. 9). While 'glacial' time 'moves back out of immediate human history and forwards into a wholly unspecifiable future' (p. 243), 'the future is dissolving into the present'. It is within this context of 'post-modern time' (p. 243) that we have to view the future of career.

Revolutions in information, communications, transport, and other technologies are having a major impact on career. According to analysts of this age of 'high modernity' (Giddens, 1991, p. 4), of 'the network society' (Castells, 1996, p. 433), 'disorganized capitalism' (Lash & Urry, 1994, p. 2), and 'flexible accumulation' (Harvey, 1990, p. 124), they are also transforming the temporal and spatial dimensions of societies and of individual lives. Indeed, Giddens 'has placed the analysis of time (and space) at the very heart of contemporary social theory' (Lash & Urry, 1994, p. 230).

Capitalism continuously promotes the reduction of turnover times, 'thereby speeding up social processes' and shrinking distances (Harvey, 1990, p. 229). Under the stress of earlier rounds of this 'time–space compression', the 'absolute conceptions' of the Enlightenment broke down and gave way to modernism (p. 252). Now with the global economy of capital flows, and further shrinking of the globe, there is a new round of time–space compression, bringing in postmodernism and new experiences of space and time. Technology has also de-materialised space. Information is conveyed, and transactions take place, electronically and instantaneously in the 'weightless economy' (Coyle, 1998). Word-processed characters 'emerge from nothingness and obediently return to nothingness, dissolving like ectoplasm' (Eco, 1989, p. 26). Society is now constructed around flows of capital, information, technology, organisational interaction, images, sounds, and symbols (Castells, 1996). The 'space of flows', constituted by exchanges and interactions between social actors in networks, now supersedes the space of places. It disorders the sequence of events, making them simultaneous, and constituting 'timeless time', which now supersedes clock time. Nevertheless, the 'multiple space of places, scattered, fragmented, and disconnected', displaying 'diverse temporalities' (Castells, 1996, p. 467), also remains. Time and space are now separated: social actions do not require the sharing of the same time or place.

In modern urban societies with their elaborate division of labour and complex web of social relationships, people have to negotiate multiple time-scales and places, but the changes taking place disrupt traditional constructions of time and space. There are significant implications, for locating oneself in time and space is inherent in constructing personal and social identity and meaning. At birth, we experience our world as 'one blooming, buzzing confusion' (James, 1890, p. 488). Our early apprehension of our 'interpersonal organisation of time and space' comes, according to Giddens (1991, p. 38), as we develop 'basic trust' (Erikson, 1950) and a sense of separate identity in response to the absences of those who are caring for us. It continues as we learn what Harvey (1990, p. 214) calls the 'symbolic orderings of space and time' that 'provide a framework for experience through which we learn who or what we are in society'. Constructs of past, present, and future, of nearness and distance, shape experiences which would otherwise be chaotic, and anchor memory, hope, anticipation, and planning.

This chapter examines how people construct their time and space, and the part career has played in this. It concludes that the future of career will both contribute to, and be influenced by, the construction and experience of 'post-modern time' (Lash & Urry, 1994, p. 243).

Time, space, and career

Time and space are implicit in career. This is recognised in various approaches, such as Super's (1980) lifespan, life-space approach to career development, the developmental–contextual approach of Vondracek, Lerner, and Schulenberg (1986), narrative approaches that give a temporal organisation to individual experiences (Cochran, 1997), and the contextual, teleological approach of Young and Valach (1996). Arthur, Hall, and Lawrence (1989), for example, define career as 'the evolving sequence of a person's work experiences over time' (p. 8), and note that 'individuals are arrayed by their relative positions' along 'some dimension of social significance' (p. 13). Because there is a dialectical relationship between time and space, '[p]rojections about careers along the time dimension have an immediate effect on how careers are viewed across social space' (p. 13).

While the discussion by Arthur, Hall, and Lawrence of the implication of time and space in career, is a brief, and relatively rare, one, spatial imagery abounds in career discourse. As well as ladders, lines, pathways, and patterns, there are escalators (Becker & Strauss, 1968), spirals (Driver, 1979), plateaux (Ference, Stoner, & Warren, 1977), vertical and horizontal careers (Wilensky, 1968), and career topography (Barley, 1989, p. 57). Stewart, Prandy and Blackburn (1980) see the occupational structure as a railway system, specific jobs as the stations, and career as the individual's journey. Gowler and Legge (1989, p. 446) introduce another image: 'careers are portrayed in a metaphorical fugue of socio-organic images woven in space and time'. This imagery also, of course, represents movement, so that career has thus been a means of conceptualising the individual's location in, and movement through, time and space – that is, social space, and the social space of organisations in particular. This movement is clearly recognised in the foundational writings of the field, in which career is 'a succession of related jobs, arranged in a hierarchy of prestige, through which persons move in an ordered, predictable se-quence' (Wilensky, 1960, p. 554); and 'a series of status [sic] and clearly defined offices' (Hughes, 1937, p. 409). However, it is also, Hughes continues, 'the moving perspective in which the person sees his [sic] life as a whole and interprets the meaning of his various attributes, actions and the things which happen to him' (1937, pp. 409–410).

The chapter moves on to examine how individuals construct time and space, understood in terms of social practices, not physics or philosophy, and then the role of career in this.

Constructing time and space

Berger and Luckmann (1971) suggest that everyday life is apprehended as an objective and ordered reality 'organized around the "here" of my body and the "now" of my present' (p. 36), experienced 'in terms of differing degrees of closeness and remoteness, both spatially and temporally' (p. 36). People understand that others have a different perspective on their 'common world': 'My "here" is their "there". My "now" does not fully overlap with theirs' (p. 37). However, they recognise that 'there is an ongoing correspondence between *my* meanings and *their* meanings, that we share a common sense about its reality' (p. 37). The everyday world, Berger and Luckmann continue, is 'structured both spatially and temporally' (p. 40). The temporal structure, upon which they focus, is complex, having personal, social, and cosmic levels which 'must be ongoingly correlated'. It confronts the individual 'as a facticity with which I must reckon . . . [and] try to synchronize my own projects . . . my existence is continuously ordered by its time . . . My own life is an episode in the externally factitious stream of time' (p. 41). It 'imposes prearranged sequences upon the "agenda" of any single day' (p. 42) and upon the biography of the individuals, and also 'provides the historicity that determines my situation in the world'. The dates of a personal history are ' "located" within a much more comprehensive history' (p. 41).

How do individuals construct their own and others' 'here' and 'now' and 'there' and 'then'? Much of this is understood tacitly and carried out unwittingly and unreflectively, and must perhaps remain so (see Featherstone's discussion of the difficulty of defining 'everyday life', 1995). However, the construction of time and space is social as well as individual. Bauman (1999, p. xxiii) writes that 'The "here" versus "out there", "near" versus "far away" oppositions . . . recorded the degree of taming, domestication, and familiarity of various . . . fragments of the surrounding world.' Further, 'the divisions of continents . . . into more or less self-enclosed . . . enclaves were the function of distances' (p. xxii), and of speed of travel. According to Harvey (1990, p. 204) 'neither time nor space can be assigned objective meanings independently of material processes'; we can only achieve a grounded conceptualisation of them if we investigate the 'material practices of social reproduction'. He illustrates this with Bourdieu's study of the domestic, social, and economic organising of the Kabyle of Algeria. Bourdieu 'shows how "all the divisions of the group are projected at every moment into the spatiotemporal organization which assigns each category its place and time" ' (p. 215). Their temporal forms and spatial structures ' "structure not only the group's representation of the world but the group itself, which orders itself in accordance with this representation" ' (p. 214). Individual and group constructions of time and space are grounded in the practices, preoccupations, and priorities of their society's religious, social, political, cultural, or other domains. It is these that give 'facticity' (Berger & Luckmann, 1971, p. 41) to the personal and social world. As Giddens (1991, p. 48) notes, tradition 'orders time' and 'creates a sense of the firmness of things', so that 'time is not empty'.

Many social roles and practices carry implications of time and space, including social space. For example, children have to start school at a given age and stay until another. Some roles are located at the inner core of a social grouping or on its outer edge. By relating their construction of their own roles and experiences to those of others, and to the social practices in their context, and by drawing on the meanings available to them there, people can locate where they are now in relation to others, where they have come from, where they could go to and when. They can trace their own and others' movement through this social space and time, its pace, trajectory, and distance covered. In reading their roles in this way, they are *mapping* the temporal and spatial dimensions of their personal world, and thus constructing their time and space.

It is difficult to discuss in a simple way and few words how people construct meaning. It is helpful to use metaphors for this, but while they can convey complex ideas, there is the danger that they will distort or objectify what they convey (see Berger & Luckmann, 1971, on 'linguistic objectification'). Metaphors are used here as a means of conveying some notion of the processes whereby individuals construct their time and space, not as descriptions of such processes.

It is proposed, then, that people construct their time and space, and their own location therein, by – as it were – taking a range of *readings* of both *latitude* and *longitude* from various *domains* of social practice. As in navigation, the reading of latitude is not sufficient to plot position: to find their longitude, voyagers have to know both the time in their present position and that simultaneously at some fixed point. Since that could be anywhere, the determination of the 'prime meridian' had to be arrived at politically (as in the choice of Greenwich in 1884: Sobel, 1996). In this argument, latitude represents the interpretation individuals make of their present location in relation to their life as a whole and/or to their interpretations of others' locations. They could, for example, compare where they are now socially (e.g. in a lower management post) with where they have come from (e.g. their father was unskilled); or with where their neighbours or others are (e.g. in semi-skilled or professional posts); or with where they aspire to be (e.g. in a senior management post). Longitude represents what they interpret as the widely shared expectations and agreed norms of their society. In this case, they could compare where they are now with where most people of their kind, in terms of age, qualifications, length of service in an organisation, etc., would normally be expected to be. Not all domains offer clear norms. While latitude and longitude have been differentiated for the purpose of this analysis, as have the various domains, it is not suggested that they would or could be clearly differentiated in the individual's process of construction. Moreover, it must be emphasised again, these metaphors are being used only to convey some notion of the processes of construction, not to describe them.

Readings of time and space

To locate themselves in time and space, individuals – as it were – take readings of both latitude and longitude from many domains. Some are taken from the natural world, such as diurnal, menstrual, and other physiological rhythms, indications of growth and ageing, and the movements of sun and moon, and the cycle of the seasons. This chapter, however, is concerned with the readings of social positions taken from the domains below and from others such as the family, the educational system, and the labour market. The domains, and hence the readings, may be intertwined, perhaps inextricably, as is to some extent represented in Super's (1980) 'life-career rainbow', but more so in Johnson's (1977, p. 81) 'social kinetics', the 'constant reverberation' of the 'careers' of marriage, work, family, health 'conceptualised as a collection of bodies operating dynamically within a limited social space and constantly interlocking with each other'.

Individuals can construct their own and others' location in time and social space through their social roles and relationships, and the practices attending them. They can take both latitudinal and longitudinal readings from, for example, occupational and economic status, type of schooling, level of educational qualifications, place of residence, and even newspapers read. There are also expectations concerning 'age-appropriate' behaviour, though these are now less clear than earlier in the century. These constitute 'an elaborated and pervasive system of norms governing behavior and interaction, a network of expectations that is imbedded throughout the cultural fabric of adult life' (Neugarten, Moore, & Lowe, 1968, p. 22), and act as 'as prods and brakes upon behavior' (p. 22). Moreover, 'certain biological and social events' mark the transition between age statuses and are 'significant punctuation marks in the life line' (Neugarten & Moore, 1968, p. 5).

Because of their relevance to career, work organisations are picked out here as another domain from which individuals can take readings. The institutional space of organisations is divided into jobs, which are often referred to as 'positions' (e.g. Becker & Strauss, 1968, p. 312). Internal boundaries are constituted by job descriptions, spans of control, and lines of authority. Jobs are linked together, often in a linear fashion, giving a pattern in social space (and time). In bureaucracies, the simplest are at the bottom, and the most complex, with the longest 'time-span of discretion' (Jaques, 1956), at the top. Their arrangement is often viewed as a pyramid (or cone: Schein, 1971). The organisation's boundary separates it from others, so there are gatekeeping, boundary-spanning, and outsider roles. Employees can read their location from, for example, the hierarchical level of their job, its distance from the core of power (Schein, 1978), or from the organisation's boundary; their period of tenure in the job; the number of increments in the pay scheme. They can thereby trace their own movement, and discern pathways taken by others through the organisation, compare themselves with others, and assess their own progress.

Large bureaucratic organisations have internal labour markets. With their several hierarchical levels, and recognised entry points, training schemes, promotion policies, management development and succession schemes, they have offered the possibilities for advancement to employees through often clearly identifiable and upward pathways. Differential financial and social rewards may mark the steps along these paths in ways that are measurable and meaningful in both the organisation and its local community. To the extent that the organisation has a continuing existence independent of the particular individuals who work in it, and that its hierarchical structure is relatively stable and visible, employees can envisage a potential future. They can envisage their movement along various pathways, on the same or to higher hierarchical levels, potentially until retirement. Thus, work organisations offer readings of potential future positions.

However, this map of the organisation is not necessarily explicit. Much is tacit, inferred through observations of what has traditionally happened. Individuals both differentiate themselves from and relate themselves to others through comparisons and competition. For example, Sofer (1970) noted an 'exquisitely sensitive awareness of each grading within the organization in relation to age, as a sign of one's chances of moving to the top. People are constantly mulling over the question whether they are up to or behind schedule' (p. 274).

Overall, then, it is suggested that, by – as it were – taking readings of latitude and longitude from these various domains, individuals cast a grid of time and space across their personal world. They thereby identify where they are in time and social space, where they are in relation to other people, and where they could be.

The role of career in constructing time and space

To construct their time and space, people will also have used career: as a domain offering latitudinal and longitudinal readings, and as an overarching construct that draws together readings from other domains.

As discussed in chapter 1, career itself is construed in different ways among and between theorists and individuals (Collin, 1990), but in many interpretations it is seen as linking the individual to the structure of society. For Goffman (1959), for example, career 'allows one to move back and forth between the self and its significant society' (p. 123). The literature often distinguishes between the individual's 'objective' and the 'subjective' career (Stebbins, 1970). Some references express the former in terms of the spatial dimension of individuals' experience (Wilensky, 1960, quoted above), and the latter in terms of the temporal dimension (e.g. Goffman, 1959; Hughes, 1937). It is tempting to assume that the objective career would give readings of longitude, and the subjective, readings of latitude. However, all these notions – of the objective and subjective career, of latitude and longitude – are just interpretations made by theorists to understand individuals' constructions. The meaning of these notions is specific to a particular interpretation, and cannot meaningfully be carried over into others. These meanings of career intersect, not coincide.

Career constitutes a domain offering readings of both latitude and longitude when it is interpreted in terms of persisting, socially recognised and sanctioned temporal and (socially) spatial patterns across a large number of people (Wilensky, 1968), with indicators of individuals' progress and social standing. Such a view is typified in the models of work-life constructed in the mid twentieth century, reinforced by research such as the Career Pattern Study (Super, Crites, Hummel, Moser, Overstreet, & Warnath, 1957). In effect, these models mapped the lifespan of that era. For example, Ginzberg, Ginsburg, Axelrad, and Herma (1951), Havighurst (1964), and Miller and Form (1951) depicted work-life in age-related stages from the period of anticipatory socialisation for work until retirement or later. Similar models of the 'subjective' career (Super, Starishevsky, Matlin, & Jordaan, 1963), or women's careers (e.g. Bardwick, 1980), were also developed. Their frameworks of specific ages and desired behaviour were normative. For example, the taking of a random succession of jobs was appropriate to the period of 'exploration' at ages 15 to 24, but thereafter such 'floundering' was expected to cease (Super et al., 1963). Other normative notions are 'timetables', 'asynchronism' (Lawrence, 1984; Sekaran & Hall, 1989), and 'career maturity', which individuals displayed when they were 'planful', looked to the future, and coped with the tasks deemed appropriate to their life-stage (Crites, 1978; Super, Thompson, Lindeman, Jordaan, & Myers, 1981).

These are theorists' models, but through their adoption by career practitioners, they can come to influence individuals' constructions of meaning. Offering explicit points for comparison between people, they have lent themselves to readings of longitude as well as latitude. However, even before the changes currently affecting career took place, their relevance had dwindled. Some authors had themselves modified their models (Ginzberg, 1972; Super & Knasel, 1981). Sociologists noted that Miller and Form's (1951) 'stable work period' was not a reality for 1970s British life, and that their own research undermined the notion of 'a normal career curve' (Goldthorpe & Llewellyn, 1977, p. 294). Nevertheless, although these models now constitute out-of-date maps of working life, some of them have continued to be referred to in discussions of theory or practice (Dalton, 1989; Kidd, Killeen, Jarvis, & Offer, 1994; Killeen, 1996; Watts, 1981), which potentially further disseminates their norms.

Because of its broad range of meanings, career has been available to individuals for more than giving latitudinal and longitudinal readings of time and space. Because it links 'the self and its significant society' (Goffman, 1959, p. 123), individuals will have used it not only to calibrate the readings they have taken from the domains, but also to weave them together with their continuing self. They have thus ordered their time and space. They have established a time-line and a trajectory, around which personal narratives, with their past, present, and future, could be woven. They have also delineated their social space: the distances, and horizontal and vertical relationships, between their various roles and those of others. These time-lines and maps, however, are not static. Career has also been the 'moving perspective' (Hughes, 1937, p. 409) in which individuals see their life as a whole. Located 'within a continuum of past and future' (Höpfl, 1992, p. 16), their vantage point – the present – is a changing one, so that they re-interpret their past and reconceptualise their future.

Career has essentially been orientated to the future, and related past and present to it. Through it, individuals have been able to construct their future, and project their sense of self around the future positions and roles identified in the readings from various domains, and especially those from the work organisation. Hence, individuals have used the ' "canopy of meaning" ' (Berger, 1967, in Roberts, 1980, pp. 163–4) of career to link their past, present, and future, and weave a continuous thread of self across and through those domains. Thus they have drawn together, orchestrated, and integrated their experiences into a personally and socially meaningful whole, and thereby woven themselves into society and society into themselves.

Changing constructions of time and space

The changes now taking place in various domains are eroding the norms that had allowed individuals to take longitudinal readings to locate themselves in time and space, and are making latitudinal readings more ambiguous. Only some of these changes, mainly in work organisations, will be noted below.

The spatial and temporal dimensions of work and of organisations are changing. The shape and nature of jobs are changing (Bridges, 1995) and the linkages between them being broken. Multiskilling, teamworking, and reorganisation, such as business process re-engineering, loosen the attachment between individual and a specified, bounded job: 'For multi-dimensional and changing jobs, companies don't need people to fill a slot, because the slot will be only roughly defined. Companies need people who can figure out what the job takes and do it, people who can create the slot that fits them. Moreover, the slot will keep changing' (Hammer & Champy, 1994, p. 72). Many people no longer work in the constrained location of the office and factory (or call centre), controlled by clock and stop-watch. Many are now working at home (though perhaps still controlled by technology). Technology also allows some to operate in several spaces simultaneously and, because of globalisation, jobs are stretched out through space. Careers can now be global and boundaryless (Arthur, 1994).

Many people no longer have permanent, full-time contracts, but temporary, part-time, and other flexible contracts. Decentralisation, total quality management, and business process re-engineering emphasise lateral rather than upward movement, which may limit the individual's future horizon. The effects of the push for organisational flexibility and of technology ('just-in-time' production, niche markets) mean that it is no longer possible, for either organisation or individual, to look to the distant future.

It is not only work organisations that are changing. Previously accepted norms indicated by age, social class, gender are either disintegrating or changing radically. Previously adopted sequences of roles dictated by the relationship between formal education and work, and the norms of marriage and the formation of a family, are breaking up. These and other changes will dislodge some of the certainties and predictabilities individuals may have hitherto experienced, 'efface . . . markers of progress', so that 'orienting oneself socially becomes difficult' (Sennett, 1998, p. 88).

These and similar changes are taking place within the context of the 'space of flows' and of 'timeless time' (Castells, 1996) and are, indeed, contributing to the new experiences of space and time. Hence, the individual's construction of time and space will change in a number of ways, and the role of career in it.

Time, space, and the future of career

'Instantaneous time', with which the chapter started, desynchronises people's 'time–space paths', thus increasing the variation between them

(Lash & Urry, 1994, p. 246). Formerly shared and collective patterns of behaviour will become more varied and segmented, leaving people without agreed norms to anchor meanings. They will thus find it more difficult to take or interpret longitudinal readings from the domains, although they would still be able to take latitudinal readings. They would not become solely self-referential, for these readings could also encompass interpretations of others' locations in relation to their own. However, they would not be able to fix their location by reference to what they construe as shared norms.

Individuals will have to generate their own 'personalized, subjective temporalities' (Lash & Urry, 1994, p. 245). As they engage in ' "an interminable series of experiments and explorations" ' (Hall, 1976, in Weick & Berlinger, 1989, p. 321), their career will be 'Protean'. Career development will not take place in terms of external markers of progress, but of personal growth. This will lead to even further divergences in individuals' 'time–space paths', and reduce the possibility of taking normative readings of time and space.

'Instantaneous time' 'dissolves the future' and creates a lack of trust in the future (Lash & Urry, 1994, p. 245). There is 'the loss of a sense of the future except and insofar as the future can be discounted into the present' (Harvey, 1990, p. 291). It is 'hard to maintain any firm sense of continuity' (p. 291). If, without the continuation of the relatively stable structures of organisations and other domains, career cannot give the individual a glimpse of the future self, there will be no motivation to delay gratification, work hard, and invest in self-development. The potential loss of a long-term future threatens career, hitherto invested with a future orientation, with an identity crisis, and this in turn will restrict individuals' construction of their future. Thus the future of career will both contribute to and result from the revolutions taking place in the construction and experience of time and space.

In the world that is emerging, not only is the 'significant society' (Goffman, 1959, p. 123), to which career refers, becoming fragmented, but so is the individual's experience of 'the self'. With increasingly flexible work organisations, time horizons are shortening, and workers are 'always starting over' (Sennett, 1998, p. 84). How, asks Sennett (p. 26), can a person 'develop a narrative of identity and life history in a society composed of episodes and fragments?' This can only result in a 'pliant self, a collage of fragments unceasing in its becoming' (p. 133). There can be 'no coherent life narrative' (p. 133), no possibility of creating 'predictive narratives of what will be' (p. 135). The sense of future hitherto implied in career, and needed by self, is eroding.

The view that 'the future is dissolving into the present' (Lash & Urry,

1994, p. 243) perhaps has to be interpreted not as the loss of a future, but as a change in its depth and direction. Rather than focusing on movement, forward direction, and long-term destination, individuals' concern may perhaps have to be with the short-term, the horizontal and lateral, the extended present, as they piece together into a narrative the 'collage' of fragments in their lives (Sennett, 1998, p. 133). In providing a 'canopy of meaning' (Berger, 1967, in Roberts, 1980, pp. 163–4) for this *bricolage* (see chapter 11), the focus of career could shift from constructing the future in primarily temporal terms (time-line, trajectory, directional continuity) to more spatial terms (horizontal, non-directional continuity). This is compatible with what Mirvis and Hall (1994) see as the challenge 'to integrate many more stimuli and experiences into [the] sense of self' (p. 373) as the boundaryless career opens up the boundaries of identity. It is also consistent with the hypothesis of Castells (1996, p. 376) that 'space organizes time in the network society', 'reversing a historical trend' (p. 465), and producing the upheavals identified at the start of the chapter. However, it appears to be at odds with the inference made earlier that the objective career focused on the spatial dimension: that inference needs further examination.

This interpretation of career also fits well with Castell's (1996) notion of the network society, and also with the interpretation that career is relational and co-constructed with others (Hall & Associates, 1996; Young & Valach, 1996). Those views imply that, rather than being individualistic, and a personal trajectory, career has strong horizontal and networking characteristics. Thus despite what are predicted to be major perturbations in the experiences of time and space, the future of career could still be a moving pattern of relationships between individuals, a dance to the music of time.

REFERENCES

Arthur, M. (1994). The boundaryless career: A new perspective for organizational inquiry. *Journal of Organizational Behavior, 15,* 295–306.
Arthur, M. B., Hall, D. T., & Lawrence, B. S. (1989). Generating new directions in career theory: The case for a transdisciplinary approach. In M. B. Arthur, D. T. Hall, & B. S. Lawrence (Eds.), *Handbook of career theory* (pp. 7–25). Cambridge: Cambridge University Press.
Bardwick, J. (1980). The seasons of a woman's life. In D. McGuigan (Ed.), *Women's lives: new theory, research, and policy* (pp. 35–55). Ann Arbor: University of Michigan Center for Continuing Education of Women.
Barley, S. R. (1989). Careers, identities, and institutions: The legacy of the Chicago School of Sociology. In M. B. Arthur, D. T. Hall, & B. S. Lawrence (Eds.), *Handbook of career theory* (pp. 41–65). Cambridge: Cambridge University Press.

Bauman, Z. (1999). *Culture as praxis*. London: Sage.

Becker, H. S. & Strauss, A. L. (1968). Careers, personality, and adult socialization. In B. L. Neugarten (Ed.), *Middle age and aging* (pp. 311–320). Chicago: University of Chicago Press.

Berger, P. L. & Luckmann, T. (1971). *The social construction of reality: A treatise in the sociology of knowledge*. Harmondsworth: Penguin.

Bridges, W. (1995). *Jobshift: How to prosper in a workplace without jobs*. London: Nicholas Brealey.

Castells, M. (1996). *The information age: Economy, society and culture. Vol. I: The rise of the network society*. Malden, MA: Blackwell.

Cochran, L. (1997). *Career counseling: A narrative approach*. Thousand Oaks, CA: Sage.

Collin, A. (1990). Mid-life career change research. In R. A. Young & W. A. Borgen (Eds.), *Methodological approaches to the study of career* (pp. 197–220). New York: Praeger.

Coyle, D. (1998). *Weightless world*. Massachusetts: Massachusetts Institute of Technology Press.

Crites, J. O. (1978). *The career maturity inventory*. Monterey, CA: CTB/McGraw-Hill.

Dalton, G. W. (1989). Developmental views of careers in organizations. In M. B. Arthur, D. T. Hall, & B. S. Lawrence (Eds.), *Handbook of career theory* (pp. 89–109). Cambridge: Cambridge University Press.

Driver, M. (1979). Career concepts and career management in organizations. In C. L. Cooper (Ed.), *Behavioral problems in organizations* (pp. 79–139). Englewood Cliffs, NJ: Prentice-Hall.

Eco, U. (1989). *Foucault's pendulum* (W. Weaver, Trans.). London: Secker & Warburg.

Erikson, E. (1950). *Childhood and society*. New York: W. W. Norton.

Featherstone, M. (1995). *Undoing culture: Globalization, postmodernism and identity*. London: Sage.

Ference, T. P., Stoner, J. A. F., & Warren, E. K. (1977). Managing the career plateau. *Academy of Management Review, 2*, 602–612.

Giddens, A. (1991). *Modernity and self-identity: Self and society in the late modern age*. Cambridge: Polity Press.

Ginzberg, E. (1972). Toward a theory of occupational choice: A restatement. *Vocational Guidance Quarterly, 20*, 169–176.

Ginzberg, E., Ginsburg, S. W., Axelrad, S., & Herma, J. L. (1951). *Occupational choice: An approach to a general theory*. New York: Columbia University Press.

Goffman, E. (1959). The moral career of the mental patient. *Psychiatry, 22*, 123–142.

Goldthorpe, J. H. & Llewellyn, C. (1977). Class mobility: Intergenerational and worklife patterns. *British Journal of Sociology, 28*, 269–302.

Gowler, D. & Legge, K. (1989). Rhetoric in bureaucratic careers: Managing the meaning of management success. In M. B. Arthur, D. T. Hall, & B. S. Lawrence (Eds.), *Handbook of career theory* (pp. 437–453). Cambridge: Cambridge University Press.

Hall, D. T., and Associates (1996). *The career is dead: Long live the career: A relational approach to careers*. San Francisco: Jossey-Bass.

Hammer, M. & Champy, J. (1994). *Reengineering the corporation: A manifesto for business revolution.* New York: Harper Business.

Harvey, D. (1990). *The condition of postmodernity.* Cambridge, MA: Blackwell.

Havighurst, R. J. (1964). Stages of vocational development. In H. Borow (Ed.), *Man in a world of work* (p. 216). Boston: Houghton Mifflin.

Höpfl, H. J. (1992). Great expectations? Toward an understanding of the life plan. In R. A. Young, & A. Collin (Eds.), *Interpreting career: Hermeneutical studies of lives in context* (pp. 15–30). Westport, CT: Praeger.

Hughes, E. C. (1937). Institutional office and the person. *American Journal of Sociology, 43,* 404–413.

James, W. (1890). *The principles of psychology.* Vol. I. London: Macmillan.

Jaques, E. (1956). *The measurement of responsibility.* London: Tavistock.

Johnson, M. L. (1977). Doctors, careers and ageing. *Concorde,* January, 65–87.

Kidd, J. M. & Killeen, J., with Jarvis, J. & Offer, M. (1994). Is guidance an applied science? The role of theory in the careers guidance interview. *British Journal of Guidance and Counselling, 22,* 385–403.

Killeen, J. (1996). The social context of guidance. In A. G. Watts, B. Law, J. Killeen, J. M. Kidd, & R. Hawthorn. *Rethinking careers education and guidance* (pp. 3–22). London: Routledge.

Lash, S. & Urry, J. (1994). *Economies of signs and space.* London: Sage.

Lawrence, B. S. (1984). Age-grading: The implicit organizational timetable. *Journal of Occupational Behaviour, 5,* 23–35.

Miller, D. C. & Form, W. H. (1951). *Industrial sociology.* New York: Harper and Row.

Mirvis, P. H. & Hall, D. T. (1994). Psychological success and the boundaryless career. *Journal of Organizational Behavior, 15,* 365–380.

Neugarten, B. L. & Moore, J. W. (1968). The changing age–status system. In B. L. Neugarten (Ed.), *Middle age and aging* (pp. 5–21). Chicago: University of Chicago Press.

Neugarten, B. L., Moore, J. W., & Lowe, J. C. (1968). Age norms, age constraints, and adult socialization. In B. L. Neugarten (Ed.), *Middle age and aging* (pp. 22–28). Chicago: University of Chicago Press.

Roberts, R. J. (1980). An alternative justification for careers education: A radical response to Roberts & Daws. *British Journal of Guidance and Counselling, 8,* 158–174.

Schein, E. H. (1971). The individual, the organization, and the career: A conceptual scheme. *Journal of Applied Behavioral Science, 7,* 401–426.

(1978). *Career dynamics: Matching individual and organizational needs.* Reading, MA: Addison-Wesley.

Sekaran, U. & Hall, D. T. (1989). Asynchronism in dual-career and family linkages. In M. B. Arthur, D. T. Hall, & B. S. Lawrence (Eds.), *Handbook of career theory* (pp. 159–180). Cambridge: Cambridge University Press.

Sennett, R. (1998). *The corrosion of character: The personal consequences of work in the new capitalism.* New York: W. W. Norton.

Sobel, D. (1996). *Longitude.* London: Fourth Estate.

Sofer, C. (1970). *Men in mid-career.* Cambridge: Cambridge University Press.

Stebbins, R. A. (1970). Career: The subjective approach. *Sociological Quarterly, 11,* 32–49.

Stewart, A., Prandy, K., & Blackburn, R. M. (1980). *Social stratifications and occupations*. London: Macmillan.

Super, D. E. (1980). A life-span, life-space approach to career development. *Journal of Vocational Behavior, 13*, 282–298.

Super, D. E., Crites, J. O., Hummel, R. C., Moser, H. P., Overstreet, P. L., & Warnath, C. F.(1957). *Vocational development: A framework for research*. New York: Teachers College Press.

Super, D. E. & Knasel, E. G. (1981). Career development in adulthood: Some theoretical problems and a possible solution. *British Journal of Guidance and Counselling, 9*, 194–201.

Super, D. E., Starishevsky, R., Matlin, N., & Jordaan, J. P. (1963). *Career development: Self-concept theory*. New York: College Entrance Examination Board.

Super, D. E., Thompson, A. S., Lindeman, R. H., Jordaan, J. P., & Myers, R. A. (1981). *Career development inventory*. Palo Alto, CA: Consulting Psychologists Press.

Vondracek, F. W., Lerner, R. M., & Schulenberg, J. E. (1986). *Career development: A life-span developmental approach*. Hillsdale, NJ: Erlbaum.

Watts, A. G. (1981). Career patterns. In A. G. Watts, D. E. Super, & J. M. Kidd (Eds.), *Career development in Britain: Some contributions to theory and practice* (pp. 213–245). Cambridge: CRAC/Hobsons.

Weick, K. E. & Berlinger, L. R. (1989). Career improvisation in self-designing organizations. In M. B. Arthur, D. T. Hall, & B. S. Lawrence (Eds.), *Handbook of career theory* (pp. 313–328). Cambridge: Cambridge University Press.

Wilensky, H. L. (1960). Work, careers and social integration. *International Social Science Journal, 12*, 543–574.

    (1968). Orderly careers and social participation: The impact of work history on social integration in the middle mass. In B. L. Neugarten (Ed.), *Middle age and aging* (pp. 321–340). Chicago: University of Chicago Press.

Young, R. A. & Valach, L. (1996). Interpretation and action in career counscling. In M. L. Savickas & W. B. Walsh (Eds.), *Handbook of career counseling theory and practice* (pp. 361–375). Palo Alto, CA: Davies-Black.

Part 2

New perspectives

7   The future of boundaryless careers

Suellen M. Littleton, Michael B. Arthur,
and Denise M. Rousseau

When massive economic restructuring forced William H. Whyte Jr's (1956) 'organization man' to walk permanently out of the front doors of the corporation, many of the assumptions of a traditional career path followed shortly behind. In the wake of his departure, people were left pondering how they would survive without a job for life, a corporate 'road map' to guide their destiny and the firm's hierarchy to define their status or place in society. Without employers' orderly structures, external guides for action, and linear career paths, however, just what is the future of career? When 'the career' devolves to the level of the individual does free agency prevail and a form of 'career anarchy' result? Is there anything that can be concluded about careers if everyone seems to be doing their own thing?

We argue here that the answer is an emphatic 'yes'. The new environment suggests a shift from pre-ordained and linear development to perpetually changing career paths and possibilities. As a result a shift from 'bounded' careers – prescribed by relatively stable organisational and occupational structures – to 'boundaryless' careers – where uncertainty and flexibility are the order of the day – is increasingly common. The concept of the boundaryless career is broadly based, and intended to reflect the emergent pace of economic change. It does not characterise any single career form, but rather 'a range of possible forms that defy traditional employment assumptions' (Arthur & Rousseau, 1996, p. 6).

The myriad interactions of a boundaryless career over a lifetime of work experiences can appear overwhelming. A complex web of relationships emerges from numerous exchanges among individuals, teams, and employers. The interplay may seem downright chaotic. So much so, that one may be tempted to think that no aggregates can be drawn from this seemingly random micro-level behaviour. Yet, despite the large amount of publicity generated as 'organization man' was shown to the door, a large proportion of people who participate in the work place, and even whole industries, never really played by the traditional rules anyway. For these people and industries the 'boundaryless career' is simply business as usual. It is business to which we can turn to understand better the future of career or – as we see the future – the boundaryless career.

We focus in this chapter on situations where boundaryless career practices appear to be well established and fruitful, involving industries where open labour markets have thrived. Our examination suggests that seemingly random micro-level activities result in the creation of emergent pattern and order. Further examination reveals not only order, but remarkable stability. In the absence of external guides, people self-organise to learn and make sense of their environments. Moreover, the resulting social interdependence provides a new form of cohesiveness that, in turn, introduces new structure. Micro-level activities gather the force and the power to shape macro-level processes and larger institutions. It is organis*ing*, rather than organisation, that is the catch-word of the boundaryless career.

In this chapter we set out to explore the pervasive nature of boundaryless careers. We present a theoretical perspective through which we can understand the dynamics of boundaryless careers followed by descriptive analysis demonstrating evidence of theory in practice in two selected industries. First we present relevant aspects of Karl Weick's work (1979, 1995, and 1996) and discuss the process of 'enactment'. We then examine the industry cases. We conclude by refining the arguments by noting key behavioural aspects of enactment and other considerations of the process.

An enactment perspective

Our exploration in this chapter is framed in the social–psychological perspective of Karl Weick (1996). Weick's work provides a theoretical lens for explaining the processes at work in boundaryless career behaviour. His conception of enactment, directly related to his previous (1995) work on sensemaking, explains the dynamics of the characteristic interdependence that operates in boundaryless careers. The enactment view emphasises that action creates the environment. That is, people create situations and understandings out of their own dispositions and backgrounds. A simple analogy is with the legal system. People enact laws, which become part of the legal system which in turn influences further behaviour, leading people to enact new laws, and so on. A legal system continually evolves from the enactment of individual laws. Similarly, career systems evolve from the enactment of individual careers.

Another way to engage with enactment is to relate it to the process of natural selection. According to Weick (1996), careers unfold through successive cycles of enactment, selection, and retention, whereby the enactment of careers gives rise to broader organising of work arrangements. From this standpoint, the 'basic theme for the entire organizing model is found in the following recipe for sensemaking: "How can I know what I think until I see what I say?"' (Weick, 1979, p. 133). In the simplest form of the recipe, enactment is 'saying' (action), selection is 'seeing what I say' (perception), and retention is 'knowing what I think' (sensemaking).

If enactment is 'saying' then it is, in essence, the action of individuals in their environment that starts the process. When someone takes action, or interacts with their environment, it immediately impacts others and hence the individual produces part of their environment. For example, if you believe a certain group of individuals to be hostile, when you interact with them your behaviour may reflect your fear. In response they may sense that fear and behave in a hostile manner. The environment becomes hostile. Moreover, you have contributed to 'enacting' that hostile environment. The result is a circular self-reinforcing relationship resembling a self-fulfilling prophecy. An alternative, perhaps more satisfactory circular relationship could result if, instead of fear, you initially showed confidence.

How do we relate this process to boundaryless careers? For this, it is important to understand that there is less room for personal inputs, manoeuvring, or 'enactment' if there are clear salient rules and structures defining behaviour. In traditional bounded organisations and careers the proliferation of structure, hierarchy, plans, detailed job descriptions, prescribed relationships, and established 'road maps' provide an armoury of articulated rules and social cues to guide behaviour. The situation is 'strong' (Mischel, 1968) in as much as it provides little scope for improvisation.

In the pure form of the boundaryless career, however, such explicit guides do not exist. Instead of providing clear guidelines, employment situations are characterised by ambiguity. 'Weak' situations fall short of providing sufficient incentives for consistent behaviour or even similar expectations for those operating within them (Mischel, 1968). In 'weak' situations individuals are not able to interpret events in the same way, and the resulting ambiguity opens the door to myriad personal interpretations and opportunities for enactment. People engage in a stable process of trial and error that resembles an evolutionary system (Weick, 1979). People join together in shared improvisation that begins to form new codes and structures to guide their further behaviour. In the process 'microstrength shapes macroweaknesses' (Weick, 1996, p. 44) through the unfolding of boundaryless careers.

To illustrate the preceding argument we will apply Weick's ideas to descriptions provided by AnnaLee Saxenian (1996) on the dynamics of the Silicon Valley and by Candace Jones (1996) on the independent film industry. We reinterpret the contributions of these authors by explicitly re-framing them within Weick's framework (and we emphasise it is these three authors, and their original descriptions and ideas, that deserve the major part of the credit for this chapter).

To show how enactment and associated principles of self-organising and learning come to life, we will trace the process of enactment in each setting. First, we will describe the factors that have contributed to boundaryless career forms in each example. Next, we will cite some of the characteristics that make the resulting circumstances 'weak'. After that we will discuss the social behaviour and collective actions that fill the resulting void in the environment. Finally, we will point out the patterns, order, and shape we see enactment bringing to each of these respective settings. By doing so we hope to convey the pervasive qualities of both the process of enactment and the vehicle through which it operates – the boundaryless career.

The Silicon Valley

The Silicon Valley is notorious for the individual and collective success of its firms. So much so that the name 'Silicon Valley' has come to be synonymous with the electronics industry. The region is regarded as the centre for excellence and innovation and has given rise to some of the world's most influential firms, including Apple, Hewlett Packard, and Intel. Since its inception the Valley has operated with an individualistic open labour market. Today, the learning advantages that emanate from associated boundaryless career behaviour are regarded as a key source of competitive advantage for the region (Saxenian, 1996). One can argue that the Valley's 'boundarylessness' is a necessary feature of operating in a dynamic industry that demands constant innovation. Proponents point out that, in order to learn and solve the problems encountered in rapid technological advancement, knowledge must be shared among firms in a symbiotic balance between co-operation and competition. Boundaryless characteristics appear more prominently when an industry is knowledge – rather than capital-intensive or when firms operate in economic clusters.

However, other industry clusters and several notable large electronics firms do not engage with boundaryless practices. We may, therefore, attribute the 'boundaryless' features of the Silicon Valley to its heritage. Some believe this is in part due to the location of the region, hosting a 'West Coast' Northern Californian alternative in geographical isolation from the established 'East Coast' industry. The greenfield site had an empty slate and no institutional rules. Others, like the late William Hewlett, a key and highly influential founder of the region, believe that success stemmed from the learning advantages of an open labour market. Hewlett 'routinely offered the following advice . . . "If you want to succeed here you need to be willing to do three things: change jobs often, talk to your competitors and take risks – even if it means failing" ' (Saxenian, 1996, p. 23). Hewlett was himself influenced by his Stanford Dean of Engineering William Terman, a mentor and an influential Hewlett Packard board member (Collins & Porras, 1995). Today, Hewlett's and Terman's philosophy permeates the region. Despite fierce inter-firm competition, open information exchange is common practice among the region's producers.

Several features of the Valley contribute to creating a 'weak' environment. The high pace of technology and product life cycles, fluidity of firm formation and failure, rapid employee turnover resulting in little company-specific socialisation, as well as a lack of meaningful institutionally based hierarchy, all contribute to an environment in which individuals rely on alternative cues to guide their behaviour. For example, in the Valley, technology moves quickly and competition is tough. New firms form almost overnight - and many disappear just as quickly. When firms come and go like ships in the night it is not surprising that employees tend to identify with their profession, not their company. Moreover, people's loyalty is not only to their profession, but to the host industry region. 'As one local semiconductor executive reportedly noted: "Many of us wake up in the morning thinking that we work for Silicon Valley Inc." ' (Saxenian, 1996, p. 23). They view job-changing as the norm.

Average job tenure is in the area of two years, and annual turnover is around 35%, and often higher for smaller firms (Saxenian, 1996). As one engineer explained: 'two or three years is about the max [at a job] for the Valley because there's always something more interesting across the street' (Saxenian, p. 28). Knowledge and practices cross company borders at a pace that defies the embedding of 'routines' within the boundaries of any single company, and instead favours inter-company exchange. Everyone knows that, upon leaving a company, they may well work together again in the future: 'A colleague might become a customer or a competitor; today's boss could be tomorrow's subordinate' (Saxenian, p. 29). Institutionally based hierarchy, therefore, loses its saliency. In the Valley, respect and authority are gained through competence, technical excellence, and market share, with the highest regard accorded to successful entrepreneurs.

In the context of this 'weak' environment, clear social behaviour emerges as structure gets built at the micro-level. People seek to form relationships and routines in order to learn and thrive in their surroundings. In the Valley, information is the life-blood of the industry and continuous learning through relationships is the key to a successful career. People build their own competence by active membership in the larger learning community. Learning takes place in the pub or club. In the Valley's early days, it used to take place in the infamous Wagon Wheel Bar and the Homebrew Computer Club. Now it takes place in one of many watering holes or hobby groups where the Valley's high-technology workers regularly meet for lunch or after work. In these meeting places, people gather to see old friends, gossip, and make new acquaintances. In the workers' adopted social settings, the transition from friendly chatter to serious business occurs naturally.

In the Silicon Valley, collective actions unfold through a combination of mutual interests, intellectual curiosity, and problem solving geared towards developing new markets, technologies, products, or applications for computers. Workers have a systemic commitment to technical excellence in their field. As one engineer explained, the process is quite simple: 'people rub shoulders and share ideas' (Saxenian, p. 27). The knowledge of these informal groups is so powerful that many 'local entrepreneurs came to see social relationships and even gossip as crucial aspects of their business' (Saxenian, p. 26) As one local manager claimed: '"Over a lunch conversation or a beer, you'll learn that company A or company B has a technology you want . . . If it fits your needs, you'll build it into your next product"' (Saxenian, p. 31). In this manner, micro-level conversations influence the creation of new technologies, products, and applications.

It is through such social interaction and collective action that we begin to understand how patterns and order emerge in the Valley. In the absence of hierarchy and centralised planning, employees in the Valley rely on their skills, rather than on formal position, to provide a reference point for their careers. Such self-generated guides are reinforced by professional social networks, which provide a tacit road map about who knows who and who does what in the industry. These networks serve as efficient job search networks and makeshift recruitment centres. As one engineer reported: '"You don't just hire people out of the blue. In general, it's people you know, or you know someone who knows them"' (Saxenian, p. 27). Social networks impose structure on larger and looser situations. It is the region and its relationships, rather than the firm, that define opportunities for individual and collective advances in Silicon Valley (Saxenian, 1996).

Thus, while Silicon Valley's high rates of job mobility and new-firm formation lead to local losses for individual firms, they also foster a dynamic process of adaptation that spurs the evolution of the region. Knowledge of the latest techniques in design, production, and marketing is diffused rapidly throughout the area. The result is an exceptional rate of technical and organisational innovation created by a 'complex mix of social solidarity and individualistic competition' (Saxenian, 1996, p. 25). The resilience of Silicon Valley's economy shows that an unpredictable open labour market and seemingly 'chaotic' career paths and relationships have led to macro-economic stability for the region and hence continued opportunity for the community at large. 'Ironically, many of these Silicon Valley job hoppers may well have led more stable lives than the upwardly mobile "organizational men" of the 1950s who were transferred from place to place by the same employer' (Saxenian, p. 28).

The independent film-making industry

Like the Silicon Valley, the independent film-making industry is noted for its innovative ability, cutting edge creativity, and overall economic success. Like in the Silicon Valley, boundaryless careers are central to independent film-making activities. These activities evolved in the wake of fierce competition posed by the proliferation of television and the need to cut fixed costs. They superseded the former studio-based model of in-house film production, and its associated restrictive practices. Since the early 1970s, the new model has persisted. Boundaryless careers provide the building blocks that combine to facilitate production of the industry's separately creative parts. Independent film production has thrived as a superior organising model to its in-house predecessor (Jones, 1996).

Several characteristics of the independent film industry favour boundarylessness, including the uncertainty in the marketplace, the limited project duration, the lack of vertical integration among industry players, and the excess supply of quality labour. The uncertainty of the market stems from the fact that production of any particular film revolves around whether or not sufficient financing is obtained to start and ultimately complete production of any given film. When financing is arranged, it is specifically for the purpose of completing a single project, the making of the film. The limited duration of the project is such that all resources, including human resources, are temporary. The assembled company is essentially wound down upon the film's release. At this time, the film's credits symbolise that those who made it have moved on to other assignments.

Uncertainty over financing and limited project duration foster a 'weak' environment in which permanent structure is dysfunctional. Studios combine with subcontractors for specific film projects and disband when the work is done. Moreover, the project-based system allows for highly complex, unique 'products' – films – to benefit from rapid and efficient allocation and re-allocation of resources. Each time a film is completed the whole process starts over again and employment relationships are re-negotiated. A ready supply of quality labour contributes to the success of the independent production model. The industry is a magnet for talented, committed workers eager for work on the industry's terms. These include being ready to depart to remote locations at a moment's notice. However, as with Silicon Valley high-technology projects, much of the work is economically 'clustered', thereby facilitating fluidity of movement from one challenge to another.

As Jones's (1996) research affirms, people's social behaviour reveals that several distinct stages can be observed over the course of a career in the film industry. At the 'beginning' stage, freelance employees are constantly vying to participate in an industry in which there are no clear rules for entry. As one grip/electrician explained: '"There's no tried and true way to get started. You have to find people you like who make movies . . . It's getting the first job that is the hardest"' (Jones, 1996, p. 62). Once inside, the worker at the 'crafting' stage finds that, 'You build your reputation every day. You're only as good as your last job' (pp. 64–5). Reputation matters, as careers are self-managed and advanced through successive 'credits' that span multiple, largely forgotten, temporary film-making companies.

Having learned key skills and become indoctrinated into the industry culture, individuals enter a 'navigating' stage, furthering their reputation and developing the personal contacts that provide the resources to navigate from one project to another. In the words of one film commissioner, '"We are a big industry but a small industry because we talk to one another"' (Jones, 1996, p. 65). It is through talking to each other that people gain access to experiences that both hone existing abilities and cultivate more complex skills. Eventually, successful careers go full circle and move to a 'maintenance' stage. Here, senior members of the industry identify and train new members, establish workshops that develop talent in the field, and co-ordinate events such as film festivals. During this period people address personal needs which may have been neglected during earlier career stages because of the necessity to survive in a relatively unforgiving industry.

In a 'weak' environment that lasts a lifetime, it is critical that non-bureaucratic forms of cohesion bring order to the industry. Part of this cohesion is provided by subcontractors, whose processes of selection, training, and socialisation bring boundaryless careers together in project-based arrangements that provide tacit infrastructure and social familiarity. However, it is at the level of the individual career that we can most clearly see the micro-level behaviour that fills the relatively structure-less context. Despite the fact that no explicit rules or operating procedures exist there is much tacit communication that binds professionals together. The aggregate effects of individuals acting independently leads to macro-level cohesion. Shared understanding and related expectations, for example regarding the need for unusual working hours and the use of 'idle' time to teach newcomers professional skills, play a key role linking identities to workplace interactions. In the process of learning the ropes, individuals are socialised and begin to make key contacts that help progress them to the next stages of their career. Once socialised, people engage in collective learning as they problem-solve on a project-by-project basis. Learning accumulates, disperses, and evolves as industry specialists enact their working environment.

From micro-level enactment we see macro-level influence and patterns, order and shape in the independent film industry. Not only do we observe distinct stages of careers, we see aggregate social norms influencing behaviour. What one can see from the pattern of progression that characterises freelance boundaryless careers in the film industry is that although few formal boundaries exist, persistent social structures and repeated patterns of interaction can be observed. In the process of enacting their careers, individuals engage in reinforcing the cohesive social patterns of the industry which serve to guide the stages of their development. In this respect careers in the Silicon Valley and the film industry have much in common, with organising in film-making resembling a 'project-based' Valley. Just as careers can be traced in the Valley through the development of technology and tightly knit project teams, in film a clear pattern also emerges that reveals micro-level organising shaping macro activity.

Refinements on enactment

Agency and communion

Both of our previous examples suggest that the enactment of boundaryless careers unfolds through a mixture of personal initiative and mutual co-operation. Marshall (1989), after Bakan (1966), refers to the elements in this mixture as *agency* and *communion*. At a very basic level agency is about control and communion is about co-operation. Agency is individualistic, and characterised by autonomy, independence, initiative, and adaptation. It is fundamental to boundaryless careers in that people are ultimately responsible for their own development. Communion, in contrast to agency, is concerned about connections, relationships, tolerance, and trust. It is fundamental to boundaryless careers in that people need to manage their own arrangements for working with others.[1]

In 'weak' environments, in which rules are not defined and behavioural responses not controlled, both agency and communion are means by which people respond to uncertainty. Agency provides direction and drive to career behaviour and helps to diffuse ambiguity by providing vision and long-term goals. Left to its own means, however, agency may cause strong hierarchies to reform, the balance of power to be lost, and, most importantly, the trust and co-operation necessary for people and information to move across boundaries to be forfeited. Communion provides the platform for mutual support and collective learning through which shared visions may be pursued. However, unbridled communion may neglect to attend to the mechanisms and rewards through which effective collaboration can occur.

The Silicon Valley and independent film-making examples illustrate the interplay of agency and communion. Agency occurs through the individual initiative and enthusiasm people bring to their careers within their adopted industries, communion occurs through the collaborative ways of working that substitute for more formal arrangements. Together, the combination of behaviours supports current high-technology or film-making projects while it simultaneously develops people for further opportunities. This development includes community-building that will influence the make-up and effectiveness of future project teams. Host industries will thrive, our examples suggest, as long as agency and communion are allowed to work in tandem (Rousseau & Arthur, 1999).

Contemporary views of work frequently lament a loss of community in restructured employment arrangements. However, in calling for a return to community, these views frequently look no further than the single company. An enactment perspective suggests that communities can be much more broadly diffused. Both the Silicon Valley and film-making stories demonstrate that host industries, as well as their embedded occupations, provide alternative contexts for community-building to occur. Other kinds of community – stemming, for example, from shared ideological, family, educational, ethnic, or gender attachments – can also provide enduring support for people's boundaryless career endeavours (Parker & Arthur, 2000).

[1] Some researchers, notably Marshall (1989), emphasise the feminine characteristics of communion versus the masculine characteristics of agency. We do not do so here, although it may be interesting to contemplate whether the Silicon Valley is, in the broadest sense, 'feminised'.

Reciprocity

A related concept is that of *reciprocity*. Since workers cannot be all things to all people all of the time, a balance of behaviours is required. Reciprocity refers to the connection between what people give to and what people take from their employment situations. Traditional career models used to prescribe that people offer loyalty in return for deferred rewards. Accordingly, deferred pension rights, vacation time, promotion opportunities, and social acceptance were most reserved for those who had 'served their time'. In contrast, those who changed employer were handicapped by the loss of the privileges that they left behind. The Silicon Valley and film-making worlds suggest a different logic: one where the old entitlement-based models are a hindrance to boundaryless career investments.

With boundaryless careers, employment relationships are too fluid to assume the trappings of traditional loyalty-based employment systems. In the simplest case, employment arrangements reflect a 'spot' contract involving a simple exchange of work for immediate financial payment. However, our examples suggest subtler forces are at work. People are recruited to participate in high-technology and film-making projects for the skills that they bring – skills that have been developed from previous projects. The system, at its best, consists of cycles in which the learning taken from previous projects is applied in the current project, which in turn provides new learning opportunities. The simple exchange of commitment to do one's best in return for learning opportunities may be a common one in contemporary employment, and one that inspires many workers to seek new employment pastures when their learning slows down (Arthur, Inkson & Pringle, 1999).

The concept of reciprocity reinforces the significance of project-based activities. Work which provides an underlying project-based structure, such as in construction ('jobs'), law (cases), or computing (programmes), provides a particular time span for reciprocities to occur. If the benefits are genuinely mutual, projects provide a basis for high commitment from both parties to the short-term employment contract. Yet, the benefits of reciprocity can accrue beyond the project's conclusion. Individuals can take their learning from projects and project participants with them. Meanwhile, their influence on other project participants can be retained in the sponsoring company, or the host industry, or both. Ultimately, other industries can also benefit as mobile workers transport best practices to new situations.

A new continuity

What general lessons can be claimed from our two examples? Many would argue that traditional employment systems, going back to the factories of the eighteenth century, do not favour boundaryless careers. We agree, but we also live in a time when those systems are failing, and where their underlying assumptions of stasis are incompatible with the emergent reality of persistent change. Moreover, those systems were designed according to a conception of 'labour capital' rather than to one of 'intellectual capital'. Yet, it is the conception of intellectual capital that is increasingly emphasised today. Readers of this chapter will most likely see themselves as having a capacity for continuous learning. Is it really too great a step to extend the same belief in the capacity for learning to the workforce at large?

If the workforce at large can learn, what are the social arrangements that best sustain new learning? Leaving the determination of what is to be learned to a few senior managers? Knowing what is best for people or trusting that they might know, or at least contribute to knowing, what is best for themselves? Having people trapped by deferred rewards (Williamson, 1975), or acknowledging that those rewards systems are grounded in distrust?

A colleague recently visited the Czech republic, and explored that country's relatively rapid adjustment to a market economy. She asked what was the single best thing a Czech worker could do to learn the underlying principles of the market. 'Work for McDonalds,' went the surprising reply, 'but only for six months.' It was explained that six months was quite long enough for the uninitiated worker to appreciate the importance of customers and customer service. After six months, the worker had learned what he or she could and it was time, from a career perspective, to move on.

The contrast between working for McDonalds for six months or working for McDonalds for a lifetime is, writ large, the contrast between boundaryless careers and their traditional bounded counterparts. Today's work is increasingly 'intelligent' work (Quinn, 1992), that calls on workers' learning capacities, and – as our examples suggest – provides an organising structure rich in project opportunities through which learning episodes can unfold. If that organising structure is lacking, the worker can heed the advice of our Czech informant and design a project for herself or himself.

In the future, we submit, most careers will be boundaryless. We have sought to illustrate the future by exploring two industries where boundaryless careers have flourished – reaping benefits for people, companies, and host industries alike. New theories, such as Karl Weick's theory on the enactment of careers, can help us to understand the underlying patterns and dynamics inherent in complex, self-organising, social phenomena. People may not need to move between firms perpetually, but they will need to take charge of their own learning agendas. As they take charge, boundaries will form and re-form, and underlying order provide a macro-economic stability in an environment in which 'organization man' has become all but extinct.

ACKNOWLEDGEMENTS

We are deeply indebted to Polly Parker of the University of Auckland, New Zealand, Anne Duncan and Svenja Tams of the London Business School, and Julian Smith for their feedback on an earlier draft of this chapter. Special thanks go to AnnaLee Saxenian, Candace Jones, and Karl Weick, authors of chapters in *The boundaryless career* in which these ideas were originally presented and on which the bulk of this text is based.

REFERENCES

Arthur, M. B., Inkson, K., & Pringle, J. K., (1999). *The new careers: Individual action and economic change.* London: Sage.

Arthur, M. B. & Rousseau, D. M. (Eds.) (1996). *The boundaryless career: A new employment principle for a new organizational era.* New York: Oxford University Press.

Bakan, D. (1966). *The duality of human existence: An essay on psychology and religion.* Boston: Beacon.

Collins, J. C. & Porras, J. L. (1995). *Built to last: Successful habits of visionary companies.* London: Century.

Jones, C. (1996). Careers in project networks: The case of the film industry. In M. B. Arthur & D. M. Rousseau (Eds.), *The boundaryless career: A new employment principle for a new organizational era* (pp. 58–75). New York: Oxford University Press.

Marshall, J. (1989). Re-visioning career concepts: A feminist invitation. In M. B. Arthur, D. T. Hall, & B. S. Lawrence (Eds.), *Handbook of career theory* (pp. 275–291). New York: Cambridge University Press.

Mischel, W. (1968). *Personality and assessment.* New York: John Wiley & Sons.

Parker, P. & Arthur, M. B. (2000). Careers, organizing and community. In M. B. Arthur, M. A. Peiperl, R. Goffee, & T. Morris, (Eds.), *Career frontiers: New conceptions of working lives* (pp. 99–121). Oxford: Oxford University Press.

Quinn, J. B. (1992). *Intelligent enterprise.* New York: Free Press.

Rousseau, D. M. & Arthur, M. B. (1999). The boundaryless human resource function: building agency and community in the new economic era. *Organizational Dynamics 27* (4), 7–18.

Saxenian, A. (1996). Beyond boundaries: Open labor markets and learning in Silicon Valley. In M. B. Arthur & D. M. Rousseau (Eds.), *The boundaryless career: A new employment principle for a new organizational era* (pp. 23–39).

New York: Oxford University Press.

Weick, K. E. (1979). *The social psychology of organizing*, (2nd edn). Reading, MA: Addison-Wesley.

—— (1995). *Sensemaking in organizations*. Thousand Oaks, CA: Sage.

—— (1996). Enactment and the boundaryless career: Organizing as we work. In M. B. Arthur & D. M. Rousseau (Eds.), *The boundaryless career: A new employment principle for a new organizational era* (pp. 40–57). New York: Oxford University Press.

Whyte, W. H. (1956). *The organization man*. New York: Simon and Schuster.

Williamson, O. E. (1975). *Markets and hierarchies: Analysis and antitrust implications*. New York: Free Press.

8   Career development in a changing context of the second part of working life

Danielle Riverin-Simard

The notion of career in the first decades of the twenty-first century will undoubtedly have a different configuration. Linear and stable dimensions will in future give way to non-linear, unstable, and even chaotic components. Young people will have to function within these contingencies in order to accomplish their specific career paths. Adults in the second part of their working lives will have already experienced numerous career transitions: job changes, disparate careers, multiple kinds of training.

Given this double complexity of an active ageing population and a society that is grappling with profound transformations, how does one conceive of career? In a world of constant change, does the term 'career' still apply to people who are forty years of age or older? Or should we speak of two early deaths: the first, given its changing meaning in a postmodern context that is increasingly characterised by precariousness, flexibility, instability, intermittance, and insecurity, the death of career in the traditional sense of the term; and the second, if we believe (in part, incorrectly, as we will later see) that adults in the second part of their working life – the vast majority – experience a certain vocational decline, the death of career among most 'active' adults? If we take into account the possible characteristics of the social and economic context of the first two decades of the twenty-first century forecast by Bridges (1994), Giddens (1990), Naisbitt and Aburdene (1990), Rifkin (1995), and Toffler (1990), should we conclude that the meaning of career will be transformed?

We can state that adults in the second half of working life experience numerous new beginnings and career transitions. Career development is in constant change. The career development of this part of working life can no longer be uniquely defined by existing models, as the American specialist Solomone (1996) indicates. Although certain research, notably by Gould, Havighurst, Levinson, Miller and Form, Neugarten, Super, and Vaillant, is very rich and rigorous (Riverin-Simard, 1998), unfortunately it cannot sufficiently answer these new questions. First of all, some of these researchers have not studied workers who are over 50 years of age. Others have developed models which can only be partially adapted to the realities of the twenty-first century. Can career development in the second half of working life be explained by a theory of disengagement (voluntary retreat from the socio-economic world and diminishing interest in it), a physiological development curve (climbing until 35–45 years of age, followed by a plateau or a period of maintenance, and then a decline that starts at age 50), or a compensatory model (where skills lost after mid-life are compensated for by other new skills)? The socio-economic context, created in part by globalisation, highlights the fact that workers continue to face renewal during the second half of working life. This context calls attention to a process to which little attention was paid twenty years ago: development that is intense, turbulent, and full of new beginnings and redefinitions of projects.

Thus, our objective in this chapter is to reflect upon and conjecture about new career configurations for adults in the second half of working life at the beginning of the twenty-first century. It is only by studying these adults' testimonies, needs, expectations, and fears that we can understand the way in which they perceive their relationships with the working world, the different phases that await them, and the inevitable transitions that are characterised by elements of continuity and rupture. A unique qualitative study of the second part of the working life is described in detail in Riverin-Simard (1988, 1990, 1991, 1998). It reveals the experiences of adults who are forty years of age or older. There are numerous ruptures (abrupt cessations of occupational tasks, of relationships between colleagues, of work environments) and new departures (job reorientations, reorganisations, renewals), continual redefinitions of occupational projects (group of work activities, or plans, which are coherent with career orientations) and novel ways of carrying out these projects, and moments of suffering and intense feelings of finitude (being mortal, or bound to die). The variables in the sample of 941 adults were age, gender, socio-economic status, employment sector, and vocational personality type – according to Holland's classification (1997). This sample allowed both time-sequential and cross-sequential data collection (Schaie, 1992). The content analysis of the semi-structured interviews followed the methods advocated by Horth (1986) and the interpretative research paradigm (Guba & Lincoln, 1994). Two types of categories were used: first, pre-existing categories; second, categories determined through data analysis that were eventually added to or replaced the pre-existing categories. These new categories were retained when more than a third of the subjects from each age strata, social class, and personality type referred to them. The detailed analysis was carried out in an intra- and inter-categorical fashion, or in other words, horizontally and vertically.

Numerous ruptures and new departures

At the start of the twenty-first century, this renewal and these constant redefinitions shed new light on the career transfigurations of people who are forty years of age or older. Let us examine the numerous ruptures and new departures they experienced during each of five phases.

During the search for the guiding thread of their career histories (phase 1), these adults (mid-forties) experienced a rupture with the past and a new departure: they gained a new understanding of their goals, their vocational identities, and the links that existed between their turbulent private and occupational lives.

A new departure was even more obvious during a career transition (at the beginning of their fifties). Equipped with updated information about their goals and their renewed vocational identities, these adults devoted this phase to making appropriate new modifications (phase 2). They aimed to achieve a change of career path in order to make the best possible compromise between the different constraints imposed by their personal demands and the always unforeseeable social expectations. Having reached the mid-fifties, these adults sought a promising exit (phase 3) from the job market by engaging in new goals that were linked to different forms of new departures: these could include training a replacement team, or highlighting qualities that had been demonstrated throughout their working lives.

Adults in their sixties experienced a particular career transition that is characterised by a great rupture. These adults eventually feel obliged to dream of other kinds of activities to fulfil their goals (phase 4). This transition also seemed to encourage them to offer advice in the form of reflection-testaments: meeting challenges; seeking to attain a certain degree of freedom at work; recognising an essential component of wisdom in this experience; maintaining a spirit of unflagging combativity.

The inevitability of retirement forced adults in their mid-sixties to face a new and definitive departure (phase 5). Different reactions could be observed: channeling energies into delaying retirement and intensifying career development in the job market; planning stimulating activities to achieve renewed career involvement or at least a certain level of social commitment in retirement.

The gradual reappropriation of opposing elements sheds light on career development, and thus is another very important part of this new rupture and departure at the end of working life. Far from continuing to pursue development in order to accentuate their vocational specificity (skills, preferences, attitudes), these adults sought to embrace the opposite elements they used to reject in order to succeed in their careers. This new departure, characteristic of the final phases of working life, was thus a turning point: these adults no longer avoided elements opposed to their own vocational personalities, and in fact sought to integrate them as they continued to pursue their vocational development.

In summary, some of my results highlight the numerous new ruptures and departures that adults over forty years of age experienced in their working lives. These results lead us to propose the law of vocational chaos (Riverin-Simard, 1998). I believe that this law could help shed light on the characteristics of the very tumultuous career of adults in our Western societies at the start of the twenty-first century. Indeed, I believe that the relatively structured instability characterising vocational development is similar to the law of chaos. This law maintains that there is an undeniable order and structure within some natural disorder. It should be remembered, moreover, that chaos theory provides the basis to find the order that is hidden in disorder, to establish a less problematic relationship with uncertainty, and to propose a new understanding of the unforeseen (Balandier, 1994). According to Gleick (1987), scientists who promoted the law of chaos met with incredulity until several experiments in fields as varied as physics, meteorology, geology, biology, and chemistry demonstrated the importance of studying chaos in the forms of instability and disorder. Yet the theory of chaos is similar to certain philosophical conceptions that are far older than recent theories about order and disorder. Lachelier (1992), for example, who integrates several philosophers' reflections on order and disorder, considers that disorder, far from being unintelligible or disruptive, might be one way of expressing a reality whose structure and intelligibility still escape us. As Bergson (1994) suggests, when all is said and done, disorder is simply confused knowledge or the absence of knowledge. This author maintains that we refer to disorder in order to note a state of facts, without being able to pinpoint any kind of definite relation between the facts.

I believe that the testimonies of close to 1,000 working adults, based on specific career paths according to diverse intra-cultural (social class) and intra-individual (personality type), variables, seem to be heading in an interesting direction. They allow us to identify the presence of a structure that is inherent to vocational chaos, or, in other words, a stable structure that underlies the omnipresent instability that is characteristic of career development. This law of vocational chaos is formulated in the following manner: first, the apparent disorder of career paths is structured, and not random or dependent on circumstances or contexts that are themselves random; instability, disorder, and chaos, therefore, are clearly distinguishable from the haphazard, or, in other words, the absence of structure and unpredictability; second, curiously, vocational instability, disorder, and chaos thus seem to be associated with a certain determinism, structure, and predictability. These are manifested, among others, in the diverse phases of working life that we have identified, and are found in a relatively predictable time-space. Above all, these phases organise these numerous – and apparently unorganised and random – ruptures and new departures into groups of vocational events that have a specific developmental meaning according to the phase of working life in which the occupational events appear.

Continuous redefinitions of vocational projects and novel ways of accomplishing them

The results of my study indicate that the numerous ruptures and new departures were also occasions for continually redefining vocational projects. This process is a central element illustrating the intensity of adult vocational development throughout all periods of life, and particularly during the second half of working life.

One thing is certain. The end of the twentieth century is probably a transitional period when the idea of work as the mainstream of existence, as it has been throughout the industrial era, is tending to disintegrate and be replaced by a diversification of activities and working times (Bridges, 1994; Rikfin, 1995). A unique, linear, and imposed temporality gives way to a plural temporality. A life cycle composed of comings and goings has already definitively replaced the three-phase cycle: education, work, retirement. People experience shifts, downgrading, and withdrawal; the majority constantly experience ruptures and discontinuities.

How can the consequences of these multiple transformations in the job market be minimised? The adult subjects of my research indicated how they succeeded in effectively managing the discontinuity, in dealing with the flexibility, and in viewing their activities differently so as to detect opportunities that are somewhat advantageous. Holding down a job did not necessarily assure a vocational identity in the sense of a social status. As the results of our research suggest, it was vocational projects (and their continuous redefinitions) that assured this identity; indeed, these projects continued while adults waited for the numerous re-entries into the job market.

The results of my research indicate increased inequalities between workers, individuals' loss of control over their work, and an increase in the unbearable ambiguity that characterises the way individuals define their activities in relation to the overall context of work. If, as a result of upheavals in the job market – which, according to Giddens (1990), result notably from globalisation – adults are only intermittently members of the active population, these same adults must thus make sure that they no longer equate economic activity with vocational activity. Though vocational identity was almost uniquely linked to having a job only decades ago, some distance must henceforth be placed between these two realities. The sociological determination that tends unquestioningly to equate adult and economically active life (Boutinet, 1993) must no longer be accepted at face value. If this distinction has been institutionalised, it must quickly be abandoned.

Vocational projects demand a notion of the future (Riverin-Simard, 1991, 1995), and the planning of current and future activities in the framework of objectives that must be achieved in the relatively near future. The results of our study highlight this constant planning through the continual redefinition of vocational projects.

How though is this notion of the future justified in our current societies? In the current socio-economic context that is characterised by job precariousness, constant changes in the job market, and numerous short-lived businesses, it can seem superfluous, unrealistic, and even idealistic to question, as demanded by the key elements of the vocational projects, the future orientations of individuals and the socio-economic world. Though the socio-economic context seems to impose a law of immediacy, on the contrary, these research results seem to propose that one must react to, and remain aware of the necessity of projecting into, the future.

Indeed, according to several philosophers, psychologists, and contemporary organisational consultants, it is precisely this future projection that guarantees the present. According to Sartre (1963), for example, existence is primarily a projection in time; individuals define themselves by the fact that they are hurtling towards a future, or that they are aware of projecting themselves towards the future. Boutinet (1993) maintains that individuals without projects risk obsolescence or an escape into activism. According to Bridges (1994), in the fields of activity where technologies and the means and demands of work are rapidly transformed, projects are already the norm.

But because the results of our research propose that vocational projects indicated intense vocational development, we need to know what, more precisely, the designation 'vocational project' means? This notion, mentioned by several authors, including Boutinet (1993), Little (1989), and Kelly (1979), is first based on the philosophical concept of personal project. Some researchers who have examined this idea have also considered its related dimensions: an individual's relation to the world and time. According to Heidegger (1962), for example, an individual is essentially a project being, a 'possible-being', and a 'being-able-to-be'. Thrown into the world, human beings are thrust into a mode of being in a project; depending on its scope, this project is always linked to the display of the being-in-the-world (Heidegger, 1962). This philosopher believes that projects signify the way individuals prefigure the world, and demonstrate their ability to transcend it. For Sartre (1963), projects are the way in which consciousness exists, or in other words, the way consciousness continually makes and remakes itself without becoming fixed in one state. According to him, nothing exists prior to projects.

In summary, this philosophical idea of personal project is closely associated with an individual's very existence. Thus vocational projects use an ontological notion of being that is essentially defined, according to certain existential philosophers, like Heidegger, Merleau-Ponty, and Sartre, as a project being (Riverin-Simard, 1995). Applied to career development, the notion of project has social meaning (Young, Valach, & Collin, 1996, p. 487) and primarily concerns the link between the individual and the socio-economic environment (Riverin-Simard, 1995). Vocational projects constitute the person's intrinsically oriented and intentional needs to seek outlets through a relationship with the world. Based on both the results of my research and these conceptual elements, I propose the following idea: given the very existence of an individual and the uniqueness of his or her existence, each person maintains, in a more or less explicit or conscious manner, his or her own vocational project; this project can be defined as an idiosyncratic mixture of dominant or secondary orientations evolving in a changing economic reality.

According to my results, vocational projects (and their constant reorientations) are an essential component of the continual redefinitions of vocational identity. They are thus deemed necessary for the individual to survive the numerous upheavals and revolving doors of the job market. They help individuals respect their vocational identity and the coherence of their occupational interests during these sporadic refusals or rejections in the job market. Vocationally speaking, a job makes no sense if it is not grafted to a vocational project. Above all, it is this project that is apt to direct an individual towards a new departure following each transition, rupture, or job loss during one of these phases of working life.

Lastly, vocational projects (and their constant redefinitions) seem to be able to assure a certain continuity throughout the phases of working life, and, above all, vocational projects are presented as one of the major elements that could contribute to the sense of self-identity. This in a way corroborates Giddens's remarks that individuals need this sense in order to face the ruptures and upheavals of high modernity: 'The individual must integrate information deriving from a diversity of mediated experiences with local involvements in such a way as to connect future projects with past experiences in a reasonably coherent fashion . . . A reflexively ordered narrative of self-identity provides the means of giving coherence to the finite lifespan, given changing external circumstances' (Giddens, 1991, p. 215).

Moments of suffering and feelings of finitude

In addition to numerous ruptures and new departures, there were multiple failed journeys that often entailed great suffering. This is another striking characteristic of careers at the start of the twenty-first century, particularly for adults in the second half of working life. Job losses, forced change of tasks, and the obligation to assume precarious jobs that are badly paid and often opposed to one's vocational personality are among the elements that cause the most occupational suffering.

Furthermore, it is unfortunately all too evident that suffering associated with the multiple failures of these numerous new departures sometimes seems more frequent and intense among workers of the disadvantaged and middle classes than among those of the advantaged class. It is in this way that our work demonstrates the traditional inequality of the class system which is at the very heart of the job market.

A completely different type of inequality, however, that also causes a lot of suffering is also indicated by the results of my research: the division between insiders and outsiders in the job market. Unfortunately, this new type of generalised inequality is also one of the elements of career transfiguration that is witnessed at the start of the twenty-first century. The observation of this new type of inequality corroborates, above all, the remarks made by several authors. Touraine (1992), for example, notes that a market society composed of insiders and outsiders has replaced the production society that had actors on the top (advantaged class) or on the bottom (middle or disadvantaged class). According to Gaujelac and Leonnetti (1994), the industrial society is built on a disciplinary and hierarchical system that is based on the notion of class, while the postmodern society is now founded on a managerial system composed of networks. Touraine (1992) thus compares the current society to a marathon which everyone can choose to enter and run. Yet there are a growing number of wounded and disabled people who are incapable of following the frantic rhythm imposed by change and the demands of competition, and others who are very simply thrown out of the race. Some are invited to attain excellence, while others are strongly encouraged to exclude themselves. According to Touraine (1992), this is the way our dual society is constructed: on one side, organisations that create a style of management that is apt to mobilise individuals who are attracted by performance; on the other side, a system that generates rejects. Whatever the situation, there seems to be a price to pay, and if, in this universe of job rationalisation, individuals' employability is often judged by the intrapersonal dimension – their ability to adapt – very real yet harmful structural factors are evoked. This new social inequality, accompanied by chronic suffering, is thus accentuated (Riverin-Simard, 1991).

Moreover, several studies corroborate the existence of this frequent suffering. According to Poulin-Simon, Bellemare and Tremblay (1992), problems arise when people stop working, whether temporarily or permanently. Their interest and motivation are weakened, their investment in their work is limited, and their feeling of belonging and identification with their work environments is suppressed. According to these authors, the alternating periods of employment–unemployment, though increasingly frequent, produce ruptures that have significant after-effects. Indeed, this entry unemployment (short-term) can degenerate into exclusion unemployment (long-term: according to the Organisation for Economic Cooperation and Development, 1995, one year or longer) for people who are unemployed for long periods of time; this is particularly true for older people. Castel (1991) observes that a growing number of individuals risk an even greater social exclusion that leads to disaffiliation or disintegration. Gaujelac and Leonnetti (1994) refer to this phenomenon as a battle for space: solitary individuals fighting society for space, or, in other words, status, identity, recognition, or social existence. Moreover, the results of our research indicated that the meaning of this suffering, tied to the numerous comings and goings in one's career, was found in the existential questioning linked to an intense feeling of finitude among adults in the second half of working life. Death played an integral part in the vocational discourse of these adults. It was integrated into the continuation of their career; in this respect, the anticipation of retirement seemed to be one of the most apparent release mechanisms. Retirement was still largely perceived to be the harbinger of the next step of biological death.

Given that the reality of death played an integral part in adults' vocational discourse (Riverin-Simard, 1991), we can assert that the identification of a career path is not limited to the execution of the immediate projects or the orientation of the whole career. Particularly at the start of the twenty-first century, it extends even more to the meaning of finitude or one's personal history or after-life. The meaning given to vocational life would thus be linked to its opposite; in other words, to death. The results of our research now lead us to an understanding of human realities that are rendered new by the intensity of their expression, yet that exist and have always been fundamental to human beings. According to Capra (1986), for example, all interpretations of existence, vocational or otherwise, that neglect biological annihilation are fatally inexistential, since death is an essential part of life. The finitude of one's own life forces human beings to confront existential questions; this is true for all phases of life, but especially for adults in the second half of working life. It is through this self-negation – that is, one's own death – moreover, that the most profound level of existence is revealed to each human being. Even if the relationship with death changes over time (through childhood, adolescence, mid-life), this preoccupation is no less present. Furthermore, the question of one's own death assumes diverse concrete forms of existential solitude, but is, when all is said and done, always the same. Does everything end with death? What is the future of the history of humanity?

Whatever the socio-economic status of workers (Riverin-Simard, 1991), or their vocational personality types (Riverin-Simard, 1998), the question of the general meaning of vocational paths, including fulfilment, seems to be irremediably present. Though swept along by the urgency and intensity of current socio-economic preoccupations at the start of the twenty-first century, adults still ponder the fundamental question of the ultimate meaning of their existence. This existential question is in fact posed with more acuity in periods of great socio-economic upheavals (Capra, 1986), like the one we are currently experiencing. This question relativises everything: our existence, our decisions, and, what is more, our actions in the world.

Faced with this significantly complex question that has been raised by our research data, should we not insert the question of the existential meaning and the reality of finitude into the identification of 'transfigured' career development (typical, notably, at the start of the twenty-first century)? After scouring diverse research, for example Savickas and Walsh (1996), we note that no conception of career truly tackles the reality, for working life, of the meaning of death; nevertheless, it is undeniably present among workers. Do current theories of career development use overly restrained horizons to view working life? Given the relatively new suffering and this accentuated existential questioning, should these theories eventually include the phenomenon of death in order to grasp better the nature of career development for adults in the second half of working life?

Based on the results of our research, we are able to propose the following principle: at the start of the twenty-first century, the phenomenon of career development must inevitably include questioning about ultimate vocational destinies, whether or not the questions raised are unsolvable or very agonising. We believe that our daily activities at work are propelled by a perception, more or less conscious and articulated, of these overall personal orientations or this ultimate direction in which our working life will emerge or vanish. We thus formulate the corollary principle of a distant future as a condition for all adult vocational development, particularly for adults in the second half of working life (Riverin-Simard, 1991, 1998). This principle highlights the obligation to envisage the general orientation of working life projects by taking into account a very distant future that simultaneously includes death and after-life; this is true whether one believes this distant space–time is defined or fabricated by the individuals themselves, or predetermined by supreme authorities (managerial gods).

Moreover, is there not a link between the increasingly intense perception of finitude observed in our research (Riverin-Simard, 1991), and the effort to integrate opposites observed in the comparative analysis of personality types in the final phases of working life (Riverin-Simard, 1998)? Should this process of integrating opposites not also be included as a new element of career development that is emerging at the beginning of the twenty-first century?

According to Jung (1976), individuals reappropriate the opposites of their personalities in the second half of their lives; this is the principle of individuation. Moreover, the psycho-social notion of individuation, proposed by Lopez (1992), is defined as a process through which individuals redefine their identities as the result of successive separations from social contexts. Using the psycho-social terminology of individuation, the end of life is viewed as the anticipation of a separation from a major context; in other words, an exit from earthly life. We believe, therefore, that the anticipation of the relatively definitive separation from the context, or in other words, leaving the job market, assumes such an importance during these phases of working life that it is somewhat similar to the anticipation of the separation from the context of earthly life. Drawing inspiration from a combination of Jungian and psycho-social notions of individuation, it henceforth demands a change in the way career development is pursued during these final phases of working life. In this new process, the integration of opposites would replace the past process of avoiding opposites.

In summary, in the socio-economic context at the start of the twenty-first century, the phenomenon of the integration of opposites, along with intense moments of suffering and the accentuation of existential worries, must play an integral part in the transfigured notion of adults' careers in the second half of working life.

Conclusion

My research results indicate that adults embrace a number of Sztompka's (1994) four visions of future societies. In fact, they appear to share a variety of simultaneous visions of high modernity: optimistic and progressive visions (through incessant departures and continuous redefinitions of their vocational projects), pessimistic visions (intense moments of suffering and existential worrying), and sober visions (acute awareness of the uncertain character and unknown direction of the socio-economic world). Adults in the second part of working life seem to anticipate that all of these aspects are simultaneously present and that they have to deal with them for their own sake.

At the start of the twenty-first century, adults' careers in the second half of working life can in no way still be described as linear. Henceforth, it is more apt to speak of zigzag or disparate careers in a post-salarial (Bridges, 1994) or post-marketable (Rifkin, 1995) world that is characterised by intermittent employment, insecurity, and instability. Our work demonstrates the intensity of the career development of adults who are forty years of age or older at the start of the twenty-first century. The careers of these adults are henceforth defined by numerous ruptures, new departures, and intense moments of suffering, by continual redefinitions of vocational projects, and by novel means of carrying out these projects. Careers now seem to be managed by a law that we call the law of vocational chaos (Riverin-Simard, 1998). This law takes into account the multiple career transitions, both linear and non-linear, continuous and chaotic. It postulates that vocational instability and disorder inherently include a certain number of predictable components; for example, the periods of uncertainty or instability are more numerous and intense than moments of relative peace of mind; vocational development unfolds through a series of increasingly complex phases; the doubts underlying this instability alternate between meta-modalities – general questions concerning one's vocational orientation: phases 1, 3, 5 – and meta-goals – questions about the vocational goals that have a major impact on the general orientation of working life: phases 2, 4; the active role of vocational opposites (elements disliked) generating different but constant questioning during the first (how should I avoid them?) and the second (how should I integrate them?) parts of working life.

My work with close to 1,000 adults thus suggests using these transitions and periods of questioning as opportunities to constantly re-examine vocational paths, redefine vocational projects, and situate them in the context of certain existential preoccupations. In the context of the twenty-first century, we cannot construct a society or help individuals develop if we continue to view instability as negative and demoralising (Riverin-Simard, 1998). On the contrary, it is by discovering a harmony within this instability that researchers and practitioners can better understand and accelerate adult vocational development and the socio-economic growth of the collectivity.

Career specialists must continue to combine their efforts in order to support adults in their vocational transitions, their career development, and, above all, their continuing search for work. The social role of career specialists is henceforth at the forefront of the body of socio-economic realities at the start of the twenty-first century. It is essential that they become increasingly aware of this role. Above all, however, they must be capable of meeting the colossal challenge presented by this social role that is so fundamental to the quality of life of all of their fellow citizens, and to achieve this role better, they must renew their knowledge of the special features of the career development of adults of all ages, particularly those in the second half of working life.

I hope this chapter will contribute in this way: I hope to promote complementary research that will refine and deepen knowledge, and attempt to answer the questions that are raised by the new career configurations of a workforce that is facing countless unknowns. Finally, I also wish to propose certain practical implications. My book, *Career transitions: Choices and strategies* (1995), proposes several of them, based on our own work. It includes details of almost twenty workshops not only to help adults in succeeding with their current transitions, but also in managing personal change and development throughout their working lives. The workshops equally assist adults who are questioning – perhaps with anxiety and misgivings – their chosen field and are considering new career directions that are more consistent with their aspirations. Above all, however, this book invites practitioners to create their own workshops on the basis of the following principle: to succeed in the numerous vocational transitions and to respond to the frequent questioning throughout working life, we must learn to redefine constantly the principal means of interacting with the socio-economic world. We must learn to negotiate the unknown and the uniqueness of each transition and period of questioning. The chaotic vocational reality at the start of the twenty-first century demands no less.

REFERENCES

Balandier, G. (1994). *Le dédale: pour en finir avec le XXe siècle?* Paris: Fayard.
Bergson, H. (1994). *L'évolution créatrice* (6th edn). Paris: PUF.
Boutinet, J.-P. (1993). *Anthropologie du projet.* Paris: PUF.

128   *Danielle Riverin-Simard*

Bridges, W. (1994). *Jobshift*. Reading, MA: Addison-Wesley.
Capra, F. (1986). *The turning point: Science, society, and the rising culture*. New York: Simon and Schuster.
Castel, R. (1991). De l'indigence à l'exclusion. In J. Donzelot (Ed.), *Face à l'exclusion* (pp. 137–168). Paris: Esprit.
Gaujelac, V. & Leonnetti, T. L. (1994). *La lutte des places*. Marseilles: EPI/ Hommes.
Giddens, A. (1990). *The consequences of modernity*. Cambridge: Polity Press.
    (1991). *Introduction to sociology*. New York: Norton.
Gleick, J. (1987). *Chaos: Making a new science*. New York: Viking.
Guba, E. G. & Lincoln, Y. S. (1994). Competing paradigms in qualitative research. In N. Denzin & Y. S. Lincoln (Eds.), *Handbook of qualitative research* (pp. 105–118). Thousand Oaks, CA: Sage.
Heidegger, M. (1962). *Being and time*. New York: Harper.
Holland, J. L. (1997). *Making vocational choices: A theory of vocational personalities and work environments* (3rd edn). Odessa, FL: Psychological Assessment Resources.
Horth, R. (1986). *L'approche qualitative*. Rimouski, Quebec: Pointe-au-Pré.
Jung, C. G. (1976). *Psychological types*. Princeton, NJ: Princeton University Press.
Kelly, G. A. (1979). The autobiography of a theory. In G. A. Kelly & B. A. Maher (Eds.), *Clinical psychology and personality* (pp. 46–65). Huntington, IN: Krieger.
Lachelier, J. (1992). *Du fondement de l'induction*. Paris: Fayard.
Little, B. R. (1989). Personal projects analysis. In D. M. Buss & N. Cantor (Eds.), *Personality psychology* (pp. 15–31). New York: Springer-Verlag.
Lopez, F. G. (1992). Family dynamics. In S. D. Brown & R. W. Lent (Eds.), *Handbook of counseling psychology* (pp. 251–285). New York: Wiley.
Naisbitt, J. & Aburdene, P. (1990). *Megatrends 2000*. New York: Morrow.
Organisation for Economic Cooperation and Development (1995). *Flexible working time*. Paris: Author.
Poulin-Simon, L., Bellemare, D., & Tremblay, D. G. (1992). La situation et les enjeux specifiques des travailleuses vieillissantes. *Recherches féministes*, 5 (2), 123–148.
Rifkin, J. (1995). *The end of work: The decline of the global labor force and the dawn of the post-market era*. New York: G. P. Putnam's Sons.
Riverin-Simard, D. (1988). *Phases of working life*. Montreal: Meridien Press.
    (1990). Adult vocational trajectory. *Career Development Quarterly*, 39, 129–143.
    (1991). *Careers and social classes*. Montreal: Meridien Press.
    (1995). *Career transitions: Choices and strategies*. Ottawa: Canadian Career Development Foundation.
    (1998). *Work and personality*. Montreal: Meridien Press.
Sartre, J. P. (1963). *The problem of method*. London: Methuen.
Savickas, M. L. & Walsh, W. B. (Eds.) (1996). *Handbook of career counseling theory and practice*. Palo Alto, CA: Davies-Black.
Schaie, K.W. (1992). The impact of methodological changes in gerontology. *International Journal of Aging and Human Development*, 35, 19–29.
Solomone, P. R. (1996). Tracing Super's theory of vocational development.

Journal of Career Development, *22*, 167–184.

Sztompka, P. (1994). *The sociology of social change*. Cambridge: Blackwell.

Toffler, A. (1990). *Powershift*. New York: Bantam Books.

Touraine, A. (1992). Inégalités de la société industrielle. In J. Affichard & J.-B. Foucauld (Eds.), *Justice sociale et inégalités* (pp. 163–174). Paris: Esprit.

Young, R. A., Valach, L., & Collin, A. (1996). A contextual explanation of career. In D. Brown, L. Brooks, & Associates, *Career choice and development* (3rd edn, pp. 477–512). San Francisco: Jossey-Bass.

9   The future of women's career

Heather Höpfl and Pat Hornby Atkinson

Despite the many changes in the organisation of work since the early 1980s, women continue to face a range of obstacles in their careers and career opportunities (Adkins, 1995; Dale, 1990). It is relatively easy to demonstrate areas of work where women have achieved success (White, Cox, & Cooper, 1992), for example in higher education, with several women now holding Vice Chancellorships of Universities, and in finance and accountancy where women appear to be able to achieve board-level appointments. However, it is extremely difficult to assess whether women's route to 'success' is different to men's and, if it is, how that difference is experienced by women. Considering the defining features of 'successful' women identified by some research (for instance, see Nicholson & West 1988; White *et al.*, 1992) as, relative to their male counterparts, more likely to be single or childless or to have children late, it seems likely that women's route to 'success' is somewhat different to that of men's. These factors, of course, not only differentiate 'successful' women from 'successful' men but also from less 'successful' women. Drawing on the literature of gender and work, this chapter will argue that, in part, this is due to the fact that the notion of career 'success' is traditionally defined in what are male terms. The chapter examines the issue of power in the work place and its implications for women's career and considers what contribution a feminist understanding of career might make to the future of work and social arrangements.

A commonsense notion of career would suggest that it is regarded as a normal and rational project that involves a linear progression and is marked by stages of achievement and, not infrequently, by tangible and personal rewards (Davidson & Burke, 1994). For most people, the term 'career' implies an engagement with work which is more than a 'job' but, perhaps, less than a 'calling' or 'vocation'. A career would tend to convey the idea of a long-term project with associated rewards. So, for example, one might speak in terms of behaviour and activities which 'would look good on' a *curriculum vitae* or might, conversely, describe an action as 'career limiting' or a poor career choice. It is perhaps the perceived nature of the rewards more than anything else, which distinguishes a 'career' from a 'job' or a 'vocation'. That is not to say that a vocation or a job is without rewards. Clearly, there are rewards and satisfactions that come from a job well done, or from the notion of service which is implicit in the idea of a vocation. In contrast, career takes on a significant role in the structuring of working life in that it links material well being with application and effort, with qualifications and their achievement, with planned progression and with land-marks in what might be described in terms of a personal development agenda (Gutek, 1987; White *et al.*, 1992). With this in mind, it is important to adopt a working definition of the term 'career' that is sufficiently rich to guide a variety of interpretations throughout the text. For example, Arnold, Cooper, and Robertson (1998) provide a definition of career that permits the inclusion of all work and non-work activities. They suggest that a career can be defined as, 'the sequence of employment-related positions, roles, activities and experiences encountered by a person' (Arnold *et al.*, 1998, p. 384). This definition deals with the problem of differentiating between job, career, and vocation (and indeed in this case unemployment) by adopting a perspective which interprets them all as part of the same activity, i.e. 'employment' activity. However, in its attempt to offer a wide interpretation it extends the definition but minimises the notions of success and power that are inherent in the way career is commonly understood. In this chapter we will explore these notions of success and power, thereby acknowledging that the difference in status and reward normally associated with career as compared with job, unemployment, or vocation, is critical.

This chapter starts from a recognition of implicit and acknowledged inequity in the workplace and yet its concerns are by no means marginal. Issues related to the meaning of women's career are extremely important for the meaning of work in both social and political terms (Knights & Willmott, 1986). The dominant approach of conventional theories of career within the literature of organisations and work tends to relegate women's career matters to concerns for obstacles to career opportunities, the equalisation of rewards and benefits, concern for child care and maternity provision (Elias, 1982; Flanders, 1994; Hewitt, 1974). All these matters are clearly important to the discussion but they fail to address more fundamental questions such as whether or not the concept of 'career' is adequate to the task of describing the range of motivations, rationalisations, and means of evaluating outcomes that might be held to characterise women's experience of work. Nor do they contemplate what social arrangements might result from a radical revision of the structuring of work. As such, the theoretical concerns raised in relation to women's career serve as a cipher for a process of change in which women and, for that matter, other disadvantaged groups, might find alternative conceptions of work (Gutek, 1987; Hanson, 1995).

There are a number of strands discernible in academic research in the area of women's career. Broadly speaking, it is possible to identify career choices (Edwards, 1980; Yeandle, 1984), career development (Gutek, 1987; White *et al.*, 1992), and career success (Flanders, 1994; White *et al.*, 1992). Although each of these areas is, in practice, interlinked with the others, each has highlighted (sometimes unconsciously) particular concerns about women's progress through their working lives.

Theories of career choice, for example, have sought to identify the basis upon which career choices and decisions are made. One of the most influential models of career choice, that is Holland's (1997) theory of vocational choice, is concerned with definitional clarity. This approach contests that individuals' choices should be based on a clear articulation of their own abilities, aptitudes, and preferences and on the characteristics of occupations under consideration. By matching individuals with occupations on the basis of identity congruence, that is, similarity of attributes of the individual and the job, it is possible for them to make successful career choices. Theories of career choice ask on what basis individuals make choices, what features of the individual and the career are most salient in accounting for the success of that choice, and how individuals can best be helped to make choices. The very clear issue here concerns individual differences, that is, is it the case that some people are better suited to some tasks/occupations than others and, if so, how can individuals be directed towards careers which are appropriate to them? Clearly, this approach to careers assumes that it is possible to identify and measure the characteristics of both individuals and occupations. It also assumes that people do not change over time, that occupations do not change much and that there are consistent differences that distinguish individuals and occupations that make different people more or less suited to different occupations. Holland suggests that there are a number of career identities that describe individuals' vocational personality and that there are types of occupational activity that roughly correspond to those identities. According to Holland, there are six ideal types of vocational personality. This simple schematisation permits the allocation of individuals to neat categories where a match can be made between individual and occupation. This is profoundly reductionist, but offers a categorical simplification for both the individual and the organisation. Such approaches, which inform the favoured techniques of career and recruitment consultants, place a great emphasis on psychometrics and their predictive powers.

Examination of the 'types' described by Holland, and their occupational counterparts, reveals gendered assumptions about organisations unintended by the theory. If, for example, a list of occupations is made under Holland's definition of the 'realistic type' it is immediately apparent that the list of occupations produced is predominantly male. On the other hand, a list of occupations under the definition of the 'social type' is clearly female dominated. There are a number of possible explanations. However, the point is that, without reflection, such theoretical models arise from a set of social constructions and then proceed to confirm and perpetuate them. Given that the theory postulates a link between congruence and satisfaction such that congruent choices are more likely to result in job satisfaction, the implications of making choices that contradict such a match are obvious. Our argument is not to challenge the theory but to encourage the interpretation and deconstruction of the link between occupation/personality match and gender during counselling. A simple 'matching' approach would not allow such deconstruction.

Theories of career development, although taking a different, longitudinal approach to career, have been seen as a reaction to some of the inadequacies of the career choice literature. The career development literature is based on theories of adult development from psychology, for example Erikson (1950) and Levinson, with Darrow, Klein, Levinson, and McKee (1978). The developmental/life stages approach to career theory – for example Super (1980) – suggests that people change over time and that what suits a particular individual at one point in their lives may not suit them at other stages. In recent years, this approach has begun to acknowledge that there are life-style constraints on women that do not apply equally to men – in particular, to recognise that women who have children are often forced to take breaks from their careers to have a family. Early career development theorists (see Fitzgerald & Betz, 1994) based their theoretical descriptions of the typical career life-cycle on empirical data collected, almost exclusively, from white, middle-class men, so ensuring that the subsequent theoretical models were devoid of any recognition of differences in life-cycle between men and women and rooted in the assumption that women's career life-cycle followed much the same route as that of men.

Although this might seem an extremely flawed position theoretically, it is not uncommon in much of the literature of organisational behaviour in general. For example, common assumptions of work motivation quite routinely offered in standard textbook accounts are based on men's experiences. Hearn (1994), for example, refers to Maccoby and Jacklin's (1974) examination of 1,400 studies of sex-role differences which suggests that assumptions of gender difference in motivation, achievement, and intelligence are rare (Hearn, 1994). Of course, there are some exceptions to this. Goffee and Nicholson (1994) are unusual in giving attention to this issue. They provide an illuminating study of the relationship between gender and the psychological contract of work and specifically advocate that researchers should give attention to differences in the career experiences of male and female managers rather than concentrate on similarities.

In general, theories of career tend to take a rational view of the story of employment histories and to represent such stories in terms of success or failure, of goals achieved or not, of material rewards and social valuations, of motivated projections and planned realisations. Such theories reflect the commonsense view of 'career' as trajectory, as a strategic life plan, as a personal application of management by objectives. Theories of career, therefore, are rooted in the idea of choice. These theories would seem to suggest that informed choices about lives and destinies translate into plans with specific outcomes and targets: a career strategy. Indeed, some of the popular self-development texts would suggest that such an approach is entirely feasible: plan, implement, monitor, evaluate. This is a very logical and sequential approach. Moreover, rational theories of career tend to be based on meritocratic assumptions about entry to occupations and about the basis for progression (Flanders, 1994). Where political factors at work are discussed, it is generally in order to define obstacles to progression, which have to be overcome. Under such assumptions, 'success' then is merely a matter of commitment and motivation. Goals can be set and only a lack of motivation to achieve stands in the way of their accomplishment. At the same time, the rational view of career assumes that it is possible to compartmentalise work and non-work life and that, while work life clearly has implications for non-work life, such implications are merely logical consequences of career choices which must be effectively managed by act of will to ensure the direction of both work and non-work life towards the fulfilment of career goals and aspirations. In short, the rational view of career is one where choice, progression, and consistency are under the control of the individual, and where personal management and planning are the keys to 'success'.

Even without a specific reference to gender, it is apparent that gender problems are already implicit in the assumptions on which the foregoing discussion is based. Men and women differ in a number of ways and, whether this is the product of socialisation or not, it has important implications for their opportunities, career choices, means of coping with competing demands, and the character and value of rewards. Many theorists have addressed these issues and presented ways in which they might be overcome either by legislation or by social change. However, validity of the concept of progression is rarely challenged.

Yet at the heart of this issue is the opportunity to consider alternative constructions and ways of working. Clearly, men and women face different conditions in relation to childbearing and child rearing and, whereas it might be possible to legislate for changes in provision for child rearing, the biological fact of childbearing introduces an immediate disjuncture in the notion of career progression for women (Dale, 1990; Edwards, 1980; Equal Opportunities Commission, 1993; Evetts, 1995; Hochschild, 1997; Nott, 1978; Yeandle, 1984). It is possible to regard childbearing as an inevitable discontinuity in a career: welcome or not. Following this line of argument, women should accept that they can only 'have it all' (Kanter, 1977) at tremendous personal cost (Hochschild, 1997); should perhaps not attempt to combine childbearing and working at all, should be corporate vestal virgins; should know their place in the general scheme of things and realise that biology relegates women to the status of inferior men. Yet it needs to be acknowledged that the power to define both the characteristics of career, and the role which women play in work, is primarily male (Collinson & Collinson, 1989; Daudi, 1983). This on its own has the potential to be responsible for the relegation of women's career issues to a marginal place on the agenda (Czarniawska, 1997) and for the lack of reflection on the meaning and values of work which a female perspective might offer (Hanson, 1995).

Labour market segregation has demonstrated that not only are jobs hierarchically segregated according to gender so that women tend to have the lower-status, lower-paid jobs but also they are vertically segregated according to gender so that some fields of employment are predominantly female and some predominantly male (Adkins, 1995). The important point here is that research that is undertaken without adequate attention to the taken-for-granted social constructions (Berger & Luckmann, 1971) that lie behind occupational typologies is frequently detrimental to the position of women. Such research can lead to a situation in which responses, career initiatives for women, and even further research on gender, tend to support and confirm the status quo. Consequently, it is important that new approaches to women's career give attention to fundamental issues in the relationship between individuals and their working lives so that remedial approaches are set in the context of the role of work as a primary source of meaning.

Taken together, these characteristics of career theory play a significant role in the structuring of experience and provide a rationale for behaviour, a purpose in life. The notions of progress and planning bring together the full range of life experiences in both work and non-work so that the individual may see the integration of non-work life into work life as an inevitable consequence of the commitment to a career plan. The career provides a meaning structure and a means of accounting for decisions, plans and progress. Non-work life will be expected to conform to and demonstrate career aspirations and progress. Partners as much as possessions play a part in this demonstration. As such, the notion of a career is fundamentally ideological in that it gives meaning to behaviour and experience. It is the inevitable implications of this which need to be given further attention.

Of course, it could be argued that such criticisms or inferences about the assumptions made by traditional theories of career are unwarranted and based on selective interpretations. This may well be the case, but the fundamental assumptions of conventional theories of career need to be subjected to scrutiny before it is possible to speculate on alternative approaches to working life and, in particular, approaches that give emphasis to the contribution that women might make to the structuring of work and styles of organising (Elias, 1982; Dale, 1990; Evetts, 1995). Therefore, in order to take this argument further it is necessary to summarise the characteristics of career theory noted above towards which this critique and evaluation is directed: first, the idea that a career is planned and involves choice; secondly, that a career is characterised by a structured approach to life which has implications and which involves a pattern of related activities; thirdly, that careers are usually seen in terms of definitions of success, with expectations fulfilled or otherwise, with power, status and influence, and with material gain, not to say wealth; fourthly, the idea that careers involve choices about the balance between work and non-work life, which might have deleterious consequences for non-work life; finally, that career is associated with satisfaction. Commitment to 'a career' suggests a degree of dedication in terms of the time spent in pursuit of career goals. Whilst this has consequences for non-work life, it is often considered that the rewards a company or occupation can offer serve as compensation for these effects. There is a wide range of compensations on offer from the obvious material gains to the more intangible satisfactions such as status, standing in a community, and, not least, the interpretation that a career 'makes sense of' life projections and events. In other words, a career when viewed as a projection of life into the future appears to give meaning to experience and a sense of order, continuity, and purpose.

Theoretical conceptualisation of the development of sex-role identity has a long history in social psychology, for example Bem (1981). Evidence suggests that the phenomenon of categorising some activities and roles as female and others as male in gender extends into the workplace. Schein (1973) demonstrated, for instance, that when people are asked to list masculine, feminine, and leadership qualities separately, there is a clear tendency for the masculine and leadership qualities lists to have most in common, and for the feminine qualities list to bear least resemblance to the other two. She and colleagues replicated this research in the late 1980s (Brenner, Tomkiewicz, & Schein, 1989), and found that there was evidence of some changes in attitude in the meantime. In particular, while women respondents were now more likely to include characteristics that appeared on both the male and female lists in their list of leadership characteristics, male respondents showed no such change and continued to have more masculine characteristics than feminine ones in their leadership list. Marshall (1995), in considering organisational cultural images of success, reflects on the words of one of the women in her study:

People have an image of what a successful [company] manager is, how they behave, how they look and are, how they communicate and manage. And that is a [company] clone. Typically it's a man who has a wife who doesn't work, so he's geographically flexible, he probably has kids, if he hasn't he is a good sportsman and has a wonderful social life. He's one of the boys, he doesn't do anything excessively, he doesn't challenge or make waves. Pretty smart. A good guy. So when women come along they don't fit into any of those things. (p. 215)

These findings tend to disconfirm the notion of employees taking a radical view of their relationship to the organisation and looking beyond work life for their source of meaning. Certainly, there is little evidence of any destabilisation of masculine notions of leadership and success in such constructions. A tension arises when one's own construction of career success is at odds with external measures, which emphasise status and money.

There is a directed rationality that drives the pursuit of career objectives. Hence, in the service of the trajectory, a man can be effective, that is, have the power to bring about a result or else he is considered effete, worn out, exhausted, no longer fertile, like a woman, effeminate. This is a very telling notion because it simultaneously defines the relationship between men and work and the position of women and, at the same time, it defines implicitly the terms under which one can enter work or develop a career. A woman can seize phallic power and become a man (albeit an effeminate man) and, in so doing, render all relationships with men homomorphic, or be different and risk censure. In other words, there is an established way of working in most work organisations that is predominantly male, defined by men for men and established as the normative basis for working arrangements. Women must, therefore, transform themselves into men or, as Kristeva (1987) points out, into men's playthings (Dougary, 1994) or they will be rejected as not fitting in. For example, they may be rejected because they do not put enough distance between themselves and their non-work life, or because they will not pursue the social rules which guide men's behaviour at work (see De Grazia, 1962). They can fit in by becoming quasi-male, by becoming a 'plaything', or becoming what has been termed a 'ladette', that is, a young woman who is 'one of the boys'. Consequently, it could be argued that women's entry into a career is regulated in much the same way that European Salic Law operated. Under the European Salic Law of inheritance a woman could not succeed. However, she could stand-in for the male heir. It seems that this is, in effect, the hidden basis of women's career choice. This is such a fundamental and taken-for-granted determinant of women's working lives that many women, and, perhaps significantly, many successful 'career women' would disclaim the influence of this implicit characteristic of entry. Martin's (1991) discussion of organisational taboos, however, puts this into perspective with her analysis of the decision by a senior female executive to have her baby induced to fit in with the organisational agenda.

Clearly, the taken-for-granted in the construction of male and female careers needs to be given some considered attention. Individuals in their strategic assumptions about the direction of their lives seek to move from one place to another over time, to achieve objectives, to reach a desired future state. The consequences of these moves for individuals are usually subordinated to the trajectory of their personal strategies and the relationship these have to the strategies of their employers. The consequences of this directedness for individuals are addressed here via a consideration of experience that might otherwise be taken-for-granted or unarticulated. In particular, the attempt here is to propose that the rational trajectory is male whereas the experiential counterpart is female. Clearly, this is a gross simplification.

A good place to start deconstructing the mythology of career lies in the language of everyday experiences. Here the accounts which people offer of their career experiences come into their own. Career stories are rarely stories of sustained success and achievement, of gains without costs, or of continuity and progress (Evans & Bartolome, 1980). For most people, men and women alike, careers are constructed in prospect and accounted for in retrospect. People make the wrong decisions, get caught in the political cross-fire, make unacceptable sacrifices, suffer remorse, lose face, lose faith even, and experience all the range of emotions that a system of life planning might produce when translated into everyday experience. Unlike the tidy plans that seem to guide 'a career', life experiences are much more messy, and decisions do not always conform to a rational pattern. For example, where the logic of a career might dictate a move into unknown territory, geographical or intellectual, an individual might decide for a variety of reasons not to pursue that opportunity but to stay with the familiar, or might decide irrationally, in terms of career logic, to move jobs because of a minor disagreement which, although easily reconciled, might initiate a career response. Clearly, the theorising of career requires a more interpretative standpoint if such non-rational aspects of experience are to be taken into account.

The presence of women in work organisations poses the threat of disjunction and of exposure of the underlying ambivalence of the psychological contract of work (see Hewitt, 1974). In part, the power of the career plan to give meaning to behaviour frustrates any immediate meaning by 'making sense of' behaviour and experience via the promise of future rewards and coherence. The difficulty here is the strength and coherence of the apparent meaning of attachment to a corporate philosophy and the range of inducements that reinforce it. However, for many people such commitment leads to a level of engagement where the need for reflexive action is minimised. The necessary conciliation between the world of the organisation and the other multiple life-worlds that the individual inhabits is achieved by an act of self-deception. Material rewards appear to compensate for personal sacrifices. In order to minimise the ambivalence, contradictions are ignored or denied. While the corporate and male definition of the situation remains the mediator of meaning, its rewards have considerable power. Disillusionment occurs when issues of choice, personal responsibilities, and personal meaning are thrown into focus. In organisational life, the irresolvable antinomies, that is, conflicts of authority which confront women who work, thrust into the arena those aspects of life which male managers would prefer to keep off-stage. Inevitably then, women can only be given minor roles, if any. They need to be kept to well-scripted roles with limited opportunities for improvisation. In other words, women's career options are limited by an anterior definition which, as things stand, they can only respond to or reject.

Neither the career-development nor the career-choice approach takes much account of societal changes that have altered the organisation of work. Technological advances since the early 1980s and changes in the global configuration of employment activity have altered and are continuing to alter the nature of paid work in ways which are fundamental, structural, and largely irreversible. These changes are important in that they determine which work activities are valued and the ways in which such value is assigned. As companies begin to alter their contractual arrangements with employees in order to enforce numerical flexibility onto the least-valued and least-rewarded activities, and to experiment with new ways of rewarding and ensuring the loyalties of those few who are perceived to possess the rarest and most valued skills, the notion of a reciprocal relationship between employer and employee is being eroded. Consequently, individuals themselves are beginning to re-evaluate the nature of their commitment to the organisation. Much of this activity has to do with people re-examining what they mean by 'success' and moving away from the view that success is inevitably tied to advancement within a work organisation (Hochschild, 1997; Kanter, 1977). However, this is easier said than done and this type of reflection may be more of a feature of successful middle-class retrospection than of the considered assessment of those who are relegated to the least-valued positions. Nonetheless, there are fundamental changes taking place in the structure of work and the impact of these changes is being felt in the way in which people understand the nature of their commitment to the organisation (Ferris & Aranya, 1983; Griffin & Bateman, 1986). To some extent, these changes expose some of the ambivalences which women have experienced in their careers through the duality of commitment to home and work. Women have frequently been unable to have the same psychological commitment as their male colleagues simply because of their awareness of their other domestic commitments. This is not, in any sense, to say that women have been less committed to their work than men but rather to emphasise the fact that women have long been aware of the problems associated with a unitary notion of organisational commitment. Women then are less threatened by current changes in working arrangements because this has been a familiar context of women's working experiences for a long time. Consequently, there is the opportunity for women to contribute to the redefinition of career and to bring some informed knowledge of working arrangements to the debate about the future of working life.

This chapter has indicated that the basis of men's and women's career options is not adequately recognised in the theories of career. In effect, this chapter has not sought to explore the more usual aspects of women's career such as barriers to success, occupational differences and preferences or even the notion of the 'glass ceiling'. Rather the concern here has been to explore some of the underlying assumptions that lead to the specifics of working arrangements for both men and women (Hanson, 1995). Certainly, corporate seductions and rewards aside, there is a need to look at the ambivalence that is at the root of women's engagement with work. This is an extremely powerful concept and one that poses a threat to the notion of a unitary trajectory of career development. The period in which women sought to define themselves as quasi-men is coming to an end and the desire for phallic-power (Kristeva, 1980) is being seen for what it is and the costs found to be too great. However, the alternative to this poses a considerable challenge to the present organisation of work.

There is a fear of such alternative definitions which threaten to expose the fragile nature of meaning as conferred by an organisation. This possibility of the collapse of the meaning that a career seems to offer is there in the tensions and oscillations which occur between the purposive nature of organisations and the ambivalence of women as corporate actors.

The paradox at the root of this argument is one of power and the power to define meanings – in particular, meanings of 'success'. Women threaten these reality definitions and therefore men seek to control the extent of their participation in work organisations. This goes some way to explaining the basis of women's engagement with the organisation and the implications of this for their career opportunities. It also lays the foundation for an examination of the future of working arrangements and, hence, the future of career, which draws more on notions of ambivalence and discontinuity than on a clear and sequential series of career advances. If fruitful advances are to be made, these should be the basis of further research on the contribution of women's work to changing conceptions of career.

REFERENCES

Adkins, L. (1995). *Gendered work: Sexuality, family and the labour market.* Milton Keynes: Open University Press.

Arnold, J., Cooper, C. L., & Robertson, I. T. (1998). *Work psychology: Understanding human behaviour in the workplace* (3rd edn). London: FT Pitman.

Bem, S. L. (1981). Gender schema theory: A cognitive account of sex typing. *Psychological Review, 81,* 506–520.

Berger, P. L. & Luckmann, T. (1971). *The social construction of reality: A treatise in the sociology of knowledge.* Harmondsworth: Penguin.

Brenner, O. C., Tomkiewicz, J., & Schein, V. E. (1989). The relationship between sex role stereotypes and requisite management characteristics revisited. *Academy of Management Journal, 32,* 662–669.

Collinson, D. L. & Collinson, M. (1989). Sexuality in the workplace: The domination of men's sexuality. In J. Hearn, D. L. Sheppard, P. Tancred-Sheriff, & G. Burrell (Eds.), *The sexuality of organizations* (pp. 91–109). London: Sage.

Czarniawska, B. (1997). On the imperative and the impossibility of polyphony in organization studies. A Keynote Address to the 'Organizing in a Multi-Voiced World Conference', Leuven, Belgium, June.

Dale, A. (1990). *An analysis of women's employment patterns in the UK, France and USA.* London: Department of Employment.

Daudi, P. (1983). The discourse of power or the power of discourse. *Journal of World Policy, 2,* 317–325.

Davidson, M. J. & Burke, R. J. (1994). *Women in management: Current issues in research.* London: Paul Chapman Publishing Ltd.

De Grazia, S. (1962). *Of time, work and leisure*. New York: Twentieth Century Fund.

Dougary, G. (1994). *The executive tart and other myths: Media women talk back*. London: Virago.

Edwards, S. (1980). *Women at work and in society*. University of Warwick Occasional Publications no. 7, Modern Records Centre Sources Booklet no. 1. Warwick: University of Warwick.

Elias, P. (1982). *Women's working lives: Evidence from the national training survey*. Warwick: University of Warwick, Institute for Employment Research.

Equal Opportunities Commission (1993). *Women and men in Britain*. Manchester: Author.

Erikson, E. (1950). *Childhood and society*. New York: W. W. Norton.

Evans, P. & Bartolome, F. (1980). *Must success cost so much?* London: Grant McIntyre.

Evetts, J. (1995) (Ed.). *Women and career: Themes and issues in advanced industrial societies*. London: Longman.

Ferris, K. R. & Aranya, N. (1983). A comparison of two organizational commitment scales. *Personnel Psychology*, *36*, 87–89.

Fitzgerald, L. F. & Betz, N. E. (1994). Career development in cultural context: The role of gender, race, class, and sexual orientation. In M. L. Savickas & R. W. Lent (Eds), *Convergence in career development theories: Implications for science and practice* (pp. 103–117). Palo Alto, CA: CPP Books.

Flanders, M. L. (1994). *Breakthrough: The career woman's guide to shattering the glass ceiling*. London: Paul Chapman.

Goffee, R. & Nicholson, N. (1994). Career development in male and female managers: Convergence or collapse? In M. J. Davidson & R. J. Burke (Eds.), *Women in management: Current research issues* (pp. 80–92). London: Paul Chapman.

Griffin, R. W. & Bateman, T. S. (1986). Job satisfaction and organizational commitment. In C. L. Cooper & I. Robertson (Eds.), *International review of industrial and organizational psychology* (pp. 157–188). New York: John Wiley & Sons.

Gutek, B. (1987). *Women's career development*. London: Sage.

Hanson, S. (1995). *Gender, work and space*. London: Routledge.

Hearn, J. (1994). Changing men and changing managements: Social change, social research and social action. In M. J. Davidson & R. J. Burke (Eds.), *Women in management: Current research issues* (pp. 192–211). London: Paul Chapman.

Hewitt, P. (1974). *Danger! Women at work*. Report of Women's Rights Conference of the National Council for Civil Liberties, London, February.

Hochschild, A. R. (1997). *The time bind: When work becomes home and home becomes work*. New York: Metropolitan Books.

Holland, J. L. (1997). *Making vocational choices: A theory of vocational personalities and work environments* (3rd edn). Odessa, FL: Psychological Assessment Resources.

Kanter, R. M. (1977). *Men and women of the corporation*. New York: Basic Books.

Knights, D. & Willmott, H. (1986). *Gender and labour process*. London: Gower.

Kristeva, J. (1980). *Powers of horror* (L. Roudiez, trans.). New York: Columbia University Press.

——— (1987). *In the beginning was love: Psychoanalysis and faith* (A. Goldhammer, trans.). New York: Columbia University Press.

Levinson, D. J., with Darrow, C. M., Klein, E. B., Levinson, M. H., & McKee, B. (1978). *The seasons of a man's life*. New York: Alfred A. Knopf.

Maccoby, E. E. & Jacklin, C. N. (1974). *The psychology of sex differences*. Stanford, CA: Stanford University Press.

Marshall, J. (1995). *Women managers moving on: Exploring career and life choices*. London: Routledge.

Martin, J. (1991). Deconstructing organizational taboo: The suppression of gender: Conflict in organizations. Paper presented to the 8th International SCOS Conference, Copenhagen, June.

Nicholson, N. & West, M. A. (1988). *Managerial job change*. London: Cambridge University Press.

Nott, F. (1978). *Women, work and family: Dimensions of change in American society*. Lexington, MA: Lexington Books.

Schein, V. E. (1973). The relationship between sex role stereotypes and requisite management characteristics. *Journal of Applied Psychology*, *57*, 95–100.

Super, D. E. (1980). A life-span, life-space approach to career development. *Journal of Vocational Behavior*, *13*, 282–298.

White, B., Cox, C., & Cooper, C. (1992). *Women's career development: A study of high flyers*. Oxford: Blackwell.

Yeandle, S. (1984). *Women's working lives: Patterns and strategies*. London: Tavistock.

10 Career or slide? Managing on the threshold of sense

Damian O'Doherty and Ian Roberts

How to 'career' has become a dominant motif for those researching career and for those individuals within careers in organisations, both of whom we want to argue in this chapter are in the end-less process of (dis)organisation. This chapter offers a challenge to traditional and more critical thinking in the broad practice and study of career. We draw our focus from intellectual developments in critical organisation studies which offer a way of developing radical neo- or post-disciplinary study that is relevant and opportune for our contemporary conjuncture. Clearly, therefore, in addressing broad ontological and epistemological phenomena – what for some might be defined as 'the human condition' – our challenge necessarily cuts across constructed micro-disciplinary boundaries such as career counselling, career development, career guidance, and career management. Thus the nature of our argument is such that we do not consider the minutiae of relationships and debates between these micro-disciplines but seek to question current understanding and practice by a consideration of what we propose to call *'metacareer' praxis*.

We first introduce and outline the relationship between so-called 'postmodernity', our views on 'meta-career thinking', and the challenge this poses to extant theory and practice in the field of career. Whilst we acknowledge that theoretical advances concerned with subjectivity, identity, and interpretation have opened up significant new ways of looking at career (e.g. Young & Collin, 1992), we argue that the literature across the micro-disciplines of career remains insufficiently self-critical and unwittingly dependent upon the fragile assumptions and constructions of Western reason and rationality.

Second we identify five key humanist 'gold standards' or anchors, namely true self, meaning, progress, order, and positioning. We argue that we have to be aware of and question our 'faith' in the persistence of a redemptive humanism in the face of what some want to call 'postmodern times'. We argue that the micro-disciplines of career theory variously dim down the nihilistic and entropic conditions of late modernity so as to pre-serve those humanist anchors. These anchors simulta-

144

neously stabilise and justify a range of orthodox and more critically inspired 'humanist' epistemologies. Whether unselfconsciously adopted in theory and research, or consciously problematised in more critically reflexive work (e.g. Collin, 1996), these anchors continue to organise and orientate understanding.

Finally we seek to demonstrate how so-called 'identity' and 'experience in organisation' have become deeply ambivalent and *aporetic* – an ambivalence we mime in this text – hence the anxiety and suspicion that *we* are just about *managing on the threshold of sense* under conditions of confusion, nihilism, and entropy.

Meta-career thinking and postmodern times

The epoch of postmodernity has variously been used to articulate what are defined as unique issues and problems associated with the period of 'late modernity' (see Jameson, 1984) or some break with the epoch of modernity. In many academic disciplines the latter is often (paradoxically) categorised and identified so that reasonable comparisons can be made, for example between the so-called modern and the postmodern organisation (Clegg, 1990; Parker, 1992).

A vast range of phenomena has been labelled as post-modern in a disparate spread of subjects and disciplinary fields but we are particularly interested in the strains of thinking which emphasise the collapse, or rather deconstruction and problematisation, of the boundaries and purchase of Western forms of reason (see Foucault, 1984). So we draw on the work of others (Bauman, 1995; Smart, 1993) who suggest that postmodernism is not so much a temporal break in social or political conditions but more an epistemological crisis/opportunity in the mode-of-being-in-the-world, a way 'of relating to modern forms of life, effectively a coming to terms, a facing up to modernity, its benefits and its problematic consequences, its limits and its limitations' (Smart, 1993, p. 23).

A number of recent critical ethnographic and experiential research studies have explored this epistemological and ontological crisis in terms of the existential anxiety associated with contemporary careers and organisations (Casey, 1995; Höpfl & Linstead, 1993; Kets de Vries & Balazs, 1997; Kondo, 1990; Watson, 1994). These studies emphasise the struggles individuals experience in positioning and making sense of themselves. Managers appear to suffer from anxiety, confusion, and loss in their attempts to de-lineate and comprehend 'their' organisation. Today, for example, competing perspectives and discourses offer contingency and an element of ambiguity and choice in how managers organise and understand themselves and their relation to their organisation. Individuals appear to float between different paradigms, shifting from one regime of signification and discourse to the next, building their own temporary cocoon (Giddens, 1991) and patch-work quilt of experiential sense and meaning. Individuals are immersed within a multiplicity of discourses. The associated sense of contingency, flux, and change which decentres them in contemporary organisations is then amplified as they struggle to compete and stay ahead of the game – to be speaking the right language, to be aligned with the ascending cabals or consultants, to be 'on-board' the latest strategic initiative of organisation (Jackall, 1988).

'Meta-career' praxis can be thought of, following Heidegger (1962), as a *mode-of-being-in-the-world* that is concerned with the emergence of these anxieties, anxieties which concern the limitations and boundaries of reason. *Being* on this edge, or in the interstices of meaning/meaningless-ness, we argue, provides the space in contemporary conditions of simulacrum, hyper-mediation, and undecidability (Baudrillard, 1983; Jameson, 1984) for coming to some kind of terms with the stresses and strains of career. Hence meta-career *praxis* invokes *existential* challenge as much as it is provokes theory or the intellect. It challenges fundamental issues that cut across the sub-territorial boundary-making of the academy. At a time when all boundaries seem in flux it might be argued that meta-career praxis is timely and urgent – an anxiety-raising but emancipatory opportunity.

The challenge to positivism in career theory

Contributions from career theory which have attended to postmodern times often emphasise notions of insecurity, flux, and change, which disturb the structures and hierarchies of modern organisation (Clegg, 1990) and impact upon the organisation of individual careers at a more general level (e.g. Collin & Watts, 1996; Schein, 1996). These emergencies are perceived as threatening but also as offering new opportunities, a new ontological and epistemological vista for those individuals 'in career' and for those who wish to study organisational careers and their management (e.g. Herriot & Pemberton, 1996; Hiltrop, 1996).

Within the specialised domain of career counselling, theorists who do not write directly from an organisational standpoint have made significant critical in-roads addressing theory, research, and practice. Here, in response to the perceived deficiencies of traditional positivist modes of social scientific enquiry, especially when confronted with the 'postmodern era', calls have been made for more interpretative and qualitative methods of study (e.g. Collin & Young, 1986; Savickas, 1994; Young & Collin, 1992).

Although Collin (1996) has begun to question assumptions about 'self', it is our belief that methodological developments in counselling psychology, involving conversation analysis (Savickas, 1993), meaning-making (Young, 1988), and hermeneutics (Young & Collin, 1992), still maintain faith in a number of humanist assumptions about self and organisation. Critical career theory remains tied to the liberal Enlightenment values of reason, organisation, and order, which betrays hope and nostalgia for a time that, we argue, has come to pass. Here, theory and practice persist in seeking ways to preserve humanist and liberal values which maintain a *modernist* commitment to the redemptive power of reason. Through trust, dialogue, empathy, and mutual understanding, it is believed that a fairly reliable picture can be constructed to re-present the situations and 'real-life' struggles of individuals. Respecting multiple view-points and valorising the interpretative capacity of individual agents provide the conditions for a dialogic and pragmatic construction of reality. Democracy and education are deemed sufficient in constructing and re-constructing a 'better reality', one that respects the individual, difference, and plurality, contributing to a more rational management and development of individual career and social relations.

Critical career theory within the discourse of postmodernity often remains embedded in a paradigm which views people as self-organising systems, by which their behaviour is deemed to be purposeful and goal-directed (e.g. Savickas, 1989). In addition, it is frequently assumed that individuals are able to construct and reconstruct meaning through personal experience and reflection, by means of which they are able to complete the modern odyssey of temporal continuity – the return to place, identity, fulfilment, and all that is secure and familiar. In effect, meaning and truth – via the agency of education, cognition, and reflection, and the practice of some form of temporal planning and ordering – are restored or constructed. In the hermeneutic approach, for example, there is an assumption that individuals can and do make or discover meaning for their lives, teased out through counselling (Young, 1984) or dialogically constructed through Habermasian-style ideal speech (Young & Collin, 1992, p. 7). Yet, in the absence of grounds or foundations for the construction of meaning, how *can* one know?

Although scholars and practitioners working within critical career theory understand that language is problematic, it is often assumed that any 'contamination' -- translation problems, bias, or political prejudice – is residual and contingent and can be removed via the humane practice of dialogue and reason. In Habermas (1984), who provides much of the theoretical inspiration for those working within critical hermeneutics, language can be purified of power distortion and preserved as a possibility for value-free communication. Habermas is harnessed to argue that a clear sense of position and self-clarification, an unveiling of truth and meaning, can be arrived at through inter-mediation and negotiation. We question the potential and reach of such reflexivity.

In addition to the recognition that bias, practical interests, ideology, repression, political allegiance, etc., distort the originary purity of communication, we need to acknowledge the constitutive lack and errancy which *both* founds *and* undoes language (Derrida, 1976). At its heart, all language is distortion and contested metaphor: an original impurity, an original void or, if you will, an *end-less un-originality* – as we indicate by hyphenation in the preceding phrase, and elsewhere in this chapter. All phrases and words are *nodal junction points* beginning from and setting off a stream of references and reverberations, an endless spiralling of associations, connections, and disconnections. As a result, 'final settlement of meaning must be continually deferred' (Game & Metcalfe, 1996, p. 46), as meaning endlessly migrates, deforms, and reforms, excessive and foreign to all purpose (Blanchot, 1982). Furthermore, we must question the 'reach' and 'hold' of language as a constitutive medium which claims to illuminate both social processes of inequality, power, and subjection, and the more micro-subjective dynamics which generate self and identity. Work by Fay (1987), Coole (1996), and Mestrovich (1993) has begun to draw attention to the alterity of irrationality, pre-discursivity, and the non-discursive which attracts but confounds language, communication, and expression. Subjects and identity are deemed to be made by factors which lie 'below the threshold of communicative reason' (Coole, 1996, p. 240), in bodies and passions, for example, which do not permit reason or language.

Thus critical career thinking remains tied into a humanist agenda of modernity, albeit a 'radical humanist' one (Burrell & Morgan, 1979), that seeks to stimulate and provide subjects with the linguistic, intellectual, and moral resources so as to enable them to respond to reality and thereby construct meaningful self-narrative, opportunity, and hope. Current conditions are therefore defined, translated, organised, and classified – today the buzzwords are simply those of uncertainty, change, and flux, instead of procedure, order, and stability – effecting what we see as a taming or 'dimming down' of nihilistic and entropic energy. Moreover, it is an energy or play which deconstructs *both* epistemology and ontology, de-differentiating author–text–world and the privileges associated with reason, theory, models, and language.

It is our view that postmodernism, or postmodernity, does not just refer to some ontological condition which stands 'over there', pristine and formed, awaiting its transcription and discursive re-presentation, an 'ontic' reality amenable to the plotting and charting of traditional logocentric practice. However spectacular, novel, or exciting the 'movements' described in the popular and academic press might be, they simply fail to recognise their own decentring, their own corrosion of author-ity (Foucault, 1969). Deconstruction as practised in the reading and writing of Derrida and those academics 'after' Derrida, including for example, Robert Smith, Nick Royle, Sam Weber, and Geoff Bennington, tries to work within this impossible position of what we call *aporetic space* (see Beardsworth, 1996), space where the oppositions which frame and form reason and understanding both emerge and collapse *into*. The affinity we find between the textual and linguistic research of Derrida and the condition of contemporary career and organisations leads us to suggest that the kind of work Derrida is doing textually, trying to find ways of articulating, speaking, and thinking while careering 'within' this aporetic space, oscillating across the undecidable co-ordinates of space and time, is exemplary for the future study and practice of career.

Faith in humanist gold standards (fool's gold?)

Our argument develops further: in *delineating* the new 'reality' as postmodern, characterised by uncertainty, flux, and struggle, much of career theory displays its attachment to modern reason. For many writers, it is as if the 'condition of postmodernity' is only happening *over there*, that is ontologically, while individuals and authors remain preserved epistemologically, a distance that allows them to carry on making sense. Postmodern conditions which threaten the 'humanist anchors' are deemed to open up a gap between the self and external conditions, a felt incompatibility which translates into personal dilemmas. Hence the role of the 'management' of career by career counsellors, organisations, or the individuals themselves, is one which helps 'soothe' this anxiety by enabling individuals to become 'useful' again (Foucault, 1977), providing individuals once more with a sense of importance, purpose, control, and centring – which we argue are (necessarily) *illusive* and *elusive*.

From 'life-design counselling' (Savickas, 1993) to experiential learning, from conversation analysis to the management of the psychological contract, the emphasis across the micro-disciplines of career theory is one of clarification, the opening up of choices, finding self, determining 'meaning', explaining the past, and predicting the future. For example, in claiming the licence to 'authorise' client stories (Savickas, 1993) or reduce cognitive dissonance (Savickas, 1991), career counselling exposes its own disciplinary technology, a self-serving power/knowledge regime (Foucault, 1980). In essence the privileged counsellor helps the individual adjust, encouraging the reconciliation of their clients' own personal concepts with those of wider social utility, thereby contributing to the *organisation* of 'social reality'. This surveillance and normalisation (Foucault, 1977) of subjects, this organisation of self in relation to the 'spirit of the times', reflects the profound generalisation of those mechanics and technics which Nietzsche identified as modernity's 'will to power'.

Similarly, writing from an organisational perspective, many observers comment on the possibilities and means by which individuals can best cope and succeed in organisation today via the lens of individualism, employability, entrepreneurialism, self-help, and initiative (e.g. Du Gay, 1996; Garsten & Grey, 1997). For example, there is a trend for organisations to present and market themselves as an arena for enterprise (e.g. du Gay, 1996), emphasising the 'resources' that are made available to all individuals but an opportunity only made use of by those 'winners' with sufficient self-motivation, initiative, and enterprise. Distance learning packages, modular based accreditation, self-reflexive practices such as work-based diaries, critical incident analysis, even team working (Barker, 1993; Ezzamel & Willmott, 1998), and the discourse of 'ownership', encourage individuals to align their existential anxieties and identity projects with those of the organisation, to take hold of their own uncertainties and respond appropriately to what they are told is an ever-changing environment.

Here too we see a form of power/knowledge (Foucault, 1980) which stimulates 'technologies of the self'. In the micro-physics of power relations, subjugation emerges in the immediacy and conduct of everyday life, a modality of power which categorises the individual, marks him by his own individuality, attaches her to her own identity, and imposes a law of truth on him which he must recognise and which others have to recognise in her. It is a form of power which makes individuals *subjects* (Foucault, 1982). This helps us to see how the discourse of community, teams, self-motivation, and self-discipline seeks to counter the disintegrative and entropic tendencies of post-industrial and postmodern life (Casey, 1995).

In sum, career theory across its micro-disciplines remains wedded to the modernist, humanist imposition of order and structure. Drawing on contemporary radical organisation theory we have sought to intimate the connections we see between developments in the logic of organ-ising and the emancipatory claims of recent career theory. It seems that we are attracted by these promises of stability, security, and order because they divest subjects from the despair that perhaps there is no purpose, meaning, or essence to self or world. What we call humanist 'fool's gold' offers some escape 'because the attainment of each one of them would reflect our individual transcendence' (Cohen & Taylor, 1976, p. 212), a transcendence which rids us of absurdity and despair. In the next section we try to prise open this space of absurdity and despair by examining in more detail these humanist pillars which animate the discourses of career management and career counselling.

'True self'

This notion assumes an essential truth and limit to 'man', 'being', or 'individual', an essence in our lives, or truth which may be latent or repressed but which can be realised (Super, 1957; Adamson, 1997), or unearthed. Individuals in modernity are required to deal with a number of competing life-spheres or, as Super (1992) suggests, life-career roles, each one demanding a slightly different 'presentation of self' (Goffman, 1959). Individuals can be simultaneously father, son, lover, divorcee, manager, working-class, and university-educated – a kaleidoscopic fracture of roles and identities which stimulates a sense of dispersion and fragmentation. The experience of disunity and contradiction is overcome by the withdrawal of full commitment from any one sphere so as to produce 'within us the sense of some entity which stands back from reality, an entity which is presented within all of them but which is fully realised in none – a sense of true self' (Cohen & Taylor, 1976, p. 205). The promise of a true self seeks to re-combine these different life-worlds where we engage separate 'modes of consciousness'. The discourse of career works to monopolise and universalise the different components of an individual's life, at times through the promise of salvation via the comforting embrace of corporate culture (see Willmott, 1993) or as a vehicle for the realisation of self (Adamson, 1997). However, at the very same time that it is becoming the site for the search of a true self, *career* today works to unravel the seams of the self as much as it unites them, adding yet one more domain which fractures and decomposes the self.

'Meaning'

The existence of different life-worlds inevitably means that it is very difficult to form any overall sense of essence or project of life. Again, full self-presence cannot be found in any one aspect of our lives and because of the incompatibility of motives, ethics, expectations, role performances, and language across the life-worlds, individuals struggle to cohere and unite meaning or purpose (Giddens, 1991; Lash & Urry, 1994). Nihilism seems to threaten at the very borders of any fragile sense of meaning individuals are able to construct or find for themselves, a threat which the confessional apparatus and 'governmentality' (Foucault, 1980) of career discourse seeks to counter. As we have noted above, a number of recent ethnographies of work are beginning to illustrate not simply the lack of ground-rules and values in organisation but the surfeit of competing messages, signs, and symbols that renders unstable today's employment. 'Where are we going now?', 'I'm not sure what might happen to me next', and 'What are we doing here anyway?' are questions which litter our own interview transcripts collected during research in the banking and financial services industry and local government organisations (O'Doherty, 1994; Holden & Roberts, 1996). As one of our managers said, 'You know that performer in the circus who balances plates on sharpened sticks? To keep them up in the air he has to keep going back to them before they stop spinning and crashing down. Well that's how I feel, that's what it's like being a middle manager' (Holden & Roberts, 1996, p. 62). These were questions and comments which *we as researchers* were increasingly forced to acknowledge applied as much to ourselves as to the subjects of our research.

'Progress'

Career theory, influenced by hermeneutics, tends to work within assumptions that individuals acquire and need to maintain a relationship with the past and the future so as to provide for the sense of continuity through position, location, and movement (Arthur, Hall, & Lawrence, 1989). Progress can be understood as the movement from a past to a projected future, a project based on ambition, purpose, and meaning.

The promise of greater happiness for the individual, through progress and novelty, is worked ideologically via the accumulation of material goods, social indicators of increased status, competencies or skills, networking, experience or expressions of our true self. It is only if we are able to experience life as progress, as ever-changing, that we can secure the dream of personal fulfilment (e.g. Kets De Vries, 1994; Lawrence, 1984). Yet, despite this projection of arrival and contentment, modern careers continually frustrate redemption. As Cohen and Taylor (1976, pp. 209–10) argue: 'despite our hidden awareness of how elusive progress is, we still maintain the idea that happiness lies ahead of us, that if only we could shift paramount reality in this way or that, then we could climb just one step nearer to nirvana'. The promise of novelty is confounded today not only by our sense of *déjà vu*, that the glitter and colour of scenery and furniture remain endless variations on a theme, but also by that suspicion, which swells up and periodically punctures our paramount sense of reality, that the packaging is perhaps all there is. So we have another paradox – constant innovation and apparent novelty concurrent with the sense that we have all seen this somewhere before – a sense that prompts the classic Baudrillardean image, that of the vacant stare of the individual watching the flickering lights of the television, a stare which betrays the shell of an empty hotel room through which we pass in the quick of life.

'Progress' is still granted the same importance even where the limitations of the traditional career ladder have been recognised by those writing in the area of 'protean' (Hall, 1996) and 'boundaryless' careers (Arthur, 1994; Arthur & Rousseau, 1996). In more recent thinking on organisational careers, the indicators or 'yardsticks' of progress now come from within the individual, the self, rather than from external sources of authority. The responsibility for establishing frameworks and co-ordinates by which progress can be charted is vested firmly in the individual. Redemption is now sought from within the self, coetaneous however with the withdrawal of spatial and temporal markers by which progress, or even stasis for that matter, can be measured.

'Order'

Modern humanist thought has been variously structured between the assumptions either that some divine natural order exists between man and her world, a fundamental and proper order which can be restored, or that man has a privileged sovereignty in constructing a secular order through the applications of scientific research and the development of modern technology (Connolly, 1995). These assumptions can be translated by the terms 'ontology' and 'epistemology' respectively, fundamental domains which anchor the modern human subject teleologically, purposively, and self-righteously.

Orthodox thinking and career theories, even those claiming the liberation of postmodernism, remain structured and limited, we argue, by such assumptions. These assumptions are expressed, often implicitly, in the ideas that individuals can order themselves and their lives, or discover some underlying order/fate in their career to which they must conform. Careers then can be ordered, whether through the relatively simple hierarchies of Weberian bureaucracy, or through some kind of flexible 'lifestyle' – which may require more complex multiple movements. Instead of a unitary and linear movement guiding careers through some pre-ordained hierarchy of 'cradle to grave', moves are required today which are lateral, diagonal, or circular (e.g. Brousseau, Driver, Eneroth, & Larsson, 1996) if order is to be 'discovered' or constructed once again.

'Position'

Modern scientific instruments have sought ever greater precision in locating and mapping man and her world. Man has sought to structure and locate movement categorically in terms of a regular and periodic timetable. In seeking to define and capture some essence, a stability and full enlightened ontic presence to phenomena, this classical mode of thinking sees the world in terms of clear-cut boundaries and entity-like objects (Cooper, 1990): an objectivity or form which is amenable to epistemological classification and categorisation. This mode of thinking is necessarily a mode-of-being in the world, a mode-of-career which maintains commitment to the sufficiency of reason and the pliability of the world.

Within careers and organisations a whole discursive economy has sought to unambiguously secure and position employees, from job titles and job descriptions, to class and gender 'locations'. For example, individuals have been located by these 'grids of specification' which attempt to routinise and predict organisational contingency and move-ment, so as to concretise exchanges between the organisation, the product and labour markets, and the wider socio-political economy of which they remain a part. Ideally, individuals knew what was expected of them, when it was expected, how much they would be rewarded for their effort, how long they could expect to wait until the next promotion – and ultimately when they would retire. These expectations should be confirmed by widely accepted organisational and society-wide norms of authority and status so that one's position was secured and esteemed by broader societal norms and objectives.

Within the 'postmodern' career, it is often argued that position can be re-established more flexibly through dialogue and reason, offering indi-viduals the freedom to establish and sanctify their own rules and understanding. Yet, the provision of these resources – 'reason', conversa-tion, counselling, and empathy – paradoxically tends to assuage, limit, and constrain the anxiety-provoking open-ness of freedom.

Unravelling of the seams

We essay the idea that the limitations of reason and rationality are increasingly being exposed by what some might see as the *a-logical*, absurd, or paradoxical movements of highly mediated capital, technol-ogy, and social relations, deconstructive movements that resemble the textual work of deconstruction in Derrida. The consequences of this complexity question the epistemological and ontological foundations of theorists, practitioners, and counsellors across the micro-disciplines of career and have implications for the possibilities for career in the process of organisation. Note we claim 'in the process of organisation', because the implications of our argument are such that it is the deconstructive erosion *between* 'the individual and organisation' and *between* 'the counselled and counsellor' which works to deny stable fixed points of reference such as individual/organisation, research/researched, and subject/object (see the discussions in *Organization Studies*, 1997). So it is not simply a hermeneutic, dialectic, or interactive *relationality* between subjects and objects, between researcher and researched, between the individual and organisation, but an *erosion of the co-ordinates by which we can identify 'relation'*. Under these conditions we are never organised but always organising and disorganising, never complete, always unfinished, never arriving but always on our 'way' (cf. Young & Valach, 1996): on our way to where, of course – and why – is increasingly unclear. Hence our 'careering', our muddling-through on the edge of reason.

The crisis which we see in re-presentation, reason, subjectivity, and language, is far more schizophrenic, nihilistic, and entropic than most observers in the field of career allow. Career theory maintains a commitment to meaning (or its restoration), progress, rationality and reason, the discovery and liberation of identity – an 'authentic' self, and the ability to organise and order work and life. Career theory still seems to offer the old humanist strategies of self-declaration and the confessional, which, by means of a mode of reflexive sociology (see Linstead, 1994), can help negotiate appropriate meaning and understanding for individuals struggling for career success. These attempts, however, become one more modernist solution, one more representation, and when it inevitably fails, the more 'frenetic' become the attempts to re-centre ontologically and epistemologically.

The individual's development of a career is like one of the rituals that Fineman (1993), building on the work of Fromm, interprets as traditional forms of protection against the 'fear of freedom'. It is a void which we argue is more and more evident today in the failure to re-present or fully reason the movements brought about by language, information, media, and technology. The concept 'career' has itself become so problematic in recent years, literally *careering*, that talk about career is perhaps only adding to this in-rushing vortex.

The, often frenetic, work of *bricolage* seeks pools of order from within an almost apocalyptic desiderata of material – fragments of texts and the ruins of strategic initiatives and change programmes – the fall-out of which casts individuals into an uncertain space of *between-ness*. In 'doing' this management (Garfinkel, 1967), employees are increasingly compelled to display and perform their competence and identity, to establish their credibility, and seek to 'position' themselves vis-à-vis others: in other words they must be 'in control'. However, it is a world which at the very same time is devoid of rules and consistency, which denies the grounds and means for establishing success and competence, the security of place, identity, of 'having achieved', of 'having arrived' at that stable centre or pinnacle of control. Constant interruptions, false trials and trails, frustrations, illusions and images devoid of anchors and referents seem to riddle organisation where, as Nietzsche argued, the 'real world' has become more than ever an elaborate and expensive myth.

It is perhaps at times of crisis, liminality, breakdown, collapse, and transgression, that we find this paradox and ambiguity forced upon us, where the promises of humanism appear hope-less. The questions are paradoxical because the more you look, or ask, or think about them, the less clarity and certitude they seem to allow. Where career begins and ends today, where an organisation starts and finishes, where the 'boundaries' of an individual are (Collin, 1996) and where the temporal markers are which delineate the 'time of work' from 'leisure-time' (Austrin, 1991; Ritzer, 1993), are all becoming far less certain, exposing individuals to paradoxical questions of this kind which riddle the heart of reason. The disturbance of fragile routines and senses of self, meaning, progress, order, and position threatens to open at many and multiple points – the Christmas party (Rosen, 1988), the accident at work (Gabriel, 1995), after-work drinking socials (Van Maanen, 1992), the appraisal interview, and even the strike ballot. 'Why work? Why try? Why bother? Why *why*? . . . What's career *for*? . . . Can career make sense without stable co-ordinates or reference?' These are questions which are being increasingly asked today, from youth culture to the growing metropolitan underworld (DeLillo, 1998) of drugs, poverty, and decay, questions which do not permit easy answers if the alternative is suburban mortgages, rented television, and hire-purchase automobiles.

In fact, rather than crisis, these openings are more like a permanent threat, always already hovering in the margins, the gaps, and fissures of reason, organisation, and career. It is an ill-defined, diffuse, and protean set of 'permanent contingencies', an Achilles heel simultaneously binding and unravelling self and organisation, drawing in discourse and reason – the in-rushing of the vortex – at the same time that it repels understanding, making a 'mockery of foresight, cunning and prudence' and thereby opening up the 'floodgates through which chaos and contingency pour' (Bauman, 1995, pp. 30–31). These floodgates disclose an always-already-there-alterity which threatens identity, sanity, and reason, dis-abling and un-securing those grounds which allow us in our day-to-day mundane reality to carry on.

In-conclusion

If the modernist/humanist certainties and guarantees no longer hold steady, if the promises of reason and rationality are ontologically and epistemologically as hollow as we suggest, perhaps it is now time to abandon the futile search for organisation and order, identity, and career.

The necessities, certainties, and structures which have regulated the careers of individuals are being replaced by a fluidity and formlessness, a dis-ordering of the traditional principles which held together the organisa-tion of society, self, and employment relations. For example, in brief moments in many organisations, the utter chaos and abyss, the founda-tion-less and groundless labyrinths of individuals are being exposed, piercing the 'thin film of order' (Bauman, 1995, p. 14) and throwing those individuals back on themselves. Many organisations seem to be going in all directions, initiative following initiative, where change *and* flux seems to be the only constant. It is this paradoxical condition – of change and stasis, of flux and stability, where everything appears to change but where things remain uncannily the same – that appears to define the space of contemporary organisation and career. Perhaps now we are witness to a condition of further implosions and collapse, where the terms of opposi-tional thinking – placement/displacement, the far and near, the present and past, the same and other, order and disorder, the real and fictional – can no longer anchor or orientate reason and understanding, a situation one theorist has recently characterised as 'pandemonium' (Burrell, 1997).

We have suggested that once so-called humanist anchors begin to lose their connection with an 'outside', some referential worldly signified, analytically they rapidly begin to collapse back on their own logic. Perhaps as subjects, therefore, we need to rid ourselves of the ritual or 'appearance' of reasoning about the 'world', the search for the *reality* of our times, and begin to problematise the process of reasoning which seems to have as its object a self-serving legitimisation.

Categories and methodologies in which we are accustomed to thinking are seemingly being by-passed by phenomena which reconfigure notions of cause, location, time, and identity. Extreme, hyper-real, excessive, chaotic, . . . the descriptions multiply as theorists attempt to make sense of conditions which stretch thinking and reason to breaking point. It is towards the thinking demanded by Derrida's concept of *différance* that may offer some kind of response to the crisis. Or perhaps we must wrestle with Bataille's labyrinth, 'where all sensations, all feelings are enhanced, but where no overview is present to provide a clue about how to get out' (Tschumi, 1994, p. 43).

No doubt man will need to lose self-importance, erasing personal history and the illusions of skin-bound identity, to seek a new relation-ship with 'self' and the earth, a new radical understanding of career which recalls Foucault's later work on the care of the self. This is a mode of being-with-others which does not seek to control or dominate, to secure or master, but celebrates the dissolution of sense and the implod-ing disconnection of signified/signifiers. It is a mode-of-being where one is abandoned to quest-ion and transgression, managing on the threshold of sense, a space(ing) from out of which are thrown the ineffable attraction and repulsion of questions of truth, meaning, and sense. It is a space where no metaphysical or transcendental guarantees confirm or sanctify the meaning of being, a meaning which we continually seek out but only ever partially construct. It 'is' literally a *no-where*, because if the oppositions and co-ordinates of reason – here and there, then and now, this and that – are without a still-point of transcendental guarantee, and therefore based on a more primordial aporetic movement, a movement of *différance* that permits, co-implicates (*complicates*), and contaminates these oppositions – then we begin to ask: 'where in comparison to what?' This is to live perhaps in the dark void of homelessness and meaningless-ness *as an achievement* (see Critchley, 1997), without grand narratives of progress and redemption, in experiment, contingency, and flux. It is where 'why' never finds an answer. A space where 'to career' is accepted with the laugh and the scream of the nihilist – literally dancing on the threshold of sense – in the quick of time, in the *vitus* of life, in errancy and vagrancy.

REFERENCES

Adamson, S. J. (1997). Career as a vehicle for the realization of self. *Career Development International*, 2, 245–252.
Arthur, M. B. (1994). The boundaryless career: A new perspective for organiza-tional inquiry. *Journal of Organizational Behavior*, 15, 295–306.
Arthur, M. B., Hall, D. T., & Lawrence, B. S. (1989). Generating new directions in career theory: The case for a transdisciplinary approach. In M. B. Arthur, D. T. Hall, & B. S. Lawrence (Eds.), *Handbook of career theory* (pp. 7–25). Cambridge: Cambridge University Press.
Arthur, M. B. & Rousseau, D. M. (1996). A career lexicon for the 21st century. *Academy of Management Executive*, 10 (4), 28–39.

Austrin, T. (1991). Flexibility, surveillance and hype in New Zealand financial retailing. *Work, Employment and Society*, *15*, 201–221.

Barker, J. (1993). Tightening the iron cage: Concertive control in self-managing teams. *Administrative Science Quarterly*, *38*, 408–437.

Baudrillard, J. (1983). *Simulations*. New York: Semiotext(e).

Bauman, Z. (1995). *Life in fragments: Essays in postmodern morality*. Oxford: Blackwell.

Beardsworth, R. (1996). *Derrida and the political*. London: Routledge.

Blanchot, M. (1982). *The space of literature* (Ann Smock, trans.). Lincoln, NE: University of Nebraska Press.

Brousseau, K. R., Driver, M. J., Eneroth, K., & Larsson, R. (1996). Career pandemonium: Realising organisations and individuals. *Academy of Management Executive*, *10* (4), 66–86.

Burrell, G. (1997). *Pandemonium*. London: Sage.

Burrell, G. & Morgan, G. (1979). *Sociological paradigms and organisational analysis*. London: Heinemann.

Casey, C. (1995). *Work, self and society: After industrialism*. London: Routledge.

Clegg, S. (1990). *Modern organizations: Organization studies in the postmodern world*. London: Sage.

Cohen, S. & Taylor, L. (1976). *Escape attempts: The theory and practice of resistance to everyday life*. London: Allen Lane.

Collin, A. (1996). Organizations and the end of the individual. *Journal of Managerial Psychology*, *11* (7), 9–17.

Collin, A. & Watts, A. G. (1996). The death and transfiguration of career – and of career guidance? *British Journal of Guidance and Counselling*, *24*, 385–398.

Collin, A. & Young, R. A. (1986). New directions for theories of career. *Human Relations*, *39*, 837–853.

Connolly, W. (1995). *The ethos of pluralization*. Minneapolis, MN: University of Minnesota Press.

Coole, D. (1996). Habermas and the question of alterity. In M. Passeron D'Entrèves & S. Benhabib (Eds.), *Habermas and the unfinished project of modernity: Critical essays on the philosophical discourse of modernity* (pp. 221–244). Cambridge: Polity Press.

Cooper, R. (1990). Organisation/Disorganisation, In J. Hassard & D. Pym (Eds.), *The theory and philosophy of organisations* (pp. 167–197). London: Routledge.

Critchley, S. (1997). *Very little . . . almost nothing: Death, philosophy, literature*. London: Routledge.

Deleuze, G. & Guattari, F. (1983). *Anti-Oedipus*. Minneapolis, MN: University of Minnesota Press.

DeLillo, D. (1998). *Underworld*. Basingstoke and London: Picador.

Derrida, J. (1976). *Of grammatology*. Baltimore, MD: Johns Hopkins University Press.

du Gay, P. (1996). *Consumption and identity at work*. London: Sage.

Ezzamel, M. & Willmott, H. (1998). Accounting for teamwork: A critical study of group-based systems of organization control. *Administrative Science Quarterly*, *43*, 358–396.

Fay, B. (1987). *Critical social science.* Cambridge: Polity Press.

Fineman, S. (1993). Organizations as emotional arenas. In S. Fineman (Ed.), *Emotion in organizations* (pp. 9–35). London: Sage.

Foucault, M. (1969). *L'Archéologie du savoir.* Paris: Editions Gallimard.

(1977). *Discipline and punish.* Harmondsworth: Penguin.

(1980). *Power/Knowledge.* New York: Pantheon.

(1982). The subject and power. *Critical Enquiry, 8,* 777–795.

(1984). What is enlightenment? In P. Rabinow (Ed.), *The Foucault reader* (pp. 32–50). New York: Pantheon Books.

Gabriel, Y. (1995). The unmanaged organization: Stories, fantasies and subjectivity. *Organization Studies, 16,* 477–501.

Game, A. & Metcalfe, G. (1996). *Passionate sociology.* London: Sage.

Garfinkel, H. (1967). *Studies in ethnomethodology.* Englewood Cliffs, NJ: Prentice Hall.

Garsten, C. & Grey, C. (1997). How to become oneself: Discourses of subjectivity in post-bureaucratic organizations. *Organization, 4,* 211–228.

Giddens, A. (1991). *Modernity and self-identity: Self and society in the late modern age.* Cambridge: Polity Press.

Goffman, E. (1959). *The presentation of self in everyday life.* Harmondsworth: Penguin.

Habermas, J. (1984). *The theory of communicative action,* vol. I: *Reason and the rationalization of society.* London: Heinemann.

Hall, D. T. (1996). Protean careers of the 21st century. *Academy of Management Executive, 10* (4), 8–16.

Heidegger, M. (1962). *Being and time.* Oxford: Blackwell.

Herriot, P. & Pemberton, C. (1996). Contracting careers. *Human Relations, 49,* 757–790.

Hiltrop, J. (1996). Managing the changing psychological contract. *Employee Relations, 18* (1), 36–49.

Holden, L. & Roberts, I. (1996). European middle managers: The search for identity in a conflicting role and an uncertain role. In I. J. Beardwell (Ed.), *Contemporary developments in human resource management* (pp. 49–64). Paris: Editions ESKA.

Höpfl, H. & Linstead, S. (1993). Passion and performance: Suffering and the carrying of organizational roles. In S. Fineman (Ed.), *Emotion in Organizations* (pp. 76–93). London: Sage.

Jackall, R. (1988). *Moral mazes: The world of corporate managers.* New York: Oxford University Press.

Jameson, F. (1984). Postmodernism, or the cultural logic of late capitalism. *New Left Review, 146,* 83–93.

Kets de Vries, M. F. R. (1994). Can you manage the rest of your life? *European Management Journal, 12,* 133–137.

Kets de Vries, M. F. R & Balazs, K. (1997). The downside of downsizing. *Human Relations, 50,* 11–50.

Kondo, D. (1990). *Crafting selves.* London: The University of Chicago Press.

Lash, S. & Urry, J. (1994). *Economies of signs and space.* London: Sage.

Lawrence, B. S. (1984). Age grading: The implicit organizational timetable. *Journal of Occupational Behaviour*, 5, 23–35.

Linstead, S. (1994). Objectivity, reflexivity, and fiction: Humanity, inhumanity, and the science of the social. *Human Relations*, 47, 1321–1345.

Mestrovich, S. (1993). *The barbarian temperament: Toward a postmodern critical theory*. London: Routledge.

O'Doherty, D. (1994). Institutional withdrawal: Anxiety and conflict in the emerging banking labour process, or, 'How to get out of it'. Paper presented to the 12th International Annual Labour Process Conference, Aston University.

Organization Studies (1997). Special edition on 'Dualisms in organizational analysis', *18* (1).

Parker, M. (1992). Post-modern organisation or post-modern organisation theory. *Organisation Studies*, 13, 1–17.

Ritzer, G. (1993). *The McDonaldization of society*. Newbury Park, CA: Pine Forge.

Rosen, M. (1988). You asked for it: Christmas at the bosses' expense. *Journal of Management Studies*, 25, 463–481.

Savickas, M. L. (1989). Annual review: Practice and research in career counseling and development, 1988. *Career Development Quarterly*, 38, 100–134.

(1991). The meaning of love and work: Career issues and interventions. *Career Development Quarterly*, 39, 315–324.

(1993). Career counseling in the postmodern era. *Journal of Cognitive Psychotherapy: An International Quarterly*, 7, 205–215.

(1994). Vocational psychology in the postmodern era: Comment on Richardson (1993). *Journal of Counseling Psychology*, 41, 105–107.

Schein, E. H. (1996, November). Career anchors revisited: Implications for career development in the 21st century. *Academy of Management Executive*, special issue: Careers in the 21st century, 10 (4), 80–88.

Smart, B. (1993). *Postmodernity*. London: Routledge.

Super, D. E. (1957). *The psychology of careers*. New York: Harper and Row.

(1992). Toward a comprehensive theory of career development. In D. H. Montross & C. J. Shinkman (Eds.), *Career development: Theory and practice* (pp. 35–64). Springfield, IL: Charles C. Thomas.

Tschumi, B. (1994). *Architecture and disjunction*. Cambridge, MA: The MIT Press.

Van Maanen, J. (1992). Drinking our troubles away: Managing conflict in a British police agency. In D. Kolb & J. Bartunek (Eds.), *Hidden conflict in organizations*. London: Sage.

Watson, T. J. (1994). *In search of management*. London: Routledge.

Willmott, H. (1993). Strength is ignorance; slavery is freedom: Managing culture in modern organizations. *Journal of Management Studies*, 30, 515–552.

Young, R. A. (1984). Vocation as relationship. *Counselling and Values*, 28, 169–178.

162   *Damian O'Doherty and Ian Roberts*

(1988). Ordinary explanations and career theories. *Journal of Counseling and Development, 66*, 336–339.

Young, R. A. & Collin, A. (Eds.) (1992). *Interpreting career: Hermeneutical studies of lives in context.* Westport, CT: Praeger.

Young, R. A. & Valach, L. (1996). Interpretation and action in career counseling. In M. L. Savickas & M. B. Walsh (Eds.), *Handbook of career counseling theory and practice* (pp. 361–375). Palo Alto, CA: Davies-Black.

11   Epic and novel: the rhetoric of career

Audrey Collin

The original idea for this chapter arose as I was reading the analysis of the genres of epic and novel by Bakhtin (1981), a major theorist of literature now regularly cited outside that field (for example Gergen, 1992; Jeffcutt, 1993; Potter, 1996; Shotter, 1992). What immediately struck me about Bakhtin's contrast between these two genres was that it could be used to illustrate the changing nature of career. Whereas, during most of the twentieth century, career had been like the traditional epic, it was becoming more like the (nineteenth-century) novel. However, in exploring these genres further, I came across the socio-historical approach to literature of Schlaffer (1989) and Moretti (1996), and this made me aware that these literary forms could perhaps have something even more significant to say about career.

Schlaffer (1989) adopts a ' "materialist" theory of aesthetic production' (p. 5): while respecting the aesthetic individuality of an artistic work, he sees it as a manifestation of a historical problem, as the 'embodiment of a social contradiction' (p. 123). Comparing some late eighteenth- and early nineteenth-century works, he concludes that their image of the hero made 'visible the complex situation of the bourgeois age: the contradiction between the narrowness of its reality and the breadth of its consciousness' (p. 15). Moretti (1996) takes a similar approach: literature 'helps reduce [the] tension' produced by the 'ethical impediments, perceptual confusions, ideological contradictions' arising from transformations in society (p. 6). He argues that what he calls the 'modern epic', with its digressions, polyphony, and polysemy, makes the tensions of modern, urban, and global experiences of the world more comprehensible and acceptable.

The division of labour, to which Schlaffer attributes the need of eighteenth-century society for the 'bourgeois as hero', has not abated over the last two centuries. Rather it has intensified and become even more widespread and, indeed, provided a structural basis for the construct of career. The arguments of Schlaffer and Moretti, then, prompted the question whether this construct was a response to the tensions of its age as much as these literary genres had been to theirs. Was the twentieth-century career being used as a rhetoric as some eighteenth- and nine-teenth-century bourgeois literature had been? With the postmodern uncertainties and ambiguities of today's experiences of work, resembling the 'modern epic', what form would the rhetoric of career take in the future? These are the questions this chapter addresses.

My purpose here, then, is to demonstrate the similarity between these literary genres and the construct of career and thus cast it and its future in a new light. To do this, I have adopted artistic licence in using material a-historically, in making connections between literary genres of one era and the social conditions of another. However, Schlaffer (1989) considers that traditional literary forms persist because they provide 'poetic sol-utions to difficulties which had been insoluble in practice' (pp. 125–126), and so this seems justified. I have also stream-lined my source material. I have not looked beyond Bakhtin (1981), Schlaffer (1989), and Moretti (1996) for other theories of the epic and the novel and, indeed, have used theirs selectively. In eliding lay and academic interpretations from the various schools of career theory, some of the differences between them will have been masked. The outcome is thus not a history of career, but an invitation to look at career differently.

Epic, novel, and 'modern epic'

The world depicted by the traditional, Homeric epic is the heroic world of the national past, separate from the everyday of the listener/reader (Bakhtin, 1981). This past is absolute; its 'single and unified world view' is 'obligatory and indubitably true for heroes as well as for authors and audiences' (p. 35). The characters of the epic are 'bounded, pre-formed, individualized by their various situations and destinies' (p. 35), and its hero – and it is taken for granted that the hero is a man – is 'a fully finished and completed being' (p. 34).

Although it proceeds through episodes, digresses, and aggregates independent elements, the epic nevertheless embodies 'a destiny, a duty, a linear teleology' (Moretti, 1996, p. 48). It is underpinned by 'the notion of following a pattern, *serving* one's destiny' (Bloomfield in Moretti, p. 48), coming close to 'the ideology of progress' (Moretti, p. 54) in a heroic world (italics in original here and in quotations throughout chapter). The epic thus exercises a centripetal influence in a culture (Moretti), 'homogenizing and hierarchicizing' (Bakhtin, 1981, p. 425).

The novel came into being as Europe developed international contacts and gained access to a multitude of different languages and cultures (Bakhtin, 1981). In contrast to the epic, the novel exerts a 'de-normatizing and therefore centrifugal force' (p. 425). The former referred to a completed world, whereas the latter reflects 'reality itself in the process of its unfolding' (p. 7). It is concerned with 'an uninterrupted movement into a real future . . . [an] unconcluded process' (p. 30). It thus recognises 'an indeterminacy, a certain semantic openendedness, a living contact with unfinished, still-evolving contemporary reality (the openended present)' (p. 7). Moreover, unlike the unitary language of the epic, the novel is polyphonous, expressing a 'multiplicity of social voices' (p. 263), and generating rich interactions, as its themes disperse into 'the rivulets and droplets of social heteroglossia' (p. 263). There is 'constant interaction between meanings, all of which have the potential of conditioning others', and 'everything is part of a greater whole' (p. 426). Specific meaning thus derives from context, and has to be interpreted through 'dialogism'.

The novel's treatment of the individual is also very different from the traditional epic's. No longer formed by and realised in a heroic role, individuals in the novel are not 'exhausted by the plots that contain them' (Bakhtin, 1981, p. 35), but have 'unrealized potential' and thus 'a need for the future' (p. 37). Thus the 'epic wholeness of an individual disintegrates' (p. 37), with a split between inner commitment to action and outer inertia (Schlaffer, 1989, p. 17), and a 'crucial tension' between 'the external and the internal man' (Bakhtin, 1981, p. 37). Thus the author has to address the subjectivity of the individual, depict a more complex individuality, with not only action but also reflection. Moreover, hero, narrator, and reader no longer have the 'single and unified world view' as presented in the epic (p. 35), and multiple perspectives emerge: 'When the novel becomes the dominant genre, epistemology becomes the dominant discipline' (p. 15).

As I read Bakhtin, the analogies between these literary forms and career sprang from the page. The traditional career, loosely interpreted as linear, upward, focused, and masculine, was like the epic, whereas the increasingly open-ended career of today was like the novel. However, when I later encountered the 'modern epic', I saw that it made an even more effective analogy for the fragmented, diverse, open-ended, postmodern career (Arthur & Rousseau, 1996; Weick & Berlinger, 1989). It is the genre which Moretti (1996) constructed to embrace those 'world texts' that defy classification   in   established   genres,   like   Goethe's   *Faust,* Melville's *Moby Dick,* Joyce's *Ulysses,* Eliot's *The Wasteland,* García Márquez's *One Hundred Years of Solitude.* It comprises fragments, assembled as collage or *bricolage,* an 'ensemble devoid of unity, an archipelago of "independent worlds"' (Moretti, 1996, p. 48). Hence the 'teleology of [the traditional epic] is replaced by the perpetual digression of *exploration*' (p. 49), with a 'perennial *ability to begin again*' (p. 48). These fragments introduce the polyphony, and the interactions between them, the polysemy, that replace the epic's 'single and unified world view' (Bakhtin,

1981, p. 35) and 'social totality' of the hero's action (Moretti, 1996, p. 17). They reflect the 'collapse' of the 'notion of the unitary individual' (p. 192) in the twentieth century. The modern epic also interweaves different times and spaces in its 'interplay of prolepsis and flashback'. Whereas the traditional epic is diachronous, the world text has synchronic breadth, and ranges across the globe during the same twenty-four hours. The 'passage of time counts for less than movement in space' (pp. 75–76).

The diversity of these fragments, their 'trivial affinities' (p. 217), and the 'unstoppable productivity' generated by their interactions, result in multiple and multiplying discourses, 'until we are given a world *full of culture* – and totally *devoid of wisdom*' (p. 211). In managing the resulting complexity, the authors of these texts achieve a heterogeneous but unified reality: 'the organized whole is more than the sum of its parts' (p. 97). It has emerging qualities, 'empirically observable', but not 'logically deducible' (p. 97). However, this whole is not homogeneous, but 'formed in extreme contrasts, rather than in their resolution' (p. 214). In the interaction of independent elements there is polarisation, 'a productive conflict of the contradictory elements' (Adorno in Moretti, p. 214), so that the whole is a 'forcefield' (Adorno in Moretti, p. 215).

In all this complexity, Moretti discerns a twofold structure. There is an 'immutable substratum' (p. 225) and a 'heterogeneous surface' (p. 226). Underneath are standardisation and commonplaces; on the surface, 'with its broken, unpredictable texture, and with the fragments triggering the most idiosyncratic associations' (p. 229), *anomie* and anarchy. There is a 'totalitarian temptation' (p. 227) in these texts to achieve the 'composure of fragments' (p. 228), but they are instead held in tension. There are 'unreconciled extremes . . . tightening the net of the world text, but without losing its boundlessness' (p. 229).

Moretti (1996) attributes to the 'silent fetter of the capitalist economy' (p. 89) this willingness to allow multiple interpretations and increased polysemy. This economic system is strong enough not to be threatened by, and can hence allow, the circulation of alternative meanings. More economically fragile societies 'have to repress the autonomy of the cultural sphere' (p. 89), but because the capitalist cultural sphere is 'neutralized', everything is possible 'because nothing is important any longer' (p. 90).

I shall return shortly to look at the analogies between career and epic, novel, and modern epic.

The hero and heroic life

The hero of the traditional epic exists in a heroic society, and 'excels at the performance of a necessary social role' (Featherstone, 1995, p. 61);

motive and action are one. The purpose for his existence, his inner world, potentials, and possibilities for action are all determined by and realised in his epic role: 'There is not the slightest gap between his authentic essence and its external manifestation . . . He has already become everything that he could become' (Bakhtin, 1981, p. 34). The hero's action, indeed, reflects and embodies the 'social totality' (Moretti, 1996, p. 142); there is 'an active epic unity of hero and world' (Schlaffer, 1989, p. 17).

However, there is a 'new modern ideal of distinction' (Simmel, in Featherstone, 1995, p. 64) that suggests that a 'form of the heroic life' (Featherstone, p. 64) persists and can be contrasted with 'everyday life'. The hero departs from the everyday world, 'of women, reproduction and care', 'only to return to its acclaim should his tasks be completed successfully'. He embarks on a series of adventures in which he struggles 'to prove himself by displaying courage', achieve 'extraordinary goals', and seek 'virtue, glory and fame'. His life has 'some higher purpose' which gives him a 'sense of destiny', enabling him to weave his adventures into a meaningful whole (Featherstone, pp. 58–60).

The bourgeois as hero

Schlaffer's (1989) socio-historical approach suggests that the image of hero reflects the otherwise unarticulated and unfulfilled longings of its age. In identifying the 'bourgeois as hero', Schlaffer discusses how, after the French Revolution, during which citizens had acted heroically, bourgeois social conditions denied the possibility of further epic heroism. The division of labour undercut the 'wholeness' of the individual (pp. 31–33), and separated work from home, enjoyment from labour, and means from ends. Traditional epic heroism and contemporary reality were now irreconcilable.

Bourgeois literature, therefore, created heroes, but heroes of a different kind, grappling with their own inner life, inactivity, reflection, and 'critical self-awareness' (Schlaffer, p. 27). Its novels recognised the limits of individual heroism, for in the bourgeois society of 'state, law, division of labour, and the separation of powers, the social totality can no longer be embodied in the action of a hero' (Moretti, 1996, p. 142). Or, as Bradley (in Moretti, 1996, p. 12) puts it: 'In a world of "trousers, machinery, and policemen . . . we have Law . . . but it is not favourable to striking events or individual actions on the grand scale"'. Schlaffer (1989, p. 121) concludes that: 'The complex, contradictory, yet consistent features of this image [of the 'bourgeois as hero'] are generated by the complex, contradictory, yet consistent features of bourgeois society.' This image reveals the 'historically specific contradiction' of that period when, with the increasing division of labour, the individual 'longs to be more than a bourgeois and to regain the lost wholeness of the hero through action' (p. 38).

A modern hero?

The period in America after the Second World War was a time of major social transformations, the American Dream, of tensions and contradictions, that gave rise to considerable analysis and discussion. The nature of mass society and of the individual within it (for example Marcuse, 1964, on th e 'one-dimensional man'; Riesman, Denny, & Glazer, 1960, on the 'lonely crowd') was much debated. The theory of mass society, according to Daniel Bell (Giner, 1976, p. 246), became probably the most influential social theory apart from Marxism in the Western world. According to Moscovici (1990, p. 70): 'Behind the person and the manner in which he or she is described, one can discern . . . the undefined mass, the anonymous crowd, a formless aggregation of little entities, each isolated from the others'. Mass society, it was argued, was creating alienation (see Giner, 1976), making individuality problematic.

Reich's (1970) exposition of the 'world-view' (p. 20) commonly found after the Second World War in the era of the 'Organization Man' (Whyte, 1956) echoes the descriptions above of the traditional epic world and the heroic life. Organisation 'predominate[d]' (Reich, 1970, p. 56), and it was accepted that the individual had to 'subordinate his [*sic*] will to it' (p. 62), 'fit himself into a function that is needed by society, make "sacrifices", deny his own feelings' (pp. 66–67). He 'had no choice but to idealize the life of the professional', for whom meaning and satisfaction in life derived from having 'the function he performs for society' (p. 59), and making a success of it. Thus life was 'a fiercely competitive struggle for success' (p. 69), but one that benefitted the corporation and society. A similar depiction is found in other writings of the same era. McClelland's (1961) cross-national study found that American managers had greater need for achievement and power than managers from less industrialised areas, and he concluded that this reflected the stage of the country's economic development. Dubin (1970) identified the importance of achievement as motivation for American, in contrast to British, managers. These interpretations recall Featherstone's (1995) 'heroic person . . . who excels at the performance of a necessary social role' (p. 61), and Schlaffer's (1989) 'epic unity of hero and world' (p. 17).

Reich (1970, p. 67) describes how the mid twentieth-century American adopted the standards of his occupation or organisation as 'his *personal values*', and dedicated himself to personal success. His motivation was towards the future, and he often seemed 'to keep pushing beyond rational limits', 'because it is not inner satisfaction that moves him, but something extrinsic to himself' (p. 67). There was an optimistic belief then in the possibility of progress, but a pessimistic view of human beings as 'aggressive, competitive, power-seeking' (p. 62). According to Reich, Americans after the Second World War were 'profoundly anti-populist' (p. 66), as Sennett (1998, p. 64) also noted: 'The masses seem not worth noticing as human beings, and so what matters is how much people stand out from the masses'. Americans believed in 'the uncommon man . . . of special abilities and effort' (Reich, 1970, p. 66), 'in meritocracy of ability and accomplishment [in order] to promote excellence' (p. 65). Hence they believed in an elitist society, where the elite was judged according to its 'utility to the technological society' (p. 66): in Simmel's words (in Featherstone, 1995, p. 64), they had an 'ideal of distinction'.

However, although Reich's description echoes the traditional epic and heroic life, there are also differences, just as Schlaffer (1989) found in bourgeois literature. Unlike the hero of the traditional epic, who had not 'the slightest gap between his authentic essence and its external manifestation' (Bakhtin, 1981, p. 34), the mid twentieth-century American experienced insecurity and fear of failure, and had self-awareness, though an inauthentic sense of self. In a meritocratic society, where recognition comes from credentials, 'to lose credentials is to cease being a human being' (Reich, 1970, p. 69); 'below the meritocracy is an abyss where people have ceased to exist altogether. Thus there is a loss of a sense of the reality of self, apart from the way in which society judges self' (p. 76). The modern American further differed from the traditional epic hero in his lack of 'wholeness' and the schizophrenic 'split between his working and his private self' (p. 71). There was 'a "public" and a "private" man . . . it is impossible to . . . confront the whole man, for the wholeness is precisely what does not exist' (p. 71). Reich also points out (pp. 57–61) that American literature and cinema of the time reflected these same anxieties and realities, as did some of the stories told by working people: ' "I think most of us are looking for a calling, not a job. Most of us . . . have jobs that are too small for our spirit. Jobs are not big enough for people" ' (Terkel, 1975, p. 14). Thus Reich presents a contradictory picture of mid-century American life. Indeed, he was using it as part of his argument that the succeeding generation was seeking and expressing very different values from those he attributed to its parents. Whyte (1956) also pointed to the emergence of a new 'social ethic', that valued group membership in contrast to the individualism of the Protestant work ethic. I shall examine these competing interpretations and contradictions shortly.

Career as epic, novel, and 'modern epic'

The most common discourse of career has depicted career in epic terms. The imagery has characteristically been that of a ladder, and career has been distinguished from just having a job (Sennett, 1998, p. 120). Careers were for the elite, the epic hero, not for Everyman. Gaining access to a career was both difficult and desirable; succeeding in it, the survival of the fittest. To identify the elite in a meritocratic society, there had to be selection between individuals, in school, and in entering work-life. Thereafter, with strenuous effort and commitment, individuals could perhaps follow pathways of upward progression and increasing status, but it was often hard, and they had to struggle to keep going. Significant decisions had to be made at every turn; indecisiveness was a weakness. To rise in a pyramid-shaped organisation, the individual had to compete with colleagues. There were thus 'winners' and 'losers' in the 'tournament' that selects 'the most talented individuals by a series of progressively more selective competitions. . . at each stage . . . [the] winners . . . compete for the next higher level' (Rosenbaum, 1989, p. 336). Other commitments and relationships in the individual's life were subordinated to this epic career, making it a driving and dominant force, and separating work from home and family (Evans & Bartolome, 1980), as in Featherstone's (1995) characterisation of the heroic life. As criticised in career theory and practice (e.g. in Arthur, Hall, & Lawrence, 1989), such a career was primarily a masculine experience. Hence, this everyday understanding saw career in terms of heroic challenges and, I suggest, offered a narrative of epic heroism.

However, this instrumental interpretation does not give the whole picture of career in the mid-century years. Just as Reich (1970) draws attention to the individual's lack of 'wholeness' and schizophrenic 'split', so recognition of the individual's self-awareness came to form the core of the humanistic psychology being developed in that same period. This gave an organic, developmental interpretation of the individual. It focused on self-concept, and self-actualisation (Maslow, 1954; Rogers, 1951), notions which were widely disseminated and applied in career theory (Super, Crites, Hummel, Moser, Overstreet, & Warnath, 1957) and work motivation theory (Herzberg, 1966). Indeed, the period of which Reich was writing was the heyday of career, what might be called the period of 'high career', when the early theories of career choice and development were being constructed and promulgated (Ginzberg, Ginsburg, Axelrad, & Herma, 1951; Holland, 1959; Miller & Form, 1951; Roe, 1956; Super et al., 1957; Super, Starishevsky, Matlin, & Jordaan, 1963). Moreover, this discourse of career allowed that, as chapter 1 identifies, individuals had a 'subjective career', whether they had an elite career or not.

Thus not only did career constitute epic heroism, but, in that it recognised the individual's inner world and potential for development, it also embodied characteristics of the novel. As in the novel, the subjective career recognised the tension between the 'internal and the external man' (Bakhtin, 1981, p. 37), and although it may have incorporated a narrative of epic heroism, it treated it as indeterminate and openended, as part of a 'still-evolving contemporary reality' (p. 7), as 'movement into a real future' (p. 30). Thus there co-existed several narratives of career: on the one hand, as heroic struggle; on the other, as a vehicle for, and expression of, self. The next section will examine this contradiction in the discourse of career further.

This epic interpretation has persisted in lay understandings and expectations of career. Nevertheless, the novel as depicted by Bakhtin, with its openendedness and heteroglossia, and, even more so, Moretti's (1996) 'modern epic', provide more appropriate analogies with today's experiences. It seems likely that, in the emerging flexible, network society (Castells, 1996), temporary, part-time, concurrent, and sequential employment contracts will proliferate. Every change in employment contract will mean starting anew, 'always starting over' (Sennett, 1998, p. 84), 'endless becoming' (p. 133). The struggle will be to reach a new accommodation over and over again. There will be the constant danger of slippage in status and rewards, the ongoing need to achieve new contracts, and to establish fallback positions (or 'employability'). Echoing Moretti and, indeed, referring to Rushdie, another author of world-texts, Sennett (p. 133) sees work-life now as 'an assemblage . . . of the accidental, the found, and the improvised'. Without a coherent narrative for life 'there is little room for understanding the breakdown of a career, if you believe that all life history is just an assemblage of fragments . . . failure is just another incident' (p. 133).

At the same time, there will be many new potentials and growth points created by the interaction between the fragments of work-life, and their association with other disparate experiences of the individual's life, and the open-endedness of the new global networking society. However, under such conditions, there is 'fragmentation of narrative time' (Sennett, p. 134). Unlike in Bahktin's (1981) novel, in the 'flexible, fragmented present' the individual may only be able to create coherent narratives about the past, and not 'predictive narratives about what will be' (Sennett, p. 135). The emerging context may not be able to sustain the kinds of continuing and coherent identities that had been generated in the more stable conditions of the past. The individual could have a more fragmented self, 'subject to the accidents of time and the fragments of history' (p. 147).

Career as rhetoric

Rhetoric 'reflects, refracts and constructs the dominant values and beliefs of society' (Gowler & Legge, 1989, p. 450). The discourse of career, with its range of meanings, has not only reflected the values and conditions of work and of the wider society, it has also put a gloss on them, given them a favourable interpretation, and, further, in Schlaffer's (1989) terms, embodied some of their social contradictions.

The rhetorical use of the discourse of career, at least in mid twentieth-century America, offered individuals an epic narrative of the heroic life, that, despite the personal costs involved, provided the meanings and motivation to engage their continuing effort, skills, and commitment. At the same time, and informed by career theory and articulated in the practices of vocational guidance, it also allowed individuals to make good what was otherwise missing in their work-lives. For those with an elite career, this rhetoric restored the wholeness and authenticity lost in the epic struggle; for those without, it allowed them to construct a sense of agency, continuity, and potential for development. This discourse of career thereby supported the vigorous development of capitalism, and, in particular, of the large-scale bureaucracies of the time: 'Career issues are . . . implicated in the current debate about the competitiveness of nations . . . The wealth of nations . . . rests on how the efforts of people are channeled into jobs' (Kanter, 1989, p. 520).

In mass society the construction of individuality is problematical: the individual is a 'mass-individual', and 'the individualism in social psychology is a fiction' (Moscovici, 1990, p. 70). Career, however, provided a rhetoric to support the discourse of individualism in the mid-century years. Indeed, career discourse and theory are criticised for the extent to which their conceptualisations are permeated by assumptions of individualism, 'embedded in an ethos of self-centred individualism' (Richardson, 1993, p. 428). Career was a means to implement the self-concept (Super *et al.*, 1957). Career, with its recognisable gateways, patterns, and pathways, was a means of differentiating self from others, or between others, where the person was only one of many. The characteristic psychometric techniques of vocational guidance assumed and constructed the concept of the individual in terms of the norms of a population. Career has also encompassed varying degrees of competition (as in, for example, selection processes, or in the 'tournament': Rosenbaum, 1989). Finally, the elitism of career provided a way of asserting, displaying, and living out one's individuality. As Reich (1970, p. 76) wrote '[w]ithout his career, without his function, [the individual] would be a non-person'.

Overall, then, career as rhetoric has performed a function similar to that Schlaffer (1989) attributes to the 'bourgeois as hero' in making visible some of the twentieth-century's 'historically specific contradictions' between 'the narrowness of its reality and the breadth of its consciousness' (p. 15). The 'bourgeois as hero', however, was just a figure in a novel. Through their career, and perhaps particularly through their subjective career, individuals have played out these contradictions both in their lives and in their society. Some may have reconciled them.

The role of career as rhetoric continues into the new millennium. Its versatility can be observed in its close resemblance to (and indeed association with) human resource management (HRM). 'Career' could easily be substituted for 'HRM' in the following statements in Legge's (1995) dissection of the latter as a rhetoric of the highly ambivalent employment relationship. A remarkable feature of the HRM [career] phenomenon is the 'brilliant ambiguity' of the term itself (Keenoy, in Legge, p. 325). HRM [career] reflects and resonates with the 'American Dream' (Guest in Legge, pp. 85–87). The central concern of HRM [career] could be interpreted as 'the symbolic rather than the social construction of "reality"' . . . it is no good carping about the differences between image and reality if it is the business of HRM [career] to shift perceptions of reality' (Keenoy & Anthony, in Legge, p. 313). 'HRM disciplines the interior of the organization, organizing time, space and movement within it' (Townley, in Legge, p. 315): career, we could say, 'disciplines the interior' of the individual's work-life, 'organizing time, space and movement' therein.

The discourse of career embodies contradictions. It has simultaneously contributed to the construction of personal meaning and identity while extracting value for society from the individual's efforts. It has accorded individuality to 'mass-individuals'. Discussing how the discourse of culture 'has been notorious for blending themes and perspectives which scarcely fit together in one cohesive, non-contradictory narrative', Bauman (1999, pp. xiii–xiv) concludes that 'the inherent ambivalence of the idea of culture which faithfully reflected the ambiguity of the historical condition it was meant to capture and narrate was exactly what made that idea such a fruitful and enduring tool of perception and thought'. This, I suggest, is also the case with career. Its power lies not only in its multiple meanings, that give it the 'ambiguity' (Watts, 1981, p. 214) that characterises it, but in its ability to contain and simultaneously express contradictory meanings without 'falling apart' (Bauman, 1999, p. xiii) or becoming meaningless.

Career theory and practice have unwittingly played a part in constructing the rhetoric of career, their humanistic and democratic intentions and values (Pope, 1999) providing the very means through which this rhetoric could be articulated. Their predominantly positivist approach (Walsh & Chartrand, 1994), consistent with social-science orthodoxy, has allowed the construction and development of a vocational guidance technology and discipline (Foucault, in Usher & Edwards, 1998) that, though indirectly, facilitated the allocation of individuals into their economic roles. Moreover, by withholding a whole-hearted approval of qualitative and interpretative research, it has also reduced the possibility of hearing the authentic voices of individuals expressing their experience of the heroic life, with its insecurities, fear of failure, and schizophrenic splits.

The future rhetorics of career

To what rhetorical purposes is the twenty-first century career likely to be put, and what form are these rhetorics likely to take?

Moretti's (1996) 'modern epic', which I have suggested is analogous to the postmodern career, suggests that one of the contradictions which future rhetoric will need to address is between the 'immutable substratum' laid down by capitalism and its 'heterogeneous surface' (pp. 225–226). To paraphrase Bradley (in Moretti, p. 12, and quoted earlier), 'in a world of call centres, mobile 'phones and the Internet, we have networks'. These constitute surface texture, but underneath the tasks and relationships demanded by capitalism remain. Will career be used as a future rhetoric to represent the tension between substratum and surface, a 'forcefield' of ' "productive conflict of the contradictory elements" ' (Adorno, in Moretti, pp. 214–215), and, if so, how?

The twentieth-century rhetoric of career, I suggested, restored lost wholeness and authenticity, and constructed a sense of agency, continuity, and potential for development. Moretti emphasises the use of collage and *bricolage* by authors of the modern epic, and Sennett (1998) the considerable fragmentation of work life. Will individuals be able to use career to create a meaningful collage for themselves, and, if so, how?

What is perhaps discernible now is a new rhetoric of the individual, seen in the now generally accepted view in organisations that individuals have to be responsible for their own development to ensure employability (Arnold, 1997). Such a rhetoric suggests that future individuals will have to have recourse to their own narratives to construct continuity and meaning for their lives. Thus they will no longer be recognisable or recognised as heroes, because there will no longer be the shared standards by which to judge their actions. In Sennett's (1998) words, in modern capitalism, '[t]here is history, but no shared narrative of difficulty, and so no shared fate' (p. 147). This lonely search for individual meaning is hinted at in the lyric used in a recent advertising campaign:

> You've got to search for the hero inside yourself.
> Search for the secrets you hide.
> Search for the hero inside yourself.
> Until you find the key to your life.
>
> . . .
>
> The missing treasure you must find.
> Because you and only you alone.
> Can build a bridge across the stream.
> Weave your spell in life's rich tapestry.
> Your passport to a feel supreme.
>
> (Pickering & Heard, 1994; performed by M People)

Will career provide a new rhetoric to articulate and embody this inner – virtual – hero?

Alternative rhetorics are also likely to arise, perhaps emerging from the present interest in the 'relational career' (Hall *et al.*, 1996), from Richardson's (1993) view of work and career, and Young & Valach's (1996) notion of 'joint action'. Without such alternatives, future individuals would be condemned to live in a world *'full of culture* – and totally *devoid of wisdom'* (Moretti, 1996, p. 211).

REFERENCES

Arnold, J. (1997). *Managing careers into the 21st century*. London: Paul Chapman.

Arthur, M. B., Hall, D. T., & Lawrence, B. S. (Eds.) (1989). *Handbook of career theory*. Cambridge: Cambridge University Press.

Arthur, M. B. & Rousseau, D. M. (Eds.) (1996). *The boundaryless career: A new employment principle for a new organizational era*. New York: Oxford University Press.

Bakhtin, M. M. (1981). *The dialogic imagination: Four essays* (Michael Holquist, Ed., C. Emerson & M. Holquist, trans.). Austin, TX: University of Texas Press.

Bauman, Z. (1999). *Culture as praxis*. London: Sage.

Castells, M. (1996). *The information age: Economy, society and culture*. Vol. I *The rise of the network society*. Malden, MA: Blackwell.

Dubin, R. (1970). Management in Britain: Impressions of a Visiting Professor. *Journal of Management Studies, 7*, 183–198.

Evans, P. & Bartolome, F. (1980). *Must success cost so much?* London: Grant McIntyre.

Featherstone, M. (1995). *Undoing culture: Globalization, postmodernism and identity*. London: Sage.

Gergen, K. J. (1992). Organization theory in the postmodern era. In M. Reed & M. Hughes (Eds.), *Rethinking organization: New directions for organization theory and analysis* (pp. 207–226). London: Sage.

Giner, S. (1976). *Mass society*. London: Martin Robertson.

Ginzberg, E., Ginsburg, S. W., Axelrad, S., & Herma, J. L. (1951). *Occupational choice: An approach to general theory*. New York: Columbia University Press.

Gowler, D. & Legge, K. (1989). Rhetoric in bureaucratic careers: Managing the meaning of management success. In M. B. Arthur, D. T. Hall, & B. S. Lawrence (Eds.), *Handbook of career theory* (pp. 437–453). Cambridge: Cambridge University Press.

Hall, D. T., & Associates (1996). *The career is dead: Long live the career: A relational approach to careers*. San Francisco: Jossey-Bass.

Herzberg, F. (1966). *Work and the nature of man*. Cleveland: World Publishing.

Holland, J. (1959). A theory of vocational choice. *Journal of Counseling Psychology*, 6, 35–45.

Jeffcutt, P. (1993). From interpretation to representation. In J. Hassard & M. Parker (Eds.), *Postmodernism and organizations* (pp. 25–48). London: Sage.

Kanter, R. M. (1989). Careers and the wealth of nations. A macro-perspective on the structure and implications of career forms. In M. B. Arthur, D. T. Hall, & B. S. Lawrence (Eds.), *Handbook of career theory* (pp. 506–521). Cambridge: Cambridge University Press.

Legge, K. (1995). *Human resource management: Rhetorics and realities*. Basingstoke: Macmillan.

McClelland, D. C. (1961). *The achieving society*. New York: Van Nostrand.

Marcuse, H. (1964). *One-dimensional man*. Boston: Beacon Press.

Maslow, A. (1954). *Motivation and personality*. New York: Harper & Row.

Miller, D. C. & Form, W. H. (1951). *Industrial sociology*. New York: Harper and Row.

Moretti, F. (1996). *Modern epic: The world system from Goethe to García Márquez* (Q. Hoare, trans.). London: Verso.

Moscovici, S. (1990). The generalized self and mass society. In H. T. Himmelweit & G. Gaskell (Eds.), *Societal psychology* (pp. 66–91). Newbury Park: Sage.

Pickering, M. & Heard, P. (1994). *Search for the hero* (sung by M People). BMG Music Publishing Ltd/EMI Publishing Ltd.

Pope, M. (1999). An historical perspective on the career development profession: Career counseling as social activism. *Career Developments*, 14 (2), 1.

Potter, J. (1996). *Representing reality: Discourse, rhetoric and social construction*. London: Sage.

Reich, C. A. (1970). *The greening of America*. Harmondsworth: Penguin.

Richardson, M. S. (1993). Work in people's lives: A location for counseling psychologists. *Journal of Counseling Psychology*, 40, 425–433.

Riesman, D., Denny, R., & Glazer, N. (1960). *The lonely crowd*. New Haven: Yale University Press.

Roe, A. (1956). *The psychology of occupations*. New York: John Wiley & Sons.

Rogers, C. R. (1951). *Client centered therapy: Its current practice, implications and theory*. Boston: Houghton Mifflin.

Rosenbaum, J. E. (1989). Career systems and employee misperceptions. In M. B. Arthur, D. T. Hall, & B. S. Lawrence (Eds.), *Handbook of career theory*, (pp. 329–353). Cambridge: Cambridge University Press.

Schlaffer, H. (1989). *The bourgeois as hero* (J. Lynn, trans.). Cambridge: Polity Press.

Sennett, R. (1998). *The corrosion of character: The personal consequences of work in the new capitalism*. New York: W. W. Norton.

Shotter, J. (1992). Bakhtin and Billig: Monological versus dialogical practices. *American Behavioral Scientist, 36*, 8–21.

Super, D. E., Crites, J. O, Hummel, R. C., Moser, H. P., Overstreet, P. L., & Warnath, C. F. (1957). *Vocational development: A framework for research*. New York: Teachers College Press.

Super, D. E., Starishevsky, R., Matlin, N., & Jordaan, J. P. (1963). *Career development: Self-concept theory*. New York: College Entrance Examination Board.

Terkel, S. (1975). *Working*. London: Wildwood House.

Usher, R. & Edwards, R. (1998). Confessing all? In R. Edwards, R. Harrison, & A. Tait (Eds.), *Telling tales: Perspectives on guidance and counselling in learning* (pp. 211–222). London: Routledge.

Walsh, W. B. & Chartrand, J. M. (1994). Emerging directions of person–environment fit. In M. L. Savickas & R. W. Lent (Eds.), *Convergence in career development theories: Implications for science and practice* (pp. 187–195). Palo Alto, CA: CPP Books.

Watts, A. G. (1981). Career patterns. In A. G. Watts, D. E. Super, & J. M. Kidd (Eds.), *Career development in Britain: Some contributions to theory and practice* (pp. 213–245). Cambridge: CRAC/Hobsons.

Weick, K. E. & Berlinger, L. R. (1989). Career improvisation in self-designing organizations. In M. B. Arthur, D. T. Hall, & B. S. Lawrence (Eds.), *Handbook of career theory* (pp. 313–328). Cambridge: Cambridge University Press.

Whyte, W. H. (1956). *The organization man*. New York: Simon and Schuster.

Young, R. A. & Valach, L. (1996). Interpretation and action in career counseling. In M. L. Savickas & W. B. Walsh (Eds.), *Handbook of career counseling theory and practice* (pp. 361–375). Palo Alto, CA: Davies-Black.

Part 3

New directions for theory, practice, and policy

12 Reconceptualising career theory and research: an action-theoretical perspective

Richard A. Young and Ladislav Valach

The thesis of this chapter is that career can be reconceptualised as an interpretative construct used by people and heuristic for counselling practice. This reconceptualisation is responsive to the current context in which both the viability of the construct of 'career' as well as 'careers' themselves have been challenged (e.g. Hall & Associates, 1996; Richardson, 1993). The reconceptualisation of career espoused here can be seen as representing one of several approaches Savickas (1995) identified as contributing to the reform of vocational psychology as an interpretative discipline (Carlsen, 1988; Cochran, 1990, 1991, 1992, 1997; Collin & Young, 1986, 1988; Csikszentmihalyi & Beattie, 1979; Neimeyer, 1988; Ochberg, 1988; Peavy, 1992; Savickas, 1993, 1994; Young, 1988). Many of these authors have attempted to address problems that have arisen in our traditional understanding of career from what can be understood as a postmodern perspective, although not all explicitly refer to their perspectives as such.

Before making a case in favour of the reconceptualised view, and thus supporting the viability of the career construct, it is pertinent to review briefly the issues that have contributed to the death of career as it has been largely understood (e.g. Hall & Associates, 1996), and then to identify the salient constructs and trends that have emerged in the discussion of career from an interpretative perspective. The reconceptualised view presented in this chapter addresses the issues relevant to the death of career, uses and extends constructs that have emerged in other interpretative approaches, and provides a conceptual framework to foster renewed research and practice in the career domain.

The death of career

Notwithstanding the significant advances that have been evident in the career literature (e.g. Walsh & Osipow, 1996) and the strong interest in career from several constituencies (business, education, policy makers: e.g. Jackson, Arnold, Nicholson, & Watts, 1996), concern has been expressed about both the 'career' construct as we have come to use it professionally and the viability of 'careers' as that word is more commonly understood (e.g. Richardson, 1993). A range of factors has contributed to a postmodern perspective on career, including an undermining of 'reality' (Held, 1995), a rejection of monistic theories and universal foundations (Hoshmand, 1998), the loss of tradition (Giddens, 1991), and lack of faith in authority and progress. However, the impact of postmodernism is not confined to academic debates – these phenomena currently reflect the experience of many people. Postmodernism has practical consequences and is relevant to our political and social condition.

Broad societal issues in the death of career

A major factor in the purported death of career is its relationship to organisational bureaucracy. Savickas (1995) associates the emergence of 'career' with the bureaucratic form of large twentieth-century organisations: '[b]ureaucratic form provided the structure for organizations, and career provided a core value' (p. 17). Kanter (1989) suggested bureaucracy's ladder metaphor and logic of advancement underlay the experience of a large proportion of employed people in industralised countries and is reflected in career theory. However, Kanter and others maintain that the bureaucratic form of career cannot be sustained in light of current changes in organisations and the workplace.

The bureaucratic structure allowed us to organise many of a person's actions over an extended period of time, that is, their actions could be understood as related. We used the term 'career' to represent our understanding of this organisation of action. However, with the shifts in bureaucratic organisation, this means of constructing long-term action is no longer as viable as it once was. Kanter (1989) identified two other pre-existing forms of career, the professional career and the entrepreneurial career. The professional career assumes growth in craft, skills, knowledge, and reputation, and the entrepreneurial career is based on the creation of new value. These forms of career represent significant alternatives in the understanding of career because they recognise the changing nature of the workplace and suggest different metaphors such as the career as portfolio.

A second factor contributing to the death of career is its emphasis on individualism. A number of authors (e.g. Bauman, 1989; Giddens, 1991) have linked individualism to market-oriented consumption, and the industrialism it is based on. In challenging industrialism and market-oriented consumption, they question individualism as well. In her critique of the concept of career, Richardson (1993) suggests career is based on an ethos of self-centred individualism that contributes to the undermining of the social fabric of society. In this, Richardson reiterates a criticism that has been directed at psychology generally (Cushman, 1990; Sampson, 1993; Smith, 1994). Gergen (1994) suggested that the ideology of individualism contributes to both trivialisation of emotional relationships and a sense of isolation.

Richardson's (1993) solution to the problem of individualism in vocational psychology is to abandon the notion of career in favour of addressing the place of work in people's lives. She uses an extension of Hall's (1986) definition of work as an activity performed for the purpose of providing goods and services to others and in some way making a social contribution. By replacing the concept of 'career' with the concept, 'the activity of work', Richardson avoids the institutional or bureaucratic conceptualisation, and is able to address purposeful activity for social ends or outcomes. What is not as explicitly addressed in Richardson's formulation is purposeful action embedded in social processes. For reasons that will be evident later in the chapter, Richardson's position can be extended by including the psychological processes of linking activities together to make sense, and address the purpose, of work activities over the long term.

Not unrelated to the individualism that has pervaded modern psychology is a third factor in the death of career, the issue of meaning. Giddens (1991) placed personal meaninglessness at the centre of the modern dilemma: 'Underlying the most thoroughgoing processes of life-planning . . . is the looming threat of *personal meaninglessness*' (p. 201). Smith (1994) points to the loss of self: the masterful self is empty; the modern self experiences a significant absence of community, tradition, and shared meaning, 'the failure of hope is at the crux of our late modern predicament' (p. 407).

From the perspective of meaning, the breakdown of career results in fewer ways in which people are able to establish connection between actions in their lives over the long term and thus construct meaning for themselves and others. For example, society's concerns about young people's motivation for, and ability to commit to, long-term action, and about their connection to community, reflect this breakdown.

A critical question postmodernists ask is whether meaning is possible at all. As Gergen (1994) points out, deconstruction theories of meaning are not about the world, but he suggests meaning is essentially arrays of signifiers within a body of interrelated texts. Thus, Gergen has described the problem of meaning as an endless search for the signification of the signifier, only to be directed to another search. He locates the problem of meaning in the belief that the individual is the centre of meaning and proposes an alternative in which human meaning is found within the process of relationships. He paraphrases Shotter (1993) in suggesting that 'meaning is not born of action and reaction but of joint action' (p. 265).

Notwithstanding the concern for meaning, it is frequently only implicitly addressed or assumed in the vocational psychology literature. For example, it is not indexed in several recent career texts (Brown, Brooks & Associates, 1996; Savickas & Walsh, 1996) and a Psychological Abstracts literature search on 'career' and 'meaning' resulted in only a few 'hits'. Yet, as Gowler & Legge (1989) point out, the possibility of having a career as well as understanding career as a construct are contingent on using language to assign meanings to actions. Young, Valach, & Collin (1996) have already indicated that meaning is a salient dimension of a contextual explanation of career and identified contributions in the career literature in the domains of meaning as object (Cochran, 1990), knowledge (Young & Collin, 1992), and practice (Cochran, 1991; Neimeyer, 1992; Savickas, 1993).

The death of career in vocational psychology

In addition to the broad social issues affecting the death of career, a number of issues within vocational psychology challenge its future. Heppner, O'Brien, Hinkelman, and Flores (1996) identified several factors contributing to the diminishing role of career counselling in the future plans of counselling psychology trainees. A number of these factors can be attributed to the rift between career theory and practice (Lent & Savickas, 1994). Although Savickas and Walsh (1996) have addressed the integration of theory and practice, a fundamental difficulty remains when 'career' is seen as a theoretical rather than a 'practice' construct. The challenge to vocational psychologists, as Young and Valach (1996) suggest, is how ' "career" is and can be used to address how people construct and resolve problems in their daily life' (p. 362).

The dichotomy between career and personal counselling has also contributed to the death of career in vocational psychology and the usefulness of the career construct. Richardson (1996) identified three 'false splits' that have contributed to this dichotomy: the split between normal and pathological, the split of the person into domains of functioning that had the effect of isolating the occupational domain, and finally the split between the public (career) and the private (personal) that further isolates the domain of career counselling within the broad field of counselling psychology. These splits reflect aspects of the fundamental issues raised earlier, and suggest the need for an approach to career and counselling that can address them.

Notwithstanding Super's (1969) differentiation between a psychology of occupations and a psychology of careers, the latter being situated in the person and grounded in phenomenological experience, work, occupation, and career are commonly associated, as Richardson (1993) points out. Those who argue that anyone with a job has a career continue to ground career in the occupational realm. At the same time, the term 'career' is also used to reflect the involvement of persons over the long term in a number of other domains. For example, the person with a chronic illness can be said to have an illness career (e.g. Robinson, 1990), there is also a patient's career (e.g. Gerherdt, 1990), a criminal career (e.g. Harvey & Osgood, 1995), and a family career. In many of these careers the individual is related to a social organisational system. Thus, career can be considered as more than an occupation.

The interpretative stance in career psychology

Savickas (1995) grouped the efforts of a number of authors who responded to both broad societal issues and issues in vocational psychology that have been raised here as contributing to the death of career. Further, he suggested that in their efforts to reform vocational psychology, these authors challenge the discipline's fundamental assumptions and methodological imperative. The six contrasts he draws between the traditional theories of vocational psychology and the interpretative approaches address epistemological differences. However, not all the salient constructs and trends that have emerged in the discussion of career as an interpretative discipline provide the same perspective. A closer examination of the specific constructs that various interpretative authors use is also warranted because these constructs provide a basis for offering and understanding the reconceptualised view to be presented later in this chapter.

The construct of narrative

It is only since the early 1980s that narrative has become an explicit construct in many fields in the social sciences, including psychology, psychotherapy, and education. With the rise of interpretative approaches, narrative has become a popular and even central construct. The argument that narrative is the fundamental way in which we endow life with coherence has been made by a number of authors, including Bateson (1979), Cochran (1986, 1997), Howard (1989), MacIntyre (1984), Polkinghorne (1988), Sarbin (1986), and Spence (1982). In career psychology, for example, Cochran (1991) equates career and life story: 'a career is a life or life story. A career is the course that a particular life took from birth to death, what one would include if one were to write the story of one's life. Career development is the continual refinement, expansion, revision, and sometimes transcendence of a life story' (pp. 6–7). Many of these authors do not make the distinction that Gergen (1994) does in contrasting the individual and social narrative. He maintains that phenomenologists, existentialists, and personologists emphasise internal processes (indexed as experience) in narrative construction. While they stress a humanistic view of the person as author or agent, they do not consider cultural determinants as foreground. Most references to the use of narrative in career counselling rely on this humanistic perspective (e.g. Cochran, 1997; Jepsen, 1994; Polkinghorne, 1988; Savickas, 1991). Gergen, however, emphasises 'self narratives as forms of social accounting or public discourse' (p. 188). He recognises that the sociocultural origins of narrative construction are not arrived at through cultural determinism but through interacting with others. He also recognises the place of personal engagement in narrative, but 'replaces the emphasis on the self-determining ego with social interchange'. This effort to bring narrative closer to its social perspective is one of the challenges facing the conceptualisation of career. It addresses the individualism that has contributed to the death of career.

In her critique of the theory of postmodern psychotherapy, Held (1995) raises a second issue regarding narrative that has implications for career. She takes the view that postmodern narrative, particularly as represented in the narrative therapy movement, is divorced from reality. Held dichotomises reality and anti-reality, suggesting that the latter, represented by authors such as Anderson and Goolishian (1988) and White and Epston (1990) depicts linguistic and not extralinguistic reality. The same critique may be made of the use of narrative in career psychology if narrative has no referent beyond language. Divorcing narrative from reality, notwithstanding the epistemological question of how we know, presents some serious problems, but it may not be the best way to address its limitations. Rather, it may be more useful to recognise that, as Shotter (1993) suggested, we do not live wholly in narrative, we live by taking practical and symbolic action in our lives. The relationships between narrative and action and narrative and culture contribute to the resolution of this problem of the separation of narrative and reality. Once we bring narrative into fields like action and culture, we begin to address the problem of the separation of narrative and reality. Narrative is more than persons spinning stories as they sit in their armchairs.

Action and project

Richardson (1993) locates the phenomena that have been the focus of career development theories, research, and practice with the activity of work in people's lives rather than with career. This useful distinction is consistent with what is proposed in this chapter because it identifies activity as the focus of attention. The notion of action reflects the emphasis on intentionality and goal-directedness. It is closely related to people's everyday experience and to narrative. Other interpretative approaches have been equally concerned with the notion of action (Cochran & Laub, 1994; Polkinghorne, 1990). Less interpretative career approaches, for example social cognitive career theory (Lent, Brown, & Hackett, 1996) also refer to action and goals. The difference, however, is that many of these authors, irrespective of how interpretative their work is, focus on individual action to the exclusion of joint or group action and they do not address long-term action other than as narrative.

'Project' is a construct that has emerged as a solution to the somewhat time-limited and focused, although molar, understanding of action. Little, Lecci, and Watkinson (1992) refer to projects as middle-level analytic constructs that emphasise intentional action in context. They describe personal projects as 'extended sets of personally relevant action' (p. 502). Cochran (1992) refers to the career project as 'a personal theme and its related sets of tasks' (p. 189).

Role of emotion

We have noted elsewhere (Young & Valach, 1996) that the place of emotion in career psychology has been underrepresented, although it is given greater attention in interpretative than in non-interpretative approaches. However, there continues to be a focus on individual emotion and on emotion separate from action. There has also been a long tradition in counselling practice of affect as being distinct from, although related to, cognition. Despite this tradition, recent theories hypothesise a relationship between discrete emotions, motivational goals, and specific behaviours (Fridja, 1986; Roseman, Wiest, & Swartz, 1994). Campos and his colleagues (Campos, Campos, & Barrett, 1989) have also proposed a view of affect as a complex relational process rather than an intrapersonal state, in which both the person's appreciation of the significance of events and the way the person deals with them are recognised. These developments suggest a direction for incorporating emotion more directly into the way career is conceptualised.

Reconceptualised view of career

A central feature of the argument for a reconceptualised view of career is the connection between action and career. Elsewhere we have described the basis for an action-theoretical approach to career and career development (Valach, 1990; Young & Valach, 1996; Young, Valach, & Collin, 1996). This perspective is based on the notion that the intentional, goal-directed actions used by agents are conceptualised and analysed as oriented towards ends and processes or means to attain the ends (Cranach, Kalbermatten, Indermuehle, & Gugler, 1982). Action theory provides a language not only for understanding people in their everyday lives but also for dealing with socially embedded behaviour. As Young and Valach (1996) point out, 'goal-directed action is represented consciously and, as such, is used by most people as a framework to understand their own and others' behavior. Thus it is a self-governing or self-organizing system' (p. 364). In this perspective, we identify career as a superordinate construct that allows people to construct connections among actions, to account for effort, plans, goals, and consequences, to frame internal cognitions and emotions, and to use feedback and feed-forward processes. Furthermore, career is embedded in a network of meaning at the social level. Career then is a construct that people use to organise their behaviour over the long term.

The salient aspects of our action theory approach to career are represented in figure 12.1 (see also Young, Valach, & Collin, 1996). Four action systems are represented in the figure. The notion of individual action which is what some theorists refer to when they speak of action is only one of several action systems, the others are joint action, project, and career. Bronfenbrenner (1979) prefigured the notion of joint action by identifying action as a characteristic of the microsystem. Joint action, project, and career refer to systems of action that are socially embedded. Project and career represent systems of action of mid- and long-term duration respectively. In other words we are proposing that people do not limit their interpretations of behaviour to single, individually based actions, but link actions over the mid and long term, represented here by constructs such as project and career.

As a mid-term construct, project provides a link between action and career. Simply put, for many individuals for whom career is not a heuristic construct for a variety of reasons, the construct of project is helpful. More

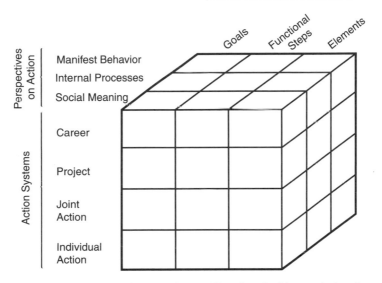

Figure 12.1. Aspects of action theory. (Reprinted with permission from D. Brown, L. Brooks and Associates, *Career choice and development* (3rd edn). Copyright 1996 Jossey-Bass, Inc., Publishers, 350 Sansome Street, San Francisco, CA 94104 (800) 956-7739.

complexly, action frequently needs to be recognised as embedded in a superordinate goal structure, represented at one level by project. For a reconceptualised view that is capable of addressing the issues raised earlier in this chapter, action also needs to be embedded in a network of meaning at the social level (Boesch, 1991) which is not explicit in all the literature that addresses action. In our conceptualisation, however, attention is directed to project as a social phenomenon. These projects (and the construct of the longer-term career) are joint undertakings that include the individual actions and goals of those involved.

The action-theoretical approach offers the basis for a reconceptualised view of career. This framework responds to the concern with the relatively tight link between career and jobs and occupations discussed earlier. The traditional career has been the culturally based means of constructing and making long-term commitments, at least for some people. In the bureaucratically based career, jobs allowed for the constructions of short-term commitments and provided simultaneous or subsequent opportunities for long-term commitments in terms of career. In our reconceptualised view, project, as we have described it previously, replaces the notion of 'jobs'. Maintaining a garden, learning to play a musical instrument, and providing good nutrition for one's children are examples of series of complex actions over a defined period of time that require commitment. As well, joint and individual actions are considered as short-term commitments.

This reconceptualisation of career involving action, joint action, and project seen in action-theoretical terms allows us to understand the apparent collapse of the traditional forms of career and their replacement by short-term jobs or contracts as a transition from the bureaucratic career to the socially embedded career. Career can still represent long-term commitments in one's life, but here career is conceptualised as a superordinate construct that organises or frames subordinate projects and actions. Thus, the changes in the bureaucratically based career that we are currently experiencing do not necessitate a shift from long-term commitments to short-term commitments or, in the case of unemployment, to no commitment at all. Rather we are proposing a shift from the traditional career to career as a superordinate construct that encompasses project and action. A more complex figure would incorporate, for example, reference to Kanter's (1989) entrepreneurial career as one of several alternatives to the bureaucratic career standing between the bureaucratic-based and the socially anchored career. The challenge to people generally, then, is how to construct socially embedded and long-term commitments from one's actions, joint actions, and projects. We suggest that career provides a viable construct for these processes.

By identifying the primary constructs of joint action, project, and career as social, this reconceptualised view of career substantially addresses the individualism that has characterised earlier career theories and research. Thus, the use of these constructs responds to Strong, Yoder, and Corcoran's (1995) recent suggestion that more counselling research should focus on joint action, a concept they see as fundamental to human agency and its enhancement. We (Young, Valach, Paseluikho et al., 1997b) have described joint action as the intentional behaviour of a group of people attempting to realise a common goal or engage in a common process. Shotter (1993) pointed out that dialogue with others is the most common place where joint action occurs and Martin (1994) uses conversation (the joint action of therapist and client) as the primary metaphor for therapy. As we noted (Young, Valach, & Collin, 1996), '[c]areer identity, values, interests, and behavior are not shaped from the outside "in"; rather, they are constructed, perhaps largely through language, in conversations with others' (p. 486). As superordinate constructs, project and career extend the assumption that many career-related actions occur between people, that is, they are social in nature.

Virtually all career development theories (e.g. Holland, 1997; Super, 1990) recognise the environment and the social context in which careers arise. However, to date, none has considered the extent to which it is constituted by joint actions. For example, we have demonstrated in research on this approach that exploration, previously associated with the career behaviour of individuals (e.g. Blustein, 1992; Thoresen & Krumboltz, 1967), is the property of joint actions in the form of conversations about career between parents and adolescents (Young *et al.*, 1997b). This is one of a number of studies that can be proposed in order to address career as a social construct. The relationships between counsellor and client, employer and employee, between coworkers, and between spouses are but a few of the significant relationships in which career (and project and joint action) are co-constructed. The contextual dimension is vitally important to the reconceptualised view because it addresses the shift from an individual to a social perspective. That is, it identifies the social unit as the unit of analyses in career research, and, for the practitioner, directs our attention to the joint construction of career.

The social basis of the action-theoretical perspective also addresses the issue of meaning. Gergen (1994) proposed that the issue of meaning is solved through joint action – which he describes as the basis of meaning. His view is that relationship rather than the individual is the fundamental unit of social life, and that social meaning precedes individual meaning. The language we have proposed – that is, action, joint action, project, and career – allows us to account for the social fabric of lives and thus respond to the relational basis for meaning. Meaning in career is constructed through common plans, joint projects, collaborative structures, etc. For example, it is in parent–adolescent conversations about career that the parties strive to establish a common ground for meaning through which issues between them, including disagreeable ones, are addressed.

In line with the recent views of emotion (Campos, Campos, & Barrett, 1989; Fridja, 1986), the role of emotion is explicitly identified in this view of career (Young & Valach, 1996; Young, Valach, & Collin, 1996). Emotion has a place in internal processes generally, it is connected to needs, goals, plans, and purposes, and is an energiser and motivator of action. It has been shown to be explicitly embedded in parent–adolescent conversations about career (Young, Paseluikho, & Valach, 1997a).

Research

In commenting on Richardson's (1993) proposal, Savickas (1994) suggested that the postmodern approach 'transforms vocational psychologists from detached testers of theory into participant observers who provide knowledge from instructive accounts provided by individual workers, accounts that describe the ordinary activities of everyday life' (p. 107). Career research from the action-theoretical perspective addresses several aspects of Savickas's (1994) statement: it is not directed as much to theory testing as it is descriptive of ordinary activities of everyday life. Where action-theoretical research differs from some interpretative research is that it does not rely solely on accounts from individuals. Rather it seeks data from three perspectives of the ordinary activities of everyday life: manifest behaviour, internal processes, and social meaning. By relying on these data sources, the focus of action-theoretical research is on action rather than on retrospective accounts. Our research (Young, Valach, Dillabough, Dover, & Matthes, 1994; Young *et al.*, 1997a, 1997b) has already developed procedures based on these perspectives. By using these procedures, we established a continuity with the long history of psychology and counselling psychology that has been concerned with manifest behaviour and internal (cognitive and affective) processes as well as with social meaning.

An action-theoretical research programme has the potential for addressing each of the cells of figure 12.1. In our own research which has focused on parent–adolescent conversations about career, we have been able to describe the cells of joint action, and infer to the cells of project and career. We have gathered parent–adolescent conversations about career through the use of video-tape and have used the video-tape immediately after the conversation to have the participants reflect on their internal processes (cognitions and emotions during the conversation) and the conversation's social meaning. When we examine these data, we are able to access career issues as a co-construction of parent and adolescent at the level of joint action. Other procedures will have to be developed to the levels of project and career more specifically.

Conclusion

This reconceptualised view of career addresses the salient issues raised broadly in society about the death of career as well as those endemic to vocational psychology. It moves away from a bureaucratically based to a socially based understanding of career that addresses both the long-, medium-, and short-term dimensions of goal-directed action. By using everyday constructs such as emotions, goals, intentions, and plans within the social context, this action-theoretical approach to career responds to issues of meaning, identity, and social change.

Our position is that by framing career from an action perspective and by identifying its component constructs, joint action and project, we offer a vocational psychology that speaks directly to practice. Thus, we are proposing a perspective that may prove helpful to both researchers and practitioners.

REFERENCES

Anderson, H. & Goolishian, H. A. (1988). Human systems as linguistic systems: Preliminary and evolving ideas about the implications for clinical theory. *Family Process*, *27*, 371–393.

Bateson, G. (1979). *Mind and nature*. New York: E. P. Dutton.

Bauman, Z. (1989). *Legislators and interpreters*. Cambridge: Polity Press.

Blustein, D. L. (1992). Applying current theory and research in career exploration to practice. *Career Development Quarterly*, *41*, 229–237.

Boesch, E. E. (1991). *Symbolic action theory and cultural psychology*. New York: Verlag.

Bronfenbrenner, U. (1979). *The ecology of human development: Experiments by nature and design*. Cambridge, MA: Harvard University Press.

Brown, D., Brooks, L., & Associates (1996). *Career choice and development* (3rd edn). San Francisco: Jossey-Bass.

Campos, J. J., Campos, R. G., & Barrett, K. C. (1989). Emergent themes in the study of emotional development and emotional regulation. *Developmental Psychology*, *25*, 394–402.

Carlsen, M. B. (1988). *Meaning-making: Therapeutic processes in adult development*. New York: Norton.

Cochran, L. (1986). *Portrait and story*. Westport, CT: Greenwood Press.

(1990). *The sense of vocation: A study of career and life development*. Albany, NY: State University of New York Press.

(1991). *Life-shaping decisions*. New York: Peter Lang.

(1992). The career project. *Journal of Career Development*, *18*, 187-198.

(1997). *Career counseling: A narrative approach*. Thousand Oaks, CA: Sage.

Cochran, L. & Laub, J. (1994). *Becoming an agent: Patterns and dynamics for shaping your life*. Albany, NY: State University of New York Press.

Collin, A. & Young, R. A. (1986). New directions for theories of career. *Human Relations*, *39*, 837–853.

(1988). Career development and hermeneutical inquiry: Part II – Undertaking hermeneutical inquiry. *Canadian Journal of Counselling*, *22*, 191–201.

Cranach, M. von, Kalbermatten, U., Indermuehle, K., & Gugler, B. (1982). *Goal-directed action* (M. Turton, trans.). London: Academic Press.

Csikszentmihalyi, M. & Beattie, O. (1979). Life themes: A theoretical and empirical exploration of their origins and effects. *Journal of Humanistic Psychology*, *19*, 45–63.

Cushman, P. (1990). Why the self is empty: Toward a historically situated psychology. *American Psychologist*, *45*, 599–611.

Fridja, N. H. (1986). *The emotions*. Cambridge: Cambridge University Press.

Gergen, K. J. (1994). *Realities and relationships: Soundings in social construction*. Cambridge, MA: Harvard University Press.

Gerherdt, U. (1990). Patient careers in end-stage renal failure. *Social Sciences and*

Medicine, 30, 1211–1224.

Giddens, A. (1991). *Modernity and self-identity: Self and society in the late modern age.* Cambridge: Polity Press.

Gowler, D. & Legge, K. (1989). Rhetoric in bureaucratic careers: Managing the meaning of management success. In M. B. Arthur, D. T. Hall, & B. S. Lawrence (Eds.), *Handbook of career theory* (pp. 437–453). Cambridge: Cambridge University Press.

Hall, D. T., & Associates (1996). *The career is dead: Long live the career: A relational approach to career.* San Francisco: Jossey-Bass.

Hall, R. H. (1986). *Dimensions of work.* Newbury Park, CA: Sage.

Harvey, J. & Osgood, D. W. (1995). Criminal careers in the short-term: Intra-individual variability in crime and its relation to local life circumstances. *American Sociological Review, 60,* 655–673.

Held, B. S. (1995). *Back to reality: A critique of postmodern theory in psychotherapy.* New York: Norton.

Heppner, M. J., O'Brien, K. M., Hinkelman, J. M., & Flores, L. Y. (1996). Training counseling psychologists in career development: Are we our own worst enemies? *Counseling Psychologist, 24,* 105–125.

Holland, J. L. (1997). *Making vocational choices: A theory of vocational personalities and work environments* (3rd edn). Odessa, FL: Psychological Assessment Resources.

Hoshmand, L. T. (1998). *Creativity and moral vision in psychology: Narratives on identity and commitment in a postmodern age.* Thousand Oaks, CA: Sage.

Howard, G. (1989). *A tale of two stories: Excursions into a narrative approach to psychology.* Notre Dame, IN: Academic Publications.

Jackson, C., Arnold, J., Nicholson, N., & Watts, A. G. (1996). *Managing careers in 2000 and beyond.* Report no. 304. Brighton: IES/CRAC.

Jepsen, D. (1994). The thematic-extrapolation method: Incorporating career patterns into career counseling. *Career Development Quarterly, 43,* 43–53.

Kanter, R. M. (1989). Careers and the wealth of nations: A macro-perspective on the structure and implications of career forms. In M. B. Arthur, D. T. Hall, & B. S. Lawrence (Eds.), *Handbook of career theory* (pp. 506–521). Cambridge: Cambridge University Press.

Lent, R. W., Brown, S. D., & Hackett, G. (1996). Career development from a social cognitive perspective. In D. Brown, L. Brooks, & Associates (Eds.), *Career choice and development* (3rd edn, pp. 373–421). San Francisco: Jossey-Bass.

Lent, R. W. & Savickas. M. L. (1994). Postscript: Is convergence a viable agenda for career psychology? In M. L. Savickas & R. W. Lent (Eds.), *Convergence in career development theories: Implications for science and practice* (pp. 259–271). Palo Alto, CA: CPP Books.

Little, B. R., Lecci, L., & Watkinson, B. (1992). Personality and personal projects: Linking big five and PAC units of analysis. *Journal of Personality, 60,* 501–525.

MacIntyre, A. (1984). *After virtue* (2nd edn). Notre Dame, IN: University of Notre Dame Press.

Martin, J. (1994). *The construction and understanding of therapeutic change: Conversations, memories, and theories.* New York: Teachers College Press.

Neimeyer, G. (1988). Cognitive integration and differentiation in vocational behavior. *Counseling Psychologist, 16,* 440–475.

(Ed.) (1992). Personal constructs in career counseling and development [thematic issue]. *Journal of Career Development, 43,* 161–177.

Ochberg, R. (1988). Life stories and the psychological construction of careers. In D. McAdams & R. Ochberg (Eds.), *Psychobiography and life narratives* (pp. 173–204). Durham, NC: Duke University Press.

Peavy, R. V. (1992). A constructivist model of training career counselors. *Journal of Career Development, 18,* 215–229.

Polkinghorne, D. E. (1988). *Narrative knowing and the human sciences.* Albany, NY: State University of New York Press.

(1990). Action theory approaches to career research. In R. A. Young & W. A. Borgen (Eds.), *Methodological approaches to the study of career* (pp. 87–105). New York: Praeger.

Richardson, M. S. (1993). Work in people's lives: A location for counseling psychologists. *Journal of Counseling Psychology, 40,* 425–433.

(1996). From career counseling to counseling/psychotherapy and work, jobs, and career. In M. L. Savickas & W. B. Walsh (Eds.), *Handbook of career counseling theory and practice* (pp. 347–360). Palo Alto, CA: Davies-Black.

Robinson, I. (1990). Personal narratives, social careers, and medical courses: Analyzing life trajectories in autobiographies of people with multiple sclerosis. *Social Sciences and Medicine, 30,* 1173–1186.

Roseman, I. J., Wiest, C., & Swartz, T. S. (1994). Phenomenology, behaviors, and goals differentiate discrete emotions. *Journal of Personality and Social Psychology, 67,* 206–221.

Sampson, E. E. (1993). Identity politics: Challenges to psychology's understanding. *American Psychologist, 48,* 1219–1230.

Sarbin, T. (1986) *Narrative psychology.* New York: Praeger.

Savickas, M. L. (1991). The meaning of love and work: Career issues and interventions. *Career Development Quarterly, 39,* 315–324.

(1993). Career counseling in the postmodern era. *Journal of Cognitive Psychotherapy: An International Quarterly, 7,* 205–215.

(1994). Vocational psychology in the postmodern era: Comment on Richardson (1993). *Journal of Counseling Psychology, 41,* 105–107.

(1995). Current theoretical issues in vocational psychology: Convergence, divergence, and schism. In W. B. Walsh & S. H. Osipow (Eds.), *Handbook of vocational psychology: Theory, research, and practice* (2nd edn, pp. 1–34). Mahwah, NJ: Erlbaum.

Savickas, M. L. & Walsh, W. B. (Eds.) (1996). *Handbook of career counseling theory and practice.* Palo Alto, CA: Davies-Black.

Shotter, J. (1993). *Conversational realities.* London: Sage.

Smith, M. B. (1994). Selfhood at risk: Postmodern perils and the perils of postmodernism. *American Psychologist, 49,* 405–411.

Spence, D. (1982). *Narrative truth and historical truth.* New York: Norton.

Strong, S., Yoder, B., & Corcoran, J. (1995). The 1993 Leona Tyler address – Counseling: A social process for constructing personal power. *Counseling Psychologist, 23,* 374–384.

Super, D. E. (1969). Vocational development theory: Persons, positions, and processes. *Counseling Psychologist, 1*, 2–9.

—— (1990). A life-span, life-space approach to career development. In D. Brown, D. Brooks, & Associates (Eds.), *Career choice and development: Applying contemporary theories to practice* (2nd edn, pp. 197–261). San Francisco, CA: Jossey-Bass.

Thoresen, C. E. & Krumboltz, J. D. (1967). Relationship of counselor reinforcement of selected responses to external behavior. *Journal of Counseling Psychology, 14*, 140–144.

Valach, L. (1990). A theory of goal-directed action in career analysis. In R. A. Young & W. A. Borgen (Eds.), *Methodological approaches to the study of career* (pp. 107–126). New York: Praeger.

Valach, L., Young, R. A., & Lynam, M. J. (1996). Family health promotion projects: An action theoretical perspective. *Journal of Health Psychology, 1*, 49–63.

Walsh, W. B. & Osipow, S. H. (Eds.) (1996). *Handbook of vocational psychology: Theory, research, and practice.* Mahwah, NJ: Erlbaum.

White, M. & Epston, D. (1990). *Narrative means to therapeutic ends.* New York: Norton.

Young, R. A. (1988). Ordinary explanations and career theories. *Journal of Counseling and Development, 66*, 336–339.

Young, R. A. & Collin, A. (Eds.) (1992). *Interpreting career. Hermeneutical studies of lives in context.* Westport, CT: Praeger.

Young, R. A., Paseluikho, M. A., & Valach, L. (1997a). The role of emotion in the construction of career in parent–adolescent conversations. *Journal of Counseling and Development, 76*, 36–44.

Young, R. A. & Valach, L. (1996). Interpretation and action in career counseling. In M. L. Savickas & W. B. Walsh (Eds.), *Handbook of career counseling theory and practice* (pp. 361–375). Palo Alto, CA: Davies-Black.

Young, R. A., Valach, L., & Collin, A. (1996). A contextual explanation of career. In D. Brown, L. Brooks, & Associates, *Career choice and development* (3rd edn, pp. 477–512). San Francisco: Jossey-Bass.

Young, R. A., Valach, L., Dillabough, J.-A., Dover, C., & Matthes, G. (1994). Career research from an action perspective: The self-confrontation procedure. *Career Development Quarterly, 43*, 185–196.

Young, R. A., Valach, L., Paseluikho, M. A., Dover, C., Matthes, G. E., Paproski, D., & Sankey, A. (1997b). The joint action of parents in conversation about career. *Career Development Quarterly, 46*, 72–86.

13 A new perspective for counsellors: from career ideologies to empowerment through work and relationship practices

Mary Sue Richardson

This chapter is written in the context of the radical economic and social changes, particularly changes in paid work, presently occurring in the United States and the rest of the world that have been addressed in earlier chapters of this book. Rapid change, while stressful and anxiety-provoking, also provides unique opportunities to see more clearly the impact of the social system on individuals in that system. My contention in this chapter is that while the career-related practice of counselling professionals in the United States developed ostensibly to aid individuals or groups of individuals with choices, plans, and development with respect to paid work, it is influenced by associated career ideologies largely serving the needs of the economy.

The goal of this chapter is to open up a space for a reflexive consideration of how the professional practice of counselling can best serve the needs of people, rather than, or in addition to, the needs of the economy. I hope to encourage a more open dialogue between the needs and desires of people and the needs of the economy. This space will be constructed through a critical analysis of career ideologies and the development of a more person-sensitive perspective on the significance of work in people's lives. It is hoped that such a perspective will encourage a professional practice of counselling supportive of personal empowerment and sensitive to the needs of all groups in society rather than a practice overly dominated by the needs of the economy and the prevailing power distributions. While this analysis is based on experience in the United States, I hope it will prove useful to counselling practitioners in other cultural contexts.

What I mean to convey by the term 'career ideology' is that the ways we think about career, reflections of theories, models, and intervention modalities in the career field, operate as a lens that shapes perceptions and experience related to work. In short, ideas about career socially construct the experience of work. To suggest that this construction is an ideology is to suggest that it serves the needs of some groups at the expense of other groups in a society (Mannheim, 1962). In this way, ideologies perpetuate existing hierarchies of privilege.

To examine the impact of career ideologies on experience, the concept of practice as it has developed in the feminist and cultural psychology literatures is useful. Both of these literatures have struggled to understand the influence of the social system on personality. Connell (1987), a gender theorist, provides a theory of mutual influence between the individual and the society in which the conception of practice is central. He defines practice simply as what people do. In his theory, the two components of the individual and society are mutually constitutive – that is, they construct each other. The individual and society also can be examined separately as coherent objects of study. His conception of practice knits together these two levels of influence. If one is interested in the perspective of the individual, that is, in what an individual does and how an individual makes sense of what he or she does, this constitutes the study of personality. A personality is a set of practices, a 'particular unification of diverse and often contradictory practices' (p. 222). Practices of individuals over time constitute the structure of personality. Work can be considered a set of important and central practices of a person.

This definition of personality is radically different from prevailing ideas of personality, at least in Western cultures, which tend to attribute personality traits and characteristics to individuals while also acknowledging the influence of the social and developmental context on traits (Maddi, 1996). Thinking of personality as a set of practices decentres the notion of personality from within a person to the actions and practices of persons operating in the world. This focus on what people do in social contexts resonates with action theory, as developed and applied to career analysis by Valach (1990) and Young and Valach (1996).

Further, according to Connell, if one is interested in the perspective of the social structure, the focus shifts to collective practices of groups of people. Collective practices, from day-to-day activities to more formal activities, in turn, become entrenched and institutionalised as social structures. Such collective practices both guide and constrain future practices, both for persons considered singly and for groups of persons. Socially structured practices exist at different levels of sophistication, formalisation, and institutionalisation. Professional practices, such as medical practice, legal practice, or counselling practice are examples of collective, institutionalised, and highly developed socially structured practices. Counselling practice, as I am using the term here, refers to what counsellors or counselling professionals do, including the production of theory and research and the provision of services to people. Counselling practice is part of the social system that influences and is constitutive of individual practices, and thereby, of individual experience and lives.

A definition of practice more inclusive than simply what people do is provided by Miller and Goodnow (1995). They define practice as 'actions that are repeated, shared with others in a social group, and invested with normative expectations, meaning, or significance that go beyond the immediate goals of the action' (p. 7). This definition more clearly conveys the ways in which practice is influenced by culture, including prevailing ideologies.

I am interested in the impact of the career-related practice of counsellors and the associated career ideologies on individual subjective experience. In order to develop the critique of the old and the new career ideologies, the model of subjective experience used in this chapter is briefly described. It is influenced by current psychoanalytic theory regarding subjectivity, identity, and multiple-self states (Kennedy, 1997; Mitchell, 1991; Seligman & Shanok, 1995), feminist writings on multiple selves (Flax, 1993), and conceptions of self in cultural psychology (Markus, Mullally, & Kitayama, 1997). It refers to consciously experienced self-experiences as well as to less conscious substrata associated with self-experience. It is as if consciously felt self-experience is the tip of the iceberg of subjective experience, with the rest of the iceberg forming and reforming with the ongoing transactions of the person with the social world. Rather than a conception of self as a single and unified centre of experience, this model of subjective experience allows for multiple centres or positions of experience, centres or positions that have some kind of organisation with a dynamic tension between fragmentation and coherence. In the language of practice used in this chapter, the multiple practices of daily life affect diverse centres of subjective experience. Subjective experience is a product of the transactions between the individual and the social world rather than solely a reflection of self or identity. Furthermore, these transactions are typically patterned by culturally sanctioned practices.

My argument is that the subjective experience of work practice in contemporary culture has been shaped by counselling practice related to career and the associated career ideologies in the United States in ways that may not necessarily be optimal for individual well-being or for the well-being of all groups in the society. Further, I argue that counselling practice, developed along the lines of a new perspective focusing on empowerment, work, and relationship practices, will contribute to a shaping of subjective experience regarding work and relationship that is more productive and useful than practice unwittingly associated with prevailing career ideologies.

Career ideologies

The notion that career ideologies affect career-related counselling practice can be traced to Sherman (1988) who analysed the development of the ideology of vocational choice in relation to the social history of the United States in the early twentieth century. While a thorough historical analysis of what I refer to as the traditional and the new career ideology is beyond the scope of this chapter, the defining attributes of the social and economic times that shaped these ideologies are briefly indicated. The traditional career ideology emerged in mid-century United States following the Second World War. The growth of the economy was fuelled by the returning war veterans and the peacetime economic expansion that followed. According to Bell (1976) the economic sector and occupational structure crossed the boundary from an industrial to a post-industrial society, with a significant shift from blue-collar to white-collar occupations and the enormous growth of the middle class. As these changes were occurring, the baby-boom generation was born and suburban America settled. These factors contributed to the increasing separation between public and private worlds, with public referring to the developing economy and occupational structure and private referring to the domain of home, family, and personal relationships. This distinction between public and private worlds was enshrined in sociological theory by Parsons and Bales (1955) as one that enabled a mutually supportive and synergistic relationship between the two domains of life. The public–private split became increasingly gendered following the Second World War with production localised in the male-dominated public domain and reproduction in the female world of home and family. This, at least, was true for the white middle class in the United States.

It was also during this time that psychology as a profession was undergoing rapid expansion and professionalisation. The vocational guidance and counselling profession that developed early in the twentieth century received a significant boost in the 1950s with its marriage to psychology, a marriage that led to the birth of counselling psychology (Whiteley, 1984). Counselling psychologists, in turn, were largely responsible for elaborating notions of career and career development constitutive of the traditional career ideology (Holland, 1959, 1973; Super, 1957, 1969, 1980).

The ideology associated with these ideas regarding career that emerged during this time period has three significant components. First, it fosters a belief that a career is a product of individual effort and talent rather than a joint product of a person, position, and an occupation or profession. One might say that the idea of career was oversaturated with psychology and an individualistic point of view. Second, an over-identification of self with career is encouraged that leads to the quintessential American experience that a person is what he or she 'does', and what he or she 'does' primarily refers to paid work in the occupational structure. What a person 'does' in other areas of life becomes marginalised (Richardson, 1993). Third, I believe that this ideology may encourage an exaggerated focus on success in paid work as a source of self-esteem, at least among some groups.

In terms of the model of subjective experience described earlier in this chapter, this ideology encourages a split between the subjective experience of paid work and the rest of life, with an overvaluation of paid work and an undervaluation of unpaid work. It contributes to an unequal distribution of self-esteem along the lines of this bifurcation, with paid work and activities in the public world having a potentially greater impact on self-esteem than unpaid work or other activities in the personal or private world. One might say that the American psyche has been powerfully shaped by mid-century capitalistic economy through this career ideology to serve the needs of the economy, and, especially, the needs of some groups. It has been highly successful in helping to produce loyal, committed, and stable workers who seek to express themselves in the line of paid work they are pursuing.

This ideology, however, has a differential impact according to privilege. To the extent that the traditional ideology of career is endorsed, and success is believed to be due to individual talents and efforts, then persons with privilege, who have greater access to 'good' careers, that is, careers that provide a high level of socially valued rewards, have greater access to more powerful sources of self-esteem. Conversely, those less favoured by privilege, who do not have the same opportunities to develop a career associated with such rewards, may not be as likely to reap the rewards of self esteem due to career success. They may be far more vulnerable to experiencing their careers as sources of diminished self-esteem.

I do not mean to imply that a privileged background is synonymous with success, that lack of privilege inevitably predicts less rewarding occupational work, or that self-esteem is largely determined by career success. I am suggesting, however, that a career system shaped by this traditional ideology of career tends to distribute self-esteem along the lines of privilege and that, in this sense, it operates in the service of the prevailing power structure.

Although the traditional career ideology has been enormously successful in the extent to which it has shaped American consciousness and subjective experience regarding careers, its power is fast eroding. According to Hall and Mirvis (1996), the contract between the individual and the organisation – what they refer to as the career contract – has been dead since the 1980s. It is only in the past few years that this death has been acknowledged. Just as the career contract is dead, so too is the traditional ideology of career for which the expected link between the individual and the organisation no longer exists.

New notions of career and a new career ideology are emerging to replace the old one (Hage & Powers, 1992; Hall & Mirvis, 1996; Howard, 1995; Waterman, Waterman, & Collard, 1994). These new notions of career celebrate change and the need for individuals to be independent of organisations in shaping their careers. They refer to self-managed careers, promote expectations for self-managed and multiple careers, for lateral career moves rather than progressive or upward ones, and encourage expectations of lifetime learning and lifetime self-development. These new notions value complex, creative, and flexible people, skilled in the symbolic communication necessary in this new world. The old notion that individuals have defining talents and capabilities that suit them for specific jobs is a liability. What is needed instead is the ability and motivation to develop new talents and capabilities in response to the changing needs and demands of the economy.

The protean career concept of Hall and Mirvis (1996) is a seemingly more psychologically sensitive version of the new career. 'Protean' refers to Lifton's (1993) suggestion that in order to adapt and survive the fragmentation of the modern world, selves need to be self-regenerating – that is, protean. The protean career has a number of distinguishing characteristics. First, it replaces the notion of a linear and progressive career path with one that acknowledges flexible and idiosyncratic career movement. The idea of career path is replaced with that of career fingerprint, prized for its uniqueness. Second, it enlarges career to include home and family commitments as part of career and encourages the valuation of these commitments in self-definitions of psychological success. Third, it places the individual at the centre of the career as figure with the organisation and occupation considered as ground.

The ideology underlying these newer notions of career has a number of facets. First, the oversaturation of the construct of career with psychological meaning, identified in the traditional career ideology, is taken to the extreme. In this new version, the person, more than ever, is his or her career. The individual now is wholly responsible for his or her career and, by implication, for his or her success in that career. Second, this career now includes both public and private spheres of life. Whereas in the traditional career ideology, the focus was limited to the developmental progression of a person in his or her paid work, the new ideology collapses the private and public domains and ignores the differences between them. A third feature of this ideology is a belief in personal self-sufficiency.

Psychological resources and personal resiliency are believed to compensate for the security, predictability, and safety formerly provided, at least in part, by stable employment. It is American individualism at its most extreme. A fourth feature of this ideology is a belief that everyone can be creative, adaptable, and flexible. It is as if everyone can or ought to have the characteristics of an entrepreneur.

It is my contention that these features of the new career ideology, in fact, serve the needs of a new capitalistic order that requires workers who do not believe that they should depend on an employer to provide the safety and security long associated with stable employment, and that enables managers more easily to dispense with workers as needed. The protean career fits all too well with what has been called a ruthless economy (Head, 1996), while, at the same time, the role of this economy in dictating the shape of the new career is either obscured or glorified.

The danger to self-esteem noted in the traditional career ideology is magnified in this new ideology. If a person essentially is his or her career, career success may have a greater impact on self-esteem. Persons without the psychological resilience or psychological resources, who do not fit the psychological profile of an entrepreneur, or who have needs for safety, stability, and economic security, may be more prone to feel like personal as well as career failures. Furthermore, the inclusion of personal, family, and paid work domains in the new career, while not falsely separating private and public life, minimises a basic distinction between these domains – that is, the distinction between paid and unpaid work. Ignoring this difference glosses over the extent to which the traditional social contract between employees and employers has been abrogated in the new economy. Workers, more than ever, are on their own. The new career ideology fully embraces this reality.

It can be expected that privilege will continue to insidiously affect access to the resources needed to succeed in this economy. Reich (1991), for example, argues that skills in symbolic analysis are necessary for success in the new economy and the new workplace. Those who lack these skills are not as likely to succeed, and, among these, it can be expected, will be a disproportionate number of poor, less educated, and non-white Americans. For these, the new career ideology may only enhance a sense of failure.

To critique this new career ideology is problematic for those involved in developing counselling practices designed to help people to cope with the changing realities of paid work. Social criticism of the ways in which a career ideology serves the needs of the economy and those who are privileged in this system doesn't do much to help those who need to survive and hope to prosper. One could argue that many of the features of the new career concepts and ideology will help people to cope with and survive in a changing world. My point, so far, however, is to argue that the ideologies of career, both traditional and new, are problematic. In the next section of this chapter I suggest a perspective that I hope will be more helpful than these career ideologies to individuals in an uncertain and changing world.

A new perspective for counsellors: empowerment through work and relationship practices

This new perspective for counsellors is responsive to the collapse of stability and long-term security in paid work. The contention by Hall and Mirvis (1996) that the old career contract is, for all intents and purposes, dead, or, at the very least, seriously ailing, is valid. It is important to note that loss of stable structures and normative expectations in adult lives is not specific to the occupational context. Loss of stable structures pervades all arenas of contemporary life, including marriage, family, and even sexual orientations.

Central to the new perspective is the notion of empowerment, drawn primarily from the literature in feminist counselling and therapy (Brown & Root, 1990; Surrey, 1987), especially the empowerment model of Worell and Remer (1992). This literature distinguishes between power over others and empowerment – that is, the power to improve one's own life without any necessary connotation that this requires power over another person (Yoder & Kahn, 1992). What is particularly significant about empowerment is that it conceptualises a person more clearly in the social contexts of her or his life. For the purposes of this chapter, empowerment is defined as the capacity to (1) identify goals, (2) develop and utilise personal resources in order best to attain identified goals, and (3) negotiate with the environment to provide needed resources for goal attainment.

This definition reframes the concept of agency in a social context (Richardson, 1994). Agency, in turn, has long been considered a central dimension of personality development, a proposition supported by theory and research (Bakan, 1966; Blatt & Blass, 1992). According to Bakan, agency encompasses the capacity to be self-directed, that is, to pursue one's goals, and to master the environment. The first component of the definition of empowerment used here refers to the goal-directionality of agentic behaviour while the second and third components refer to mastery. Each of these components of empowerment are critical in enabling persons to respond to the new and emerging social contexts of contemporary life.

Narrative theory, which seeks to understand how people make sense of or give meaning to their lives (Polkinghorne, 1988), sheds additional light on the significance of the ability to identify goals. At the centre of the search for meaning, according to Bruner (1990), is an agentic self guided by intentional states, that is, beliefs, desires, and needs. These intentional states are goals towards which people strive. Goal-directed behaviour, then, can be construed as enhancing the development of meaning and the enrichment of the narrative texture of individual lives. In the language of narrative theory, the collapse of old story lines provided by a fast receding social order creates the opportunity to develop new story lines in response to individually generated goals.

The identification of goals is complicated by a postmodern worldview in which subjectivity has been problematised. The postmodern position questions whether goals can, indeed, be self-generated or whether such goals merely reflect what social structures and contexts allow. In response to this challenge, proponents of feminist theory and other philosophically oriented theorists (Flax, 1993; Kruks, 1992; Mahoney & Yngvesson, 1992; Williams, 1994) have argued persuasively for the possibility of agentic self-direction despite its problematised status.

Furthermore, identification of goals needs to be construed as a process. In light of the conceptualisation of self and subjectivity developed in the introduction to this chapter, subjective experience arises in interaction with the multiple social contexts of life. If it is posited that these contexts are rapidly changing, then, so too, is subjective experience, including subjectivity regarding goals. A consideration of goals and goal identification as a process shifts the notion of planning from projection into a more or less distant future, to a process in need of continual revision in relation to the changing contexts of daily life.

The second and third components of empowerment – that is, to develop personal resources and to negotiate with the environment – can be construed as reflective of competence motivation, that is, the motivation to interact effectively with the environment (White, 1959). This motivational theory, highly relevant to work issues, has been eclipsed by the focus in career practice over the past several decades on motivational theories based on self-expressive needs and motivations (e.g. Super's theory that people are motivated to express themselves in choosing an occupation or career). In the language of this chapter, competence motivation refers to the motivation to be competent in the multiple practices constitutive of personality enacted in the multiple and changing contexts of contemporary life. It is my contention that placing competence motivation at the centre of this new counselling perspective enables a broader scope for personal development than self-expressive needs and motivations.

The third component of empowerment, to negotiate with the environment, further distinguishes this perspective from traditional counselling theory in that it acknowledges the social context of peoples' lives and the ways in which this context can be either supportive or undermining, empowering or disempowering. Current research on early child development provides a metaphor illustrative of its meaning. Infant–caregiver interactions reveal a finely attuned social system in which infant attributes both are shaped by, and shape, the caregiving adult (Beebe & Lachmann, 1988; Sander, 1991; Stern, 1985). Infant goal-directed and competent behaviours emerge in a caregiving environment in which the infant is able to influence the caregiver to give the needed and desired responses (Rustin, 1997). Implicit in this description of the infant is the ability or willingness of the caregiver to be so influenced. Conversely, lack of goal-directed competent behaviour results either from the infant's inability to influence the caregiver and/or the caregiver's inability or unwillingness to be so influenced. Similarly, this third component of empowerment construes the individual as able to identify and pursue goals only in a system that is willing and able to provide needed resources.

While the definition of empowerment here does not assume oppressive or discriminatory external conditions, it does include that possibility. The capacity to negotiate with and influence the social context to provide needed resources may or may not require one to challenge oppressive social conditions. In any case, attention to and sensitisation regarding external conditions and their impact on people's lives is more protective of self-esteem than the career ideologies analysed earlier. Responsibility for outcome is shared by the individual and the social system. Self-reliance is not privileged nor are potentially aversive social forces ignored. This is an important corrective both for clients in understanding their lives and for counsellors in their efforts to help clients improve their lives. An awareness that people can only be empowered in a social system that is committed to empowering them directs attention and efforts of counsellors and counselling practice both to individual lives and to social conditions. In other words, the world is changing and people need to be empowered both to adapt to this world and to influence the world to adapt to their needs, desires, and goals. The perspective for counsellors that I propose is responsive to both sides of this interaction, while, at the same time, recognising the forces of social construction that are shaping both the individual and the social world.

Work as empowering practice

Up to this point the description of this new perspective has focused on empowerment without specific regard to work practice as a critical venue for empowerment. For my purposes, work practice is defined as practice that provides goods or services of value to others in both public and personal domains of life, or that prepares one to produce such goods or services. Work practice may be paid or unpaid. This is, in part, a fairly traditional definition, similar to that provided by Hall (1986). It is nontraditional in that it explicitly includes both paid and unpaid work practices. By defining work practice instead of work, it distinguishes between work – that which is accomplished by the worker – and the activity of the worker – that is, work practice.

As argued earlier, to focus only on paid work marginalises unpaid work, most of which is performed by women, and perpetuates the split between the private and the public spheres of life. Though this split was considered functional by Parsons and Bales (1955), it may be increasingly dysfunctional in the contemporary world for both genders (Kanter, 1977). Further, this definition of work practice, while acknowledging work practice in both spheres of life, enables the recognition of differences between work practices that are paid and those that are unpaid, a distinction minimised in the new career ideology.

It is a central thesis of this chapter that work practices in both public and private domains of life are critical empowering practices. They are socially located practices that provide significant opportunities for the development of socially valued, goal-directed activities that foster and enable the development of competence and mastery. The identification of goals in relation to work practices is enriched by the action theory of careers (Young & Valach, 1996), particularly the idea of project. Project is described as a construction superordinate to actions and goals that extends over a longer time frame than action and that serves to knit together a set of inter-related goals and actions. Similarly, in the application of an empowerment model to work practices, it is useful to include the identification of work-related projects as well as goals, with project referring to a set of evolving, interconnected, and socially located goals and practices. Personal narratives evolve, in part, through the process of identifying and pursuing work-related goals and projects that, in turn, give direction and meaning to work practices.

The location of competence motivation at the centre of the empowerment model is particularly important. While people may have a wide range of goals across multiple domains of life, work practices, in particular, in both public and private domains, enable and require competence. As such, work practices may be especially important for counselling practices committed to the empowerment of clients. To include both paid and unpaid work practices in public and private domains of life enlarges the possibilities for empowerment across the varied and shifting social contexts of contemporary life. Conversely, to ignore work in either domain diminishes the possibilities for empowerment and may, in fact, be construed as disempowering. If counselling practice does not attend to the full range of human intentionality and competence, it participates in a socially induced diminution of the potential meanings available to human beings for living full and productive lives.

The emphasis on negotiation in the empowerment model resonates with current hermeneutic interpretative research on career counselling. This research has identified the client's active negotiation with the social context, including the social context of the counselling dyad and the larger social context of the client's life, as the central metaphor of the counselling (Vähämättönen, 1998). This contrasts with a more traditional focus on client change that puts the onus of adaptation on the client.

So far, the use of the term 'career' has been deliberately avoided in the description of this new perspective. Although it is possible to include both paid and unpaid work in a new definition of career, I prefer work for several reasons. First, it is not invested with the ideologies of career. Second, it emphasises the social values of work, regardless of whether it is paid or unpaid, as opposed to the individual achievement values with which career is invested. Thereby, it provides a more solid foundation for self-esteem for a broader range of people. In this light, the term 'career' diminishes the significance and meaning of work, especially the social values of diverse work practices across life domains.

Empowerment through work and relationship practices

Although the focus in this chapter is on career and work, the definition of empowerment can refer to intentionality or goal-directed behaviour and the development of competence in relation to communal or relationship issues and practices as well as to work practices. While it is tempting to limit the focus in this perspective to work, a more holistic perspective is suggested that encompasses empowerment across both work and relationship practices (Surrey, 1987). This more holistic approach is an attempt to avoid dualistic thinking that tends to split reality and promotes both hierarchy and marginalisation (Griscom, 1992). Particularly in the kind of challenging contemporary world that is presently taking shape, people need to be fully empowered across the multiple contexts of their lives and in relation to both work and relationship practices. It is the thesis of this chapter that counselling practice is a significant social practice that can make a major contribution not only in helping people through services provided, but, in fact, in shaping how people think about their work and their relationships. In so doing, counselling practice is a powerful force that shapes subjective experience in the first place.

REFERENCES

Bakan, D. (1966). *The duality of human existence: An essay on psychology and religion.* Chicago: Rand McNally.

Beebe, B. & Lachmann, F. (1988). The contribution of mother–infant mutual influence to the origins of self and object representations. *Psychoanalytic Psychology,* 5, 305–337.

Bell, D. (1976). *The coming of post-industrial society: A venture in social forecasting.* New York: Basic Books.

Blatt, S. J. & Blass, R. B. (1992). Relatedness and self-definition: Two primary dimensions in personality development, psychopathology, and psychotherapy. In J. W. Barron, M. N. Eagle, & D. L. Wolitzky (Eds.), *Interface of psychoanalysis and psychology* (pp. 399–428). Washington, DC: American Psychological Association.

Brown, L. S. & Root, M. P. P. (Eds.) (1990). *Diversity and complexity in feminist therapy.* New York: Haworth Press.

Bruner, J. S. (1990). *Acts of meaning.* Cambridge, MA: Harvard University Press.

Connell, R. W. (1987). *Gender and power: Society, the person and sexual politics.* Stanford, CA: Stanford University Press.

Flax, J. (1993). *Disputed subjects: Essays on psychoanalysis, politics, and philosophy.* New York: Routledge.

Griscom, J. L. (1992). Women and power: Definition, dualism, and difference. *Psychology of Women Quarterly,* 16, 389–414.

Hage, J. & Powers, C. (1992). *Post-industrial lives: Roles and relationships in the 21st century.* Newbury Park, CA: Sage.

Hall, D. T. & Mirvis, P. H. (1996). The new protean career: Psychological success and the path with a heart. In D. T. Hall, & Associates, *The career is dead: Long live the career: A relational approach to careers* (pp. 13–45). San Francisco: Jossey-Bass.

Hall, R. H. (1986). *Dimensions of work.* Beverly Hills, CA: Sage.

Head, S. (1996). The new, ruthless economy. *New York Review of Books,* 29 February, 47–52.

Holland, J. L. (1959). A theory of vocational choice. *Journal of Counseling Psychology,* 6, 35–45.

(1973). *Making vocational choices: A theory of careers.* Englewood Cliffs, NJ: Prentice Hall.

Howard, A. (1995). Rethinking the psychology of work. In A. Howard (Ed.), *The changing nature of work* (pp. 513–555). San Francisco: Jossey-Bass.

Kanter, R. M. (1977). *Work and family in the United States: A critical review and agenda for research and policy.* New York: Russell Sage Foundation.

Kennedy, R. (1997). On subjective organization: Toward a theory of subject relations. *Psychoanalytic Dialogues, 7,* 553–582.

Kruks, S. (1992). Gender and subjectivity: Simone de Beauvoir and contemporary feminism. *SIGNS, 18,* 89–110.

Lifton, R. J. (1993). *The protean self: Human resilience in an age of fragmentation.* New York: Basic Books.

Maddi, S. R. (1996). *Personality theories: A comparative analysis.* Pacific Grove, CA: Brooks/Cole.

Mahoney, M. A. & Yngvesson, B. (1992). The construction of subjectivity and the paradox of resistance: Reintegrating feminist anthropology and psychology. *SIGNS, 18,* 44–73.

Mannheim, K. (1962). The meaning of ideology. In S. Nosow & W. H. Form (Eds.), *Man, work, and society: A reader in the sociology of occupations* (pp. 404–410). New York: Basic Books.

Markus, H. R., Mullally, P. R., & Kitayama, S. (1997). Selfways: Diversity in modes of cultural participation. In U. Neisser & D. Jopling (Eds.), *The conceptual self in context* (pp. 13–61). Cambridge: Cambridge University Press.

Miller, P. J. & Goodnow, J. J. (1995). Cultural practices: Toward an integration of development and culture. In J. J. Goodnow, P. J. Miller, & F. Kessell (Eds.), *Cultural practices as contexts for development: New directions in child development* (pp. 5–16). San Francisco: Jossey-Bass.

Mitchell, S. (1991). Contemporary perspectives on self: Toward an integration. *Psychoanalytic Dialogues, 2,* 121–148.

Parsons, T. & Bales, R. F. (1955). *Family socialization and interaction process.* Glencoe, IL: Free Press.

Polkinghorne, D. E. (1988). *Narrative knowing and the human sciences.* Albany, NY: State University of New York Press.

Reich, R. B. (1991). *The work of nations.* New York: Knopf.

Richardson, M. S. (1993). Work in people's lives: A location for counseling psychologists. *Journal of Counseling Psychology, 40,* 425–433.

   (1994). Agency/empowerment in clinical practice. *Journal of Theoretical and Philosophical Psychology, 14,* 40–49.

Rustin, J. (1997). Infancy, agency, and intersubjectivity: A view of therapeutic action. *Psychoanalytic Dialogues, 7,* 43–62.

Sander, L. W. (1991). Recognition process: Specificity and organization in early human development. Paper presented at University of Massachusetts Conference on the Psychic Life of the Infant: Origins of Human Identity.

Seligman, S. & Shanok, R. S. (1995). Subjectivity, complexity, and the social world: Erikson's identity concept and contemporary relational theories. *Psychoanalytic Dialogues, 5,* 537–566.

Sherman, P. R. (1988). *The origins and meaning of the ideology of vocational choice for women.* Unpublished doctoral dissertation, New York University, School of Education.

Stern, D. (1985). *The interpersonal world of the infant.* New York: Basic Books.

Super, D. E. (1957). *The psychology of careers.* New York: Harper and Row.

   (1969). Vocational development theory: Persons, positions, and processes. *Counseling Psychologist, 1,* 2–9.

(1980). A life-span, life-space approach to career development. *Journal of Vocational Behavior*, *13*, 282–298.

Surrey, J. L. (1987). *Relationship and empowerment*. Work in Progress no. 30. Wellesley, MA: Stone Center.

Vähämättönen, T. (1998). *Reframing career counselling in terms of counsellor–client negotiations. An interpretive study of career counselling concepts and practice.* Joensuu, Finland: University of Joensuu.

Valach, L. (1990). A theory of goal-directed action in career analysis. In R. A. Young & W. A. Borgen (Eds.), *Methodological approaches to the study of career* (pp. 107–126). New York: Praeger.

Waterman, R. H., Jr, Waterman, J. A., & Collard, B. A. (1994). Towards a career-resilient workforce. *Harvard Business Review*, *72*, 87–95.

White, R. W. (1959). Motivation reconsidered: The concept of competence. *Psychological Review*, *66*, 297–333.

Whitcley, J. M. (1984). A historical perspective on the development of counseling psychology as a profession. In L. D. Brown & R. W. Lent (Eds.), *Handbook of counseling psychology* (pp. 3–55). New York: John Wiley & Sons.

Williams, R. N. (1994). The modern, the post-modern, and the question of truth: Perspectives on the problem of agency. *Journal of Theoretical and Philosophical Psychology*, *14*, 25–39.

Worell, J. & Remer, P. (1992). *Feminist perspectives in therapy: An empowerment model for women.* New York: John Wiley & Sons.

Yoder, J. D. & Kahn, A. S. (1992). Toward a feminist understanding of women and power. *Psychology of Women Quarterly*, *16*, 381–388.

Young, R. A. & Valach, L. (1996). Interpretation and action in career counseling. In M. L. Savickas & W. B. Walsh (Eds.), *Handbook of career counseling theory and practice* (pp. 361–375). Palo Alto, CA: Davies-Black.

14   Adapting to the changing multicultural context of career

Frederick T. L. Leong and Paul J. Hartung

An increasingly global economy and the steady stream of immigrants and refugees from developing to developed nations have prompted many changes in our conceptions of career. One significant change arises from a major demographic trend towards increasing cultural diversity of populations in many parts of the world. This trend will have significant impact on both the practice of and theoretical developments in career psychology. The future of career, how it is conceptualised, experienced, and addressed in counselling, will be shaped by this significant demographic trend. A monocultural, or ethnocentric approach to careers will no longer be viable as the *modus operandi* for either career theorists or career counselling practitioners. In this chapter, we discuss the changing multicultural context of career. Although a multicultural mindset is developing, career theory, research, and counselling interventions still have a long way to go to attend to the increasing cultural diversity within the population. Our thesis posits that cultural issues will feature largely in the future of career.

Multiculturalism: from demographics to mindsets

Through the confluence of several different factors, many psychologists have come to realise that theories and models based on a Eurocentric paradigm fail to apply to a significant portion of their students, clients, and research participants. These factors range from the increasing cultural diversity in the demographics of many Western nations (Triandis, Dunnette, & Hough, 1994) to the development of a 'global community' made possible by the explosive growth of the Internet and the World Wide Web, to the development of satellites and international (versus primarily national) news bureaus such as Cable Network News. With these developments has come a movement towards multiculturalism in both research on cross-cultural differences (Markus & Kitayama, 1991) and approaches to psychology (Triandis, 1994). The changing demographics and accompanying increase in ethnic-minority and cross-cultural research are producing a particular mindset in the field of psychology. This developing mindset has also come to influence career theories and approaches to career interventions (e.g., see Fouad & Bingham, 1995, and Leong, 1995).

Describing how this multicultural mindset is likely to influence future career psychology research and practice requires first detailing our conception of this mindset. Research in social cognition indicates certain predictable patterns in people's cognition about themselves and others (Fiske & Taylor, 1991). A major pattern in our social cognition is our tendency to use heuristics in our social judgements and decision making. One consequence of our use of heuristics is our susceptibility to availability bias. How we respond to and interact with research subjects, clients, or supervisors who are culturally different from us will be limited by the elements of experience and memory we have available to us at any moment. To the extent that these elements are monocultural (for example, we have had limited interactions with Asians), then our repertoire of responses is limited to the cognitive elements that are available to us. In a monocultural environment where cross-cultural or cross-ethnic communication and interactions are limited, availability bias severely restricts our flexibility in responding to persons who are culturally different from us. On the other hand, with the increasing multiculturalism in our societies, the type and range of cognitive elements that guide social interactions available to us are likely to increase, and with them our cross-cultural competencies. The trend towards multiculturalism in our societies will give rise to a 'multicultural mindset'. This multicultural mindset will be central to our understanding of the changing multicultural future of career.

In order to understand how the changing multicultural context will affect our research and practice in career psychology, we need to understand the process by which this multicultural mindset will develop in researchers, practitioners, clients, and coworkers. In the lead article of a special issue of the *Journal of Counseling and Development*, Pedersen (1991) proposed that we are moving towards 'multiculturalism as a fourth force in psychology', following the three major forces, namely psychodynamic, behavioural, and humanistic. While some authors have proposed that multiculturalism is upon us, others have argued that its espousal is more similar to an evolution than a revolution. For example, while it is true that culture is beginning to play an increasingly important role in psychological research and theory building, multiculturalism remains far from becoming a dominant force in psychology (Leong & Santiago-Rivera, in press).

One need only review recent introductory psychology textbooks and the role of culture in the graduate psychology curriculum to see that multiculturalism is far from taking centre stage in psychology. Appropriately recognising culture in psychology, as well as other disciplines, will involve a long and often tedious journey which has just begun.

Various social-psychological factors will both facilitate and inhibit movement towards multiculturalism in counselling and psychology (Leong & Santiago-Rivera, in press). Countervailing forces against a multicultural conception of career include ethnocentricism, the false consensus effect, the attraction selection–attribution framework, psychological reactance, the values-as-beliefs fallacy, and conformity to majority influences. The combined action of these various social-psychological factors will significantly impede the multiculturalism movement. The dominance of the Eurocentric mindset in career psychology gives further evidence to support the argument that a multicultural mindset will be slow to develop.

Fitzgerald and Betz (1994) examined the cultural context of career development research and theory as reflected in the attention paid to gender, race, class, and sexual orientation. As they noted, career psychology pays little, if any, attention to cultural factors and career development theories have traditionally held relevance for only a small segment of the population, namely, white, middle-class, heterosexual men. Although research has significantly advanced our knowledge of women's career development since the early 1980s, similar gains in our understanding of the vocational behaviour of non-white women and men and of nonprofessional workers have not been achieved. Data indicate that a significant portion of the United States population consists of non-white people and their representation in the labour force continues to increase dramatically (Fitzgerald & Betz, 1994). Despite this increase, the vocational behaviour research literature continues to report data almost exclusively on college-level, white, middle-class individuals.

Fitzgerald and Betz (1994) used the 1987 volume of *Journal of Vocational Behavior* to illustrate their point. Similarly, we reviewed the 1997 volume of that journal and this ten-year update resulted in little or no change to the pattern observed by Fitzgerald and Betz. More specifically, of the twenty-seven articles within the 1997 volume only one of the articles dealt directly with cultural factors (Ensher & Murphy's article on the effects of race, gender, perceived similarity, and contact on mentor relationships). To be fair, two of the four issues within the 1997 volume were devoted to special topics but cultural factors in those special topics could have been considered.

In time, the multiculturalism movement in psychology will gradually introduce a multicultural mindset that will replace the still-dominant Eurocentric one. This shift will not occur rapidly but it will take place due to a myriad of forces. The changing demographics of our societies will result in career clients from diverse cultural groups who will require career practitioners to become familiar with cross-cultural research and theories more relevant to these groups. Concurrently, more culturally different (non-White-European) students will graduate and become career counsellors and professors in counselling and psychology programmes. Consequently, we will see more theory building and research on cultural factors in career as well as more culturally diverse curricula in graduate training programmes. As more culturally different persons enter counselling and psychology, they will begin to demand that their professional associations pay attention to cultural factors in their range of activities. A recent example is the election of the first Asian American President of the American Psychological Association. Eventually, these significant movements in graduate training programmes, career counselling centres, and professional association activities will come to influence licensure and certification processes which in turn will come full circle and influence graduate training programmes and new professionals entering the field. This process of evolution or paradigm shift from a Eurocentric to a multicultural mindset has already begun and we will use the remainder of the chapter to outline the significant changes in both career research and approaches to career counselling that have taken place thus far.

Career interventions in a multicultural context

Many calls have been made and some responses generated for renovating and enriching career choice and development theories and research to address issues of culture (for example, Arbona, 1995; Fitzgerald & Betz, 1994; Savickas, 1995a). Concurrently, there have been calls made and initial strategies devised for conducting career interventions that effectively take account of cultural influences on career development and vocational behaviour (for example, Bowman, 1995; Fouad & Bingham, 1995; Subich & Billingsley, 1995). Thus, as our fundamental notions about and approaches to the empirical study of career have begun to change, so too have our basic approaches to career counselling within a multicultural context.

Increasing communication, collaboration, cooperation, and contact among career theorists, researchers, and practitioners should help accomplish the goal of providing culturally sensitive career interventions to clients representing a variety of diverse groups (Collin, 1996; Leong, 1996). Culturally sensitive career intervention involves a web of complex, if rarely synergistic, relationships among career theorists, researchers, and practitioners (Leong, 1996; Savickas, 1996). Rarely do individuals participate in or represent all three groups. More typically, members of each group work in isolation from members of the other groups with a particular division between theory and research on the one hand and practice on the other (Leong, 1996; Savickas, 1995a).

Successfully elaborating career interventions to incorporate important cultural variables such as identity development, value orientation, language, communication style, time perspective, and decision-making style will involve nurturing these relationships to be more interactive and synergistic. Edited textbooks by Leong (1995) and Savickas and Walsh (1996) represent pivotal steps towards such integration of career theory and research with career counselling and career intervention whereby each informs the other. Other specific writings on career counselling and assessment in a multicultural context have also articulated the central role of cultural variables in individual career development and vocational behaviour (for example, Fouad, 1993; Leong & Brown, 1995; Tinsley, 1994; Walsh, 1994). This work translates into modifying existing conceptualisations of career. It also involves developing alternative approaches that effectively consider and take account of cultural variables that influence the process and outcomes of career counselling. Examples of some of these alternatives and modifications of existing conceptualisations can be found in a recent special issue on international perspectives on vocational psychology in the *Journal of Vocational Behavior*, guest-edited by Leong, Hesketh, and Savickas (1998).

Savickas (1996) developed a career services model that explicates the dimensions, types, and domains of career intervention. In the future of career, these interventions must derive from, respond to, and take place within a multicultural context. As described in the model, counsellors provide specific career interventions relative to six different domains of career service including occupational placement, vocational guidance, career counselling, career education, career therapy, and position coaching. The extant and growing multicultural career literature addresses interventions across these domains. Much of this literature focuses on vocational guidance with objective career assessment as the primary intervention, and career counselling with subjective career self-exploration as the primary intervention. These two basic domains of career services will therefore be considered in order to illustrate how the changing multicultural context of career influences approaches to career intervention.

Culturally sensitive career assessment and counselling

As the context of career changes to incorporate issues of culture, several models for effective career counselling and intervention in a multicultural context have emerged (Fouad & Bingham, 1995; Leong, 1993; Leong & Brown, 1995). Two such models exemplify how the changing multicultural context of career prompts theoretical, research, and practical innovations in career interventions. The first model explicates a conceptual framework for cross-cultural career assessment and counselling using an integrative tripartite approach (Leong & Hartung, 1997). Like models of similar purpose (Fouad & Bingham, 1995; Leong & Brown, 1995), the integrative-sequential model situates career interventions in a cultural context. Moreover, the model recognises how culture influences what individuals identify as career problems, whether they seek professional help for any work or career-related problems identified, and how counsellors evaluate those problems prior to identifying culturally appropriate interventions. This model will be presented in further detail in the last section of this chapter as a framework for guiding future research in multicultural career psychology.

A second model for culturally sensitive career assessment and counselling focuses on appraising and attending to cultural identity in career counselling (Hartung, Vandiver, Leong, *et al.*, 1998). This scheme elaborates the Career Development Assessment and Counseling model (C-DAC; Super, Savickas, & Super, 1996) to include cultural issues. The elaborated C-DAC model addresses cultural identity concerns throughout career assessment and counselling, and adds formal cultural identity assessment to step one of the model. This model thus incorporates assessment and counselling interventions that consider cultural identity as a significant variable in career development and vocational behaviour.

In addition to innovative theoretical models, other approaches to career intervention have emerged that support and advance culturally sensitive career counselling and assessment. These approaches include contextual (Collin, 1996; Young & Valach, 1996; Young, Valach, & Collin, 1996), personal construct (Savickas, 1995b, 1995c; Super, 1954), and narrative (Cochran, 1997; Jepsen, 1990, 1994) strategies for assisting individuals to make improved career decisions. Consistent with a multicultural mindset, all of these perspectives on career counselling and intervention emphasise exploring each client's subjective, qualitative, and personal career reality.

Major trends in multicultural career research

Trends in research give further evidence of an evolving multicultural mindset in career psychology. A perusal of the career research literature reveals a significant, albeit gradual, shift towards infusing cultural variables (e.g. race, ethnicity, gender, sexual orientation, and socio-economic status) into basic and applied research programmes on career development and vocational behaviour. Prompting this shift has been a dynamic voice intensifying among theorists, researchers, and practitioners that underscores the need to examine empirically the multicultural context of work and career. This voice resonates throughout textbooks (Leong, 1995; Savickas & Walsh, 1996; Walsh & Osipow, 1995) and journal issues (Leong, 1991; Savickas, 1993; Tinsley, 1994; Walsh, 1994) specifically devoted to addressing how culture influences individual career development and vocational behaviour.

The future of career relative to its changing multicultural context will witness the continued evolution of two overarching research trends. These research trends will both echo and amplify the basic rationale for conducting multicultural career research proffered in a host of recent writings (e.g. Fitzgerald & Betz, 1994; Fouad & Bingham, 1995; Subich & Billingsley, 1995). One fundamental trend is to investigate the applicability of constructs from existing career theories for understanding the career development and vocational behaviour of people comprising traditionally under-represented groups in career research. These groups include racial and ethnic minorities in the United States, women, the economically disadvantaged, and various other cultural groups outside the United States. This trend of research addresses issues of *cultural validity* by examining the relevance of career theories and models for individuals within various cultural groups (Leong & Brown, 1995). A second basic trend is to examine the influence of specific cultural variables on career development and vocational behaviour. This includes such variables as identity development, acculturation, and a variety of worldview dimensions such as value orientation, time perspective, and decision-making style. This second area of research addresses issues of *cultural specificity* which Leong and Brown (1995) noted pertains to determining the role of particular culturally based variables in explaining and predicting career development and vocational behaviour outcomes. Let us consider these emerging research trends in turn.

Cultural validity of career constructs

Theories of career choice and development offer various conceptualisations of how people make career choices, adjust to those choices, and manage work relative to other life roles. Constructs within these theories range from those concerned with person–environment fit, efficacy beliefs, and career-choice readiness, to those that describe vocational personality development and decision-making styles. Many of these constructs may lack utility for understanding individual career development and vocational behaviour in culturally diverse contexts (Arbona, 1995; Fitzgerald & Betz, 1994; Richardson, 1993). However, this may in time change because the major theoretical constructs in career 'have not been tested, or tested adequately, with culturally diverse groups' (Leong & Brown, 1995, p. 173).

In some cases, research has begun to determine the cultural validity of particular constructs derived from the predominant career theories. As examples, consider the theories of Super and Holland, widely regarded as the two preeminent approaches to understanding career choice and development. A significant body of research provides support for the constructs of role salience and work values central to Super's lifespan, life-space approach to careers (Niles & Goodnough, 1996). Similarly, a review of Holland's personality and environmental types model concluded that '[t]he ordering (RIASEC) of types or occupational categories is similar even when the data, sexes, and cultures vary' (Holland, 1997, p. 138). The most recent update of the Strong Interest Inventory (Strong, Hansen, & Campbell, 1994), which uses the RIASEC model originated by Holland, incorporated key revisions that support its cultural relevance.

Cultural specificity in career research

Empirical study of the influence of specific cultural variables, such as acculturation level and value orientation, on career development and vocational behaviour represents a second major trend in the multicultural career research. Acculturation refers to the process by which a member of one cultural group identifies with members of another cultural group which he or she has entered. Leong and Tata (1990) found that Chinese-American children who were more highly acculturated to European-American culture in the United States held work values consistent with Euro-American culture, such as self-realisation. Other variables related to acculturation levels include occupational segregation, stereotyping, discrimination, prestige, mobility, attitudes, aspirations and expectations, stress, satisfaction, choice and interest (Leong, 1985; Leong & Serafica, 1995).

Cultural value orientation refers to the perspectives individuals develop on what is defined as meaningful. Individualism–collectivism represents an important cultural value orientation on which people differ (Triandis, 1994) and plays a potentially significant role in career development and vocational behaviour (Hartung, Speight, & Lewis, 1996; Leong, 1993). Individuals from groups with more collectivistic value orientations (for example, Asian Americans, Hispanic Americans, and Native Americans) may conceive of the 'self' as interdependent, whereas persons from individualistic cultures view the self as independent. One study found support for this latter notion by indicating that, for individualists, career decision making may be an individual rather than collective matter based mainly on personal interests, values, and aspirations (Hartung *et al.*, 1996). That is, individualists were found to base their career choices more on their own personal needs and values, rather than on the needs and expectations of their in-groups, such as family.

A framework for guiding multicultural career research

A conceptual framework may help guide career research in a changing multicultural context (Leong & Hartung, 1997). To understand the mental health of ethnic minority groups, it is important to have an integrated and sequential model that accounts for the cultural context in which mental health services are provided (Rogler, Malgady, & Rodriguez, 1989). This argument extends to career counselling services. Rogler *et al.* proposed an integrated-sequential model to guide minority mental health research in which cultural factors influence what happens both within each stage and during the transition from one stage to another. This model, consisting of five stages, can be adapted for use in cross-cultural career counselling and career assessment and could guide future research (Leong & Hartung, 1997).

Stage 1. Emergence of career and vocational problems

All too often, both in our theories and in our career counselling practice, we forget that clients' career problems emerge within their homes, workplaces, and communities rather than our consulting rooms. In this stage, cultural differences in conceptions of normality and work will influence what experiences are perceived as a 'career problem'. Two clients could have similar experiences with one client considering it a career problem amenable to counselling and the other not so due to cultural differences. How a client's family or ethnic community reacts to the emergence of a career problem is another important factor in this stage. Hence, cultural differences in values, norms, and expectancies play an important role in the emergence, recognition, and acceptance of career and vocational problems in racial and ethnic minority communities.

Stage 2. Help-seeking and career services utilisation

The second stage of the model addresses how culturally different clients' conceptions of work and normality will influence their attitudes towards help-seeking and career services utilisation. For example, for some culturally different youth not knowing what one is going to do for a career at the end of high school may not be viewed as a problem, especially if one lives in a community where most available jobs are low-paying or not intrinsically satisfying or dignified. This stage is concerned with all the various cultural factors that influence whether culturally different clients will seek career counselling. For example, an important question in this stage is whether different racial and ethnic minority groups underutilise career counselling services and why. At the same time, this stage also involves determining the client's referral source (for example, self, social network, professionals) and how he or she felt about it (for example, accepted referral or resisted it for months). It is important for us to assess whether different cultural factors serve as barriers to culturally different clients seeking career counselling services. Some cultural factors that may influence such underutilisation include: (a) lack of bicultural and bilingual staff, (b) lack of culturally appropriate services, and (c) cultural mistrust or systems distrust.

For the culturally different individual to move from identifying a career problem and being a 'prospective career client' in Stage 1, to actually seeking professional career services and entering the client role to deal with the problem in Stage 2, depends on a variety of factors. One is the extent to which the prospective client's racial or ethnic group uses counselling and mental health services generally. As has been widely noted (Akutsu, Snowden, & Organista, 1996; Sue & Sue, 1990), many such groups tend not to use traditional mental health services. Instead, they may turn to more informal help-giving networks such as nuclear and extended family, friends, community, traditional folk healers, clergy, and other naturally available supports. Culturally different individuals may avoid professional counselling because of cultural sanctions against discussing personal issues and revealing emotionally laden material outside the family or other group with which he or she identifies. This often relates to issues of mistrust of mental health and related health and social service systems as well as to the need to protect the sanctity and integrity of the family over and above all else. At the same time many racial and ethnic minority individuals may believe a permanent job will never be a reality and thus they never seek career services because they do not perceive a problem in the first place. When the culturally different individual faces an educational or vocational problem, however, the likelihood of seeking career services may increase because they often perceive such problems as more circumscribed, concrete, specific, and nonemotional (Sue & Sue, 1990). Consequently, racial and ethnic minority group members may be expected to seek out career counselling more readily than they would other types of mental health services (Tracey, Leong, & Glidden, 1986). It thus becomes vitally important for counsellors who deal with issues of work and career especially to understand and conduct career counselling that uses culturally-appropriate process and goals (Leong, 1993).

Stage 3. Evaluation of career and vocational problems

In crossing the threshold, either alone or with the support and/or pressure of the family, to seek professional help for a career problem, the individual reaches the third stage of the model: 'Evaluation of career and vocational problems'. Cultural factors influence the threshold itself in the same way that they influence this evaluation process. At this stage, two events usually take place. As the first event, the career counsellor conducts an intake interview to evaluate and assess the client's problem. Typically, this diagnostic interview will result in the client being referred for career and/or personality tests. To the extent that career assessment guides career interventions, then any mis-diagnosis or mis-assessment in the diagnostic interview due to cultural biases in our theoretical models or to training biases among career practitioners may lead to culturally inappropriate career interventions. As the second event, using psychometric instruments to evaluate career problems and their treatments and outcomes presents another area of concern.

Stage 4. Career interventions

At the end of the evaluation process, two decisions are possible. The client is either assigned to some form of career counselling or is determined to be not in need of intervention. If some career intervention is recommended, the counsellor and client select and use appropriate career interventions and the same cultural factors that operated in the evaluation process also enter into the career counselling process (Leong, 1986; Sue & Morishima, 1982). Career interventions take many forms and ultimately comprise any activity designed to enhance an individual's ability to make optimal career decisions (Spokane, 1991). Assessment constitutes a primary career intervention and often represents a fundamental element of the career counselling process (Betz, 1992; Herr, 1994; Spokane, 1991). In many approaches to career counselling, a significant portion of the time in counselling involves interpreting vocational and personality test results.

Stage 5. Outcomes of career interventions

At the end of career counselling, the client returns fully to the community. The outcomes of career interventions, the client's status and functioning at the end of counselling, represents the 'bottom-line' of our enterprise. Identifying and using both culturally appropriate process and goals are central to career counselling that provides effective and culturally relevant career interventions and appropriate and desirable outcomes for the client (Leong, 1993). Failure to attend to the cultural dimension is likely to lead to culturally inappropriate processes and culturally inappropriate goals in career counselling which in turn are likely to result in premature terminations and undesirable counselling outcomes. Despite the importance of outcomes as the very reason we do what we do for our clients, there is a tremendous dearth of research on this phase of the model.

Overall, this five-stage framework will hopefully serve as a valuable guide to future research on cross-cultural career counselling and advance the multicultural perspective in career psychology. A review of the existing literature indicates most of the existing models for cross-cultural career counselling and assessment tend to address only the third and fourth stages in our model, that is, evaluation of the career problem and career interventions. There is a dearth of research for Stages 1 and 2 (i.e., emergence of career problems and help-seeking / service utilisation). For example, there is little or no research on whether racial and ethnic minorities underutilise career counselling services as they do mental health services (Sue, Zane, & Young, 1994). Furthermore, there remains a need for empirical work on career intervention outcomes for racial and ethnic minorities. Because this framework is more sensitive to cultural contexts, an often neglected dimension in counselling research, using it should encourage us to attend to the transitions between stages as well as what occurs within each stage. Ultimately, it may prove effective as a guide for future research on the multicultural dimensions of career psychology.

REFERENCES

Akutsu, P. D., Snowden, L. R., & Organista, K. C. (1996). Referral patterns in ethnic-specific and mainstream programs for ethnic minorities and whites. *Journal of Counseling Psychology*, *43*, 56–64.

Arbona, C. L. (1995). Career intervention strategies and assessment issues for African Americans. In F. T. L. Leong (Ed.), *Career development and vocational behavior of racial and ethnic minorities* (pp. 37–66). Mahwah, NJ: Erlbaum.

Betz, N. E. (1992). Career assessment: A review of critical issues. In S. D. Brown & R. W. Lent (Eds.), *Handbook of counseling psychology* (pp. 453–484). New York: Wiley.

Bowman, S. L. (1995). Career intervention strategies and assessment issues for African Americans. In F. T. L. Leong (Ed.), *Career development and vocational behavior of racial and ethnic minorities* (pp. 137–164). Mahwah, NJ: Erlbaum.

Cochran, L. (1997). *Career counseling: A narrative approach*. Thousand Oaks, CA: Sage.

Collin, A. (1996). New relationships between researchers, theorists, and practitioners: A response to the changing context of career. In M. L. Savickas & W. B. Walsh (Eds.), *Handbook of career counseling theory and practice* (pp. 377–399). Palo Alto, CA: Davies-Black.

Fiske, S.T. & Taylor, S.F. (1991). *Social cognition* (2nd edn). New York: McGraw-Hill.

Fitzgerald, L. F. & Betz, N. E. (1994). Career development in cultural context: The role of gender, race, class, and sexual orientation. In M. L. Savickas & R. W. Lent (Eds.), *Convergence in career development theories: Implications for science and practice* (pp. 103–117). Palo Alto, CA: CPP Books.

Fouad, N. A. (1993). Cross-cultural vocational assessment. *Career Development Quarterly*, *42*, 4–13.

Fouad, N. A. & Bingham, R. P. (1995). Career counseling with racial and ethnic minorities. In W. B. Walsh & S. H. Osipow (Eds.), *Handbook of vocational psychology: Theory, research, and practice* (2nd edn, pp. 331–365). Mahwah, NJ: Lawrence Erlbaum Associates.

Hartung, P. J., Speight, J. D., & Lewis, D. M. (1996). Individualism–collectivism and the vocational behavior of majority culture college students. *Career Development Quarterly*, *45*, 87–96.

Hartung, P. J., Vandiver, B. J., Leong, F. T. L., Pope, M., Niles, S. G., & Farrow, B. (1998). Appraising cultural identity in career-development assessment and counseling. *Career Development Quarterly*, *46*, 276–293.

Herr, E. L. (1994). The counselor's role in career assessment. In J. T. Kapes, M. M. Mastie, & E. A. Whitfield (Eds.), *A counselor's guide to career assessment instruments* (3rd edn, pp. 13–22). Alexandria, VA: National Career Development Association.

Holland, J. L. (1997). *Making vocational choices: A theory of vocational personalities and work environments* (3rd edn). Odessa, FL: Psychological Assessment Resources.

Jepsen, D. A. (1990). Developmental career counseling. In W. B. Walsh & S. H. Osipow (Eds.), *Career counseling: Contemporary topics in vocational psychology* (pp. 117–158). Hillsdale, NJ: Erlbaum.

(1994). The thematic-extrapolation method: Incorporating career patterns into career counseling. *Career Development Quarterly*, *43*, 43–53.

Leong, F.T.L. (1985). Career development of Asian-Americans. *Journal of College Student Personnel*, *26*, 539–546.

(1986). Counseling and psychotherapy with Asian-Americans: Review of the literature. *Journal of Counseling Psychology*, *33*, 196–206.

(Guest Ed.) (1991). Special issue on career development of racial and ethnic minorities. *Career Development Quarterly*, *42*, 196–198.

(1993). The career counseling process with racial/ethnic minorities: The case of Asian Americans. *Career Development Quarterly*, *12*, 26–40.

(Ed.) (1995). *Career development and vocational behavior of racial and ethnic minorities*. Hillsdale, NJ: Erlbaum.

(1996). Challenges to career counseling: Boundaries, cultures, and complexity. In M. L. Savickas & W. B. Walsh (Eds.), *Handbook of career counseling theory and practice* (pp. 333–345). Palo Alto, CA: Davies-Black.

Leong, F. T. L. & Brown, M. T. (1995). Theoretical issues in cross cultural career development: Cultural validity and cultural specificity. In W. B. Walsh & S. H. Osipow (Eds.), *Handbook of vocational psychology: Theory, research, and practice* (2nd edn, pp. 143–180). Mahwah, NJ: Lawrence Erlbaum Associates.

Leong, F. T. L. & Hartung, P. J. (1997). Career assessment with culturally-different clients: Proposing an integrative-sequential conceptual framework for cross-cultural career counseling research and practice. *Journal of Career Assessment*, *5*, 183–202.

Leong, F. T. L., Hesketh, B. L., & Savickas, M. L. (1998). Guest editors' introduction: International perspectives on vocational psychology. *Journal of Vocational Behavior*, *52*, 271–274.

Leong, F.T.L. & Santiago-Rivera, A. (in press). Climbing the multiculturalism summit: Challenges and pitfalls. In P. Pedersen (Ed.), *Multiculturalism as a fourth force*. Washington, DC: Taylor and Francis.

Leong, F. T. L. & Serafica, F. (1995). Career development of Asian Americans: A research area in need of a good theory. In F. T. L. Leong (Ed.), *Career development and vocational behavior of racial and ethnic minorities* (pp. 67–102). Hillsdale, NJ: Lawrence Erlbaum.

Leong, F. T. L. & Tata, S. P. (1990). Sex and acculturation differences in occupational values among Chinese American children. *Journal of Counseling Psychology*, *37*, 208–212.

Markus, H. R. & Kitayama, S. (1991). Culture and the self: Implications for cognition, emotion, and motivation. *Psychological Review*, *98*, 224–253.

Niles, S. G. & Goodnough, G. E. (1996). Life-role salience and values: A review of recent research. *Career Development Quarterly*, *45*, 65–86.

Pedersen, P. B. (1991). Multiculturalism as a generic approach to counseling. *Journal of Counseling and Development*, *70*, 6–12.

Richardson, M. S. (1993). Work in people's lives: A location for counseling psychologists. *Journal of Counseling Psychology*, *40*, 425–433.

Rogler, L., Malgady, R., & Rodriguez, D. (1989). *Hispanics and mental health: A framework for research*. Malabar, FL: Krieger.

Savickas, M. L. (Ed.) (1993). Special section: A symposium on multicultural career counseling. *Career Development Quarterly, 42* (1), 3–55.

(1995a). Current theoretical issues in vocational psychology: Convergence, divergence, and schism. In W. B. Walsh & S. H. Osipow (Eds.), *Handbook of vocational psychology: Theory, research, and practice* (2nd edn, pp. 1–34). Mahwah, NJ: Lawrence Erlbaum Associates.

(1995b). Examining the personal meaning of inventoried interests during career counseling. *Journal of Career Assessment, 3,* 188–201.

(1995c). Constructivist counseling for career indecision. *Career Development Quarterly, 43,* 363–373.

(1996). A framework for linking career theory and practice. In M. L. Savickas & W. B. Walsh (Eds.), *Handbook of career counseling theory and practice* (pp. 191–208). Palo Alto, CA: Davies-Black Publishing.

Savickas, M. L. & Walsh, W. B. (Eds.) (1996). *Handbook of career counseling theory and practice.* Palo Alto, CA: Davies-Black.

Spokane, A. R. (1991). *Career intervention.* Englewood Cliffs, NJ: Prentice-Hall.

Strong, E. K., Jr, Hansen, J. C., & Campbell, D. (1994). *Strong Interest Inventory.* Palo Alto, CA: Consulting Psychologists Press.

Subich, L. M. & Billingsley, K. D. (1995). Integrating career assessment into counseling. In W. B. Walsh & S. H. Osipow (Eds.), *Handbook of vocational psychology: Theory, research, and practice* (2nd edn, pp. 261, 293). Hillsdale, NJ: Lawrence Erlbaum Associates.

Sue, D. W. & Sue, D. (1990). *Counseling the culturally different: Theory and practice* (2nd edn). New York: John Wiley & Sons.

Sue, S. & Morishima, J. (1982). *The mental health of Asian Americans.* San Francisco: Jossey-Bass.

Sue, S., Zane, N., & Young, K. (1994). Research on psychotherapy with culturally diverse populations. In A. E. Bergin & S. L. Garfield (Eds.), *Handbook of psychotherapy and behavior change* (4th edn, pp. 783–817). New York: Wiley.

Super, D. E. (1954). Career patterns as a basis for vocational counseling. *Journal of Counseling Psychology, 1,* 12–20.

Super D. E., Savickas, M. L., & Super, C. M. (1996). The life-span, life-space approach to careers. In D. Brown, L. Brooks, & Associates, *Career choice and development: Applying contemporary theories to practice* (3rd edn, pp. 121–178). San Francisco: Jossey-Bass.

Tinsley, H. E. A. (Ed.) (1994). Special issue on racial identity and vocational behavior. *Journal of Vocational Behavior, 44* (2).

Tracey, T. J., Leong, F. T. L., & Glidden, C. (1986). Help seeking and problem perception among Asian-Americans. *Journal of Counseling Psychology, 33,* 331–336.

Triandis, H. C. (1994). *Culture and social behavior.* New York: McGraw-Hill.

Triandis, H. C., Dunnette, M. D., & Hough, L. M. (1994). *Handbook of industrial/organizational psychology* (2nd edn, vol. IV). Palo Alto, CA: Consulting Psychologists Press.

Walsh, W. B. (Ed.) (1994). Special feature: Career assessment with racial and ethnic minorities. *Journal of Career Assessment, 2* (3).

Walsh, W. B. & Osipow, S. H. (Eds.) (1995). *Handbook of vocational psychology:*

Theory, research, and practice (2nd edn). Mahwah, NJ: Lawrence Erlbaum Associates.

Young, R. A. & Valach, L. (1996). Interpretation and action in career counseling. In M. L. Savickas & W. B. Walsh (Eds.), *Handbook of career counseling theory and practice* (pp. 361–375). Palo Alto, CA: Davies-Black.

Young, R. A., Valach, L., & Collin, A. (1996). A contextual explanation of career. In D. Brown, L. Brooks, & Associates, *Career choice and development* (3rd edn, pp. 477–512). San Francisco: Jossey-Bass.

15 Managing careers in organisations

Mike Doyle

Introduction

The aim of this chapter is to explore the future of career from the perspective of work organisations. For the purposes of this chapter, career will be defined as 'a sequence of employment-related positions, roles, activities and experiences encountered by a person' (Arnold, 1997, p. 16) and career management as interventions to shape careers in organisations, not only by the individuals concerned, but also formally and informally by their managers (Arnold, 1997; Mayo, 1991). The chapter will take as its focus the changing nature of the employment relationship to explore the way organisational change is affecting existing career management procedures and practices. It will be argued that emergent ambiguities, contradictions, and dilemmas may require a reframing of current career management practice.

The idea that careers can and ought to be managed on behalf of the individual and the organisation is part of a wider debate surrounding the objective/subjective nature of career in work organisations (Fish & Wood, 1993; Nicholson & West, 1988). Notwithstanding this debate, career management remains a key activity within the philosophy of human resource management (HRM; e.g. Beardwell & Holden, 1997; Bratton & Gold, 1994; Mabey & Salaman, 1995). It also forms an important element within the theory and professional practice of human resource development. This is most apparent in the field of management development where career planning, guidance, and counselling for the individual are vital requisites to any investment by the organisation or the individual in management training and education (Nicholson & West, 1988; Tate, 1995; Woodall & Winstanley, 1998).

Broadly speaking, the theory and practice of career management is based on two assumptions. First, career should not, indeed could not in a business sense, be considered exclusively from within the context of an individual's subjective experience. Subjective notions of career may be shaped by personal perceptions of role, attitudes, identity, and self-worth, and broader social factors such as class and gender. A more rational, managerialist view of career is captured in Garavan and Coolahan's (1996a) observation that careers are 'usually made within organisations and therefore career dynamics are influenced to a considerable degree by *matters organisational*' (p. 35, emphasis added). This perspective suggests that individuals may be considered as stakeholders in their career and, to that end, are expected to own and take responsibility for their own career development. Support is usually forthcoming through established or-ganisational frameworks of career management procedures and practices. Individuals may elicit the help and support of their boss who, in turn, may draw on the expertise of HR professionals or consultants.

The second assumption is that there exists a common, shared interest between the strategic aims and business objectives of the organisation and the personal aspirations and ambitions of the individual (Bratton & Gold, 1994). The organisation seeks to manage an individual's career in a way that ensures it is strategically focused to promote and contribute to business goals whilst at the same time providing the individual with the opportunity to fulfil their personal needs and aspirations (Fish & Wood, 1993; Mayo, 1991, 1992).

Both assumptions have provided the rationale and legitimacy for career management interventions in the past, and both remain influential in shaping current career management thinking and practice. However, it is increasingly apparent that radical organisational change is creating 'significant career problems for individuals and organisations alike' (Fish & Wood, 1993, p. 7). In this chapter, evidence will be presented to suggest that traditional, orthodox career management models and structures are struggling to adapt and cope with what is becoming an increasingly complex, diverse, and fluid organisational context (Brousseau, Driver, Eneroth, & Larsson, 1996). If this leads to disillusionment and frustration amongst employees and managers, it is not difficult to imagine that those affected will perceive career management as meaningless and, conse-quently, may be reluctant to make a personal investment in their career – especially if they suspect that their individual aspirations are going to be subverted to the business priorities of cost-reduction, productivity im-provement, and efficiency savings (Ebadan & Winstanley, 1996; Hirsh & Jackson, 1996a, 1996b; McDougall & Vaughan, 1996).

Against this backdrop, analysing and understanding the way managers and HR professionals think about and practise career management becomes of paramount importance. In the past, managers and profes-sionals took what could be construed as a largely dutiful, almost philanthropic stance towards the career management of their subordi-nates. Constructive feedback and advice would be given, sponsorship afforded, networking opportunities created – all aimed at successfully advancing the career of the employee or protégé whilst at the same time providing a measure of personal or professional satisfaction to the boss, HR practitioner, or mentor. For some, this stance still remains an appropriate basis for their career management thinking and practice. But for others – especially those in the middle tier of management who are themselves experiencing difficulties in adapting to the changing demands and effects of the new psychological contract – perceptions are changing (Hallier & James, 1997; Hendry & Jenkins, 1996; Newell & Dopson, 1996). For example, there may be an emotional and political backlash from managers against what they perceive to be the negative effects of downsizing and delayering on their own roles, jobs, and personal career prospects. Some may see it as 'legitimate' to place their personal interests and goals ahead of those of the organisation or the employees for whom they have responsibility (Ebadan & Winstanley, 1996; Hallier & James, 1997; McDougall & Vaughan, 1996; Newell & Dopson, 1996; Sparrow, 1996).

But as they place their own interests ahead of their employees, it is important for managers to recognise and appreciate that they have a stake in their employees' career. Their futures are inextricably linked through a complex network of dependencies, interrelationships, and interactions to the eventual career outcomes of their subordinates. To this end, managers may choose to intervene (or not intervene) and shape their subordinates' career in the knowledge that there are long-term consequences for their personal careers. In some senses, this realisation may explain why some managers and employees are, unwittingly or otherwise, colluding to deny reality in the career management process. For instance, when they are discussing an individual's suitability for promotion, for political or emotional reasons, both parties may 'decide' it is in their interests that unattainable expectations should not be openly discussed or confronted. This creates a sense of false confidence leading to a preservation of the status quo (Herriot, Pemberton, & Pinder, 1993). This may bring emotional and political benefits in the short term but there is a risk of eventual frustration and demotivation as employees discover that the reality of the situation is that their aspirations and hopes are never going to be fulfilled. Not only will this adversely affect individual performance (perhaps far more so than if reality had been addressed earlier), but poor employee attitudes and performance may reflect negatively on the managerial or professional capabilities of the manager or HR practitioner who had allowed these false expectations to continue. Ultimately, it is these perceptions that may jeopardise the career opportunities of these managers and in extreme circumstances even their position and job security (Hallier & James, 1997).

The picture emerging then is one of traditional career management structures and approaches struggling to balance and reconcile organisational and individual goals which themselves are changing in response to an increasingly self-centred, instrumental climate. This is affecting the nature of the social exchanges where career opportunities and directions are decided and planned (Ebadan & Winstanley, 1996; Newell & Dopson, 1996). This chapter will argue that if the employment relationship is shifting in this way then its impact on career management may have to receive greater acknowledgement by those who theorise and practise in the field. This may involve a move away from highly structured, somewhat mechanistic approaches to career management, towards a more holistic and integrated approach. This new approach involves efforts to analyse, and make sense of, the complex and dynamic social interactions occurring between the different stakeholders involved and affected by the process of career management, and how the process can be made more responsive and adaptive to change. The chapter concludes with some speculation about the short- and long-term future of career management theory and practice.

Career management in an organisational context

In many organisations, career management would seem to be synonymous with sophisticated structures, processes, and methodologies designed to align the often diverse career needs and aspirations of individuals with business goals. Career ownership and participation on the part of the individual are achieved through conformity and compliance with career planning structures, for example, career planning workshops and career counselling seminars. The overall aim is to ensure that any investment in career is achieved through the preparation of personal growth profiles that are then matched to short- and long-term organisational goals. Typically, this is achieved through the use of instruments such as competency frameworks and human resource forecasts (Bratton & Gold, 1994; Mayo, 1992; Rothwell, 1995).

Having negotiated career plans, a range of career activities will follow. For example, training and development programmes, appraisal systems, participation in incentive and reward systems, mentoring arrangements may all be implemented and utilised to ensure that both the organisation and the individual benefit from any subsequent investment. As their career unfolds, individuals are urged to climb career 'ladders' and cross career 'bridges' as they seek to advance themselves and thereby contribute to the overall management of their personal career and the organisation's strategic goals (Arnold, 1997; Mabey & Iles, 1994; Mabey & Salaman, 1995; Mayo, 1991, 1992).

In addition to career management being viewed as a series of functional activities and processes designed to meet organisational and individual needs, it must also be viewed as an integral part of the complex framework of social interactions that define work organisations. As members of an organisation, individuals participate in a series of 'strategic exchanges' in which they are shaped by their social interactions with others (Watson, 1994a, 1994b). With respect to career management, these strategic exchanges are enacted through 'dyadic relationships' (Hall & Associates, 1996). Here, the individual interacts formally or informally with a superordinate or significant 'other'. This may be their boss or a HR professional, or, in a less formal context, their work colleagues and friends. Through social interaction, the potential for human initiative and autonomy (agency) is seen in the individual's desire to influence the forces that shape their destiny. However, in work organisations, the scope for autonomous decision making and action may be circumscribed by the 'interplay between the intentions of the person acting and the constraints (and opportunities) of their circumstances' (Watson, 1994a, p. 27). In career terms, it is not unusual for the individual to be aware of the fact that their career transition experiences 'are structured for him or her by others in the organisation' (Van Maanen, 1982, p. 86). For example, as pointed out earlier, the superordinate 'other' may decide to use their power or expertise to shape the relationship in a way that may have more to do with the achievement of their own cultural or political advantage or personal aggrandisement than advancing the career of their subordinate (Hallier & James, 1997; McDougall & Vaughan, 1996).

The significance and importance attached to this shaping process and the extent to which agents or 'significant others' influence an individual's career, and the value that individuals attach to the opportunity for social interaction and exchange, can be sensed in a recent study by Mabey and Iles (1994). In their study, the career management techniques that individuals felt most positive about were those which were less formal and more socially oriented. For instance, it was found that the one-to-one career reviews with a superior, gaining feedback from psychometric testing and development centres, and informal mentoring arrangements were the methods judged by participants to be more effective than passive and structured techniques such as the provision of career guidance information or self-assessment information. Interestingly, many individuals appeared to place considerable value on the opportunity to engage in personal interaction with their bosses and mentors which they felt enabled them to tap into the 'power nexus' and 'reality of the organisation' (p. 127).

The changing nature of career management in organisations

As discussed in chapter 2, there has been a significant shift in some organisations away from a psychological contract which traditionally embodied the values of mutuality and reciprocity, towards one that represents a more calculative and instrumental relationship between employees and their work organisations. One effect of this new contract has been that traditional, onwards-and-upwards planned, accessible, and secure careers are being replaced by an 'over-to-you' philosophy where ownership and responsibility for career management are transferred or delegated to the individual employee (Hirsh & Jackson, 1996a, 1996b; McDougall & Vaughan, 1996). Organisations now expect their employees actively to create and manage a form of personalised 'employability' in what is becoming a jobs-for-now structure and culture (Germain & Heath, 1994; Wills, 1997). Employees and managers are being reminded that they have to remain more realistic about their career futures as restructuring and new technology reduce career opportunities (Inkson, 1995).

Such changes in the nature of the employment relationship suggest significant implications for career management. Future success, it is claimed, may now depend less on the efficacy of the relationship between subordinate and boss and mentor and protégé – largely founded in the past on power and patronage and a sense of philanthropy – and more on a reconfigured approach that is founded on a greater sense of co-learning in a spirit of mutuality and reciprocity 'in which both parties would benefit from being in connection with each other' (Hall & Associates, 1996, p. 142). This suggests there is a need for those who have a stake in career to generate a more open, communitarian spirit in which a willingness to learn, self-disclosure, active listening, reflection, and empathy will predominate. But such idealism may have to be tempered by the recognition that in the practical/pragmatic reality of some organisational contexts, changes to the employment relationship may have rendered the notions of mutuality and reciprocity in it vulnerable to subversion by wider organisational factors and conditions. In these situations, it may be difficult to 'build relationships that support learning through connections with others' (1996, p. 147).

There is no doubt that some organisations are facing or will face conditions of extreme uncertainty and turbulence. In such situations, there is a risk that a short-termist, self-calculative, individualistic culture (captured in Herriot and Pemberton's (1995) euphemistic New Deal) will act to deter or undermine these more idealistic models of career management. Because these models seek to promote high levels of trust, openness, self-reflection, and learning, significant changes in the nature of the psychological contract represent a clear challenge to the sense of duty and philanthropy traditionally shown by 'significant others' towards career management responsibilities. Such a challenge may have concomitant implications for the way careers are viewed and managed in the future. Evidence for this can be detected in two recent studies exploring career management where managers and HR professionals are having to respond to changes in the employment relationship.

The first is a study of career management processes within a large private sector organisation (McDougall & Vaughan, 1996). The company sought to transfer responsibility for career development away from its managers and towards the individual. However, traditional expectations remained firmly entrenched amongst employees who saw career management as very much the company's responsibility. Managers were made aware of the company's need to shift responsibility onto the shoulders of employees but felt ill-equipped to handle this task. They had reservations about individuals who did not appear to have the capabilities to manage their careers. There was little information available about company strategy, future headcount projections, and skills requirements on which they could construct appropriate career maps. Performance review interviews were more concerned with performance and training needs and less with giving career planning assistance which was judged a low priority. There were also concerns expressed by HR specialists that line managers were not competent to give career advice, for example in acknowledging that there were differences between the career patterns of women and men.

In many respects, the second study reinforces and adds to the findings of the first. It highlights the way ambiguous messages can attach themselves to efforts aimed at transferring career responsibility from the organisation to employees leading to frustration and demotivation (Hirsh & Jackson, 1996a, 1996b). The study, involving fifteen major UK employers, revealed a complex framework in which a sense of career ownership and responsibility were closely linked to perceptions of job security and access to training. The study's findings suggest that the main aim of career management was to negotiate a partnership deal that matched the interests of each partner - to create a mutually beneficial, win-win situation. This was seen as largely unproblematic where it involved professional and highly skilled groups who were felt to have the motivation, skills, and educational capabilities to manage their own careers. However, in other sectors of the workforce, ambiguity and contradiction about career prospects emerged, largely as a consequence of the actions and rhetoric of 'misguided' senior management and HR professionals. Moreover, judgements were made that some managers did not have the right career management capabilities and/or were avoiding any objective reflection on the realities of the organisation even when they impacted directly on an employee's career and future job security, for example in those organisations experiencing turbulence and uncertainty. In one instance, managers in a financial services organisation were accused of misleading their workforce into believing they had clear support for their career development. What was not being communicated effectively by these managers to their subordinates was the message that career development should now be viewed in the context of a 'job-for-now deal'. The consequence was disillusionment and demotivation. The researchers concluded that 'in many organisations the pendulum of career development ownership has swung back and forth and sometimes it has seemed that there are a variety of unsynchronised pendulums swinging completely independently in different parts of the same organisation' (Hirsh & Jackson 1996b, p. 17).

On the face of it, perhaps the logical conclusion to draw from both studies is that good practice would appear to lie in finding a logical and rational response to the exigencies of the changing employment relationship by, for example, urging organisations to be more 'up-front' in their communications and to close the rhetorical gap (Hirsch & Jackson, 1996a, 1996b; Wills, 1997). Organisations must persuade their managers to become more involved and supportive in managing their employees' career (Garavan & Coolahan, 1996b). However, even at this pragmatic level it might be claimed that such solutions are overly optimistic, even naïve when set against what might be construed as somewhat brutal, calculative, and self-centred messages emanating from these and other studies (see e.g. Ebadan & Winstanley, 1996; Newell & Dopson, 1996; Sparrow, 1996). Indeed, in all of these studies, there is a risk that greater intervention by HR professionals and line managers may appear, at best, insincere and ineffective to employees, and, at worst, incompetent, obstructive, and damaging to their interests.

These studies would seem to support the argument that orthodox career management policies and practices are struggling to find an effective response to a changing psychological contract. This may, in part, be due to the inadequacies of current career structures and processes but it may also – and somewhat paradoxically – be due to the changing attitudes and the behaviour patterns of line managers and HR professionals. This is resulting in tensions and dysfunction in the career management process.

The changing role of line managers and HR professionals

The preceding discussion suggests that career outcomes are intertwined and thus affected by changes in the way managers and/or HR professionals perceive their role. As radical change grips organisations, managers are increasingly finding their roles being actively reinterpreted by their organisations and by themselves (Salaman, 1995; Stewart, 1994). As well as having to absorb and meet new job demands and expectations, they are discovering that their traditional role – which in the past combined social as well as functional duties and responsibilities conducted in an atmosphere of mutuality, paternalism, and patronage – is being replaced by something akin to the role of 'contracting agent', responsible for enacting and administering a more transactional employment relationship often with the expertise and support of their HR professional colleagues (Hallier & James, 1997; Sparrow, 1996).

In a number of ways, this new role of 'contracting agent' poses challenges to the efficacy and sustainability of the traditional manager/employee relationship as it has existed and operated within a mutual and reciprocal framework of relationships (Sparrow, 1996; Watson, 1996). In particular, it presents managers with a duality in their role as they become 'contract makers with subordinates and parties to their own organisational relationship' (Hallier & James, 1997, p. 706). What emerges from these developments is a 'double control' dilemma (Watson, 1994b). On the one hand, managers are encouraged to take responsibility for shaping the organisation and its performance by controlling those who deliver performance through techniques such as career management. On the other hand, they are having to 'control their own personal lives and identities and make sense of the work they are doing, both on behalf of the employing organisation and in terms of their own personal and private purposes and priorities' (Watson, 1994b, p. 895). The prospect therefore facing managers is one of 'contractual dissonance' as they have to reconcile their 'commitment to the employee contract and fulfilling their own contractual priorities' (Hallier & James, 1997).

A feasible and perhaps understandable reaction to this dilemma is for managers to exploit their traditional frameworks of managerial autonomy and agency which confer on them a right to make choices and decide particular courses of action. To preserve and minimise risk to their own functional, emotional, and psychological security, identity, and well-being, they may exploit this conferred right in a way that puts their self-interest ahead of employees, work priorities, and even the expectations of senior managers (Hallier & James, 1997; Herriot & Pemberton,

1995). But for many, such a value-system will run counter to their management philosophy and beliefs (Watson, 1996). Instead of permitting change to undermine mutuality and reciprocity in the employment relationship, managers may now be recognising that their future prospects are inextricably bound up with those of their employees. This may encourage them to try and protect elements of the traditional employment relationship by re-evaluating their existing obligations – including those they have with the organisation. It might be concluded therefore, that what appear to be dysfunctional attitudes and behaviour in career management – such as those suggested by the studies discussed earlier – may in fact be a reflection of managerial efforts to reconcile and come to terms with some of the more fundamental contradictions that have crept into the employment relationship. For example, it may now be considered legitimate by some managers to collude with their employees in areas such as appraisals to avoid communicating and acknowledging the message of new realism about career prospects which they perceive will have adverse consequences for employee commitment and performance and ultimately perceptions of the manager's personal performance (Herriott, Pemberton, & Pinder, 1993).

In the case of HR professionals, the evidence presented suggests two core issues to be addressed. First, it would appear that some HR professionals have yet to discover and adapt to a new role within the framework of the new psychological contract and its implications for employees, line managers, and the contracting process (Sparrow, 1996). Second, their efforts to adapt career-related HR policies and practices to meet organisational restructuring exigencies and the realities imposed by the psychological contract may be proving increasingly ineffectual (Fish & Wood, 1993; Newell & Dopson, 1996).

Conclusions and prospects for the future

For some organisations, the outlook would appear to be a bleak one. As the evidence presented in this chapter has suggested, they have not responded well to the career consequences of change and things may well reach crisis proportions as a growing number of line managers and HR professionals find themselves working within career management structures and systems that are seemingly inflexible and unable to handle the implications of a new employment relationship (Ebadan & Winstanley, 1996; Hallier & James, 1997; Newell & Dopson, 1996; Sparrow, 1996). The impression from a number of recent studies is that current frameworks are outdated and overly mechanistic (Fish & Wood, 1993; Newell & Dopson, 1996). Efforts by managers and HR professionals at amelioration appear to be meeting with little success. Instead, there is a risk that their efforts are contributing to greater employee cynicism with concomitant risks for motivation and labour retention and ultimately organisational performance (Hirsh & Jackson, 1996a; McDougall & Vaughan, 1996).

The possibility of crisis is further increased when career management procedures and practices begin to break down as more calculative and instrumental ideologies permeate the employment relationship. The potential is therefore created for 'career pandemonium' (Brousseau *et al.*, 1996). The message to those responsible for managing career would appear to be 'there are markedly different ways of defining career success and consequently markedly different approaches to career management and development in organisations' (p. 56). It would seem there has to be greater diversity and a more contingent, individualised approach to career management in organisations (Arnold, 1997; Brousseau *et al.*, 1996; Herriot & Pemberton, 1995).

Within the context of radical organisational change there must be doubts about the continuing efficacy and sustainability of the traditional, dyadic model – so long the foundation of the career management process. As stated at the beginning of this chapter, managers and employees are increasingly confronted with an uncertain business and organisational environment over which neither party can exert control and yet from within which they have to frame and enact their career management strategies (Garavan & Coolahan, 1996a; Giles & West, 1995). Crisis is likely to emerge if things do become so chaotic, so uncertain (Guest & Mackenzie Davey, 1996), and if the influence of 'anti-career drivers' (fewer promotion prospects, a loss of job security, a short-term performance culture) becomes so strong that they serve to destabilise career management processes by undermining openness and trust (Hirsh & Jackson, 1996a, 1996b). The risk is that career management then becomes a sham. At best, managers and HR professionals will view participation as a waste of time and resources. At worst, they may accuse it of demoralising employees by sending mixed messages about career motives and intentions. However, the evidence suggests they may seek to maintain the illusion of effectiveness in career management practice as long as it is in their political or emotional interest to do so.

Increased investment in communication techniques and other devices may not solve the problem. If the message is deemed to be suspect, people will continue to interpret their identity, role, career prospects, and job security in the reality of the situation in which they find themselves (Gollan, 1996; Hirsh & Jackson, 1996a, 1996b). Without any action, managers and employees may continue to collude with one another to obscure or avoid confronting reality and, in doing so, will preserve the illusion of an efficient and relevant career management system, and protect both their futures.

What action might be taken? To begin with, there has to be a greater understanding and awareness on the part of career theorists and practitioners about individual career patterns and motives and the way they are transformed in the organisational change process (Fish & Wood, 1993). As Nicholson and West (1988) argue, career theorists 'seem to have put all of their emphasis on the individual at the expense of the organisation' (p. 224) whilst practitioners have not replaced 'conventional but inaccurate paradigms of managerial careers with a new realism' (p. 225). As this chapter has suggested, a possible way forward might lie in promoting a greater understanding and appreciation of the way organisational role and job change are interpreted and of the nature of the social interactions that occur between key stakeholders in a complex and dynamic context (Fish & Wood, 1993). A future strategy based on formalised career structures and systems is unlikely to cope with the diversity and 'messiness' that is likely to characterise career management in the future (Bolton & Gold, 1994; Jackson et al., 1996).

Given the problems and issues identified in this chapter and the changes to the employment relationship discussed in chapter 2, it may be that future career management will only ever be effective if organisations can persuade their managers and HR professionals to relinquish their formalised career management roles and intervene less directly in shaping and managing the careers of others. Instinctively, managers may view this idea as an abrogation of professional and managerial responsibility. However, their views may change as they realise they do not have the time, energy, or information to form the productive social relationships required for effective career management (Hirsh, Jackson, & Jackson, 1995). A further impetus may be gained as the everyday experience of career management becomes more and more uncomfortable, tense, and risky, with managers increasingly feeling the effects of an employee backlash from changes to the employment relationship (Gollan, 1996).

This leads to speculation that future career management may be less concerned with one-to-one, dyadic interactions which attempt to shape career through direct social interaction and more with organisational strategies founded on a less interventionist, second-order approach that seeks to 'interfere with the interference' (Tosey, 1993). In practice – and despite reservations to the contrary (Mayo, 1992) – this will necessitate a far more laissez-faire posture from managers and HR professionals with regard to 'up-front' career management. Career can no longer be controlled and manipulated through the exercise of professional expertise, power, and patronage. Instead, energy and resources are diverted to addressing those contextual factors and influences that shape career, for example developing the right cultural orientation for self-ownership and development and thereby contributing to a more realistic and pragmatic process of HR planning and policy making. There is, after all, little merit in continuing to try and manage careers in a conventional manner if the management process itself does not confront and address the structural, cultural, and political barriers brought about by organisational change and which are increasingly undermining its effectiveness (Rajan, 1996; Wills, 1997). In the same vein, organisational efforts to change the balance of power by invoking the spirit and practices associated with the new employment relationship (of which career management is an important consideration) will receive little support from managers if all that is achieved is to undermine their power and status and add more hassle to an already hassled life!

This places a question mark over the efficacy of current career management systems and the way they contribute to organisational success. It suggests that on the evidence presented in this chapter, there may arise circumstances where career management, as an explicit organisational process, can be deemed dysfunctional to organisational performance if it creates unnecessary and avoidable frustration and disillusionment amongst employees. This might prompt a close examination of the benefits derived from career management and it is not inconceivable that such a review would lead some organisations to take a strategic decision to remove any pretence at being able to control or manage career in any centralised or formalised sense. What the impact of such a decision might be remains to be seen.

REFERENCES

Arnold, J. (1997). *Managing careers into the 21st century*. London: Paul Chapman.
Beardwell, I. & Holden, L. (1997). *Human resource management: A contemporary perspective* (2nd edn). London: Pitman.
Bolton, R. & Gold, J. (1994). Career management: Matching the needs of individuals with the needs of organisations. *Personnel Review, 23*, 6–24.
Bratton, J. & Gold, J. (1994). *Human resource management: Theory and practice*. Basingstoke: Macmillan Press.
Brousseau, K. R., Driver, M. J., Eneroth, K., & Larsson, R. (1996). Career pandemonium: Realising organisations and individuals. *Academy of Management Executive, 10* (4), 66–86.
Ebadan, G. & Winstanley, D. (1996). Downsizing, delayering and careers: The survivor's perspective. *Human Resource Management Journal, 7* (1), 79–91.
Fish, A. & Wood, J. (1993). A challenge to career management practice.

International Journal of Career Management, 5 (2), 3–10.

Garavan, T. & Coolahan, M. (1996a). Career mobility in organisations: Implications for career development – Part 1. *Journal of European Industrial Training, 20* (4), 30–40.

(1996b). Career mobility within organisations: Implications for career development – Part 2. *Journal of European Industrial Training, 20* (5), 31–39.

Germain, C. A. & Heath, C. E. (1994). Career development 2000. *Training and Development UK, 12* (5), 12–14.

Giles, M. & West, M. (1995). People as sculptures versus sculptures that shape career development programmes. *Journal of Management Development, 14* (10), 48–63.

Gollan, P. (1996, May). The revenge of the employee. *Management Australia,* 21–23.

Guest, D. & Mackenzie Davey, K. (1996, February). Don't write off the traditional career. *People Management, 2* (4), 22–25.

Hall, D. T., & Associates (1996). *The career is dead: Long live the career: A relational approach to careers.* San Francisco: Jossey-Bass.

Hallier, J. & James, P. (1997). Middle managers and the employee psychological contract: Agency, protection and advancement. *Journal of Management Studies, 34*, 703–728.

Hendry, C. & Jenkins, R. (1996). Psychological contracts and new deals. *Human Resource Management Journal, 7* (1), 39–43.

Herriot, P. & Pemberton, C. (1995). *New deals: The revolution in managerial careers.* Chichester: John Wiley & Sons.

Herriot, P., Pemberton, C., & Pinder, R. (1993). Misperceptions by managers and their bosses of each other's preferences regarding the manager's career: A case of the blind leading the blind? *Human Resource Management Journal, 4* (2), 39–51.

Hirsh, W. & Jackson, C. (1996a). *Strategies for career development: Promise, practice and pretence.* Report no. 305. Brighton: Institute for Employment Studies.

(1996b). Ticket to ride or no place to go? *People Management, 2* (13), 20–23, 25.

Hirsh, W., Jackson, C., & Jackson, C. (1995). *Careers in organisations: Issues for the future.* Report no. 287. Brighton: Institute for Employment Studies.

Inkson, K. (1995). Effects of changing economic conditions on managerial job changes and careers. *British Journal of Management, 6*, 183–194.

Jackson, C., Arnold, J., Nicholson, N., & Watts, A. G. (1996). *Managing careers in 2000 and beyond.* Report no. 304. Brighton: IES/CRAC.

Mabey, C. & Iles, P. (Eds.) (1994). *Managing learning.* London: Routledge.

Mabey, C. & Salaman, G. (1995). *Strategic human resource management.* Oxford: Blackwell.

Mayo, A. (1991). *Managing careers: Strategies for organisations.* London: Institute of Personnel Management.

(1992, February). A framework for career management. *Personnel Management,* 36–39.

McDougall, M. & Vaughan, E. (1996). Changing expectations of career development. *Journal of Management Development, 15* (9), 37–46.

Newell, H. & Dopson, S. (1996). Muddle in the middle: Organisational restructuring and middle management careers. *Personnel Review, 25* (4), 4–20.

Nicholson, N. & West, M. (1988). *Managerial job change: Men and women in transition*. Cambridge: Cambridge University Press.

Rajan, A. (1996). Employability in the finance sector: Rhetoric vs reality. *Human Resource Management Journal, 7* (1), 67–78.

Rothwell, S. (1995). Human resource planning. In J. Storey (Ed.), *Human resource management: A critical text* (pp. 167–202). London: Routledge.

Salaman, G. (1995). *Managing*. Buckingham: Open University Press.

Sparrow, P. (1996). Transitions in the psychological contract: Some evidence from the banking sector. *Human Resource Management Journal, 6* (4), 75–92.

Stewart, R. (1994). *Managing today and tomorrow*. Basingstoke: Macmillan.

Tate, W. (1995). *Developing corporate competence: A high performance agenda for managing organisation*. Aldershot: Gower.

Tosey, P. (1993). Interfering with the interference: A systemic approach to change in organisations. *Management Education and Development, 24* (3), 187–204.

Van Maanen, J. (1982). Boundary crossings: Major strategies of organisational socialisation and their consequences. In R. Katz (Ed.), *Career issues in human resource management* (pp. 85–115). Englewood Cliffs, NJ: Prentice-Hall.

Watson, T. J. (1994a). *In search of management*. London: Routledge.

(1994b). Management flavours of the month: Their role in managers' lives. *International Journal of Human Resource Management, 5*, 893–909.

(1996). How do managers think: Identity, morality and pragmatism in managerial theory and practice. *Management Learning, 27*, 323–341.

Wills, J. (1997, June). Can do better. *Personnel Today*, 31–34.

Woodall, J. & Winstanley, D. (1998). *Management development: Strategy and practice*. Oxford: Blackwell.

16   Learning for work: global causes, national standards, human relevance

Bill Law

Everybody has an interest in education. Nowhere is that more so than in the relationship between education and work. It may seem that 'vocational education' is the main arena for examining the relationship; but 'general education' and 'liberal education' are also deeply implicated.

How can education help in working lives?

General education is the transmission of knowledge, concepts, and methods, from a range of academic disciplines, which cover what all members of society should know. Part of it is thought to be for helping people, as one Prime Minister put it, 'to do a job of work'. The movement to identify work relevance in general education is world-wide (Oxenham, 1988). Employers are thought of as wanting young men and women to stay at school for long enough to gain qualifications; and qualifications are thought to be reliable guides to employability. Such assumptions shape the curriculum to employers' needs, so that students learn to communicate clearly, calculate precisely, key-board accurately, and work with others flexibly. These are 'key skills' for employability. Such thinking is now a feature of the education of young children (Lauglo & Lillis, 1988). The pressure is to raise standards because, it is assumed, work productivity will then increase (Department of Trade and Industry, 1994).

Vocational education is more specifically shaped, enabling people to develop employability for work roles. Where employability becomes a dominant feature of a secondary programme it is called pre-vocational education. Governments target money into schools on criteria associated with vocational relevance. Pre-vocational programmes are organised around work clusters rather than specific occupations; they can therefore have a more exploratory quality than vocational courses. In Britain they lead to general vocational qualifications, which compete for credibility with 'academic' qualifications.

Liberal education acknowledges that learning is for roles other than employment – as citizen, consumer, partner, and parent. Such roles are interleaved in domestic, neighbourhood, and community settings, and are addressed to more than economic tasks. Liberal education develops the qualities of mind required to reform society (Dewey, 1916). It includes questioning the purposes of what is being learned (Wirth, 1991). An aim is to inform consenting participation in society (Law, 1996b). Its more sceptical approach transposes consideration of 'key skills' into another discourse: we can help students to scrutinise communication for *value* as well as clarity; we can invite students to wonder about values that numbers *cannot* represent; we can value their questions concerning the *penalties* of information technology; and we can engage learners in a consideration of who they will, and *will not*, cooperate with. Education then becomes more contentious: 'why do this work?', 'who thinks it a good idea?' and 'what else might be done?'. As Hoggart (1995) acidly observes 'some people want children to be literate enough to be handed over to the persuaders, not literate enough to blow the gaff on them!' (p. 34).

Education can, then, examine answers to questions concerning, academically, 'knowing that' and, vocationally, 'knowing how' (cf. Pring, 1995). But it can also be concerned with, liberally, 'knowing why'.

The boundaries are permeable; some academic education pursues vocational purposes, some vocational programmes include liberal elements (Law, 1986). But the centres of gravity are distinct.

Understanding working life

'The principal purpose of education is to produce understanding' (Gardner, 1997). Understanding is more than 'knowing that'; it identifies the links between causes and effects that underpin 'knowing how'; and it is able to confront the difficulties and conflicts entailed in 'knowing why'. The centre column in table 16.1 lays out such elements for working life; the right-hand column suggests an agenda for education.

World-wide causes – in economics and technology

Some of the implications of the global economy are discussed in chapter 2 and elsewhere in this volume. The educational agenda is explained below.

Global commerce reaches into the social and political as well as the economic life of nations. It would be naïve to assume the benign intentions of all its movers and shakers (Hutton, 1995). The most powerful of them can undermine a state's control of its own economy (Marr, 1995).

Table 16.1. *Understanding contemporary working life*

1. CONCERNING WORLD-WIDE CAUSES		learning objectives
Global commerce	We compete in a low cost, low-public-investment environment, dominated by multi-nationals – and their customers	• understanding what global and domestic economies do • understanding the extent and limitations of domestic government influence on working lives
New technologies	Capital-intensification of production, distribution, and exchange confront all parts of society	• skill in new technologies at work • understanding change in work roles
Smaller government	Competitiveness releases businesses from regulation, affects social fabric, and develops a 'flexible' workforce	• ability to deal with a flexible labour market • understanding a reduced welfare provision
2. CONCERNING CHANGING PATTERNS OF EMPLOYMENT		learning objectives
Changing economic structures	Effects are cyclical, demographic, and structural – varying between sectors	• knowledge of causes and effects in variable work distribution • understanding who is most at risk
Extending concepts of work	More of what is done in domestic, freelance, voluntary, and other modes is thought of as 'proper work'	• understanding why people work • appreciating alternatives to employment and unemployment
Adapting work locations and requirements	Firms are smaller, 'flatter', cleaner – more work is done at home – skill requirements are changing	• ability to deal with contemporary work locations and procedures • ability to respond to changing requirements
3. CONCERNING PERSONAL AND SOCIAL EFFECTS		learning objectives
Transitory work contracts	Collective, full-time contracts are less common; serial or portfolio careers more common	• ability to find and approach work opportunities • ability to negotiate with recruiters
Discontinuous experience	Individual experience is increasingly fragmented offering lower levels of sustained contact	• ability to make continuing sense of fragmented experience • ability to maintain identity – even in rejection
Reconstructed community	Work connects people to neighbourhood and community – a stake in society lost to those without work	• appreciation of supportive social attachment • ability to discriminate who and who not to attend to

The educational task is therefore broader than vocational; people need to understand that it is a global empire of production, distribution, and exchange upon which the sun never sets. And it changes their lives.

New technologies. Commerce and technology are in global partnership. Its effects are accumulating and irreversible; they change what we all do at work. Work once done by muscle has for some time been done by hydraulic lift, more recently by magnetically controlled automata, now by digitally programmed warehousing. If the owner of the muscle still has a job his wages are no longer calculated by cranking comptometers, they are silently computed, and instantly credited. The balance is available at a call-facility, and accessed with a swipe card. You can buy much of what you need with a card number, a personal computer, and a modem.

Of course people need rudimentary IT skills. But workers need to understand that if they are not prepared to lose some of their jobs to technology, they risk losing all of them to a more efficient competitor elsewhere on the globe.

Smaller government. Competitiveness seeks environments where enterprise is less shackled by regulation and investment less penalised by tax. Government is urged to slim. Post-war Europe's standards of welfare are now said to be unsustainable, because national frontiers – protecting Keynesian solutions – have been eroded (Giddens, 1994). The effect is to relinquish protective social fabric to commerce.

Education is part of that fabric, and is not exempt. Relatively moderate commercial interests in education argue that the UK suffers a skills deficit, that private individuals must learn to manage their own career development in a market place, that careers guidance should be subject to market forces, and that education should develop vocationally relevant skills recorded on a life-long basis (e.g. Confederation of British Industry, 1995). Attention to education as a remediable cause of decline is not unwelcome to politicians. They sense their inability to deal in other ways with the global causes of domestic failure.

But, for people seeking work, the future is as much a threat as a promise. Though young people are reported to see their lives as better than those of their parents, they are troubled by insecurity and by perceptions of work as unfriendly to life-style concerns (Wilkinson & Mulgan, 1995). Dealing with this must rest on an educated understanding of global causes and their consequences.

Changing patterns of work – and forms of disengagement

Global causes have domestic effects, in places of employment and other locations now used as work places. They are referred to elsewhere in this volume.

Changing economic structures. Informed planning for work needs to understand that no economy is static. There are rhythms in levels of employment and shifts in the demand between sectors, bringing changes in who is most likely to get employment. Some of these effects are 'frictional' (unemployment while the next job is found); some 'cyclic' (caused by recurrent down-turns in economic activity); some are 'demographic' (when population change puts too many people in the labour market); and some are 'long-wave' (while we wait for the next phase of economic activity to gather momentum). In all these cases the effects come and, eventually, go.

But global commerce exports work to cheaper markets and new technologies replace workers with more cost-effective machines. These effects are structural – cumulative, accelerating, and irreversible. They come, they keep on coming, and they stay. They mean loss of jobs; but complex causes have variable effects – unemployment differently impacts different age groups, genders, levels of qualification, employment sectors, and geographic areas.

Over-employment – having too much work to do – is also an effect of change. An irony of contemporary street life is people with no time to read a street paper, buying one from people with little left to them but to try to sell it. A flexible and frantically busy worker, using new technology, can engage in tasks which would have formerly required design, production, secretarial, and management people. Many such traditional work titles lose their meaning (Hirsh, Kidd, & Watts, 1998).

Bad employment is a third effect of change. The badly employed are abused in work below their attainment level, and – often – with unfair pay and conditions.

Disengagement from employment is a commonly reported response to all three effects. But disengagement is itself not one thing:

- *'Can't work'* means a person has not risen to employability levels for available work. He or she may live in an area of skill shortage, but is not a credible candidate. Such people are in a 'frictional' relationship with a current demand, they are disengaged until they become employable.
- *'Excluded-from-work'* means a person is living in an area where there is not enough work to go round. He or she may be highly employable but labour supply exceeds demand. 'Long-wave', 'cyclic', and 'structural' changes have such effects.
- *'Won't-work'* means that people avoid work on offer. Some welfare dependants and people who live off crime are here. So are more respectable 'down-shifters'. Freelance, voluntary, and domestic work are among their options. All risk becoming 'outsiders'; not necessarily a dishonourable position (Wilson, 1956).

- *'Separated-from-work'* means that people lose contact with the means to improve their position. There are areas of economic depression where you may never meet someone who can help you find work. A good many welfare dependants are here, for whom disengagement is a self-replicating social script.

Not to understand the risks of disengagement is to be at a serious career disadvantage. Helping people to understand this is an educational task.

Extending concepts of work. But disengagement from employment is not disengagement from all *work* (cf. Bayliss, 1998). Work-for-wages is a recent invention. Many so-called 'disengaged' forms of work are longer-standing.

Diversity in work reflects the range of human motivation. Assumptions that people work solely for wages insults that diversity (Law & Ward, 1981). Indeed, contemporary work values are reported to be shifting away from economic concerns (Wilkinson & Mulgan, 1995).

Some disengagement from employment can be re-engagement in community. Giddens (1994, p. 167) enthuses about 'the survival and perhaps re-creation of local traditions, a bursting variety of activities carried on by neo-artisans, living off their locally developed skills as well as catering to the needs of the neighbourhood'. Maybe. But learning all they need to know about work in work-for-wages would be an impoverished education for people. In societies where forms of employment are increasingly problematic, and forms of disengagement are increasingly prevalent, education must extend concepts of work (Law & Storey, 1987).

Adapting work locations and requirements. This volume refers to changes in the places where people work, the equipment they use, the operations they engage in, and the relationship they make.

The obvious implications for education are vocational, helping people to deal with new technologies. Less obvious is the need to help them anticipate and plan for work in sparsely populated work environments, with flatter and more pressurised management. Less obvious still is the need to help them anticipate work outside paid employment – with 'sweated home-labour' and 'electronic cottage' as increasingly common locations.

Enthusiasts for the technological triumphs of the global economy are quick to point to the need for appropriate skills – which are often quite rudimentary. A more demanding need is to learn how to survive, cope, and thrive in contemporary working conditions.

Personal and social effects – and the reconstruction of communities

More deeply implicit in this is a concern not just with functional efficiency but with sustainable meaning. As Hutton (1995, p. 11) points out, places of employment were themselves once 'at the heart of society, where people work and define their lives'. Work-for-wages once provided workers and their families with a culture, an identity and means of attachment to community (Law, 1986). If changed work changes meanings, then education must respond.

Transitory work contracts. Work is a contract. A worker's gain has been security. Salary scales, pension arrangements, and leisure activities ranging from company health clubs to brass bands, manifest a culture of attachment. But contracts are changing. Part of the psychological contract workers are now said to make requires employers to offer re-saleable employability rather than sustained attachment (Herriot & Pemberton, 1995).

Operational contracts are increasingly for part-time and short-term work. We speak of portfolio and serial careers. Such flexibility makes paid employment more like other forms of work: self-employment and voluntary work combine portfolio and serial features. Marriages and other domestic partnerships are, if not portfolio, increasingly serial.

Young people seem ready for such flexibility (Wilkinson & Mulgan, 1995); they are reported to assemble work life from elements of employment, self-employment, and voluntary work (Cannon, 1997). The 're-newal' and 'invigoration' (Handy, 1995) they find may or may not be due recompense for loss of attachment.

The implications for education are extensive. People must learn to rely on personal resources rather than institutional support to manage their careers (Jackson, Arnold, Nicholson, & Watts, 1996). Education for work cannot therefore ignore the needs to seek out shifting opportunities and to negotiate the psychological and operational contracts they now entail.

Discontinuous experience. Disturbances in work disturb the way in which identity is known. Sacks (1997) specifies the threat:

> It will not be surprising if a person's life consists in a series of temporary engagements – jobs, relationships, lifestyles – none of which, since they come and go, gives shape and unity to a life. He may even have little relationship with his parents or his children. Perhaps the cruellest realisation will be that for no one does he hold unconditional worth. A world without moral bonds, of free floating attachments, is one in which we are essentially replaceable – as employees, sexual partners, or members of a lifestyle enclave. (p. 97)

Sack's particular analysis of the fear is rooted in Judaeo-Christian cultures. There are other ways of manifesting identity. Any adequate conception of education must offer ways of making continuing personal sense of fragmented experience. A severe test of that need is the ability to deal with rejection, and move on, intact. Vocational education cannot do this; it needs something more.

Reconstructed community. To work is to occupy a role – such as 'colleague', 'entrepreneur', or 'performer'. Roles are reciprocating relationships: colleague with mates, entrepreneur with competitors, performer with audience. Some roles are assigned; but many are achieved by people who enrich work with a commitment above and beyond the call of the pay-cheque. This criss-cross of relationships offers 'ligatures' for social membership (Dahrendorf, 1979). Work is a cultural and social, as well as an individual and economic, phenomenon. If this is so, then changed work will change society.

The evidence accumulates: change in contemporary working life has marginalised significant numbers of British people. Galbraith (1992) characterises the group as 'the underclass'. It is calculated (Hutton, 1995) that 30% of contemporary Britain is disadvantaged by being part of a family in which there is no adequately paid work. Most Brits, he argues, now find it difficult to think of themselves as social stakeholders. Meanwhile, the contented minority is characterised by Galbraith as assuming themselves to be receiving their just desserts.

Damaged social fabric is more than the erosion of welfare. We are speaking here of 'damaged solidarities' (Giddens, 1994). Fukuyama (1995) highlights the importance of damage to attachments wider than the family and narrower than the state – in neighbourhood and work place. The problem is this: people start from marginal roles, such as 'child' and 'student'; their maturational task is to achieve recognisable roles in a proximate society – if people do that, they have a stake in something shared; if they don't, they don't. This is disengagement.

The comfortable also disengage, according to Hutton, by establishing a 'caste-status causing them to withdraw from the public life of the country' (1995, p. 34).

Disengagement determines what shall be attended to and ignored. Ignoring can be rational where it ignores what cannot be managed (Marr, 1995). There may be a rationality in ignoring some aspects of global commerce. But ignoring the condition of members of your own community gnaws at the weft of social fabric. Is that what can be traced in the experience of young men and women who take pride in being 'outsiders'? They are reported to be sceptical concerning education, politics, and work (Wilkinson & Mulgan, 1995).

Fukuyama (1995) offers a diagnosis of damage by 'horizontal solidarities' separating society into levels – a level for the middle-aged and another for the young, one for management and another for labour, somewhere for the contented and somewhere else for the disadvantaged. There is less exchange between levels than within them. The British, argues Fukuyama, are particularly good at this.

Fukuyama also refers to 'vertical solidarities', attachments between levels. A lack of vertical attachment, argues Fukuyama, breeds a distancing and blaming distrust. Fukuyama cites world-wide evidence that distrust is associated with social and economic decline.

There is no way back to the comfortable attachments of middle-aged nostalgia; but – developing Fukuyama's imaging of 'horizontal' and 'vertical' attachment – social fabric is constituted by both warp and weft.

A question is: 'What social weft binds business managers to welfare dependants and the contented to the disadvantaged?' It is not a market-driven Press that creates these connections (cf. Engel, 1996). Cyber-space's 'society of networks' separates people as much as it connects them (cf. Mulgan & Briscoe, 1997). Perhaps one contemporary thread in social fabric, on which many of these people *might* meet many of the others, is in the comprehensive networks still set up by some schools.

But education's contribution to the recovery of social engagement is increasingly outside formal institutions – in adult literacy schemes and community regeneration projects (Coombs, 1985). As Illich's (1971) use of the term 'conviviality' long ago implied, such education draws on authority which is *available* not imposed, *tested* not assumed, *democratic* not hierarchical.

The remaining question is, 'Can formal education achieve such an authority?'

Deeper challenges to education

People now need to understand work to a depth and extent as great as their need to understand anything. Some of the elements, and some implications for education, have been set out in Table 1. We turn now to wider and deeper implications.

Education, community, and authority

Learning for work does not occur in a social vacuum. In developing working lives people change their own and their loved ones' life chances, they determine their relationship with tax–welfare–debt–insurance systems, they impact the built and natural environment and – so – they influence the lives of people they will never meet. Everybody has an interest in what we each do about work. Career development is besieged with argument, blandishment, and enticement. Employers are major persuaders. Freedom from pressure is not an option.

And so, the 'what?', 'how?', and 'why?' questions extend to their supplementaries: 'who else has an interest in this?', 'why do I care about her?', 'how can I know whether I can trust him?', 'how do I get to grips with what people are saying here?'.

If these questions are real, contemporary education needs a non-authoritarian rationale which enables *autonomy* in being with *others* (Law, 1992). Giddens (1994) nicely counterpoises the elements: 'compliance', he says, 'is freely given'. How can that be: *free* compliance? free *compliance?*

Understanding requires an education that reaches beyond a process of matching unproblematic information about work to a readily defined self, equipped with clearly prescribed skills. The agenda is more subtle, layered . . . and fraught. People need to be able to examine the conflict between argument and pressure, to probe rhetoric, and to realise when advice is self-serving.

Career learning can be understood in such terms. Educated career learning is a progressive process leading to an understanding of where significant causes and effects lie – in work, roles, and self. It subjects all action, one's own and others', to *due process*. This evocation of a legal procedure is appropriate: due process does not elevate process over outcome; it requires that process shall be fairly conducted, in response to evidence, and in accordance with reason. In career learning this means gathering, sifting, focusing, and hypothesising the relevant knowledge (Law, 1996a). Without due process both compliance and defiance are dependent. With it even compliance – while not free from pressure – autonomously determines whose voice shall be ascribed authority . . . and whose shall not. Such processes abandon distinctions between hierarchical and lay authority (cf. Giddens, 1994). They manifest authority where it is found – among the 'disengaged' as well as the 'establishment'.

All of this locates learning for work as part of a discourse where traditional authority is exposed to scrutiny (Marr, 1995) and where populism is rejected in favour of thoughtful democracy (Hoggart, 1995). It is a long way from training people in the unscrutinised demands of employability. It evokes a liberal agenda. Through such an agenda social fabric repairs its weft.

Taking learning out of its box

A problem for education is transferability: how is learning in a 'classroom' made re-usable outside? Academic learning comes boxed in subjects.

Transfer means enabling students to use learning in another setting, in another role, on another task.

Maclure (1991) disentangles three approaches to transfer. His analysis returns us to a consideration of general, vocational, and liberal education.

a. The 'by-product' approach assumes that what people need to do is embedded in the general curriculum, and that transfer will happen spontaneously: where we teach it well, people will pick it up and use it.
b. The 'skills' approach favours setting up additional programmes dedicated specifically to what people need to do in clearly identified settings. This is a rationale for vocational education.
c. The 'infusion' approach agrees with the 'by-product' approach concerning the life relevance of general education, but insists that its usefulness must be made explicit, so that people can see how it might be used in life. Such an approach would transpose general education into a liberal mode.

The kind of spontaneous combustion assumed by the *by-product approach* no doubt occasionally occurs. Where people recognise learning as useful, it is impossible to stop them learning.

Such transfers occur in narrative subjects – history, literature, religious education – where other people's work biographies offer us each a clue to our own. It may be easier to recognise the work relevance of the knowledge, concepts, and methods of dispositional subjects – science, technology, geography. But ability in expressive subjects – language, mathematics, the arts, and physical education – underpins much of what we do in any setting (at least as surely as the playing fields of Eton influenced the outcome at Waterloo).

Transfer depends upon people understanding the purposefulness of learning. Otherwise it is difficult for them to imagine how they would continue to use in their lives what they encounter in education. For reasons set out below, it may be over-optimistic for Prime Ministers, employers, or anybody else to assume that learners frequently make such links.

That is why the *skills approach* favours dedicated vocational and pre-vocational programmes. Perkins and Salomon (1989) characterise this as a battery of procedures linked to focused tasks. Evidence is collated by Meadows (1993) that transference is triggered where learners recognise this specific 'encoding' of the learning to the task, so that the learning- and life-situation are seen as similar.

Programme development here is largely one of importing the knowledge and concepts of 'pure' disciplines and applying them to the tasks, roles, and settings of working life. Some careers education, as it is taught in specialised classroom work in Britain, employs this approach.

But Perkins and Salomon (1989) characterise it as 'low-road' transferability. It is directed at a narrow range of applications which must be anticipated in advance. It cannot address the range of skills or the depth of understanding demanded by hard-to-anticipate contemporary changes in working lives. Importantly, in the context of this discussion, it does nothing for the ability to explore sceptically the 'why?' as well as the 'how?' questions of work.

Perkins and Salomon's 'high-road' transferability more closely resembles what Maclure (1991) calls the *infusion approach*. Where learning is deliberately and specifically given richer and deeper associations, it is likely to be linked to a range of tasks, roles, and settings. Indeed links can occur to situations that might not have been anticipated in the classroom.

There is a problem for infusion; it is that a single discipline or subject rarely offers a sufficiently wide range of knowledge for the resolution of any real-life event. Solutions to the simplest of working-life tasks require the simultaneous use of communicating, calculating, visualising, prioritising, and hypothesising abilities – from a range of disciplines. No academic discipline covers enough ground; the nature of academic specialism ensures that it will not. Academe puts asunder what life must join together. Furthermore a non-authoritarian education – for a thoughtfully democratic work force, in a diversifying but fragile social fabric – requires other-than-academic authority. Transfer of learning requires widely associated and flexibly applied learning and that cannot be achieved on a subject-by-subject basis or in the tightly 'classified and framed' curriculum of closed institutions (Bernstein, 1973).

There are further problems for transfer. Learners are reported (Meadows, 1993) to be reluctant to 'go beyond the information' in order to link it to novel situations. Where they are prepared to take that step they need time to learn how to do it. The evidence suggests that practice and support is essential, if people are to recognise and appropriately re-use the underpinning principles of learning.

A rationale for a general national curriculum can include the view that people have entitlement to a broad and balanced range of commonly required learning. Exponential growth in knowledge is making this increasingly hard to attain. 'Breadth and balance' are, in any event, arbitrary concepts, dependent upon whose point-of-view is adopted. A more contemporary strategy would be to address the need to learn how to learn; a refocusing of attention from the content to the processes of education. Command of process is, argues Meadows (1993), essential to all flexible and extendable transfers of learning. She lists the processes:

'students who are good at transfer are inclined to plan problem-solving approaches, seek additional information, search for and use analogies, check their reasoning, monitor progress, engage in efficient fix-up strategies when getting off track, and so forth' (p. 86).

We have identified six conditions for the transferability of learning. People will be able to link learning to work where they:

- appreciate that learning has a purpose beyond gaining qualifications, so that it is seen as valuable – having a point;
- recognise a specific use for each piece of learning, so that people link learning to life;
- make multiple associations, so that one piece of learning can be linked to a range of tasks, settings, and roles;
- integrate learning, so that understanding from different subjects or disciplines can be brought to bear upon a single problem or decision;
- take possession of due processes as well as the content of learning – learning how to learn, so that when unforeseen situations arise people know how to approach them;
- are practised and supported, so that there is time and space to develop and adjust their use of the learning.

This is a tall order. It is hardly surprising that transfer of learning is not commonly observed (cf. Rowe, Aggleton, & Whitty, 1993). The practical implications are daunting: learners need to learn both inside and outside the school or college; and they need time to find, practise, develop, and refine widely associated learning. Liberal manifestations of pre-vocational education have commonly employed the required apparatus: time to develop learning, community-linked activity, in inter-disciplinary schemes of work, addressed to tasks rather than subjects (Law, 1986). Such programmes are squeezed in Britain by the subject-framed and standards-driven National Curriculum.

A culture of relevance

Transfer of learning is a key concept in developing education for contemporary working life. It can be applied in general education, and vocational education; but an important theme in this chapter concerns the liberal agenda.

Where transfer is achieved learning will remind students of their lives and their lives will remind them of their learning. This means that learning is more likely to be sought, remembered, used, and developed. If these things happen, standards will rise. But that is not the rationale; indeed, an exclusive preoccupation with measurable standards has the effect of locking learning in categorised boxes – the antithesis of transferability.

The liberal agenda requires an education culture which restores balance to an obsessional concern for standards. This chapter has led to a definition of transfer-of-learning which links purpose to process and all to the problems and decisions of widely conceived work. It therefore speaks not just of standards but of relevance.

The concept of relevance stretches beyond any particular interest in education – certainly beyond employer interests. Now more than ever, work life impacts consumer choice and income maintenance, it also concerns the built and natural environment and the social fabric. Education for one of these concerns must be education for them all; in the contemporary world the boundaries between them are increasingly meaningless. Indeed, consumer action may be at least as important as politics and work, as a lever for shaping the environment we must all now share.

A feature of culture is that we notice it most when it changes. The growth of a world-wide preoccupation with standards was one such change. It was a legitimate correction to some ill-thought-through mid-century so-called liberal pretensions. There is no way back, and this chapter is not seeking one. But, whatever new culture for world-wide new-millennium education is now developed, it must pursue relevance. For if, without standards, learning is unreliably flaky, without recognisable relevance it is entirely futile.

REFERENCES

Bayliss, V. (1998). *Redefining work*. London: RSA.
Bernstein, B. B. (1973). On the classification and framing of educational knowledge. In K. Brown (Ed.), *Knowledge, education and cultural change* (pp. 363–392). London: Tavistock.
Cannon, D. (1997). The post-modern work ethic. In G. Mulgan (Ed.), *Life after politics: New thinking for the twenty-first century* (pp. 41–48). London: Fontana.
Confederation of British Industry (1995). *Realising the vision – a skills passport*. London: Author.
Coombs, P. H. (1985). *The world crisis in education*. Oxford: Oxford University Press.
Dahrendorf, R. (1979). *Life chances*. London: Weidenfeld and Nicolson.
Department of Trade and Industry (1994). *Competitiveness – helping business to win*. London: HMSO.
Dewey, J. (1916). *Democracy in education*. London: Macmillan.
Engel, M. (1996). *Tickle the public*. London: Victor Gollancz.
Fukuyama, F. (1995). *Trust: The social virtues and the creation of prosperity*. London: Hamish Hamilton.
Galbraith, J. K. (1992). *The culture of contentment*. London: Sinclair Stevenson.

Gardner, H. (1997). Opening minds. In G. Mulgan (Ed.), *Life after politics: New thinking for the twenty-first century* (pp. 101–110). London: Fontana.

Giddens, A. (1994). *Beyond left and right: The future of politics.* London: Polity Press.

Handy, C. (1995). *Beyond certainty: The changing worlds of organisations.* London: Hutchinson.

Herriot, P. & Pemberton, C. (1995). *New deals: The revolution in managerial careers.* Chichester: John Wiley & Sons.

Hirsh, W., Kidd, J. M., & Watts, A. G. (1998). *Constructs of work used in careers guidance.* Cambridge: National Institute for Careers Education and Counselling.

Hoggart, R. (1995). *The way we live now.* London: Chatto and Windus.

Hutton, W. (1995). *The state we're in.* London: Cape.

Illich, I. (1971). *De-schooling society.* London: Calder and Boyars.

Jackson, C., Arnold, J., Nicholson N., & Watts, A. G. (1996). *Managing careers in 2000 and beyond.* Report no. 304. Brighton: Institute for Employment Studies.

Lauglo, J. & Lillis, K. (1988). Vocationalisation in international perspective. In J. Lauglo & K. Lillis (Eds.), *Vocationalising education: An international perspective* (pp. 3–28). London: Pergamon.

Law, B. (1986). *The pre-vocational franchise: Organising community-linked education for adult and working life.* London: Harper and Row.

(1992). Autonomy and learning about work. In R. A. Young & A. Collin (Eds.), *Interpreting career: Hermeneutical studies of lives in context* (pp. 210–232). Westport, CT: Praeger.

(1996a). A career learning theory. In A. G. Watts, B. Law, J. Killeen, J. M. Kidd, & R. Hawthorn (Eds.), *Rethinking careers education and guidance: Theory, policy and practice* (pp. 46–71). London: Routledge.

(1996b). Careers education in a curriculum. In A. G. Watts, B. Law, J. Killeen, J. M. Kidd, & R. Hawthorn (Eds.), *Rethinking careers education and guidance: Theory, policy and practice* (pp. 210–232). London: Routledge.

Law, B. & Storey, J. (1987). *Is it working?* Hertford: National Institute for Careers Education and Counselling.

Law, B. & Ward, R. (1981). Is career development motivated? In A. G. Watts, D. E. Super, & J. M. Kidd (Eds.), *Career development in Britain: Some contributions to theory and practice* (pp. 101–154). Cambridge: CRAC/Hobsons.

Maclure, S. (1991). Learning to think: Thinking to learn – an overview. In S. Maclure & P. Davies (Eds.), *Learning to think: Thinking to learn* (pp. ix–xxvii). London: Pergamon.

Marr, A. (1995). *Ruling Britannia: The failure and future of British democracy.* London: Michael Joseph.

Meadows, S. (1993). *The child as thinker.* London: Routledge.

Mulgan, G. & Briscoe, I. (1997). The society of networks. In G. Mulgan (Ed.), *Life after politics: New thinking for the twenty-first century* (pp. 339–345). London: Fontana

Oxenham, J. (1988). What do employers want from education? In J. Lauglo & K. Lillis (Eds.), *Vocationalising education: An international perspective* (pp. 69–80). London: Pergamon.

Perkins, D. N. & Salomon, G. (1989). Are cognitive skills context bound? *Educational Researcher, 18* (1), 16–25.

Pring, R. (1995). *Closing the gap: Liberal education and vocational preparation.* London: Hodder and Stoughton.

Rowe, G., Aggleton, P., & Whitty, G. (1993). *Subjects and themes in the school curriculum: The national survey.* London: Institute of Education.

Sacks, J. (1997). *The politics of hope.* London: Jonathan Cape.

Wilkinson, H. & Mulgan, G. (1995). *Freedom's children: Work relationships and politics for 18–34-year-olds in Britain today.* London: Demos.

Wilson, C. (1956). *The outsider.* London: Victor Gollancz.

Wirth, A. G. (1991). Issues in the vocational–liberal studies controversy – 1900–1917: John Dewey v. the Social Efficiency Philosophers. In D. Corson (Ed.), *Education for work* (pp. 55–64). Clevedon, Avon: Multilingual Matters.

17   The new career and public policy

A. G. Watts

Careerquake

The concept of career has been a significant feature of advanced industrial societies in the twentieth century. For individuals, it has provided the structure for a coherent and continuous working life which has helped to shape and sustain social identity, linked to a faith in the future and a sense of the future self. For organisations, it has provided a means of motivating employees, and a structure through which their development can be linked to organisational goals. It has also bound individuals to the wider society, and so helped to stabilise it (Wilensky, 1961).

But career structures in many countries are now being fractured (see chapter 2). Work organisations are less prepared to make long-term commitments to individuals. Many have been reducing their size, and seeking to operate in more flexible ways through a small core of key workers and a growing contractual periphery.

This process has gone further in some countries than in others. It is strongly evident in English-speaking countries, and particularly in the USA, which has been concerned to restrict labour-market regulation and to trust the free flow of market forces. Although deregulation has created jobs, many have been low-skill in nature. Combined with low levels of social-welfare expenditure, this has resulted in marked social disparities, linked to high levels of crime, drugs, and violence.

In other countries, the process has been constrained by cultural and political factors (Albert, 1993; Hutton, 1995). In Japan, for example, the 'lifetime employment system' has been eroded somewhat but remains influential; economic relationships are based on trust and continuity, supported by an interventionist state providing the infrastructure for economic development. Continental European countries like Germany, France, and the Scandinavian countries, too, have sought to regulate markets, underpinned by corporate partnerships between the state, employers, and unions, in order to encourage employment security and social protection. It seems, however, that relative stability in these countries is being bought at the price of higher levels of unemployment.

The UK could be in a position to offer a 'third way'. It has traditionally had a stronger welfare ethos than the USA. But its tentative flirtations with corporatism have been largely abandoned, and in recent years it has engaged in extensive US-style deregulation aimed at securing greater labour-market flexibility. Its task now is to see whether it can re-cast its welfare ethos in forms which can be reconciled with such flexibility.

Labour-market flexibility is not necessarily unwelcome to those affected by it. But for many, it is seen as offering a threat rather than an opportunity (National Association of Citizens Advice Bureaux, 1997). This is particularly the case for the low-skilled, who can be exploited on low wages, without benefits or security, and then thrown back on to the labour market when no longer needed. Flexibility here becomes a euphemism for the naked exercise of employers' labour-market power.

This raises the critical issue of how flexibility can be reconciled with the need to secure the high skill levels required for economic competitiveness. As Reich (1991, pp. 264–265) points out, well-trained workers and modern infrastructure attract global webs of enterprise, which invest and give workers relatively good jobs; these jobs, in turn, generate additional on-the-job training and experience, thus creating a powerful lure to other global webs (see also Porter, 1990). High levels of skill make it possible to generate products which compare on the basis of quality rather than purely on the basis of price: this alone can yield the high returns that sustain high wages. But in flexible labour markets, employers tend to restrict their training commitment to their limited core workers. While some peripheral workers may be prepared to plan and finance their own training to maintain employability, those with lower skills and lower pay are unlikely to do so; even less so are those caught in poverty traps and cultures of unemployment which limit their hold on the labour market.

This in turn poses threats to social cohesion. Hutton (1995) has described the emergence of the 40:30:30 society: the growing divisions between the 40% who are relatively privileged, in reasonably secure employment or self-employment; the 30% who are marginalised and insecure, in jobs that are poorly protected and carry few benefits; and the 30% who are disadvantaged, being either unemployed or economically inactive. Such divisions threaten a decline into an ever more selfish, splintered, violent society. In the USA, Reich (1991, p. 303) has pointed to the risk that what he calls the 'symbolic analysts' – the new work aristocracy, with the high-level skills that can make flexibility work to their advantage – are losing their sense of belonging to a wider community, and becoming resentful of any support for the well being of others. He notes that their sense of enclosure is illusory: that 'the peace of mind potentially offered by platoons of security guards, state-of-the-art alarm systems, and a multitude of prisons is limited'.

The key policy question, therefore, is whether it is possible to reconcile social equity and upgrading of skills with a flexible labour market. One response is to view low-skill jobs in life-cycle terms (Esping-Andersen, 1994). Instead of being a life sentence for certain groups, such jobs could be seen as a temporary phase, giving individuals an initial experience of work disciplines, filling in gaps, or helping to fund further education, after which they can move on to more demanding roles. The Confederation of British Industry (1989) has advanced the concept of 'careers for all' – linked to continuous learning throughout life as the means of achieving the 'skills revolution' needed to achieve competitive advantage in the global economy.

This suggests that what is needed is a much broader concept of career, supported by appropriate social institutions and incentives. In the industrial era, the dominant concept of career has been progression up an ordered hierarchy within an organisation or profession. Instead, career should now be viewed as the individual's lifelong progression in learning and in work. 'Learning' embraces not only formal education and training, but also informal forms of learning, in the work place and elsewhere. 'Work' includes not only paid employment and self-employment, but also the many other forms of socially valuable work, in households and in the community (including child-rearing and elder care). 'Progression' covers not only vertical but also lateral movement: it is concerned with experience as well as positions; with broadening as well as advancing. 'Progression' does however retain the sense of development: career is more than mere biography.

Such a concept recognises not only skill development but also fluctuations in the life-cycle due to changing family commitments and changing values. It provides a framework for encouraging everyone to continue to learn and develop throughout life, linked to a sense of having a stake in society. It thus makes it possible to reconcile flexibility with a just society, in Rawls's (1972) challenging definition of the term: one we would choose to live in if we did not know what position within it we ourselves would occupy.

If future careers in this broader sense are to be accessible to all, new social ligatures are needed: new bonds between individuals and social structures. These are the issues for public policy which this chapter discusses. Much of it is drawn from a pamphlet written for the policy think-tank Demos (Watts, 1996); many of its themes have also more recently been addressed by Bayliss (1998). Whilst written mainly from a UK perspective, most of the issues are of broader international relevance.

More flexible financial-support structures

The most fundamental ligature is to reform the welfare state to provide support to more flexible and individually driven careers, linked to a wider concept of work. The welfare state that emerged after the Second World War was based on a series of assumptions about the family, work, and the life-cycle (Esping-Andersen, 1994). The family was assumed to combine a full-time stably employed male wage-earner, with a wife primarily devoted to her work within the home. It was further assumed that their life-cycles were orderly, standardised, and predictable, that male employment was assured, and that the welfare state could therefore concentrate on childhood (schooling) and old age (pensions), being largely passive during the active middle part of the life-cycle except in supporting men affected by frictional or cyclical unemployment.

All of these assumptions are now in question. Women are now spending much longer periods in the labour force, with shorter gaps for child-rearing. Young people are entering the labour force later, and taking longer to secure an independent foothold within it. Dislocation and significant changes in mid-career are more common. Some older workers are adopting a more gradual process of disengagement from full-time employment. In short, the life-cycle is becoming more flexible and diverse (e.g. Gaullier, 1992).

These changes place an ever-greater burden on the welfare system as currently constructed, with longer periods of dependency during the lifespan and shorter periods of contribution. This is producing a fiscal crisis in which the basic tenets of welfare as a basis for social equity and citizenship are being increasingly challenged, and levels of support eroded.

The most radical proposal for supporting a more flexible concept of career is to collapse the present tax and social-benefits systems into a basic citizen's income, received as a right by every individual – man, woman, and child. This would enable people to make flexible choices about the extent of paid employment in which they engage. The concept of unemployment – an industrial-era notion (Garraty, 1978) – would be redundant. With it would go poverty traps and the alternative lure of the black economy. More flexible patterns of work would be positively encouraged rather than – as at present – discouraged. The concept has appeal both to the political left, because it provides an egalitarian base, and to the right, because it liberates the market.

There are, however, objections to the citizen's income. The first is *fiscal*: the costs of the level needed to provide the basis for a satisfactory quality of life. After exhaustive costings of alternative models, Parker (1989) concluded that while it is not politically realistic to move immediately to a full citizen's income, it could be phased in. The second objection is *political*: a basic income would not of itself solve the problems of social exclusion, but might erode the political will to do anything further to address them. Certainly there would be a need for further measures to transform, for example, the infrastructure of poor neighbourhoods in terms of resources, housing, education, and economic opportunities. The third objection is *ethical*: by providing income without duties, the basic income undermines the concept of reciprocal obligation, traditionally the basis of active citizenship (Gray, 1996). It would however recognise that social contribution can take a variety of forms other than paid employment; and would be preferable to the present benefit system, which provides income only so long as people can demonstrate that they are doing little or nothing of social value.

To those who regard the ethical objection as decisive, the debate moves to some form of 'work test'. Taken to its logical conclusion, it leads to the notion of replacing current benefit systems with a 'workfare' scheme, in which unemployment benefits are paid only to those who engage in work constructed through public-policy interventions. The administrative costs of such schemes are, however, considerable, and there are difficulties in ensuring that they do not undermine the operations of the market. They also, if too narrowly drawn, tend to have a stigmatising effect, associated with 'make-work' rather than 'real work'. If, however, the boundaries of what is regarded as acceptable social contribution are broadened to include voluntary work, childcare, and education and training – as suggested by the concept of a 'participation income' (Commission on Social Justice, 1994) – this danger is more easily avoided. It then becomes a matter of balancing the costs of policing such a system – and the invasion of individual dignity which such policing systems can involve – against the benefits of maintaining an assurance of social obligation.

In the meantime, steps need to be taken to devise ways of coping with the effects of more flexible and discontinuous career patterns on mortgages, pensions, and private health-care insurance, all of which have hitherto been based on assumptions of continuous employment. Thus the great majority of those whose homes are repossessed because of mortgage default are people who have lost their job, whose earnings have fallen, or whose businesses have failed (Ford, Kempson, & Wilson, 1995). Wider use of payment 'holidays' and similar devices is needed to help mortgage payers to schedule their payments in line with their fluctuating career commitments, including helping them through temporary loss of work or the birth of children.

Stronger incentives to learning

Learning is the key to progression in work. If workers are to be able to move from contract to contract with some sense of development rather than mere survival, they need to find ways of enhancing their skills and knowledge on a continuing basis. Some of this will happen informally; some will happen formally alongside their work; some will require breaks from work.

Within a flexible labour market, employers need to be encouraged to replace a narrow approach to training with a broader approach to career development. This would include development in the work place as well as on training courses, and focus on future employability as well as the skills required for immediate use. Some organisations are already doing this, as part of a new 'psychological contract' in which they seek to assure employees' security not by offering a 'job for life' but by providing training and development which will extend their marketable skills and sustain their 'career resilience' (Herriot & Pemberton, 1995; Waterman, Waterman, & Collard, 1994).

In general, however, the rhetoric here is running well ahead of the reality (Hirsh & Jackson, 1996). Employers readily acknowledge the need to encourage people to participate in learning throughout their working lives. Most, however, are unwilling to provide any training that is not strictly related to immediate job needs (Metcalf, Walling, & Fogarty, 1994), and their performance management systems pressure individuals to perform rather than to learn. In a market environment, the rational self-interest of employers requires access to skills, but offers little incentive to invest in their development, because they cannot be privately appropriated (Streeck, 1989, 1992). Employers investing in skill development are adding to a common pool which is accessible to other employers, including direct competitors, in their industry or locality. The result is that most firms have a chronic tendency to invest less in training and development than their own longer-term interest demands. Flexible labour markets greatly accentuate this tendency.

On the other hand, training is not an area where state provision is able readily to respond to market failure (Streeck, 1989). The record of government training schemes is not impressive. The notion that places of work and places of learning should be kept neatly apart, to serve their separate interests, is now widely questioned. Work places – particularly those using state-of-the-art technology – are engines of learning as well as of production.

A key policy question therefore is what measures need to be taken to encourage employers to invest in training and development in their collective interest, and whether these measures should be voluntary or include an element of compulsion. An idea of particular interest in this respect is individual learning accounts, to which government, employers, and individuals would all contribute, thus providing a mechanism for recognising mutuality of interest by sharing the costs (Commission on Social Justice, 1994). For the unemployed or self-employed, the lack of an employer contribution could be compensated through enhanced state contributions.

A more flexible and responsive learning system

Stronger incentives to learning require a learning system able to respond to learners' more flexible needs. In the industrial era, learning structures have tended to reflect work structures. Both work and learning have been concentrated in large bureaucratic organisations. Young people have been concentrated in schools and colleges, where they have acquired the attitudes and behaviours, plus the base of skills and knowledge, required for their likely future in the work place (Bowles & Gintis, 1976). An important role of these institutions has been to sort out those destined for different levels of careers and of jobs – largely on the basis of examination performance (Dore, 1976).

Within this model, formal education has largely *preceded* employment. As the demands of the work place have grown, the minimum school-leaving age has been progressively raised, further and higher education expanded, and the age of entry to the work place deferred. But education has continued to be heavily 'front-loaded'. The relatively stable nature of work organisations has meant that any subsequent work-related learning has been largely provided within the organisation, with little need for further recourse to formal learning systems.

Now, however, new models of career are calling these traditional models of learning into question. The pace of technological change means that the 'shelf-life' of work skills and knowledge is getting ever shorter. 'Just-in-time' work systems require 'just-in-time' learning. More frequent movement between jobs requires regular acquisition of new competencies. More and more jobs require 'multi-skilling': a broader and more flexible range of skills, demanding a wider base of understanding. Learning no longer precedes work: it is interwoven with work, on a lifelong basis.

Lifelong learning does not necessarily mean lifelong education. It embraces training, as well as more informal learning in the work place and outside it. The education system has, however, an important role to play in supporting such varied forms of learning, as well as providing formal learning opportunities detached from the immediate concerns of the work place. It accordingly needs to be much more flexible than in the past. It needs to establish much stronger links with the world of work: to view employers as its partners in learning, not as receivers of its products. In addition, course structures need to be adapted to enable individuals to move easily in and out of the formal learning system, and to design their own learning pathways, drawing from provision in different kinds of institution where appropriate. In other words, education institutions need to be integrated into a flexible and co-ordinated learning system, providing resources for individuals to use as and when they have particular learning needs.

Technology is likely to play a powerful change-agent role in this respect. It liberates knowledge, and the learning process, from institutions (Hague, 1991). The traditional emphasis on class attendance is outdated. Learning packages can now be used in the home, the work place, community centres, and elsewhere. Learners can start when they like, work at their own pace, and complete when ready to do so. The value added by more direct forms of learner support needs to be more personal and more interactive: in one-to-one or small-group situations, and focused not on transmitting information but on deepening understanding.

More flexible learning systems imply new roles for teachers, with implications for their staff development and career structures. The first role is as a learning *designer* – with 'products' ranging from books and video lectures to programmed-learning packages, multi-media learning kits, and various forms of experiential learning. The second is as a learning *co-ordinator*, linking human and material resources to objectives and methods so that they meet the needs and readiness of the learner. The third is as a learning *consultant* or *mentor*, helping the learner to overcome learning blockages and to engage at a deeper level with the meaning of what they are learning. The fourth is as a learning *assessor*, evaluating and accrediting the individual's learning regardless of where and how it has been obtained.

Such a concept of lifelong learning transforms the role of schools. Hitherto their models of learning have been dominated by public examinations, linked to their 'sorting' function. This has tended to encourage a narrowly instrumental approach to learning, focused on the 'exchange value' of examination certificates rather than the 'use value' of the learning itself (Saunders, 1993). Now, however, the key role of the school is to foster young people's motivation and confidence, and to develop their skills for learning how to learn. This requires very different curriculum models, with weaker emphasis on the boundaries between traditional school subjects, more stress on the interaction between theory and practice, and more use of community resources. Kolb's (1984) four-stage learning cycle – concrete experience, reflective observation, abstract conceptualisation, and active experimentation – needs to be built more strongly into school curricula.

This implies that relationships between learning and work need to be established more strongly at an earlier stage. Perhaps because of education's early-industrial-era role of protecting young people from child labour, its boundaries with the world of work have been sharply marked, and tightly patrolled. This has begun to change, and needs to change further. Experience-based learning in work places and other forms of education–business partnership enrich the learning process, and help young people to engage at an earlier age in the interaction between learning and work which is the essence of lifelong learning (Miller, Watts, & Jamieson, 1991): such activities need to be extended, with stronger employer commitment. This could be linked to other changes in schools, mirroring those in the world of work: more 'portfolio' teachers combining teaching with other work roles, more 'contracting out' of parts of the curriculum to business and industry, more use of information technology for independent learning, more opportunities for problem-solving projects involving students working in supervised teams in varied settings, and more flexi-time arrangements that give teachers and students a stronger sense of control and reduce the sense of oppressive routine and predictability (Hargreaves, 1994).

Lifelong learning can be viewed as comprising three overlapping stages: *foundation* (up to the age of 16), instilling the habit of learning; *formation* (ages 14–21), developing work place readiness; and *continuation* (age 18+), based on independent learning (Ball, 1991). A more flexible learning system constructed along these lines would mirror the new more flexible work system, and enable individuals to construct career paths intertwining the two.

A national qualifications framework

Within this new model of learning, the role of accreditation is critical. If individuals are to move more regularly between different work organisations, their learning must be accredited in ways which make it portable. This means accreditation not only of formal learning, but also of informal learning, including learning in the work place. Individuals who are responsible for their own career development need to be assured that the learning they have acquired in the course of any work contract is accredited, to enable its value to be recognised by other possible employers. This could be the basis of a new mutually beneficial 'psycho-logical contract' focused around employability rather than secure employ-ment.

In the UK, the structure of National, and Scottish, Vocational Qualifi-cations (NVQs/SVQs) represents an important move in this direction. It is competence-based, but does not prescribe the process by which the individual should achieve this competence. The framework is designed to cover all work-related learning, and to facilitate movement between as well as within particular occupations (Jessup, 1991). The framework has been extended to cover competences acquired through unpaid work in the home and the community. Its approach is, however, widely criticised for being narrowly behaviourist in nature and not paying sufficient attention to underpinning knowledge and theory (e.g. Hodkinson & Issitt, 1995). This could be a particularly significant limitation at higher occupational levels, where progress is still at an early stage.

As the same time, the post-compulsory education system is increasingly developing credit accumulation and transfer systems (CATS) to enable students to move more easily between different courses and institutions. The pace of such development is still uneven, with different credit 'tariff' systems being used by different institutions, with a continuing divide between the systems used within further and higher education respective-ly, and with some institutions being concerned with intra- rather than inter-institutional mobility (Robertson, 1994).

In principle, the roles of these two systems are complementary. The criticisms of NVQs/SVQs for neglecting knowledge and theory are mirrored by criticisms of educational courses accredited in CATS schemes for neglecting skills (in particular, transferable core skills). Effective learning experiences are likely to need to encompass attention to knowledge/theory *and* skills, though in varying balance – *both* need to be accredited. Whether this is based on a system of dual accreditation of single learning experiences, or on an integrated accreditation system, is open to debate. But whichever approach is adopted, the new model of career requires an integrated qualifications framework. Such a framework will provide a clear, comprehensible, and widely recognised climbing-frame for career development for all. Schools should then be seen as providing young people not with life-sentences based on terminal assess-ments, but with their initial foothold within the frame.

Action is also needed to make the resulting framework the basis for a 'licence to practise' in work roles. At present, such requirements exist in Britain only within occupations dominated by strong professional associ-ations (e.g. medicine, the law, architecture, accountancy) and within some skilled trades (e.g. welding, electrical work). Such professional licencing could be applied to other occupational groups, as in Germany, both by legislation and by other forms of pressure and encouragement. It could be extended by requiring evidence of continuing professional development to maintain one's licence. The result would be greater protection of the consumer through product and service quality, plus a stronger incentive for individual career development.

Lifelong access to career guidance

Within the industrial era, the role of career guidance has been limited. The destiny of individuals within both the education system and the employment system has been determined largely by selection processes. Career guidance has been a limited switch-mechanism to fine-tune the passage from one system to the other. Hence career guidance services have been concentrated around the transition from full-time education to employment. In practice, the two systems have usually been so well synchronised that it has not had too much to do. It has been a marginal and low-status activity.

Now, however, its role is moving centre-stage. If individuals are to take responsibility for their career development, career guidance is critical, in three respects: helping individuals to clarify and articulate their aims and aspirations; ensuring that their decisions are informed in relation to the needs of the labour market; and empowering them in their negotiations with employers and other purchasers of their services. Careers are now based not on single decision points, but on a long series of iterative decisions made throughout life. Guidance needs to be available at all these decision points.

This means that a national strategy is required for lifelong access to guidance in support of lifelong career development for all (Watts, 1994a; Watts, Law, Killeen, Kidd, & Hawthorn, 1996). No single agency can deliver what is needed. A three-pronged strategy is required, with each prong supported by strong and clear quality standards (Hawthorn, 1995).

First, career guidance should be an integral part of education. In particular, compulsory schooling should lay the foundations for lifelong career development. This emphasises the importance of career education within the curriculum, designed to develop competence in career self-management: the skills, knowledge, and attitudes which will enable young people to make and implement career decisions both immediately and in the future. Career education has traditionally been marginal to a curriculum dominated by academic subjects. It now needs to be the core of a new curriculum, preparing students for lifelong learning.

In addition, within but also beyond compulsory schooling, all educational provision should provide regular opportunities for students to relate what they are learning to their future career development. This has implications for the whole curriculum. It also requires tutorial support, and specialist guidance services within the institution. The importance attached to such services is likely to grow as course structures become more flexible, with the development of modular courses and systems of credit accumulation and transfer.

A particularly significant development both in schools and in further and higher education is the growing practice of encouraging students to engage in regular recording of achievement (reviewing their learning experiences, inside and outside the formal curriculum, and defining the skills and competencies acquired) and action planning (reviewing their long-term goals, their short-term learning objectives, and ways of achieving these objectives). These processes are of value in their own right; they also help to develop and support the skills of reviewing and of planning which are crucial to career self-management.

Second, guidance should be an integral part of work organisations. Here, too, individuals are increasingly being given opportunities to review their progress and their future plans – either within appraisal systems, or through parallel systems of development reviews. In addition, a growing number of organisations are introducing other activities to support career self-management, such as career planning workshops, assessment centres, career resource centres, and mentoring programmes (Kidd, 1996). Such practices tend, however, to be more common in larger organisations.

A potential advantage of embedding career guidance within educational and employing organisations is that they have more continuous contacts with individuals based within them, and so are able to deliver more substantial and sustained support than any external service can do. In particular, through their processes of regular development reviews, they are able to deliver the career equivalent of the dental check-up (Goodman, 1992). Furthermore, they are in a stronger position to influence the opportunities they offer in response to individuals' needs and demands, as revealed through the guidance process (see, e.g., Oakeshott, 1990). Guidance can thus not only help individuals to choose between the opportunities already available, but also encourage organisations to develop new opportunities to meet individuals' preferences and requirements.

But career guidance within education and employment will not cover everyone: many people spend significant parts of their lives outside such organisations – because they are unemployed, for example, or engaged in child-rearing. Moreover, guidance provision within organisations does not always have a sufficiently broad view of opportunities outside that organisation. Again, the organisation can have a vested interest in the outcomes of the individual's decision, which can make it difficult to provide guidance that is genuinely impartial. In the UK, for instance, schools with sixth-forms are rewarded financially if their students stay on beyond the age of sixteen: some are tempted to bias their guidance in favour of their own offerings at the expense of the opportunities available elsewhere. Employers, too, may be reluctant to encourage valued employees to explore opportunities in other organisations.

For these reasons, individuals also need access to guidance with a broader and more impartial perspective. Some will be able to gain sufficient help and support from friends and relatives. Many, however, will need access to a neutral service with professional counselling skills and access to high-quality information. This could have two levels (Watts, 1994b). Its *foundation* provision would be available free of charge to all. It could comprise a national telephone helpline (now available in the UK), plus open-access information centres in every sizeable town and city, with 'satellites' in rural areas. These centres would offer high-quality information, supported by brief 'diagnostic guidance' interventions designed to identify guidance needs for which further provision might be needed. This *enhanced* provision – counselling interviews, psychometric testing, etc. – would be available from a range of accredited providers, and would be costed: those able to pay would be expected to do so, perhaps from their individual learning accounts; public funding would be targeted at groups where the ability to pay was low and/or the public interest in take-up was high (notably the unemployed, women returners, and the low-waged).

To bring together these various strands of guidance provision within a coherent strategic framework, strong co-ordinating structures are needed. At national level, the National Advisory Council for Careers and Educational Guidance in the UK now brings together the major stakeholder organisations and guidance professional organisations, with observers from the relevant government departments. Strategic frameworks for lifelong access to guidance are also needed at local level (Watts, Hawthorn, Hoffbrand, Jackson, & Spurling, 1997).

The changing concept of career has considerable implications not only for the structure of guidance delivery, but also for its processes. Full use needs to be made, for example, of the opportunities for global access to information and contacts offered by the Internet. It also seems likely that there will be a need for stronger links between career guidance and financial guidance (Collin & Watts, 1996).

Stronger intermediary organisations between individuals and employers

Independent guidance services are intermediaries between individuals and employers. Other intermediary organisations need to be strengthened too, to provide additional supports on which individuals can draw, and where appropriate to act as brokers in their relationships with employers.

The main social institutions which exist to provide such support to individuals at present are professional associations and trade unions. Unions have hitherto tended to be pre-occupied with collective wage bargaining, but this role has been in decline in the UK. Both they and professional associations now need to pay more attention to supporting individual career development within a flexible labour market. This requires greater attention to services to individual members, including professional development and career guidance, and possibly acting as agents and advocates for individuals in their negotiations with employers. Use of commercial agents is already common in fields like sports and the arts where the practice of short-term contracting is well established: professional associations and unions could take on similar roles as such contracts are introduced elsewhere. Their concern should be more with maintaining their members' employability than with seeking to protect their existing jobs; their role should be heightened rather than weakened when their members experience unemployment. Where the collective bargaining role of unions survives, it should cover employers' career management practices, and pay more attention to the procedural equity of the individual contracting process than to the pursuit of common outcomes (Herriot & Pemberton, 1996). It may be that the roles of professional associations and unions in these various respects will increasingly blur into one another.

There is also a growing role for 'deployers' – firms with a long-term relationship with individuals whose labour they deploy to others. Other intermediary organisations with increasingly significant roles include commercial agents, voluntary organisations representing particular client groups (e.g. one-parent families), self-help groups, and networks. Social networks represent personal communities (Wellman, Carrington, & Hall, 1988): they are important in providing colleagueship and support, in exchanging ideas and information, and in supplying links to potential customers and employers. The Internet is likely to provide a powerful impetus to networks of all kinds.

The social importance of these various intermediary organisations needs to be publicly recognised, and where appropriate supported by facilitative legislation and in other ways. In recent years, legislation in the

UK and elsewhere has been used to restrict the power of (particularly) trade unions, based on their traditional functions. In other countries, however, it is recognised that – effectively channelled – they form part of a structure of civil society which can greatly aid economic performance (Streeck, 1992). The task now is to strengthen the new social forms that will perform this function in a post-industrial society characterised by a flexible labour market.

Conclusion

Flexible labour markets could make it possible for more individuals to achieve more of their potential than has been the case in the past. But they will only do so if they are linked to a new concept of career, made available to all, and buttressed by appropriate support structures. Some of these structures should continue to be provided by employers: appropriate forms of regulation and encouragement are needed to ensure that employers carry out their responsibility in offering such support, in their own longer-term self-interest. But increasingly, within a flexible labour market, more support structures need to be available directly to individuals. Assuring the availability of such support is an important issue for social policy. Attending to the implications of the new career is one of the most pressing tasks for public policy as we enter the new millennium.

REFERENCES

Albert, M. (1993). *Capitalism against capitalism*. London: Whurr.
Ball, C. (1991). *Learning pays*. London: Royal Society of Arts.
Bayliss, V. (1998). *Redefining work*. London: Royal Society of Arts.
Bowles, S. & Gintis, H. (1976). *Schooling in capitalist America*. London: Routledge and Kegan Paul.
Collin, A. & Watts, A. G. (1996). The death and transfiguration of career – and of career guidance? *British Journal of Guidance and Counselling*, 24, 385–398.
Commission on Social Justice (1994). *Social justice: Strategies for national renewal*. London: Vintage.
Confederation of British Industry (1989). *Towards a skills revolution*. London: CBI.
Dore, R. (1976). *The diploma disease*. London: Allen and Unwin.
Esping-Andersen, G. (1994). Equality and work in the post-industrial life-cycle. In D. Miliband (Ed.), *Reinventing the left* (pp. 167–185). Cambridge: Polity Press.
Ford, J., Kempson, E., & Wilson, M. (1995). *Mortgage arrears and possessions: Perspectives from borrowers, lenders and the courts*. London: HMSO.
Garraty, J. A. (1978). *Unemployment in history*. New York: Harper and Row.
Gaullier, X. (1992). The changing ages of man. *Geneva Papers on Risk and Insurance*, 17, 3–25.

Goodman, J. (1992). The key to pain prevention: The dental model for counseling. *American Counselor, 1* (3), 27–29.

Gray, J. (1996). *After social democracy.* London: Demos.

Hague, D. (1991). *Beyond universities: A new republic of the intellect.* Hobart Paper 115. London: Institute of Economic Affairs.

Hargreaves, D. (1994). *The mosaic of learning.* London: Demos.

Hawthorn, R. (1995). *First steps: A quality standards framework for guidance across all sectors.* London: RSA/National Advisory Council for Careers and Educational Guidance.

Herriot, P. & Pemberton, C. (1995). *New deals: The revolution in managerial careers.* Chichester: John Wiley & Sons.

——— (1996). Contracting careers. *Human Relations, 49,* 757–790.

Hirsh, W. & Jackson, C. (1996). *Strategies for career development: Promise, practice and pretence.* IES Report 305. Brighton: Institute for Employment Studies.

Hodkinson, P. & Issitt, M. (Eds.) (1995). *The challenge of competence: Professionalism through vocational education and training.* London: Cassell.

Hutton, W. (1995). *The state we're in.* London: Cape.

Jessup, G. (1991). *Outcomes: NVQs and the emerging model of education and training.* London: Falmer.

Kidd, J. M. (1996). Career planning within work organisations. In A. G. Watts, B. Law, J. Killeen, J. M. Kidd, & R. Hawthorn, *Rethinking careers education and guidance: Theory, policy and practice* (pp. 142–154). London: Routledge.

Kolb, D. A. (1984). *Experiential learning.* Englewood Cliffs, NJ: Prentice-Hall.

Metcalf, H., Walling, A., & Fogarty, M. (1994). *Individual commitment to learning: Employers' attitudes.* Research Series no. 40. London: Employment Department.

Miller, A., Watts, A. G., & Jamieson, I. (1991). *Rethinking work experience.* London: Falmer.

National Association of Citizens Advice Bureaux (1997). *Flexibility abused.* London: author.

Oakeshott, M. (1990). *Educational guidance and curriculum change.* London: Further Education Unit/Unit for the Development of Adult Continuing Education.

Parker, H. (1989). *Instead of the dole.* London: Routledge.

Porter, M. (1990). *The competitive advantage of nations.* London: Macmillan.

Rawls, J. (1972). *A theory of justice.* Oxford: Oxford University Press.

Reich, R. B. (1991). *The work of nations.* London: Simon and Schuster.

Robertson, D. (1994). *Choosing to change.* London: Higher Education Quality Council.

Saunders, M. (1993). TVEI and the National Curriculum: Culture clash between use and exchange value. *Evaluation and Research in Education, 7,* 107–115.

Streeck, W. (1989). Skills and the limit of neo-liberalism: The enterprise of the future as a place of learning. *Work, Employment and Society, 3,* 89–104.

——— (1992). *Social institutions and economic performance.* London: Sage.

Waterman, R. H., Jr, Waterman, J. A., & Collard, B. A. (1994). Towards a career-resilient workforce. *Harvard Business Review, 72,* 87–95.

Watts, A. G. (1994a). *Lifelong career development: Towards a national strategy for careers education and guidance.* Cambridge: Careers Research and Advisory Centre.

(1994b). *A strategy for developing careers guidance services for adults.* Cambridge: Careers Research and Advisory Centre.

(1996). *Careerquake.* London: Demos.

Watts, A. G., Hawthorn, R., Hoffbrand, J., Jackson, H., & Spurling, A. (1997). Developing local lifelong guidance strategies. *British Journal of Guidance and Counselling, 25,* 217–227.

Watts, A. G., Law, B., Killeen, J., Kidd, J. M., & Hawthorn, R. (Eds.) (1996). *Rethinking careers education and guidance: Theory, policy and practice.* London: Routledge.

Wellman, B., Carrington, P. J., & Hall, A. (1988). Networks as personal communities. In B. Wellman & S. D. Berkowitz (Eds.), *Social structures: A network approach* (vol. II, pp. 130–184). Cambridge: Cambridge University Press.

Wilensky, H. L. (1961). Orderly careers and social participation: The impact of work history on social integration in the middle mass. *American Sociological Review, 26,* 521–539.

18   The future of career

Audrey Collin and Richard A. Young

This book has brought together authors from different countries, disciplines, traditions, and fields of practice to take a view of the future of career. From their different perspectives, they address various aspects of career, of what it is and has been. They point to actual and potential changes not only in career paths and patterns, and in individuals' experiences of career, but also in the construct and discourse of career, and consider issues for theory, practice, and policy arising from them. The book thus presents a kaleidoscopic view of career and its future. Implicitly, some chapters challenge others, interrogate others, or resonate with others. While the juxtaposition within this book of their differing angles and perspectives has the potential to stimulate new understandings of and questions about career, it also fragments and refracts any glimpse of its future they may afford. However, there are also common themes and issues running through the book. The challenge of this closing chapter is to celebrate these multiple interpretations, yet draw their various messages into a greater whole.

We open by highlighting the key themes of the book, and then set out to join-the-dots of our contributors' perspectives within a long-term view of the context of career. This enables us to draw out how career is multi-layered, and intertwined with other significant social constructs and processes, and to highlight the stakeholders in it, such as employers, individuals, and the career 'industry' as a whole. Having discussed some of the key issues for its stakeholders, we then propose a reframing of career that captures and makes sense of the issues raised in the book, and ways forward in the twenty-first century for those concerned with career.

Major themes in the book

It is neither possible nor necessary to mention all of the many themes and issues in the book: the chapters speak for themselves. The themes we have chosen to highlight are those that reiterate through the book, resonate with one another and with other literature, and raise significant questions about the future of career.

The future of the construct of career

A question running through the book is whether the changes reported would result in a discontinuity in the meaning of career, and a dwindling in its utility. The clear message is that the meaning of the construct of career will change, but will have continuing value. For example, Watts suggests that career should now be understood as lifelong progression in learning and work. Young and Valach interpret that one version of career has come to an end, but propose a reconceptualisation of it. Richardson, however, urges that the construct of career should be abandoned in favour of the construct of work practice.

Two chapters voice caution on the extent of the changes taking place. Littleton, Arthur, and Rousseau suggest that some people have always had boundaryless careers. Storey cites research that suggests that bureaucratic careers cannot be written off, and argues that what is happening is not a 'radical shift', but the evolution of a concept that 'contains many layers of meaning'. She considers that a revised definition of career needs to encompass a greater diversity of experiences than before, although these experiences in themselves are not new.

Continuity and discontinuity

As would be expected in any consideration of the future of career, many chapters refer to the individual's actual and potential experiences of change and discontinuity. Savickas notes how 'postmodern' workers encounter 'twists and turns'. Riverin-Simard writes that the career of older workers is no longer linear, but 'zig-zag' and 'disparate', so that they experience 'ruptures, departures and suffering'. Collin (chapter 11) likens such experiences to the collage and *bricolage* of the 'modern epic', in which the interaction of fragments generates heteroglossia and polysemy.

This discontinuity arises because of the fragmentation of work life created by changes in work contracts and patterns described throughout the book. Its impact upon the individual's experience and sense of identity is compounded by other changes taking place in what is, according to Doyle, 'an increasingly complex, diverse and fluid organisational context'. Traditional boundaries between the organisation and the world outside it are being eroded by approaches such as 'total quality management', whereas internal boundaries are being eroded by 'business process reengineering' (Hammer & Champy, 1994), and becoming redrawn through team- and project-working. Thus it is increasingly difficult for individuals to experience the definition and security of a specific job for which, in more sophisticated organisations at any rate, they have been particularly selected. Increasingly, people are being left to experience what Höpfl and Hornby Atkinson see as the ambivalence and contradictions of working in an organisation.

The increasingly complex context, intra- and interorganisationally, as well as globally, makes it impossible to map all the potential contingencies individuals will meet in their career. This is reflected in the view of Littleton, Arthur, and Rousseau that there is 'career anarchy'; the multiple relationships in boundaryless careers, 'perpetually changing career paths and possibilities', make career seem 'random'. There is, however, pattern within this seeming chaos. Riverin-Simard is also aware of 'structured instability', which she, too, interprets as chaos. Nevertheless, she proposes that, through what she calls the vocational project, individuals can continually redefine their vocational identity, and so achieve a degree of continuity, and a container for their identity, during the periods of transition.

However, it is important to note that some chapters indicate that the impact on individuals of the changes highlighted is not necessarily always negative or destructive. Littleton, Arthur, and Rousseau paint a positive picture of self-organising, entrepreneurial individuals, sharing identity and friendships, engaged in continuous learning. They also point out how the 'chaotic patterns' of boundaryless careers contribute to the economic and social stability of a region. Watts suggests that the new forms of career will embrace non-elites as well as elites. Riverin-Simard recognises that the transitions adults now experience give them opportunities to re-examine their lives. By managing the discontinuity, they can find opportunities and, by re-appropriating 'opposing elements', achieve a new wholeness. O'Doherty and Roberts, looking beyond what they see as the current epistemological and existential crisis, present a more ambiguous and darker view. In their new 'ontological and epistemological vistas', the individual is free, but divested of the protection from freedom.

The individual in context

This book looks beyond the experiences of individuals to raise questions about the concept of the individual, and the relationship between individuals and their context. Several chapters explicitly or implicitly refer to the constructed, rather than essential, nature of individual identity, and to the cultural reference points used in this construction. For example,

Collin (chapter 6) discusses the role of the latter in the individual's construction of time and space, and suggests that the reference points give 'longitudinal readings'. Collin (chapter 11) notes the construction of individuality in terms of the relationship between the individual and the collective, and suggests that individuals construct their identity through comparison and contrast with others, with career playing a part in their differentiation.

Other chapters express concern about the decontextualised construction of the individual in career theory. Höpfl and Hornby Atkinson challenge the gendered assumptions made there, and Leong and Hartung the inappropriate assumptions for a multicultural society. Patton refers to the social construction of the individual's values.

Young and Valach, and Richardson, challenge the individualistic assumptions underpinning career theory and, in particular, the assumption of individual autonomy in career. In response to such assumptions, Young and Valach have developed an action-theory approach, in which career represents the long-term construction of socially embedded actions. Richardson considers that work cannot be separated from the rest of the individual's life (as Patton also acknowledges). These chapters are, in effect, arguing for the need to recognise that both the individual's construction of self, and the construction of the concept of the individual, are contextualised. Both chapters reflect efforts to address the 'relational' interpretations of career, as Hall and Associates (1996) have done.

Although they do not discuss the construct of the individual, other chapters appear to support a relational view of career. Hence, Maranda and Comeau recognise the need to approach dysfunctional experiences in the work place at the level of the group rather than of the individual. Littleton, Arthur, and Rousseau suggest that both individualistic 'agency' and relational 'communion' (Bakan, 1966), as well as reciprocity, are at work in boundaryless careers. Doyle identifies how managers play a part in their subordinates' careers. However, Storey, Höpfl and Hornby Atkinson, and Doyle cite the literature on the psychological contract that argues that, whereas it had formerly had a 'relational' nature, it has now become 'instrumental'.

Finally, the relationship between the individual and his or her wider society is addressed both implicitly and explicitly throughout the book. It underpins the classification of theories that Maranda and Comeau present. It arises again in Leong and Hartung's discussion of an appropriate form of counselling in a multicultural society. In discussing the future role of education, Law argues that individuals do not exist as separate units, that they are a part of the social fabric. Watts urges the need to safeguard social cohesion by developing new 'social ligatures'.

The construction of the future

Chapter 1 suggested that career connected the individual's past, present, and future, and made the construction of the future possible. Some contributors to the book raise important questions about individuals' orientation to the future and how it will be constructed. Collin (chapter 6) suggests that career may no longer construct a long-term view for the individual, but rather an all-embracing view of the individual's present, making coherent the simultaneous experiences across the individual's life. Riverin-Simard also questions the possibility of maintaining a future orientation, in the sense of the traditional single, linear temporality, for this is 'giving way to a plural temporality'. She proposes that individuals can and, indeed, must have a view of the future, and that the 'vocational project' affords such a view, albeit a limited one. Riverin-Simard also suggests that death and the after-life play a part in the 'vocational discourse' of older adults, extending the future horizon beyond the project, while at the same time presaging the 'finitude' of life.

Young and Valach's reconceptualisation of career through an action-theoretical approach addresses the same issue. They argue that the systems of goal-directed action – joint action, project, and career – link the individual's actions over the short, medium, and long term. They suggest that the medium-term project provides a more appropriate construct for many people than the longer-term career.

Whereas for Riverin-Simard the project achieves the continuity of identity over time, Littleton, Arthur, and Rousseau emphasise its spatial rather than temporal nature. In the film industry, with its 'fluid labour market, pervasive social networks and continuous learning', subcontractors construct their boundaryless careers by moving 'from project to project across firms over time'. The project results in the individual's continuous learning, and development of reputation, as well as the development of the whole industry through the social networks built through projects. These two perspectives upon project suggest that we should examine the view of Castells (1996, p. 376) that 'space organizes time in the network society', and its implications for the future of career, as Collin (chapter 6) has started to do.

Making meaning

Underlying many of the issues raised in the book is that of the construction of meaning, and the role of career in it. Meaning is not given: individuals construct and negotiate it. Collin (chapter 6) examines how individuals construct their time and space, and suggests that they do this through comparison with others. The starting-point of the action-theory approach of Young and Valach is the individual's intentional goal-directed action, which is 'embedded in a network of [social] meaning'. Richardson adopts the concept of 'practice', by which she means repeated, shared actions, carrying normative expectations. She argues that looking at work as practice rather than in terms of career will help counsellors to empower individuals.

Other chapters emphasise that the construction of meaning is problematic. O'Doherty and Roberts draw attention to the fragility of meaning and how this is easily shattered. They argue that whereas career had been used by individuals as a 'traditional ritual' to make meaning, and 'fill the inevitable void', it could no longer do so in the 'nihilistic and entropic conditions of late modernity'. Previously 'stable fixed points of reference' are eroding, leaving individuals experiencing existential anxiety. Höpfl and Hornby Atkinson also refer to the fragility of the meaning which is conferred by organisations, and which the presence of women in organisations threatens. They, too, see career as providing a framework of meaning. Law recognises the difficulty of sustaining meaning in situations where temporary work contracts make experience discontinuous. Leong and Hartung draw attention to the cultural variables in the construction of meaning.

Power and conflict

The exercise of power in and through career is an issue that is made explicit in several chapters, and implied in others. Maranda and Comeau set the scene in their classification of the sociological theories of career according to their focus on whether the individual or society has to change, and whether people are free to determine their own actions, or are constrained by social structure. Other chapters also recognise the power relations that attend career. Richardson points to how they are embodied in the ideology of career, and argues for the need for counselling to empower people through their work and relationships. In looking at career as rhetoric, Collin (chapter 11) highlights the social contradictions that are the results of the economic power relations within a society. Höpfl and Hornby Atkinson, and Leong and Hartung, point to the effects of the unequal distribution of power in society. The former argue the need to widen the concept of career to embrace the needs of women and of a multicultural society. They express this graphically by referring to 'the hidden basis of women's career choice' as being like the Salic Law for inheritance: the most a woman could do would be to 'stand-in for the male heir'. Chapter 1 and a number of others discuss the charge that career has been largely for elites – that is, they look at career in terms of the reproduction of society. Riverin-Simard points to the development of new inequalities for older adults.

Issues of power in the employment relationship are also discussed in the book. Maranda and Comeau allude to labour struggles over the organisation of work in the work place. Patton notes how the construct of job satisfaction masks some of the conflicts inherent in the work place. Doyle makes it explicit that organisational career management is fuelled by the need to meet organisational goals, and that managers carry it out in the light, not only of their own career needs, but also of the need for both their own and the organisation's survival.

The issues of power in career that derive from social class, ethnicity, and gender, and the issues of ideology present in the construction of knowledge through theory, research, and the techniques of practice, are discussed in the career psychology literature written from a critical perspective. In this book, these issues are raised by O'Doherty and Roberts, who argue that the 'humanist gold standards' represent constructed meanings supporting certain kinds of social practices, and are hence about the exercise of power. However, the issues of power inherent in the employment relationship are rarely if at all discussed in the career field. This may be because, as Collin has argued (1996a), organisations have been left invisible in the career psychology literature. Once they are recognised, as in Doyle's chapter, then it becomes impossible to regard career solely as the manifestation of individual autonomy. For example, the literature, referred to by Storey, O'Doherty and Roberts, and Doyle treats the 'psychological contract', in rational terms, as an exchange, but it could also be regarded as, at best, an unequal, and, at worst, an exploitative, relationship. Similarly, although the purpose of guidance interventions is to assist the client, the power inherent in the practitioner–client relationship also needs to be examined.

The need to develop career theory and practice

A number of chapters point to the limitations of existing career theories. Leong and Hartung point out that multiculturalism has so far made little impact on psychology generally, and career psychology in particular still scarcely acknowledges differences in gender, race, class, and sexual orientation. Höpfl and Hornby Atkinson also challenge the gendered assumptions of career theories, while Young and Valach, and Richardson, question their individualistic assumptions and, in particular, their assumption of individual autonomy in career. Patton argues that, although career theories acknowledge the importance of values in career, they fail to represent them effectively. O'Doherty and Roberts interpret that the whole range of career theory is underpinned by what they believe is a failing ontological and epistemological paradigm.

Savickas argues that the changes currently taking place are so challenging that vocational psychology has to become more 'self-reflective'. He points to the need to build bridges between existing factions, while Leong and Hartung, and Watts, focus on extending and developing existing approaches to career. However, throughout the book, arguments are made to replace interpretations that are no longer meaningful with more appropriate understandings: a psychodynamic theory of work (Maranda & Comeau), chaos theory (Riverin-Simard), feminist thinking (Höpfl and Hornby Atkinson), a more explicit relation of work and education (Law). Young and Valach offer an action-theory approach to career. Richardson's theory of work in people's lives would not have the elitism and limitations of the present construct of career. These are all attempts to achieve interpretations that will make a difference to the experience, construction, research, and theories of career of the future.

One of the two axes used in the classification of the sociological theories of career by Maranda and Comeau is that of adaptation–transformation. A question hinted at in a number of chapters, but not fully addressed, is where the various practices of career should be located along this axis. Maranda and Comeau, Savickas, Riverin-Simard, Young and Valach, and Leong and Hartung all advocate forms of intervention that, they would argue, facilitate transformation. However, Richardson expresses concern about the degree of empowerment such approaches, tied into the construct of career rather than work, have so far achieved. O'Doherty and Roberts categorise them all as built on increasingly untenable assumptions.

Grounding the future of career in the past

For a book concerned with the future, this one pays, perhaps, unexpected attention to the past. While Part 1 starts by looking at the present and immediate past, and takes a synchronic view of career in terms of contextual changes, subsequent chapters also take a longer and diachronic view of what is happening to career. Several return to the early years of the twentieth century, or even before, to enable them to consider the changing present and potential future of career. The overall stance of the book, then, is to adopt a longer view to approach the challenge of understanding and delineating complex, far-reaching, and dynamic change.

Thus this book recognises the three co-existing 'registers' of time proposed by the historian Braudel (1973). It looks at recent and contemporary events in what he calls the *courte durée*, but also at aspects of career that have changed over the longer term, and at the even slower changes in the epistemological assumptions underpinning them which are visible only in the *longue durée*. To focus on the *courte durée* is to emphasise the disjunction from the past, the loss of old industries, tasks, and skills, and the increasing demands for new tasks, skills, and patterns of working. This directs our eyes towards a particular vision of the future, which may be incomplete and misleading. As Storey points out, it is by no means entirely clear what is currently happening. While there is disjunction, this may not be the whole picture, so we also need to look at what is happening in those other aspects of career that may be changing more slowly over time.

This approach enables us to recognise that career is multilayered. It is made up of a number of strands that overlap, interweave, and resonate as they slowly change, underpinned by the deep epistemological structures of meaning in Western society that change even more slowly, so slowly that their change can be seen only in the *longue durée*. Some of the themes of this book – concern with the concept of the individual, the epistemology of theory and practice – arise from changes in these deep underpinnings of career; others – the fragmentation of experience, issues of power – from the continuous interweaving of the strands. As these strands have changed, so career has changed, and, to consider the future of career, we must attend to how these strands are changing further.

In taking this approach in what follows, we not only contextualise the various perspectives, themes, and issues in the book, but can also see how deeply embedded career is in the fabric of Western society so that its future cannot be clearly identifiable.

Epistemological assumptions underlying career

The assumptions of an ordered, objective reality that have framed the dominant understanding of career go back to the seventeenth century, and the start of the modern period with the emergence of Western rationality, its positivist and technocratic approach to knowledge, and hence the making of the individual as an object of knowledge. Positivism has held sway in the career field (Walsh & Chartrand, 1994), and underpinned the psychometric techniques that have been so important in it. Other significant assumptions that have informed our understanding of career emerged from the Romanticism of the eighteenth century (Taylor,

1989), and led to the interpretation that the individual was unique and a source of significant truths.

The final decades of the twentieth century saw the development of alternative epistemologies that, through their focus on language (Derrida, 1973) and the social construction of meaning (Gergen, 1985), held that meaning had to be continuously deconstructed and negotiated, and problematised the relationship between objective and subjective. These views prompted challenges to the established understanding of, and approach to, career (e.g. Collin & Young, 1986; Young & Collin, 1992), as recognised in Arthur, Hall, and Lawrence's (1989) identification of the 'competing views' of 'social science orthodoxy' and 'social science reform' (p. 18). However, the spread of postmodern approaches at the century's end (Savickas) is defusing the original impact of these challenges.

Moreover, changes taking place in the science of knowledge, arising from, for example, quantum mechanics (Wheatley, 1992) and chaos theory (Gleick, 1987), raise questions about the 'apparent certainty, linearity, and predictability' of the Newtonian universe and perhaps offer new ways of understanding the 'uncertainties, nonlinearities, and un-predictable aspects' of what social scientists study (Elliott & Kiel, 1997, p. 1). As these new ways of thinking work their way through into social science generally, and the career field in particular, they will come to affect how we understand and study career. Some of their shock-waves have been registered by Littleton, Arthur and Rousseau, and Riverin-Simard, and may also be felt in what O'Doherty and Roberts, in the most uncompromising discussion in the book, assert is a crisis in ontology and epistemology. They argue that previously 'stable fixed points of reference' are eroding, leaving the individual exposed to the 'nihilistic and entropic conditions of late modernity'.

Constructions of the individual and society

The Western concept of the individual, assumed to be a bounded, reified self, an autonomous, self-actualising agent, was unknown in pre-modern times (Giddens, 1991). It emerged in the period of the Reformation and Enlightenment, and has become a fundamental assumption of Western society. It has been argued that this conceptualisation was ideological, and served the needs of liberal capitalism which was developing over this period (Sampson, 1989, pp. 4–5). Alongside this, Protestantism, with its work ethic, 'laid a massive stress on the individual, on a striving for individual achievement, on human competitiveness' (Watson, 1980, p. 86).

This construction of the individual allowed an atomistic view of society, and the setting of the individual as a single social unit against the conglomerate of such units, the group or society (Sullivan, 1990). From this also flowed the differentiation of individuals, specialisation, the stratification of society. However, as seen in the discourse of individualism discussed by Collin (chapter 11), the relationship between individual, as defined above, and society was problematical, giving rise to a significant role for career. It not only connected individuals with work organisations but, Collin suggests, like the modern epic, it has provided a means of bringing disparate elements together in an organised whole.

The nature and primacy of this Western concept of the individual is being challenged and problematised by postmodernism (Edwards, Harrison, & Tait, 1998; Kvale, 1992). Sullivan (1990) argues that the person should be seen not as an autonomous social unit, but in relation to others, and his view is reflected in this book by Young and Valach, and Richardson, and in other career literature. It is seen in, for example, Hall & Associates' (1996) relational approach to career, and in Blustein's (1994) endorsement of Josselson's (1988) notion of the 'embedded self', which 'rests on the assumption that we are inextricably related to others, even within our core self experiences' (Blustein, 1994, p. 145).

The relationship between the individual and the wider context is also recognised in this book. Maranda and Comeau classify the sociological theories of career in terms of this relationship, and other chapters register the role of career in articulating it, for example in the references to elitism in the opening chapter and in the chapters by Richardson and Watts, and by implication in Law's discussion of the role of education. Several chapters note the relevance for career of the individual's changing social contexts. Some refer to the social institutions of marriage and the family: Savickas traces the development of the construct of career in association with changes in community, education, and the family; Richardson refers to the loss of stable structures such as family and marriage; Höpfl and Hornby Atkinson refer to the implications for a woman's career of having children. Also mentioned are education (Law; Watts); tax and welfare systems (Watts); the qualifications system and training for employment (Watts); demography (Patton refers to the new values of 'Generation X'); a multicultural society (Leong and Hartung refer to a 'multicultural mindset').

The role of psychology

The Western concept of the individual is central to psychology (Sullivan, 1990), and psychology has helped to construct a particular version of it. The techniques of psychology 'individualiz[ed] humans' through 'classifying them, calibrating their capacities and conducts, inscribing and recording their attributes and deficiencies, managing and utilizing their individuality and variability' (Rose, 1989, pp. 121–123). During the two world wars (Rose, 1978; Seymour, 1959), psychologists made major strides in selection, appraisal, and allocation techniques that were then adapted for use in industry. Thus it has been argued (Rose, 1989) that Western psychology has had a symbiotic relationship with capitalist work organisations. Its objectification of individual subjects facilitated the rational control of the new industrial work places, where success depended on 'the organization of the capacities and attributes of those individuals, [how] they were fitted to the demands of the tasks to be undertaken, [how] individuals could or should be co-ordinated with one another in space, time and sequence, and [how] those lacking appropriate capacities could be identified and excluded' (p. 120).

Psychology has been a major influence on the theory and practice of career, and its conceptualisation of the individual has dominated North American career theory, whether utilising psychometric or developmental approaches. Although constructivist, interpretative, and narrative approaches that regard the individual as a social construction have now taken root in the theory and practice of career (Cochran, 1997; Young & Collin, 1992), nevertheless Savickas indicates that the psychometric approach still remains at the core of the dominant theories and techniques of career. How long that will continue is a matter of conjecture, for there are many new developments taking place in psychology: postmodern psychology (Kvale, 1992), societal psychology (Himmelweit & Gaskell, 1990), global and community psychology (Marsella, 1998). Moreover, North American psychology is not the only approach to career. Structural constraints have received greater attention in Britain (Watts, 1981), and sociology (Maranda & Comeau) has interpreted the individual differently. The Chicago School (Barley, 1989) saw career as the 'enacted attributes of the collectives to which individuals belonged', persons being 'less defined by their uniqueness than by their membership in a category of actors that populate some setting' (p. 51).

The organisation of work

The nature of the tasks to be undertaken, their organisation into jobs and occupations, the relationships between jobs and within occupations, and the overall structure of organisations and occupations, have all constituted structures for career, and have all changed over time. The Industrial Revolution led to the organisation of work based on the detailed division of labour, and the introduction of the manager, as distinct from the owner, to control work in the new factories. By the early 1900s, the basic framework for organisational careers was in place. The typical pyramid shape of organisations meant that only the elite would have an upward moving, future-orientated career, not the industrial work force in general, whose tasks were geared to those of machines, and whose work was minutely fractionated (Braverman, 1974).

The nature of the organisational career, with its pathways, patterns, delayed gratification, and future orientation, became established with the widespread development of bureaucracies in the middle years of the twentieth century. Work-study structured basic tasks, job descriptions shaped jobs, set their boundaries, and the relationships between them, and job specifications shaped individuals to fill those jobs. It was now, Collin (chapter 11) suggests, that the period of 'high career' began, the early theories of career started to appear, and the rhetorical discourse of career began to flourish. Thereafter, with the growth of organisations and development of internal labour markets, the opportunity for career advancement grew.

In 1984 it was still possible to assert that 'the "upward and onward" view of career is still the most prevalent conception of what a career is all about' (Williams, 1984, p. 31). Since then, considerable changes have taken place. Jobs are becoming more temporary, flexible, and fluid (Storey; Littleton *et al.*; Riverin-Simard; O'Doherty and Roberts), individuals' time horizons are shortening (Collin, chapters 6 and 11; Riverin-Simard), boundaries within and between organisations are becoming more permeable, boundaryless careers are developing (Littleton *et al.*). Globalisation, networking forms of organisation, and the concomitant separation of space from place (Castells, 1996) are changing the nature of tasks and, to some extent, detaching jobs (or tasks) from organisational structures. Such developments will continue into the future of career.

The employment relationship and its management

Another strand in career is the nature of the employment relationship and how people are managed at work. In the capitalist process of production, the purpose of employing labour is to create a surplus value in order to accumulate capital. Thus the employer has to increase the output of the labour power purchased, and derive the greatest benefit from the distinctive qualities and potentials of the individuals employed. However, these potentials are indeterminate (Braverman, 1974), and a key challenge to employers is to find ways of realising them. The conditions in which this has to be done present a further challenge. There is an inherent contradiction between the economically efficient organisation of work –

from Adam Smith's (1776/1910) detailed division of labour, through the Fordist modes of production, to the development of bureaucracies in the middle years of the twentieth century – and the attempt to realise the potentials of those employed: 'The organization . . . *pays* people only for certain of their *activities* . . . but it is *whole persons* who come to work' (Schein, 1978, p. 17, quoting Barnard, 1938). The construct of career, however, has offered a connective tissue across fragmented tasks, work-lives, and work and personal lives, and hence employers and managers are stakeholders in it, for it has provided a narrative connecting individuals to employing organisations.

In most organisations, the relationship between employer and employee is inherently unequal; the employer has the greater power but may exert or restrain it, or even purport to share it by 'empowering' the employee. During the second half of the twentieth century, with economic expansion, greater stability, and a degree of social mobility, the balance of power shifted to some extent. Buttressed by protective legislation and collective bargaining, individuals became sufficiently secure to be able to consider their potential future, and make a career for themselves. Nevertheless, though rarely discussed in the career literature – but touched on by Patton, Höpfl and Hornby Atkinson, Richardson, Leong and Hartung, and Doyle in various ways – the balance of power intrinsic to the employer–employee relationship remains constituted in career.

Considerable changes have taken place in the management of the employment relationship that have reflected the increasingly sophisticated response to the contradiction in the need not only to control but also to motivate and develop employees. The emphasis shifted from making welfare provisions in the early years of the twentieth century, to the introduction of personnel management (Child, 1969), and its increasing professionalisation from mid-century onwards, until the emergence of human resource management (HRM) in the later years of the century (Legge, 1995). Personnel management and HRM have influenced the context in which organisational careers are played out, and elaborated the structures, processes, and practices underpinning them. Selection, training, employee and management development, and performance appraisal have shaped the skills, opportunities, and expectations of the individual, and thus the individual's career. Over the years, the opportunity within an organisation to have a career, and support for it, have become terms in the 'psychological contract' (Doyle, Storey).

However, more recently, in response to the pressures from employers to make organisations more flexible, the legislative protection of the employee has been greatly lessened, and the powers of the trades unions curtailed. For the most part, the employment relationship is no longer shaped collectively but individually. This has led to a considerable increase in employee insecurity (Gallie, White, Cheng, & Tomlinson, 1998), a change in the 'psychological contract', and a limiting of the employee's future horizon. These changes, Höpfl and Hornby Atkinson suggest, are uncovering the 'underlying ambivalence' of the psychological contract which is largely disguised or suppressed in the male-defined notion of career. Moreover, HRM has colonised career, using 'career management' in its discourse, as Doyle's chapter shows, to retain, reward, motivate, and manage the individual. The similarity between the discourses of HRM and career in addressing the highly ambivalent employment relationship is noted by Collin (chapter 11).

Key issues for the stakeholders in the future of career

The preceding analysis of the strands of career makes it clear that, as well as individuals, there are a number of other stakeholders in it. Over and above those we highlight below, the chapters by Maranda and Comeau, Savickas, Collin, Law, and Watts emphasise the stake which Western societies at large have in career (see also Kanter, 1989). By developing the implications of the chapters further, we shall now identify some of the key issues in the future of career for these stakeholders, for their interests will in part construct its future.

Issues for employers and managers

Employers and managers will continue to have a stake in career. They will need to continue to control and extract value from employees while maintaining commitment and motivation. However, future developments in the employment relationship – whether it continues to be shaped individually rather than collectively – and in the organisation of work – whether organisations become even more flexible – will raise issues about control and motivation. Employers will face new contradictions. Increasing globalisation and networking forms of organisation will change the nature of tasks and, hence, the nature of labour required. 'Self-programming' labour will be differentiated from 'generic' labour because of its 'capability to redefine the necessary skills for a given task' (Castells, 1998, p. 341). Although a key resource, self-programming labour will be difficult to control. Generic labour will be more controllable, but difficult to motivate. Individuals who comprise it will be like 'human terminals'; they could be replaced by machines or other people, perhaps anywhere around the world, 'collectively indispensable' but 'individually expendable' (p. 341). The continuing separation of space from place (Castells,

1996) will detach jobs (or tasks) from organisational structures, and boundaryless careers will proliferate (Littleton, Arthur, and Rousseau).

These issues will challenge employers' modes of managing: their existing rhetorics of HRM and 'empowerment' may be insufficient to contain these new contradictions. Equally, the existing rhetoric of career that once sealed, or glossed over, the relationship between employers and their employees may also be inadequate for these emerging conditions, and new forms of rhetoric may have to be constructed.

Issues for individuals

Individuals clearly have a major stake in the future of career. Some of them could construe as opportunities the very conditions that seem likely to challenge employers. They could experience these projects and contingencies as opportunities to construct the world anew each day, free themselves from societal chains, and gain control over their own constructed world. Others could experience them as threats. The loss of a clear and long-term view of the future, of stable reference points by which they can construct meaning, of a clear-cut and contained sense of self, could for some spell insecurity and ambiguity.

To become effective actors in the new social and informational networks, as Law observes, individuals will need a new understanding of work and new skills, including the skill to negotiate new projects, the ability to adapt to new situations, and work with a changing cast of colleagues, perhaps even across the globe. They will need learning-to-learn skills, the personal skills to be entrepreneurial, and to cope with ambiguity.

The remaining questions are more difficult to address. How will individuals construct their sense of self in this emerging world, and in a relational career? How will they construct their identity, which Castells (1996, p. 3) says is the main source of meaning in this increasingly fragmented world? How will they achieve the reflexive project of the self (Giddens, 1991)? Will the networking self be a 'project self' (Castells, 1997), a more tentative and fluid self, an interdependent rather than an independent self (Arthur & Rousseau, 1996), more like a non-Western self (Leong and Hartung)? How will such individuals construct coherence, continuity, and meaning in their lives, a sense of future, their relationships with others and with their society as a whole? How will they avoid the 'corrosion of character' feared by Sennett (1998)?

One way of looking at these questions is through Giddens's (1976) concept of structuration. This refers to the dialectical relationship between agency and structure: society both constitutes and is constituted by the actions of individuals. An associated notion is that of praxis. This captures the act of constructing meaning. As in Young and Valach's notion of socially embedded action, the individual's action, the 'transformative capacity of human action' (Giddens, 1976, p. 110), constructs the world. Thus 'human beings change themselves through changing the world around them in a continual and reciprocal process' (Giddens, 1976, p. 100). Of relevance to the issues in this book, Giddens notes how power is involved in this transformative capacity. The capacity to change the world raises the possibility of changing it and self in ways that are liberating and fulfilling, as in Richardson's 'empowerment' or emancipatory praxis (Sullivan, 1990, p. 127). Much of what is being argued in our book concerns the potential role of career as praxis for the individual.

Issues for career theorists, researchers, and practitioners

Guidance and counselling, education, and a supportive infrastructure of policies and provisions, will have a significant role to play if individuals are to achieve emancipatory praxis. These will have to be underpinned by appropriate and relevant assumptions, theories, and research.

One of the two axes in Maranda and Comeau's classification of the sociological theories of career is that of adaptation–transformation. The call made by Arthur, Hall, and Lawrence (1989, p. 20) for 'transformational career theory' implies that many theories have congregated at the adaptation pole. Although critical interpretations, such as Foucault's view of the practices whereby ' "inner" lives are brought into the domain of power' (Usher & Edwards, 1998, p. 216), are not yet commonly found in the career literature, the roots of career theory and practice are at the transformation pole. Pope (1999), president of the National Career Development Association, explains that the origins of career counselling are in 'social activism'. He cites Whiteley (1984) who suggests that career counselling was a ' "progressive social reform movement aimed at eradicating poverty and substandard living conditions spawned by the rapid industrialization and consequent migration of people to major urban centers at the turn of the Twentieth century" ' (Pope, 1999, p. 1). Pope concludes that: 'The career counselling profession has provided important aid to the workers of the United States and around the world in finding their life's work and in alleviating some of the misery resulting from social and economic change. Our legacy has been one of life-affirming work' (p. 1). The emerging world at the start of the twenty-first century calls for similar 'social activism'.

Underpinning guidance and counselling practices must be appropriate and relevant assumptions, theories, and research. However, in identifying what these might be, it has to be borne in mind that our basic grounds for knowledge may be changing (Wheatley, 1992), and that what is now taken for granted may shortly become irrelevant or obsolete. Nevertheless, on the basis of our present state of understanding, the directions in which Marsella (1998) argues that psychology should go would open the new avenues for our understanding of the future of career which this book suggests are needed. To be responsive to the needs of a changing world, psychology should recognise the global dimensions and scale of our lives; limit the ethnocentric bias in theories, methods, and interventions; develop indigenous psychologies; emphasise the cultural determinants of behaviour; use systems, contextual and nonlinear conceptualisations of behaviour; and adopt qualitative, naturalistic, and contextual research methods.

It would seem that the best way of addressing the complex and multilevel relationships that comprise career has to be multidisciplinary. However, this has been called for previously (Arthur, Hall, & Lawrence, 1989), but the field of career remains largely fragmented, with a major division between those concerned with organisational careers (Collin, 1996a) and others concerned with individual careers. The latter has been primarily the territory of psychology: Maranda and Comeau note how sociology has been less involved, but suggest it should now pool its ideas with psychology. Career psychology is also divided. In his chapter Savickas identifies two camps in terms of epistemology and methodology, but there are also other significant differences among theorists (Savickas & Lent, 1994), and between theorists and practitioners (Savickas & Walsh, 1996). Thus, as well as paying attention to developments in the other areas of psychology that were noted earlier, and to the 'new sciences' (Elliott & Kiel, 1997; Wheatley, 1992), attempts must be made to share knowledge, collaborate, and achieve synergy across the existing field.

Several approaches referred to in this book will repay further investment: action theory, chaos theory, Weick's (1979) notion of enactment. Moreover, relational theories of career and theories of the boundaryless career have considerable further potential. Actor network theory (Callon, 1986; Latour, 1987, 1991; Law & Hassard, 1999) is a new and increasingly influential approach that should also be considered.

A number of issues raised in this book need to be addressed in research and theory: power and career, and not only in relation to elitism, ethnicity, and gender; the impact on the individual of project working; the experience of not having a long time horizon. A further issue is that of emotion in career (see also Kidd, 1998; Young, Paseluikho, and Valach, 1997). The question of how to conduct multidisciplinary research into career, and how to study the complex and multilevel relationships that comprise career, will also have to be addressed.

If career practice is to empower clients (Richardson), more attention has to be given to its nature. A question that is not asked in this book, but which needs attention, is the relationship between the various forms of vocational guidance, career counselling, and career management in organisations. At which pole of chapter 3's adaptation–transformation axis are they located? Would all three forms of practice be located together, or are there significant differences between them? The existing separation between the counselling and organisational branches of the career field, and hence the lack of opportunity for shared knowledge, collaboration, and potential synergy, and the tension between career theory and practice, must be addressed. Further, attempts must be made to overcome the problem of the timelag in a fast-moving world between research being carried out, the development of theory, and its availability to practitioners. One way forward is for practitioners to practise reflectively and to become small-scale researchers themselves (Collin, 1996b), but in this they need the support of academic researchers and theorists.

Reframing career

The overall message from this book suggests that we have to reframe our understanding of career, not only to accommodate the changes taking place at this particular conjuncture in time, but also those that are still slowly building up from the past, and those aspects of it we have previously neglected. We need to recognise that career has a wider scope than we have previously seen, and that it is not only ambiguous, but also ambivalent.

In the world outside the immediate concerns of this book, the violent, political upheavals of our time remind us of the contingency of human life and our personal worlds. The book itself has emphasised that, even in more secure societies, the personal worlds of individuals are becoming disrupted as their shorter work-runs or projects fragment their working lives. Such conditions suggest that the linear, future-orientated, view of career that we had taken for granted was a construct of its time. People may increasingly need to be able to make sense of their actions in and across the various domains of their lives, and link them together into meaningful sequences, in the shorter term as projects, and in the longer term as their careers. Thus career has to be reframed as a construct, an unfolding narrative, that gives coherence laterally across the individual's life in addition to the meaning it can give to the future; and career theory, research, and practice have to be developed to support this.

In the newly emerging network society, with its complex and dynamic web of global and local, real and virtual, interconnections between individuals, it will no longer be meaningful to conceptualise career as individualistic, as in the past. This book has emphasised how individuals co-construct their career with others, and this relational view of career has to be accommodated in its reframing.

This book has referred to the dialectical, ambivalent, and contradictory relationship between individual and society. This relationship recurs in various forms: individualism is prized in a mass society; the construction of the individual is in part based on comparison with others; the individual gains some security and hence freedom by being part of a wider group that can bargain collectively. These various forms of this relationship are all interconnected, and constitute a matrix of social meanings that are constantly changing in response to one another. This book has shown how in the past career as a cultural construction has mediated, contained, and hence defused some of the contradictions in the various forms of the individual–society relationship, and embodied its reciprocal nature. As rhetoric, it has expressed individualism in the mass society, and given a means of differentiating between individuals. As praxis, it has enabled the individual to create a personal world out of collective experiences. Thus, threading its way throughout the web of social meanings which constitute the individual–society relationship, career has played a significant role in tightening or slackening its tensions. At this time, when there is increasing individualisation of labour (Castells, 1996), and individuals are under increasing threat from society/employer, there are nevertheless being noted less individualistic, more relational, or even community, approaches to career. It would seem that career, with its rich ambiguity, is continuing to adjust the tensions in the relationship between individual and society.

Contradictions in the discourse of career have been noted or implied throughout the book. Career simultaneously constitutes a means whereby the person can construct their autonomy using empowering social meanings, a private refuge from the disempowering claims and definitions of the social world, a rhetoric disguising those social claims and definitions, and an arena in which the individual can embody or display those claims. These are not new understandings of career. However, the fragmented nature of the field of study has allowed them to be glossed over, or at most recognised in references made to the 'ambiguity' of the construct of career, or to its Eurocentric construction. Unless in our reframing of career we recognise not only its ambiguity but also its duality – or multiple dualities – we shall prevent ourselves from making an adequate response to its future. Career, we suggested in chapter 1, relates past and present to the future; it can be interpreted as being both objective and subjective. It is also, we are arguing here, both rhetoric and praxis. It has multiple dualities: it is not either/or, but both/and. Its inherent ambivalence allows it to reflect the ambiguity and contradictions of its time, just as, according to Bauman (1999), 'culture' does. Even if the experiences of individuals in the emerging world become more fragmented and atomised, career could continue to act as a magnet that sets up a force-field among the disparate particles of individual experiences, creating 'a productive conflict of the contradictory elements' (Adorno, in Moretti, 1996, p. 214: see chapter 11). To create such a force-field, one of its poles would, for example, be rhetoric and control, the other praxis and potential emancipation. In this way career would continue to provide a source of meaning for both individuals and society.

Constructing the future of career

The contributors to this book have suggested that the opportunities and threats in the new millennium will continue to challenge the traditional philosophies, theories, prescriptions, and practices of career. There seems little doubt, however, that career will continue into the future. It will continue to reflect the nature of society, contribute to its coherence, and give it a discourse and a rhetoric. At the same time, it will offer the framework for a narrative that fulfils, energises, and empowers individuals.

Society will no doubt take care of itself, but what is the way forward for those of us who are committed to career as emancipatory praxis? We need to find ways to support the directions that have been advocated in this book, including achieving synergy across the fragmented career field and ensuring that our theories and research are relevant and accessible to practitioners, and heard by policy-makers. We must be constantly aware of the dual faces of career, and of how our efforts could be translated into disempowering ends. We have to be more knowing in our theorising, research, and practice, and recognise more clearly the politics of career. Moreover, if career is to remain meaningful and accessible to all, then its dualities have to be addressed in the future. This must start with education, as Law argues. It must be continued through the empowering practices which Richardson, and Leong and Hartung, urge, and the public provision of guidance and structures advocated by Watts.

As theorists, researchers, and practitioners, we need to assert our confidence in and commitment to our values, so that we can pass on to the new millennium the 'legacy . . . of life-affirming work' (Pope, 1999, p. 1) we ourselves inherited from a more certain world. At the same time, however, we have to recognise that our basic assumptions may not survive the ontological and epistemological upheavals now believed to be taking place, so we must move forward with 'thoughtful uncertainty' (Covino, 1988).

REFERENCES

Arthur, M. B., Hall, D. T., & Lawrence, B. S. (1989). Generating new directions in career theory: The case for a transdisciplinary approach. In M. B. Arthur, D. T. Hall, & B. S. Lawrence (Eds.), *Handbook of career theory* (pp. 7–25). Cambridge: Cambridge University Press.

Arthur, M. B. & Rousseau, D. M. (Eds.) (1996). *The boundaryless career: A new employment principle for a new organizational era.* New York: Oxford University Press.

Bakan, D. (1966). *The duality of human existence: An essay on psychology and religion.* Boston: Bcacon.

Barley, S. R. (1989). Careers, identities, and institutions: The legacy of the Chicago School of Sociology. In M. B. Arthur, D. T. Hall, & B. S. Lawrence (Eds.), *Handbook of career theory* (pp. 41–65). Cambridge: Cambridge University Press.

Bauman, Z. (1999). *Culture as praxis.* London: Sage.

Blustein, D. L. (1994). 'Who am I?': The question of self and identity in career development. In M. L. Savickas & R. W. Lent (Eds.), *Convergence in career development theories: Implications for science and practice* (pp. 139–154). Palo Alto, CA: CPP Books.

Braudel, F. (1973). *The Mediterranean and the Mediterranean world in the age of Philip II* (Vol. 2). London: Collins.

Braverman, H. (1974). *Labor and monopoly capital: The degradation of work in the twentieth century.* New York: Monthly Review Press.

Callon, M. (1986). Some elements of a sociology of translation: Domestication of the scallops and the fishermen of St. Brieuc Bay. In J. Law (Ed.), *Power, action and belief: A new sociology of knowledge?* (pp. 196–233). Sociological Review Monograph 32. London: Routledge & Kegan Paul.

Castells, M. (1996). *The information age: Economy, society and culture. Vol. I: The rise of the network society.* Oxford: Blackwell.

(1997). *The information age: Economy, society and culture. Vol. II: The power of identity.* Oxford: Blackwell.

(1998). *The information age: Economy, society and culture. Vol. III: End of millennium.* Oxford: Blackwell.

Child, J. (1969). *British management thought.* London: Allen and Unwin.

Cochran, L. (1997). *Career counseling: A narrative approach.* Thousand Oaks, CA: Sage.

Collin, A. (1996a). *Integrating neglected issues into the reconceptualization of career.* In M. Savickas (Chair) The birth and death of career: Counseling psychology's contribution. Symposuim conducted at the 104th Annual Convention of the American Psychological Association, Toronto.

(1996b). Re-thinking the relationship between theory and practice: Practitioners as map-readers, map-makers – or jazz players? *British Journal of Guidance and Counselling,* 24 (1), 67–81.

Collin, A. & Young, R. A. (1986). New directions for theories of career. *Human Relations, 39*, 837–853.

Covino, W. A. (1988). *The art of wondering.* Portsmouth, NH: Boynton/Cook.

Derrida, J. (1973). *Speech and phenomena.* Evanston, IL: North-Western University Press.

Edwards, R., Harrison, R., & Tait, A. (Eds.) (1998). *Telling tales: Perspectives on guidance and counselling in learning.* London: Routledge.

Elliot, E., & Kiel, L. D. (1997). Introduction. In L. D. Kiel & E. Elliott, *Chaos theory in the social sciences.* Ann Arbor, MI: University of Michigan Press.

Gallie, D., White, M., Cheng, Y., & Tomlinson, M. (1998). *Restructuring the employment relationship.* Oxford: Oxford University Press.

Gergen, K. J. (1985). The social constructionist movement in modern psychology. *American Psychologist, 40*, 266–275.

Giddens, A. (1976). *New rules for sociological method.* London: Hutchinson.

(1991). *Modernity and self-identity: Self and society in the late modern age.* Cambridge: Polity Press.

Gleick, J. (1987). *Chaos: The making of a new science.* New York: Viking.

Hall, D. T. & Associates (1996). *The career is dead: Long live the career: A relational approach to careers.* San Francisco: Jossey-Bass.

Hammer, M. & Champy, J. (1994). *Reengineering the corporation: A manifesto for business revolution.* New York: Harper Business.

Himmelweit, H. T. & Gaskell, G. (Eds.) (1990). *Societal psychology.* Newbury Park, CA: Sage.

Josselson, R. (1988). The embedded self: I and thou revisited. In D. Lapsley & F. Clark (Eds.), *Self, ego, and identity: Integrative approaches* (pp. 91–106). New York: Springer-Verlag.

Kanter, R. M. (1989). Careers and the wealth of nations: A macro-perspective on the structure and implications of career forms. In M. B. Arthur, D. T. Hall, & B. S. Lawrence (Eds.), *Handbook of career theory* (pp. 506–521). Cambridge: Cambridge University Press.

Kidd, J. M. (1998). Emotion: An absent presence in career theory. *Journal of Vocational Behavior, 52*, 275–288.

Kvale, S. (Ed.) (1992). *Psychology and postmodernism.* London: Sage.

Latour, B. (1987). *Science in action: How to follow scientists and engineers through society.* Milton Keynes: Open University Press.

(1991). Technology is society made durable. In J. Law (Ed.), *A sociology of monsters: Essays on power, technology and domination* (pp. 103–131). London: Routledge.

Law, H. & Hassard, J. (Eds.) (1999). *Actor network theory and after.* Oxford: Blackwell/The Sociological Review.

Legge, K. (1995). *Human resource management: Rhetorics and realities.* Basingstoke: Macmillan.

Marsella, A. J. (1998). Toward a 'global-community psychology': Meeting the needs of a changing world. *American Psychologist, 53*, 1282–1291.

Moretti, F. (1996). *Modern epic: The world system from Goethe to García Márquez* (Q. Hoare, Trans.). London: Verso.

Pope, M. (1999). An historical perspective on the career development profession: Career counseling social activism. *Career Developments, 14* (2), 1.

Rose, M. (1978). *Industrial behaviour: Theoretical developments since Taylor.* Harmondsworth: Penguin.

Rose, N. (1989). Individualizing psychology. In J. Shotter & K. J. Gergen (Eds.), *Texts of identity* (pp. 119–132). London: Sage.

Sampson, E. E. (1989). The deconstruction of the self. In J. Shotter & K. J. Gergen (Eds.), *Texts of identity* (pp. 1–19). London: Sage.

Savickas, M. L. & Lent, R. W. (Eds.) (1994). *Convergence in career development theories: Implications for science and practice.* Palo Alto, CA: CPP Books.

Savickas, M. L. & Walsh, W. B. (Eds.) (1996). *Handbook of career counseling theory and practice.* Palo Alto, CA: Davies-Black.

Schein, E. H. (1978). *Career dynamics: Matching individual and organizational needs.* Reading, MA: Addison-Wesley.

Sennett, R. (1998). *The corrosion of character: The personal consequences of work in the new capitalism.* New York: W. W. Norton.

Seymour, W. D. (1959). *Operator training in industry.* London: Institute of Personnel Management.

Smith, A. (1910). *The wealth of nations* (Originally published 1776.) London: Dent.

Sullivan, E. V. (1990). *Critical psychology and pedagogy: Interpretation of the personal world.* New York: Bergin and Garvey.

Taylor, C. (1989). *Sources of the self: The making of the modern identity.* Cambridge, MA: Harvard University Press.

Usher, R. & Edwards, R. (1998). Confessing all? In R. Edwards, R. Harrison, & A. Tait (Eds.), *Telling tales: Perspectives on guidance and counselling in learning* (pp. 211–222). London: Routledge.

Walsh, W. B. & Chartrand, J. M. (1994). Emerging directions of person–environment fit. In M. L. Savickas, & R. W. Lent (Eds.), *Convergence in career development theories: Implications for science and practice* (pp. 187–195). Palo Alto, CA: CPP Books.

Watson, T. J. (1980). *Sociology, work and industry.* London: Routledge and Kegan Paul.

Watts, A. G. (1981). Introduction. In A. G. Watts, D. E. Super, & J. M. Kidd (Eds.), *Career development in Britain: Some contributions to theory and practice* (pp. 1–6). Cambridge: CRAC/Hobsons.

Weick, K. E. (1979). *The social psychology of organizing* (2nd edn). New York: Random House.

Wheatley, M. J. (1992). *Leadership and the new science: Learning about organization from an orderly universe.* San Francisco: Berrett-Koehler.

Whiteley, J. M. (1984). Historical periods in the development of counseling psychology: Formative influences in the first half of the 20th century: The first historical period. *Counseling Psychologist, 12* (1), 7–20.

Williams, R. (1984). What's new in . . . career development. *Personnel Management,* March, 31–33.

Young, R. A. & Collin, A. (Eds.) (1992). *Interpreting career. Hermeneutical studies of lives in context.* Westport, CT: Praeger.

Young, R. A., Paseluikho, M., & Valach, L. (1997). The role of emotion in the construction of career in parent–adolescent conversations. *Journal of Counseling and Development, 76,* 36–44.

Author index

Subject index